The Decisive Battles of India

From 1746 to 1849 Inclusive

Second Edition
with an additional chapter

by

Colonel G.B. Malleson

Low Price Publications

Low Price Publications
2016

George Bruce Malleson (1825-1898)

First Published 1885
Reprinted in **LPP** 2002, 2016

ISBN 10: 81-7536-291-X
ISBN 13: 978-81-7536-291-8

Published by
Low Price Publications
A-6, 2nd Floor, Nimri Commercial Centre,
Ashok Vihar Phase 4, Delhi 110052 (INDIA)
tel.: +91-11-27302453 fax.: +91-11-47061936
url: www.LPPindia.com e-mail: info@LPPindia.com

Printed at
D.K. Fine Art Press Pvt. Ltd.
Delhi

PRINTED IN INDIA

THE DECISIVE BATTLES OF INDIA

FROM 1746 TO 1849 INCLUSIVE.

WITH A PORTRAIT OF THE AUTHOR, A MAP, AND FOUR PLANS.

LONDON:
W. H. ALLEN & CO., 13 WATERLOO PLACE.
PUBLISHERS TO THE INDIA OFFICE.
1885.

TO

St. Mary's College, Winton,

IN WHOSE CLASSIC HALLS

I NURTURED THAT LOVE OF LITERATURE

WHICH HAS BEEN THE JOY AND CONSOLATION OF MY LIFE,

AND ON THE HILLS IN WHOSE VICINITY

I LEARNED TO FIGHT MY "DECISIVE BATTLES,"

THIS VOLUME IS INSCRIBED

ITH REVERENCE AND AFFECTION.

PREFACE TO THE SECOND EDITION.

When the first edition of this work appeared, two years ago, the dark cloud now threatening our Indian Empire was but a little speck on the horizon, no bigger than a man's hand. The book simply—to use the expression of the critics—told the story of how we had won India. We are now entering upon a period when we shall be called upon to defend the Empire we so greatly gained. Upon this point let there be no mistake in the public mind. Let us at least be honest to our own consciences. A great Power does not go to enormous expenditure to conquer merely sandy deserts. Every previous conqueror of the deserts which Russia has subdued has aimed at the subjugation of the fertile lands beyond them. The rulers of Russia are not less intelligent than were Alexander, Mahmoud of Ghazni, Chengiz Khán, Taimúr, Bábar, Nádir Sháh, and Ahmad Sháh Duráni. Since the days of the first Peter they have pursued a steady and persistent course towards a definite end. Russia is now at the very gates of Herat. No one can peruse the admirable paper by Captain Holdich,

R.E., which, written on the spot, was read at the Royal Geographical Society on the 23rd March last, without being convinced that the present vacillating rulers of India have allowed her to take possession of the several points which command the passes leading to that city. The acquisition of such positions is the natural step to the possession of Herat itself. Nor should any man delude himself with the belief that the possession of the valley of the Herirúd will satisfy the ambition of Russia. Why should it? It did not satisfy the greed of the conquerors in whose footsteps she is treading. When those conquerors had seized the outer gate of India, they naturally passed through it. Much more readily will Russia do so, when she notices that we have neglected to secure the inner gate—the gate of Kandahar—which, if strongly barred and defended by men the equal of those whose exploits are described in this volume, would yet check her advance!

It is, then, at a time when we may at any moment be called upon to defend the great Dependency of Hindustan, that I offer to the public the second edition of a work which has endeavoured faithfully to describe the mode in which that Dependency was acquired. The thoughtful reader will not fail to discern an enormous difference between our method and the method of Russia. In the tenth chapter of another work, now about to appear, "AMBUSHES AND SURPRISES," I have indicated Russia's principle. I have shown how she watches, intriguing with its principal inhabitants, on the border of a doomed country till she feels herself strong enough to step across it. No sooner does she achieve complete success than she intimidates the aboriginal inhabitants by wholesale slaughter. Thus did she act towards the Tartars of the Crimea; towards the Circassians of the Caucasus; towards the Nomads of the Kizil Kúm and the Kara Kúm; thus, within the last five years, towards the Akhal Turkomans. Not in this way did the British behave towards the races of India. In all their onward progresses they had the assent and support of the populations who desired to maintain law and order. The decadence of the Mughul rule was proceeding rapidly when Clive first landed in Bengal. Then the buffalo was to the man who held the bludgeon. These pages show how, under English rule, the buffalo is the property of the man, woman, or child who has the legal right to possess it. We have shed no blood except on the battle-field, and the blood we have shed there has been the blood of the oppressors of the people.

I am anxious to take this opportunity of expressing my acknowledgments of the very kind manner in which this work has been received by the Press and by the Public. The verdict of the former has been unanimous in its favour. Two days after it was ushered into the world the *Times* honoured it with a leading article. The reviews of the journals more particularly devoted to literature were equally encouraging. I have taken advantage of some of these to correct one or two errors which had escaped me in the first reading. I have profited, likewise, by a well-founded suggestion made by the *Athenæum*, to add a chapter containing an account of the two sieges of Bharatpúr. This chapter is based mainly upon Thorn's *War in India* and the *Memoirs of Viscount Combermere.*

One word more. Heretofore the invader from the north, who, holding Herat, has endeavoured to penetrate into India, has invariably succeeded. He had to contend either against a feebler race or degenerated descendants from his own parent stock. That is no longer the case. India is held by men who have in no way degenerated from their forefathers. Some of the Englishmen now in India helped to fight the four last battles recorded in this book. The men who won India, and their comrades not one whit inferior to them, can, if not thwarted by timidity at home, successfully defend India. This is a conviction which, I am confident, will not fail to force itself upon the minds of everyone who shall read and ponder over the great record contained in this volume!

G. B. MALLESON.

27 West Cromwell Road,
1st *June* 1885.

PREFACE TO THE FIRST EDITION.

This volume contains the story of the conquest of the several races of India by our countrymen. To this purpose are devoted eleven out of the twelve chapters of which it is composed. The remaining chapter, the first in order in the book, is the key to all others; for it records an event, but for the occurrence of which the battles which follow might have been indefinitely postponed. It was the victory of Paradis on the Adyar, over the army of the native ruler of the Karnátak, which inverted the position of the Europeans on the eastern coast and the children of the soil.

The battles which illustrate the story were all, in the truest sense of the term, decisive battles. It cannot be denied that some of them showed a small list of casualties, and, in many, the numbers on one side at all events were few. If I may judge from some criticisms which have appeared, this fact alone would be held to be sufficient to remove those battles from the category I claim for them. There are some critics who judge of the importance of a battle solely by the amount of the slaughter produced on both sides.

There is no need for me, I am certain, to point out to the intelligent reader that the criterion thus set forth is altogether a false one. The status of a battle can be decided only by its results. If those results prove decisive—decisive, that is, of the campaign, decisive as to the consequences, decisive as to the future permanent position of the combatants—then, though the casualties be ever so few, that battle is a decisive battle. Take, for example, the first battle described in this book, that between the French and the Karnátak troops at ST. THOMÉ. The French numbered two hundred and thirty Europeans and seven hundred sipáhís. Their loss did not exceed twenty men. Yet that battle changed the face of southern India. It made the European traders the masters, whose aid was eagerly sought for by the native princes who had previously despised them.

That battle brought the French and English face to face in the Karnátak. The contest took, almost at the outset, the form of a duel between two men, both men of consummate genius, Clive and Dupleix. The ability of Clive to carry out himself the conceptions of his teeming brain—an ability denied to his rival—gave him an advantage which turned the contest in his favour. That contest cannot be said to have been decided by the splendid defence of Arkát, for, a few weeks later, the French had re-occupied the province of which Arkát was the capital. But it was decided at KÁVÉRIPÁK, a battle passed over with singular neglect, relative to its importance. by such historians as Mill and Thornton, by a biographer such as Malcolm, and even by Macaulay. Yet it is not to be questioned but that the victory of Kávéripák, promptly followed up, caused the surrender of the French army before Trichinápallí, and gave the British a preponderance which they never after entirely lost.

That battle, won by the daring, the coolness, the resolution of Clive, against numbers greatly superior, settled for the time the pretensions of the French in southern India. In Bengal, the intervention of the conqueror was called for a few years later, to avenge the cruelties inflicted by the native ruler upon his countrymen. Those cruelties were avenged at PLASSEY, one of the most decisive battles ever fought. Plassey gave the English a position in Bengal, Bihár, and Orísá, akin to that of overlord. The native ruler whom they appointed paid them homage, and agreed to undertake no foreign enterprise without their approval.

But other European nations had planted settlements in Bengal, and, after the capture of Chandranagar, the chief of these was the Dutch. That people, jealous of the advantages which Plassey had gained for the English, made a great effort to surprise and trip them up. But Clive, cool and ready, was too much for them, and the decisive battle of BIDERRA quenched for ever their aspirations.

Then came another, a very desperate and final struggle for the possession of the three provinces. The native troops, led by men with their hearts in the national cause, fought better than they had ever fought before. But again were the English, commanded by a warrior of the first class, the careful and daring John Adams, too much for them

The battles of Katwá and Ghériah, and finally the decisive battles of ÚNDWAH NÁLÁ attested the superior discipline of the British soldier, the more skilful leading of his general.

Úndwah Nálá decided for ever the fate of the three provinces, and brought the English frontier to the Karmnásá. There it touched the territories of the vassals and tributaries of the Núwáb-Vazír of Awadh (Oudh). The contact produced war—a war unsought by the British, who desired nothing so much as to consolidate the territories they had but just acquired—but a war caused solely by the desire of the Núwáb-Vazír to aggrandise himself at their expense. After some fluctuations of fortune, the result of the hesitations of Carnac, that war was terminated by the brilliant victory gained by Munro at BAKSAR. Baksar advanced the English frontier to Allahábád, and even to detached positions beyond it.

The scene had shifted, even before this, to southern India. The French there had made a desperate effort to recover their fallen fortunes. Not only did the attempt fail, but, by a stroke of genius, Clive, through his lieutenants, wrested from them, by the victory of KONDÚR and the storming of MACHHLÍPATANAM, a province the importance of the possession of which could not be too highly estimated; for the manner in which that province was gained, more, even, than the actual gain, secured for the English an influence at Haidarábád which has ever since gone on increasing.

But the British hold on southern India was not yet secure. In the decay of the Mughul empire, an adventurer of low birth, but of commanding talents, had usurped authority in the Hindú kingdom which had existed on the highland plateau overlooking the Karnátak towards the east and the sea coast towards the west. Having by degrees absorbed all the petty native states within his reach, and having measured his strength—not, on the whole, unequally—with the English, that adventurer determined at length to make a supreme effort to become the arbiter of India south of the Krishna. The war that ensued became, then, a war of life and death for the foreigners who had by degrees constituted themselves the protectors of the Karnátak. Never were the English in such danger. But for the obstinacy of one solitary Frenchman—the Chevalier D'Orves—they must have succumbed. Saved for the moment by that obstinacy, they were still forced to risk the fate of their dominion on the issue of a single battle. It was the hard-fought victory of PORTO NOVO which, giving the first check to the conquering career of Haidar Alí, secured for the English time to accumulate their resources, and eventually to baffle his aims. Those aims once baffled, the invader once forced to retire within the limits of his dominions, his entire subjugation became the object which no Governor of Madras could omit from his political calculations. When, at last, the opportunity did offer, this object was achieved without much difficulty.

The overthrow of the Muhammadan dynasty in Maisúr, made possible by Porto Novo, brought the English face to face with the Maráthás. The aggressive action of those hardy warriors had, even in the time of Aurangzíb, shaken the Mughul empire to its very basis. After the death of that sovereign they, too, began to dream of universal dominion. Everything seemed to favour them. They gradually absorbed the larger part of western and central India, and made rapid strides towards the Jamná. Suddenly they met with an unexpected opponent in the shape of Ahmad Sháh Duráni, the leader of the Afghán invaders. The hotly-contested battle fought at Pánipat (1763), gave the Maráthás their first decisive check. Gradually, however, they recovered from that terrible overthrow, and, under the leadership of a very remarkable man who had fled from the field, not only reconquered all they had lost, but gained infinitely more. Masters of the imperial cities of Dihlí and Agrá, of the north-western provinces as far as Alígarh, they at length beheld before them only two possible rivals—one of them, indeed, the Sikhs, almost too young to be seriously regarded as a rival—and the English, ruling from the mouths of the Ganges to Kánhpúr, and possessors of Bombay and Madras. The inevitable contest with the more powerful of the two rivals, preceded by circumstances which not only deprived the Maráthás of their great leader, but which paralysed one and forced to temporary inaction another of their four great confederacies, came at last. It was a fight for supremacy throughout India. For southern and western India the question was decided at ASSAYE; for northern India at LASWÁRÍ. Though further lessons became necessary, no serious question of rivalry for empire between the British and the Maráthás was possible after Laswárí.

The victorious issue of the Maráthá campaign extended the English frontier virtually to the Satlaj. For forty years the great sovereign who ruled beyond that river recognised, often sorely against his will, the policy of keeping on terms with his powerful neighbours. His death, and the anarchy which ensued in his kingdom, broke the spell. It is hard to say how Ranjít Singh, had he been then alive and in the prime of life, would have acted during the Kábul disasters of 1840–41. In a military point of view, he would have been master of the situation. Fortunately for the English, the Sikh chieftains were, at the critical time, occupied with intrigues for power; they had no guiding mind to direct them, and the occasion was allowed to pass. But, from the day of Ranjít's death, the contest between the two nations had become inevitable. For four years before the invasion occurred warnings of its certain proximity had been incessant. The English had made such preparations to meet it as were possible without exciting the jealousy of a high-spirited people. When, at length, inspired by chiefs who only desired to ensure their own safety by the destruction of the Prætorians who threatened them, the Sikh army crossed the Satlaj, and the English hurried up their troops to meet them, the greatness of the danger was recognised. Two things alone, at this conjuncture, preserved India to the English. The first was the unaccountable halt of the invaders for several days on the south bank of the Satlaj; the second, the detachment of a few troops only instead of a whole army to Múdkí. There was even then time to repair mistakes. But the splendid valour which had all but won Fírúzshahar on the first afternoon of the fight, was neutralised by the treachery of the Sikh leaders. The battle which might have been a victory became a defeat; a defeat which virtually decided the campaign, for Sobráon was but the complement of Fírúzshahar.

The peace which followed was but a patched-up peace. The Sikh nobles had been gained over, but the Sikh people had not been subdued, and they knew it. Resolutely they bided their time, seized the first opportunity to rise, and fought their old enemy once more; this time, not for empire, but for independence. How the contest, undecided by Chiliánwálá, was brought to a final issue at Gujrát I have told at considerable, but I hope not unnecessary, length, in the last chapter.

It will be seen, then, that this book has for its aim to describe the steps by which the English, after subduing their European rivals, conquered, one after another, the several races which inhabit India; how Bengal, the provinces north of the Karmnásá, Maisúr, the Maráthá confederacies, the Panjáb, received the blow which paralysed them. Sometimes the paralysed territories were swallowed up at once; sometimes they were left paralysed, to be swallowed on the first fitting opportunity. But there they were, harmless, impotent as far as rivalry was concerned; capable of making, indeed, a blow for defence, but never again striking for victory. Such was the state of the Bengal of Mír J'afar after Plassey; of the Bengal of Mír Kásim after Úndwah Nálá; of southern India north of the Krishna after Machhlípatanam; of the same region south of that river after the peace which followed Porto Novo; of the Maráthá confederacies after Assaye and Laswárí; and, I may say, notwithstanding Chiliánwálá, of the Sikhs after Fírúzshahar.

One word more regarding the method of the book. The reader will perceive that whilst each chapter describes the particular battle which gives it its name, it is linked informally, yet very really, to the chapter which precedes it. Further, that wherever it has seemed necessary—in the chapters, for instance, describing the battles of Plassey, of Baksar, of Porto Novo, to a certain extent of Assaye, and of Fírúzshahar and Sobráon—I have given a sketch either of the previous history of the people, or of the family which gave political existence to the country they inhabited. This is especially the case with the chapters referring to Haidár Ali and the Sikhs.

In writing this book I have gone as far as possible to original documents, or to the writings, published and unpublished, of contemporaries. Thus, for the first chapter, that on St. Thomé, and for the third, that on Kondúr and Machhlípatanam, I have relied on the memoirs of Dupleix and Moracin, with the correspondence attached to each (*pièces justificatives*), on Orme, on Colonel Stringer Lawrence's memoirs; for the second chapter, relating to Plassey and the early history of Bengal, and for the fifth, Biderra, I have consulted Stewart's *History of Bengal*, Orme's *Military Transactions*, the *Siyar-ul-Muta'akherin*, Caraccioli's *Life of Clive*, Ive's *Voyage and Historical Narrative*, Grose's *Voyage to the East Indies*, Holwell's *Indian Tracts*, and Broome's *History of the Bengal Army*; for the sixth,

Úndwah Nálá, and for the seventh, Baksar, the *Siyar-ul-Muta'akherin*, Vansittart's *Narrative of Transactions in Bengal*, the *Asiatic Annual Register*, Williams's *Bengal Native Infantry*, Francklin's *Life of Shah Aulum*, Verelst's *English Government in Bengal*, Wheeler's *Early Records of British India*, and Broome's *History of the Bengal Army*; for the eighth chapter, Porto Novo, I have relied mainly on Wilks's *History of Southern India*, on *Transactions in India*, on *Mémoire de la dernière guerre*, on Grant Duff's *History of the Maráthás*, and on information acquired during a residence of seven years in the Maisúr country; for the ninth and tenth, Assaye and Laswárí, I have depended on the despatches of the two Wellesleys, on Grant Duff's history, on Thorn's *War in India*, on the *Annual Register*, and on the *Asiatic Annual Register*. I am indebted likewise to the writer, whose name I have been unable to ascertain, of an article in the *Calcutta Review*, on the Duke of Wellington's career in India, for many useful indications.

The eleventh chapter demands a more special notice. The portion relating to the rise of the Sikh nation is based upon Cunningham's *History of the Sikhs*; the account of the battles on Cunningham's history, on an article in the *Calcutta Review* (vol. vi.), by the late Sir Herbert Edwardes, on private letters, and on minute personal investigation. I dismiss the despatches of the day as utterly unreliable, abounding in exaggerations of all sorts; worthy, in that respect, to be classed with the bulletins of Napoleon. But Cunningham is a great authority. His history is a very remarkable one. Joseph Davey Cunningham belonged to the corps fruitful of great men, the Bengal Engineers.* His talents early attracted the attention of Lord Auckland, anxious to select a young officer to train for the work of a political agent on the Satlaj frontier; and, without any solicitation on his part, he was appointed assistant to Colonel Wade, then in charge of the British relations with the Panjáb, and the chiefs of Afghánistán. Holding that office, Cunningham was present at the interview which took place, in 1838, between Lord Auckland and Ranjít Singh. In 1839 he accompanied Shahzádah Taimúr and Colonel Wade to Pesháwar, and he was with them when they forced the Khaibar pass and laid open the way to Kábul. In 1840 he was placed in administrative charge of the district of Lodíáná; towards the end of that year, he, then under the orders of Mr., now Sir George, Clerk, the agent for the Governor-General, once more traversed the Panjáb to Pesháwar; during part of 1841 he was in magisterial charge of the Firúzpúr district; and towards the close of that year he was, on the recommendation of Mr. Clerk, deputed to Thibet to see that the ambitious rájahs of Jamú surrendered certain territories which they had seized from the Chinese of Lhassa, and that the British trade with Ludákh was restored to its old footing. He returned in time to be present at the interview between Lord Ellenborough and the Sikh chiefs at Firúzpúr (December 1842). Appointed subsequently personal assistant

* The names of the first-class men, whom I have known personally, rise at once to the recollection; men, for instance, like Lord Napier of Magdála, Sir Henry Durand, Baird Smith, George Chesney; but the list is too long, for other names remain.

to Mr. Clerk's successor, Colonel Richmond, and then employed in important duties in the Baháwalpúr territory, Cunningham, very studious by nature and greedy of knowledge, was able to acquire a fund of information regarding the Sikhs, unequalled at the time in India. It was by reason of this knowledge that, when the Sikh war broke out, Sir Charles Napier ordered him at once to join his army then occupying Sindh. For the same reason, Sir Hugh Gough, after Firúzshahar, summoned him to join his head-quarters; detached him to accompany Sir Harry Smith to Badiwál and Aliwál, and retained him near his person on the day of Sobráon.

Cunningham, then, had enjoyed peculiar opportunities of knowing the Sikhs. He had lived with them for eight years during a most important portion of their history. He had enjoyed intercourse, under every variety of circumstances, with all classes of men, and he had had free access to all the public records bearing on the affairs of the frontier. It had even been one of his duties to examine and report upon the military resources of the country, and, being essentially a worker, a man who, if he did a thing at all, could not help doing it thoroughly, he had devoted to the task all his energies and all his talents.

No one, then, was more competent than this honest and experienced officer to write a history of the Sikh people—a history which should tell the truth and the whole truth. Circumstances favoured the undertaking of such a task by Cunningham As a reward for his services he had been appointed to the political agency of Bhopál in Central India. He found the life in that quiet part of the world very different to the all-absorbing existence on the frontier. To employ the leisure hours forced upon him then he conceived the idea, as he knew he had the means, of writing a history of the Sikhs. This intention he communicated to superior authority, and he certainly believed that his plan was not disapproved of. The work appeared in 1849. Extremely well written, giving the fullest and the most accurate details of events, the book possessed one quality which, in the view of the Governor-General of the day, the Marquis of Dalhousie, rendered the publication of it a crime. It told the whole truth, the unpalatable truth, regarding the first Sikh war: it exposed the real strength of the Sikh army; the conduct of, and the negotiations with, the Sikh chiefs.

The book, if unnoticed by high authority, would have injured no one. The Panjáb had been annexed, or was in the process of annexation, when it appeared. But a despotic Government cannot endure truths which seem to reflect on the justice of its policy. Looking at the policy of annexation from the basis of Cunningham's book, that policy was undoubtedly unjust. Cunningham's book would be widely read, and would influence the general verdict. Now, Lord Dalhousie was not only a despot, but a despot who hated the expression of free opinion and of free thought; he would be served only by men who would think as he bade them think. That an officer holding a high political office should write a book which, by the facts disclosed in it, reflected, however indirectly, on his policy, was not to be endured. With one stroke of the pen, then, he removed Cunningham from his appointment at Bhopál.

Cunningham, stunned by the blow, entirely unexpected, died of a broken heart!

Lord Dalhousie could crush Cunningham, but he could not crush his work. The truths given to the world by this conscientious and faithful historian will for ever be the basis upon which a history of the Sikh war, worthy of the name of history, will be written. In my chapter on Fírúz-shahar and Sobráon, then, I have adopted the view which Cunningham put forward, and which my own subsequent investigations absolutely confirmed. The conclusions arrived at regarding the Sikh leaders obtain a strong support, moreover, from the fact that, after the war, the men who received the largest rewards, and the greatest share of the British confidence, were Lál Singh and Téj Singh, the two leaders who, nominally at the head of the war party, had betrayed their followers!

With respect to the actual fighting, I have consulted, I repeat, and to a great extent followed, the narrative of the campaign written by Sir Herbert Edwardes in 1846, in the *Calcutta Review*. The article has since been republished with the name of the author attached to it.*

I have relied on the same authority (Edwardes's *Year on the Panjáb Frontier*) for the true story of the events which preceded, and which immediately followed, the rebellion of Mulráj in 1848. The campaign which ensued was described and criticised at the time by one who took a part in it—the late Sir Henry Durand. A cool, able, and impartial critic, favouring no one and blaming where blame was deserved, Durand has left a record which it is impossible to ignore.

* *Selections from the Calcutta Review.* Calcutta: Thos. S. Smith.

The article, which appeared in the *Calcutta Review* for June 1851, and which has since been republished with the name of the author attached (*Selections from the Calcutta Review*), must be consulted and studied by everyone who would wish to understand events as they actually happened. Indeed, Durand's article bears the relation to the second Sikh war which Cunningham's book bears to the first. One remarkable fact in connection with it is that both articles were written by Engineers, and both were written at Bhopál. Durand succeeded Cunningham as political agent at that place! The fact that Durand's article was unsigned, and that it criticised only military manœuvres, saved him from any open expression of the wrath of the Saturn who had devoured his predecessor!

The military despatches of the second Panjáb campaign are as unreliable and as worthless as those of the first. They were denounced at the time, in the most uncompromising manner, by the Indian press. Some other contemporary memoirs are not much better. But I have studied very carefully, for the purposes of this as I did for the purposes of the first Sikh campaign, the letters of officers written at the time. I have likewise made considerable use of a little work written on the campaign, some five years ago, by an officer formerly in the 24th Foot, Captain Lawrence-Archer,* and which appears to me to be a model of the style in which such a work should be written.

It remains now to add that these decisive battles have during the past twelvemonth appeared as articles in the

* *Commentaries on the Panjáb Campaign of* 1848–49. London: W. H. Allen & Co.

pages of the *Army and Navy Magazine*; that the actual fighting details of one of them, Plassey, occur in my *Life of Lord Clive*. In the same work appears also a description of the battle of Kávéripák; but, in this volume, many details have been added to it. The other battles have been compiled and written expressly for this series.

I have found it difficult to obtain reliable plans of the earlier battles. I have given, therefore, but three, relating to those not of the least importance—Plassey, Chiliánwálá, and Gujrát. To supply, as far as possible, the omission, I have arranged that the map accompanying the book shall contain the name of every important place mentioned in its pages.

CONTENTS.

INSTRUCTIONS TO THE BINDER.

Portrait . . .		*to face title page.*	
Map of India		*in pocket.*	
Plan of the Battle of Plassey		*to face page*	60.
"	Fortress of Bharatpúr .	"	326.
"	Battle of Chiliánwálá .	"	417.
"	" Gujrát .	"	431.

THE

DECISIVE BATTLES OF INDIA.

CHAPTER I.

ST. THOMÉ.

The story of the rise and progress of the British power in India possesses peculiar fascination for all classes of readers. It is a romance sparkling with incidents of the most varied character. It appeals alike to the sympathetic qualities of the heart and the colder calculations of the brain. Whilst it lays bare the defects in the character of the native races which made their subjugation possible, it indicates the trusting and faithful nature, the impressionable character, the passionate appreciation of great qualities, which formed alike the strength and the weakness of those races—their strength after they had been conquered, their weakness during the struggle. It was those qualities which set repeatedly whole divisions of the race in opposition to other divisions—the conquered and the willing co-operators to the sections still remaining to be subdued. There are few studies more alluring than the study of the habits and manner of thought which made this process possible. The student will most certainly discover faults, indigenous and imported, the former the result mainly of an over-refinement of civilisation, the latter pertaining to or derived from the Muhammadan invader. But in the combination of astuteness with simplicity, of fearlessness of death and conspicuous personal daring with inferiority on the field of battle, in the gentleness, the submission, the devotion to their leader which characterised so many of the children of the soil, he will not fail to recognise a character which demands the affection, even the esteem, of the European race which, chiefly by means of the defects and virtues I have alluded to, now exercises overlordship in Hindústán.

Of the different sections of the story of the rise and progress of the British power, not one so well illustrates the qualities I have referred to as that which relates the earlier phases of the conquest of the country. In those earlier days the position of the European trader and the native of India was the direct converse of the position of the present day. Then, the European trader was the vassal, holding his lands as a rent payer and on condition of good behaviour, recognising the native ruler of the province as his overlord. It was a consequence of this well-recognised position that, when, in 1744, war broke out between France and England, and the governor of Madras made preparations to attack the French settlement of Pondichery, the governor of that settlement, M. Dupleix, appealed to the Núwáb of the Karnátak, not, indeed, to afford him aid, but to command his English tenants to renounce the threatened attack. It never entered into the head of the Madras governor either to question the right of the Núwáb to issue the order, or to dispute it. Nay, more: when the English governor, professing his readiness to obey the Núwáb as faras his own power extended, expressed a regret that his authority did not reach the English fleet, which, he stated, was under the separate orders of the English commodore, and when the Núwáb answered that he should expect all English officers who came to the Koromándal coast to respect his government, the English governor, far from remonstrating, hastened to prevail upon the commander of the fleet to abstain likewise from all attack upon the French. Such was the state of affairs in Southern India so late as the year 1745. The European trader was simply the permanent occupier, on a fixed rental, of a portion of the lands of the lord of the country. He possessed the right only to claim the protection of that overlord when he might be attacked.

In one year—I might almost say in a few months—this position became practically inverted. The marvellous combination of circumstances by which this result was attained is known to every student of early Indian history. Until recently, however, the majority of students have cared only to examine the action on the part of the rival European traders which precipitated the change. But few have taken into consideration the workings of the native mind which enormously aided it. Had all classes of natives been able to combine as the inhabitants of a European country invaded by a foreign foe would combine, such a revolution would, at that time at all events, have been impossible. I may go even further, and affirm that if the English had been the only settlers on the coast, the revolution would not even have been thought of. It is a remarkable fact, but a fact which cannot even be questioned, that the English owe their empire in India to two causes—the first, French ambition; the second, that combination of virtues and defects in the native character of which I have already spoken.

How French ambition acted as a main factor in the events which followed the assertion, in 1745, by the Núwáb of the Karnátak of his supreme authority over all the Koromándal coast and in the waters of the Indian seas adjacent to that coast, has been told by every writer of Anglo-Indian history. The subject has been treated as a matter concerning principally the two European nations. Undoubtedly it did greatly concern them. Although subsequently to 1746 the French and English fought as the partisans of rival chiefs struggling for supremacy, they became within a very few years the arbiters of the positive. The dynasties and chiefs under whose shadow and on whose behalf they fought have for the most part disappeared or been despoiled—despoiled in course of time, after success had been attained, by the very European race enlisted in the beginning to support their claims. Tanjúr, the Karnátak, Trichinápalli, Madura, all tell the same story. Rightly, then, in one sense, have English historians of the period treated the subject as a matter affecting principally the rival European traders who, under the shadow of native chieftains, were really fighting for predominance, I might even say for supremacy, in Southern India.

Sufficient attention has not, I think, been paid, hitherto, to the train of thought which influenced many of the natives of that and of later periods, nor has it been duly considered how the combination of the qualities I have referred to, their fidelity to their temporary masters, and their appreciation of heroic qualities displayed by those masters, contributed to bring about the result. These are questions which must be examined in connection with the scenes which occupy the most prominent position in the drama—the scenes in which the Europeans fill a prominent place. In each successive scene of each successive drama, there was always one decisive point. Round that point were grouped the hopes, the wishes, the fears, the secret ambitions of thousands. In those days, and even to the present day in India, the decisive point of each scene was and is a battle. Whether it were a battle of giants or a battle of pigmies, whether the slain were many or were few, that battle, when it was decisive, changed the destinies of princes and of peoples. It has appeared to me, then, that a short and succinct account of the decisive battles of India—decisive as they affected the predominance of one European race, first over its European rival, and secondly over the children of the soil—would afford an opportunity to bring into prominence those qualities of the natives to which I have so often alluded.

The battles I have selected mark, each one, a new epoch, some of them even a revolutionary epoch, in the history of India, and contain within themselves a full and complete explanation of the sudden and remarkable transformation of which I have spoken—the transformation within a few short months of a vassal tenantry into a position of virtual sovereignty. They will explain even more than that; they will explain how it was that the natives of India worked freely, loyally, with their eyes open, and with all their might and main, for their own subjection to a foreign power.

By a striking example I have shown how the relative positions of the native rulers and the European traders towards each other were from the beginning placed on a distinct and well-defined basis. The established order of things which forced the governor of the English settlement to obey, sorely against his inclination, the command of the Nuwáb of the Karnátak to abstain from all hostile action against the French, revealed relations between the two races which were not, apparently, lightly to be shaken. That command, and the obedience paid to it, made it abundantly clear that the European settlers occupied towards the ruler of the country a position precisely analagous to that now maintained by the native princes of India towards their European overlord. The European settlers were allowed then, as the native princes are allowed now, complete administrative action within the territory held by them, but they, like the native princes of the present day, were prohibited from waging war against each other. For defence against an enemy, the native ruler had then, as the European overlord has now, to be trusted to. The principle acts well now, because the European overlord really possesses the power to carry it out. It failed on the Koromándal coast because, on the first attempt to enforce his authority, the native ruler was baffled. His failure manifested itself in the first pitched battle between the European settlers and the native overlord. The battle was perhaps more than any, certainly as much as any, ever delivered, a decisive battle. It was fought on the same lines as subsequent battles between the Europeans and the natives of India have been fought; it showed the discipline, the skill, the inventive power of the few, opposed to the bad generalship, the untutored valour, the want of cohesion, the absence of patriotic feeling, of the many. But it was the first of its kind. It broke a spell which, unchallenged, might have exerted its influence for many years. It inverted, almost immediately, not openly, yet most really, the positions of the vassal and the overlord. From the day on which it was gained, supremacy in Southern India became the fixed idea in the brain of the illustrious governor of the people who had won it. In the course of time the idea passed, almost unconsciously, to his successful rivals. They certainly had not dreamed of it in the earlier days. That it finally became a part, though for long years an unwritten part, of their creed, was, however, the certain and logical consequence of the battle which first conveyed to the native rulers of Southern India the conviction that the Europeans, whom they had allowed to settle on their coasts, were able to dictate terms even to them. Thenceforth the position of vassal and overlord, recognised as binding in 1745, was broken, never to be re-imposed.

It happened in this wise. The English, ordered by the Núwáb in 1745 to abstain from all hostilities against their French rivals, had obeyed; but in 1746, the French finding themselves superior on the coast to the English, possessing a fleet which had driven away that of their rivals, an army largely outnumbering theirs, deemed the moment too opportune to be lost. The clumsy action of the English governor came to aid their endeavours to persuade the native overlord, the Núwáb of the Karnátak, to allow them power of unrestricted action. That governor, warned of the French intentions, had appealed to the

Núwáb to issue to his rivals the prohibition which had been imposed upon himself the preceding year; but, whether from ignorance or from thoughtlessness, he had committed the grave offence of sending his messenger empty-handed into the presence of the Núwáb. The latter was still smarting under this barbaric insolence, as he considered it, when there arrived, laden with choice and costly presents from Europe, a messenger from M. Dupleix, Governor of Pondichery. The Núwáb was an old man, and he had the reputation of being a capable man; but on this occasion, he allowed his feelings to dictate his policy. One word from him, and the French preparations would have been stayed. He would not speak that word. Whilst his better instincts withheld him from giving absolute sanction to the plans of the French, his preference for that people, and his anger against the English, combined to stifle the prohibitory sentence which would have enforced his true policy. The silence was fatal to him and to his race. Unfettered by prohibition, the French sent an expedition against Madras (September 1746). Before the place had actually fallen, the Núwáb, recovering from his infatuation, had despatched to Pondichery, on a swift dromedary, a messenger bearing a letter to Dupleix, in which he expressed his surprise that the French should have waged war in his territories, and threatening to send an army to enforce his orders unless the siege were immediately raised. Dupleix was too accustomed to deal with the natives of India to hesitate as to the reply he should give to this citation. His main object was to expel the English from Madras. Whether that place should fall permanently to the French or to the Núwáb was a matter, for the moment, of only secondary importance. He, therefore, replied that his object in attacking Madras was to secure the interests of the Núwáb, as on its conquest the English would gladly pay him a large ransom for its restoration; that for that purpose the French would at once make it over to him on its surrender. These were mere words intended only to gain time. Before the Núwáb could form a decision to act, or not to act, Madras had surrendered to the French (21st September 1746).

As soon as the Núwáb learned that Madras had fallen he despatched his son, Máphuz Khán, at the head of 10,000 men, mostly horsemen, to take up a position in the vicinity of the fort so as to be ready to receive it when the French should be ready to evacuate it. But when one week, then two, three, and even five weeks passed, and the French still answered all his demands for the surrender with evasions, the suspicion that he had been duped began gradually to take possession of the mind of the Asiatic ruler. Up to the end of the fifth week the French had been able to offer an excuse for their conduct, which had, at all events, the appearance of validity. The disputes between La Bourdonnais and Dupleix—the former pledged to restore Madras to the English for a consideration, the latter resolved to keep it for his nation—had—La Bourdonnais being in possession—tied the hands of Dupleix. But on the 23rd October the departure of La Bourdonnais left Dupleix free to act. Still he did not keep his promise to the Núwáb. He had no intention of keeping it, for he had resolved to risk rather the fury of his overlord; he had transmitted orders to his lieutenant, Duval d'Esprémesnil, to hold Madras at all hazards, and against all enemies whatsoever.

The Núwáb, for a long time cajoled, lost patience at last. Two days after the departure of La Bourdonnais, he directed his son, Máphuz Khán, to lay siege to Madras, and to drive out the French just as the French had driven out the English. He had no idea whatever that this would be a matter of any difficulty. The French had always carried themselves so humbly, they had professed so much respect for himself, for his officers, and for his people, that he had believed that this behaviour was but the outward expression of conscious inferiority. He knew that their white soldiers numbered from five to six hundred, and that their native levies were as numerous. His son commanded ten times that number, and many more levies were marching to support him. He had, then, but to demand admittance within the fort. Who would venture to refuse to comply?

Sharing such thoughts, Máphuz Khán presented himself, on the 26th October, before the town. Entrance having been refused, he took up a position commanding its water-supply. The French governor, M. Duval d'Esprémesnil,* father of the politician who made himself so prominent in the last of the old French *parlements*, had not been bred a soldier, but he possessed courage, common-sense, and energy, which, against such an enemy, more than supplied the want of military training. Under instructions from Pondichery he had, on the approach of Máphuz Khán, drawn the whole of his troops within the walls of the fort, determined to offer only a passive resistance to the army of his suzerain. But when Máphuz Khán showed himself very earnest in the attack, when he began to erect a battery, and when he occupied a position which cut off the water-supply of the town, then d'Esprémesnil found it necessary to abandon his passive attitude. At first he ventured only to fire upon the men engaged in erecting the battery; but though this act of vigour drove away the assailants from the mound on which they were working, it did not affect those engaged in diverting the water, for these were out of range. More decisive measures were thus forced upon him. It had become a question either of unconditional submission to a suzerain who had been irritated and defied, or of an attack upon his troops. D'Esprémesnil wisely chose the

* Duval d'Esprémesnil was likewise son-in-law of Dupleix, and second member of the Council of Pondichery. He possessed, to a degree which would be considered rare even in these days, a knowledge of the people of India, their languages, and their customs. In 1747, he had the hardihood to disguise himself as a Brahman, and visit the most famous temples and pagodas of India. He succeeded, without being discovered, in penetrating the holiest recesses into which no one but a member of that sacred caste was allowed to enter.

second course. On the night of the 1st November he made all the preparations for a sortie. Early on the following morning 400 men with two field-pieces sallied from the fort to attack the portion of the besieging force which was guarding the spring which supplied the town. As this handful of men advanced, the guns behind their centre, on the point previously indicated, the enemy's horsemen, who had mounted in all haste, moved towards them with the intention of charging them. The French at once halted, extended from the centre to allow their guns to move to the front, then, when the enemy had come within range, they opened fire.

That the reader may understand the feelings which animated the horsemen of Máphuz Khán before the French guns had fired at all, and the bewilderment which came over them after the second discharge, it is necessary I should state that the practice of artillery, as understood by European soldiers, was not at all comprehended in Southern India. It is true that the native chiefs possessed guns, but not only were these guns, as a rule, uncared for, or so old that it was a positive risk to fire them, but the natives were so unskilful in their management, that they thought they had done well when they discharged them once in a quarter of an hour. Never having been engaged in warfare with Europeans, they had no idea that it was possible to fire the same piece five or six times in a minute. Their invariable practice, then, was to await the first discharge of an enemy's artillery, then, in the full belief that they had a good quarter of an hour before them before the fire could be renewed, to advance boldly and rapidly.

Their feelings, then, when the French guns opened upon them on the occasion of the sortie I am describing, may be easily imagined. That discharge killed two or three horses only. What other thought could then have possessed the Indian horsemen but this, that at the expense of those horses they had the enemy in their power? Amongst themselves, cavalry could always ride down infantry; and now the infantry before them had thrown away their one solid support. They were preparing to use to the best advantage the quarter of an hour thus, in their belief, foolishly granted them, when another flash from the same guns, followed with great rapidity by another and another and another, came to show them that they had been living in the paradise of fools, that they had before them a new kind of enemy, an enemy of whose strange and fearful devices they knew nothing. More even than the sight of the emptying saddles in their midst, the contemplation of the unknown process came to weaken their morale. Imagination added horrors to visible slaughter. After a few moments' hesitation, they turned and fled in disorder. D'Esprémesnil had not only regained his water-supply—he had not only forced the enemy to raise the siege—he had gained a victory over the minds and imaginations of the Indian soldiers, the consequences of which were permanent. He had driven in the thin end of the wedge which was to bring to the ground the whole fabric of the Mughul empire.

There was needed, however, a stronger, a more decided blow of the mallet to drive in the wedge a little further, to prevent the close of the fissure caused by the first. A comparatively few men of the army of Máphuz Khán had witnessed the magic power of the French guns. Those few men had been panic-stricken; they had communicated their panic to their comrades; their comrades had fled they knew not why. The original fugitives when questioned doubtless varied their replies. No one could positively declare the actual number of hostile guns. After all, they began to argue, the victory might have been the result of skilful management. They came by degrees to the belief that the French must have had several guns, and that they had fired only two at one time, then two more, whilst the others were reloading. This would explain much of the mishap. At the end of a few hours, after the subject had been well ventilated, and the heroes of the flight had recovered their equanimity, it probably was so explained. At all events, the dismay of the native soldiers evaporated.

Máphuz Khán had lost seventy men by the fire of the French guns. He had raised the siege and had taken up a position two miles to the westward of Madras. He was there, when, on the day following his discomfiture, he learned that a French force, marching from Pondichery to Madras, would arrive at St. Thomé, four miles to the west of that place, the following morning. By this time big talk and bluster had succeeded the panic of the previous morning. Máphuz Khán, who had not been one of the fugitives, and who probably attributed the defeat of his soldiers to a sudden but ordinary panic, was burning to avenge himself on the audacious Europeans. He immediately, then, took a step worthy of a great commander. Resolving to intercept the approaching force before it should effect its junction with the garrison of Madras, he marched that evening (3rd November) on the town of St. Thomé, and took up a strong position on the northern bank of the river Adyár, at the very point where it would be necessary for the French to cross it, and lined the bank with his guns.

The detachment which was approaching consisted of 230 Europeans and 700 sepoys. There were no guns with it. But its commander, Paradis, was a man to supply any deficiency. A Swiss by birth, and an engineer by profession, Paradis had been selected by Dupleix, in the dearth of senior officers of the military service, for command in the field. Paradis amply justified the discernment of the French governor, for he had been born with the qualities which no soldier can acquire—decision of character, calmness, and energy.

The movements of Máphuz Khán had not been so secretly carried out as to escape the notice of the French within Madras. Aware of the approach of Paradis, and divining the motives of Máphuz Khán, d'Esprémesnil had at once despatched a messenger to the former, recommending him to defer an engagement with Máphuz Khán until the garrison of Madras should have time to operate on his rear. But events would not allow Paradis to delay the contest. At daybreak on the morning of the 4th November, that officer approached the south bank of the Adyár. He beheld the whole space between the north bank of that river and the town of St. Thomé—a space about a quarter of a mile in length—occupied by the hostile army—the bank itself as far as eye could reach lined with their guns, each gun well-manned. There they were, horse, foot, and artillery, more than 10,000 in number, barring the road to Madras.

If Paradis entertained any doubt as to the motives which swayed the leader of the masses on the northern bank, a discharge of artillery directed against his advancing troops quickly dispelled it. Under such circumstances, to await on the south bank the promised co-operation appeared to him a proceeding fraught with peril. A halt where he was would be impossible, for he was under the fire of the enemy's guns; he must fall back, even though it should be only a few hundred yards. Such a movement would, he thought, expose him, unprovided with guns, to a charge from the enemy's horsemen, eager to avenge their defeat of two days' previously. His Europeans were fighting for the first time on Indian ground, his native troops were raw levies. With such material, could he, dare he, encounter the risk of retiring? On the other hand, a bold advance would inspire his men and discourage the enemy.

Such thoughts coursed through the brain of Paradis as his men were advancing under fire. His resolution was immediately taken. His bold spirit had solved in an instant the problem as to the method to be pursued when European troops should be pitted against the natives of India. That method was, under all circumstances, to advance to close quarters. With a cool and calm decision, then, he plunged without hesitation into the waters of the Adyár, and led his infantry to attack the three arms of the enemy, ten times their superior in numbers.

Up to the moment of reaching the south bank of the Adyár, the French force had not suffered very much from the fire of the enemy's guns. The aim had been bad and the guns had been ill-served. They were still, however, dangerous, and the troops felt that their capture would decide the day. Without drawing trigger, then, they followed Paradis to the bank of the river; then, wading through it, delivered one volley and charged. The effect was electric. The Indian troops, unaccustomed to such precipitate action, gave way, abandoned their guns, and retreated as fast as they could into the town. The walls of the town had many gaps in it, but the Indians had taken the precaution to cover these on the western face with palisades. Behind these palisades they now took refuge, and from this new position opposed a strong front to the advancing force. The French, however, did not allow them time to recover the spirit which alone would have made a successful defence possible. Advancing and always advancing, in good order, and firing by sections as they did so, they forced the enemy to abandon these new defences. The defeat now became a rout. Falling back on each other in the narrow streets of the town, the enemy's horse and foot became mixed in hopeless confusion, exposed, without being able to return it, or to extricate themselves, to the relentless fire of the French. Máphuz Khán himself, mounted on an elephant, had made his escape early in the day. His troops were less fortunate. Their very numbers impeded their movements. When, at last, in small bodies, in twos and threes, they made their exit from the northern gate and attempted to hurry away with the baggage and camp equipage that yet remained to them, they found themselves face to face with the body of Europeans sent by d'Esprémesnil from Madras to co-operate with Paradis. Then they abandoned everything, baggage, horses, oxen, rams, even hope itself, and fled across the plain in wild confusion. The French were too much occupied in plundering their camp to pursue them further. But the terror which had struck into their souls was proved by the fact that they made no attempt to unite in masses till they had covered many miles in the direction of Arkát, and then only to fall back with all possible speed upon that capital of the Karnátak.

Such was the decisive battle of St. Thomé. "It was now," writes Mr. Orme, the contemporary historian of that period, "more than a century since any of the European nations had gained a decisive advantage in war against the officers of the Great Mughul. The experience of former unsuccessful enterprises, and the scantiness of military abilities which prevailed in all the colonies, from a long disuse of arms, had persuaded them that the Moors were a brave and formidable enemy; when the French at once broke through the charm of this timorous opinion, by defeating a whole army with a single battalion."

"It may be well asserted," writes another author,* in language which I now reproduce, "that of all the decisive actions that have been fought in India, there is not one more memorable than this. Not, indeed, that there has not since been displayed a daring equal to that of Paradis, or that numbers as disproportionate have not, within the memory of the living, achieved a victory as important. The circumstance which stamps this action as so memorable is that it was the very first of its kind, that it proved, to the surprise of both parties, the overwhelming superiority of the European soldier to his Asiatic rival. Up to that moment the native princes of Southern India had, by virtue of their position as lords of the soil, or as satraps of the Mughul, arrogated to themselves a superiority which none of the European settlers had ever thought of disputing. With the French, as we have seen, it had been a maxim of settled policy to avoid the semblance of hostility towards them. We have noticed how Martin and Dumas and Dupleix had toiled to effect this end. When at last Dupleix, to avoid a more dangerous contingency, accepted the

* *History of the French in India.*

dreaded alternative of hostility, he did so more in the hope that he might find some means to pacify the Núwáb whilst the siege was in progress than in any expectation of routing him in the field. And now, suddenly, unexpectedly, this result had been achieved. From being the suppliants of the Núwáb of the Karnátak, the vassals whose every movement depended upon his license, the French, in a moment, found themselves, in reality, his superiors. The action at St. Thomé completely reversed the positions of the Núwáb and the French governor. Not only that, but it inaugurated a new era, it introduced a fresh order of things, it was the first decided step to the conquest of Hindústán by a European power. Whether that power were French or English would depend upon the relative strength of the two nations, and even more on the character of the men by whom that strength should be put in action. The battle which introduced this change deserves, then, well to be remembered; and, in recalling it to our memories, let not us, who are English, forget that the merit of it is due, solely and entirely, to that great nation which fought with us the battle of empire on Indian soil, and did not win it."

I find it difficult to add anything to this true description of the consequences of this most decisive battle. It was the prelude to many more resembling it in results. But not one of those which followed was fought under circumstances precisely similar. Prior to the sortie of d'Esprémesnil from Madras, which may be taken as the first part of the battle which so quickly followed it, the prestige, the morale, were on the side of the children of the soil. The humble traders had, before 1746, never thought of questioning the authority, or of doubting the power, of the satraps of the Indian provinces. It was the striking, the momentous, I might almost say the eternal, consequence of those two acts of the same drama that the prestige and the morale were transferred from the natives—from chief and follower alike—to the European settlers. Of almost every subsequent battle between the European and the Asiatic, it may be said that, in consequence of that transfer, it was half won before it had been fought. This was the magic power which the France of the Bourbons won in November 1746, and which she subsequently transferred, not willingly, to England.

CHAPTER II.

KÁVÉRIPÁK.

The results of the decisive victory gained by Paradis at St. Thomé were soon manifested. The influence of the French became supreme in the Karnátak. Three years after that event, the governor of Pondichery was able to establish the prince whose cause he had espoused in the Subadárship of the Dakhan, a position greater than that now occupied by the Nizám. Another nobleman, likewise protected by him, he had proclaimed Núwáb of the Karnátak, with the possession of the whole of that province except Tanjúr and Trichinápalli. The time had not arrived when a European power could openly assert supreme dominion, but in January 1751 almost the whole of south-eastern India recognised the moral predominance of Pondichery. The country between the Vindhayan range and the river Krishna, including the provinces known as the Northern Sirkárs, was virtually ruled by the French general whose army occupied the capital of the Subadár of the Dakhan. South of the river Krishna, the country known as the Karnátak, including Nellúr, North and South Arkát, Madura, and Tinnevelli, was ruled virtually from Pondichery. The only places not subject to French influence were Madras, restored to England by the Treaty of Aix la Chapelle; Fort St. David, within a few miles of

Pondichery, held by the English; Tanjúr, whose Rájah had not acknowledged the supremacy of the French nominee; and Trichinápalli, held by a rival candidate for the Núwábship, supported by the English. Madras and Fort St. David were, under the circumstances of the peace with England, unassailable; but everything seemed to point to the conclusion that Trichinápalli and Tanjúr would speedily fall under the supremacy which had successfully asserted itself over the other portions of the Karnátak. A large army, supported by a French contingent, was marching on Trichinápalli. The English, by the loss of Madras, by the failure of an attempt made in 1748 to capture Pondichery, and by the ill-success which had attended them when opposed to the French at Valkunda, had gained the unhappy reputation of being unable to fight. There seemed to be no power, no influence, capable of thwarting the plans which the brain of Dupleix had built up on the firm base of the victory gained by Paradis at St. Thomé.

Nor, had the French possessed a real soldier capable of conducting military operations—had their troops been led by a Clive, a Stringer Lawrence, or even by a Paradis—could those plans have failed of success? It happened, however, for their misfortune, that at this particular epoch their forces were commanded by men singularly wanting in the energy, in the decision, in the rapid *coup d'œil* essential to form a general. At first it seemed that this misfortune would not be necessarily fatal; for if it were true that their army besieging Trichinápalli was led by men who would dare nothing, the English allies of the defenders possessed commanders of mental calibre certainly not superior. As the French were vastly superior in numbers it was clear that, the commanders on both sides being equal, the victory must in the end be with them. But they had made no provision either for time or for the unforeseen. When their plans seemed gradually verging towards success, and the fall of Trichinápalli—by the slow process of famine—seemed to loom in a not very distant future, a young Englishman, not yet a soldier, though endowed by nature with the talents which go to form a finished commander, had suddenly burst into the province of Arkát, had seized the capital; then resisting for fifty days, and finally repulsing, a besieging native army, aided by Frenchmen exceeding his own European garrison in numbers, had proved conclusively to the world of Southern India—to use the actual words used by the famous Marátha leader, Murári Rao—"that the English could fight."

The splendid diversion made by Robert Clive in northern Arkát was not in itself decisive of the fate of Trichinápalli. The French and their native allies continued to press the siege though in the same slow and perfunctory manner as before. The fate of Southern India depended upon the fall of that place. The time employed to besiege Clive in Arkát gave the French precious opportunities to take it. They threw them all away. They attempted nothing. Fancying that Clive was, at Arkát, in a trap whence he could never emerge to trouble them, they still trusted to the slow process of starvation. They were roused from their fools' paradise by the intelligence that the young Englishman had forced the besiegers to retire; had subsequently beaten them in a pitched battle, and was then engaged at Fort St. David in raising troops to march to the relief of the besieged of Trichinápalli.

Fortune, however, had not yet abandoned the French. The blind goddess was content to give them one more chance. Whilst Clive was preparing a force to march to the relief of Trichinápalli, the energetic governor of Pondichery incited his native allies to raise a fresh army, and to send it—well supported by French soldiers—not only to reconquer north Arkát, but to threaten Madras itself. He argued, and argued soundly, that such a diversion would, in the attenuated condition of the English garrisons, render it imperative on Clive to forego his march on Trichinápalli, and hasten to the defence of the threatened posts.

These—if the French and their allies would only display energy and resolution—might be captured. The fall of Trichinápalli would not fail to follow.

At first, events fully confirmed the anticipations of Dupleix. No sooner had Rizá Sáhib, the Indian chief whom Clive had repulsed from Arkát and defeated at Ární, felt that the province was relieved from the awe inspired by the presence of the young Englishman who had conquered him, than, re-uniting his scattered troops, and calling to him a body of 400 Frenchmen, he appeared suddenly at Punamallí (17 January 1752). The only English troops that could possibly oppose him were shut up, to the number of about a hundred, in Madras; about two hundred and fifty were in Arkát. The allied French and Indian forces were, therefore, practically unopposed in the field. Using their advantages—I will not say to the utmost, for, placed in their position, Clive would have employed them far more effectively—the allies ravaged the territory belonging to the East India Company down to the very sea-side; burned several villages, and plundered the country houses built by the English at the foot of St. Thomas's Mount. The fact that peace existed between France and England probably deterred them from attempting an attack upon Madras. They worked, however, as much damage in its neighbourhood as would affect very sensibly the revenues of the country, and then marched on Kánchipuram (Conjeveram). Having repaired the damages which the English had caused to the fortified pagoda of this place only a very short time before, they placed in it a garrison of 300 native troops; then moving to Vendalúr, twenty-five miles south of Madras, established there a fortified camp, from which they levied contributions on the country around. Although the forts of Punamallí and Arkát invited attack, they attempted no serious military enterprise. Their aim was so to threaten the English as to force them to send all their available troops into the province of north Arkát, and thus to procure for the French besiegers of Trichinápalli the time necessary to capture that place. They were to run their heads against no walls, to keep their troops fresh for the emergency which was certain, when it should come, to demand all their energies, and then suddenly to strike the one blow which would secure the supremacy of the French in Southern India. It was an extremely well-devised plan, and it very nearly succeeded.

In the outset it met with the success which had been hoped for. It procured a respite for Trichinápalli. Clive, engaged at Fort St. David in making preparations for the relief of that place, was suddenly ordered to proceed to Madras, and to use there to the best advantage the means he would find at his disposal. Clive set out, reached Madras early in February, found there about 100 Europeans and a few half-drilled native levies, and expectations of the daily arrival of about the same number of Europeans from Bengal. A few days later these expectations were fulfilled. The interval had been employed in ordering up four-fifths of the Europeans and 500 of the sepoys forming the garrison of Arkát, in drilling the native levies, in raising others, in laying in stores for a campaign, and in obtaining information regarding the enemy. Clive soon learned that the allies lay still at Vendalúr, apparently waiting to receive him there. On the 20th February the troops from Bengal arrived; on the 21st, Clive received information that the garrison of Arkát would march in the following morning. No time was to be lost if Trichinápalli were to be saved. On the 22nd, then, Clive set out from Madras, and, joined that day by his old soldiers from Arkát, marched at once in the direction of Vendalúr. His united force consisted of 380 Europeans and 1,300 sepoys, with six field-pieces. Marching all night, he hoped to be able to surprise the enemy early the following morning. But it formed no part of the French plan to await the arrival of Clive in their camp at Vendalúr. Well served by their spies, they were acquainted with all the movements of their enemy

On the night preceding the day, then, on which Clive set out from Madras, the French and their allies, acting on a plan preconcerted to puzzle the English leader, quitted Vendalúr, and marched in different directions. Re-uniting at Kánchipuram, they hurried by a forced march to Arkát, hoping to surprise its reduced garrison. With this object in view they had corrupted some of the native soldiers within the fort, and had pre-arranged with these to make a signal, to which, if all were satisfactory, their friends were to reply. They entered the town of Arkát very early in the morning, and made the signal. Receiving no response, they concluded—what was the fact—that the plot had been discovered. Then, reverting to their tactics of marching away in different directions, they quitted Arkát, only to reunite at Káváripák and occupy there a position, in which it had been pre-determined, even should the attempt on Arkát succeed, to receive Clive. They had marched fifty-eight miles in less than thirty hours.

The French plans showed very skilful calculation. It will be clear to the reader that their object had been to alarm Clive regarding their real aims, to draw him on by forced marches towards a position where he could only fight at disadvantage. The attempt on Arkát would, they knew, incite the English leader to desperate exertions. They divined, moreover, that pressing to its relief, and marching by night, he would fall into the trap they had laid for him, for marching on Arkát he must traverse the town of Kávéripák. Before he could reach it, they would have several hours for rest and preparations. Their anticipations were realised almost to the letter.

Clive, we have seen, had set out from Madras, on the 22nd, with the object of surprising, by a forced march, the hostile forces at Vendalúr. He had not proceeded quite half-way, however, when intelligence reached him of their sudden disappearance from that place and their dispersion in different directions. The second portion of the intelligence left him no option but to push on to

Vendalúr with all speed to make there the necessary inquiries, He arrived there about 3 o'clock in the afternoon to find the enemy had disappeared, no one knew, or no one would say, whither. A few hours later, certain intelligence reached him that they were at Kánchipuram. That place was twenty miles distant. It was 9 o'clock; his men had that day marched twenty-five miles; but they had had a rest of five hours, had eaten, and were in good spirits. Clive, therefore, pushed on at once, and by a forced march reached Kánchipuram about 4 o'clock on the morning of the 23rd, to find that the French and their allies had been there only once again to disappear. He felt certain now that they would attempt Arkát. Without positive intelligence, however, and with troops, who, for the most part, without any previous training, had marched forty-five miles in twenty-four hours, he felt it unadvisable to move further. Contenting himself with summoning the pagoda, which surrendered on the first citation, he ordered his troops to rest. A few hours later his conjecture was confirmed by positive information that the French were in full march on Arkát. Certain that a crisis was approaching which would demand all the energies of his men Clive did not disturb their slumbers.

Arkát is twenty-seven miles from Kánchipuram. Although Clive entertained no doubt whatever that the former place would resist successfully the attempt which, he now felt sure, the French and their allies would make upon it, he was naturally anxious to reach it with as little delay as possible. Accordingly, after granting his troops a few hours sleep and a meal, he started a little after noon, on the road to Arkát. Towards sunset his troops had covered sixteen miles, and had come within sight of the town of Kávéripák. They were marching leisurely, in loose order, totally unsuspicious of danger, when suddenly, from the right of the road, from a point distant about 250 yards, there opened upon them a brisk artillery fire. That fire proceeded from the French guns.

That the reader may clearly understand the position, I propose to return for a moment to the French and their allies. I have already related how, in the early part of this very day, their combined forces, after having vainly attempted Arkát, had marched on Kávéripák, and taken up there a strong position, barring the road to Clive. In numbers they were superior to him, but mainly only in cavalry. Clive had no horsemen with him. His enemy had 2,500. In other respects they exceeded him only slightly, having 400 Europeans to his 380, 2,000 sepoys to his 1,300, and nine guns and three mortars to his six guns. I have searched the French records in vain to find the name of their European commander. In this respect he has been fortunate, for the conduct he displayed on this occasion was not of a character to evoke the gratitude of his nation. The commander of the natives and nominal commander of the whole force, was Rizá Sáhib, son of the titular Núwáb of the Karnátak.

The position they occupied had been extremely well chosen. A thick grove of mango-trees, covered along its front on two sides by a ditch and bank, forming almost a small redoubt fortified on the faces towards which an enemy must advance, and open only on the sides held in force by the defenders, covered the ground about 250 yards to the left of the road looking eastward. In this the French had placed their battery of nine guns and a portion of their infantry. About a hundred yards to the right of the road, looking eastward, and almost parallel with it, was a dry watercourse, along the bed of which troops could march, sheltered, to a great extent, from hostile fire. In this were massed the remainder of the infantry, European and native. The ground between the watercourse and the grove and to the right of the former was left for the cavalry to display their daring. The allies were expecting Clive, and were on the alert. They had hoped that, marching unsuspiciously along the high road, he would fall into the trap they had laid, and that what with the guns on his right, the infantry on his left, the cavalry in his front, and his own baggage train in his rear, escape for him would be impossible.

We have seen that Clive did fall into the trap. Marching unsuspiciously along the high road, the fire from the guns in the grove on his right gave him the first warning of his danger. That fire, fortunately, was delivered just a little too soon, before the infantry had reached a corresponding point in the watercourse. Still his position was full of peril. He was thoroughly surprised. Before he could bring up his own guns, many of his men had fallen, whilst the sight of the cavalry moving rapidly round the watercourse, and thus menacing his rear, showed him that the danger was not only formidable but immediate.

It was ever a characteristic of Clive that danger roused all his faculties. Never did he see more clearly, think more accurately, or act with greater decision than when the circumstances were sufficiently desperate to drive any ordinary man to despair. He was true to his characteristic on this eventful evening. Though surprised, he was in a moment the cool, calculating, thoughtful leader, acting as though men were not falling around him, and the difficulties to be met were entirely under his control. As soon as possible he placed three guns in a position to reply to the enemy's fire. Detecting at the same time the use which might be made of the watercourse, both for him and against him, he directed the main body of his infantry to take shelter within it. Then, to check the movement of the enemy's horsemen round the watercourse, he hurried two of his guns, supported by a platoon of Europeans and 200 sepoys, to a position on his own left of it; whilst at the same time, to clear the space around him, he directed that the baggage carts and baggage animals should march half a mile to the rear under the guard of a platoon of sepoys and two guns. Giving his orders calmly and clearly, with the air of a man confident in himself and in his fortunes, he saw them carried out with precision, before the enemy, using badly their opportunity, had made much impression upon him.

Still the chances were all against him. He could not advance under the walls of that mango grove fortress bristling with guns. He could not retreat in the face of that cavalry. He must fight at great disadvantage on the ground he occupied. The truth of the last proposition soon made itself apparent. On his left, indeed, his men in the watercourse just held their own. They exchanged a musketry fire with the French advancing from the other end, but neither party cared or dared to have recourse to the decisive influence of the bayonet. Beyond that, the enemy's cavalry were kept in check, for though they made many charges against the infantry and two guns on the English left of the watercourse, and even against the platoon in charge of the baggage, they made them in a manner which showed that the *morale* of the European gave him a strength not to be measured by numbers. In a word, they did not dare to charge home. But though he held his own in the other parts of the field, Clive was soon made to feel that on the right he was being gradually overpowered. The vastly superior fire from the guns in the grove fortress came gradually to kill or disable all his gunners and to silence his guns.

It was a situation which, Clive felt, could not be borne long. Those guns must be silenced or else ——. The historian of that period, Mr. Orme, says that "prudence seemed to dictate a retreat." If prudence so counselled, it was that bastard prudence, the bane of weak and worn-out natures, the disregard of which gained for Clive all his victories, which alone made possible the marvels of the Italian campaign of 1796, the too great regard to which made Borodino indecisive and entailed all the horrors of the Russian retreat. Such prudence, we may be sure, presented itself to the minds of many fighting under the orders of Clive, but not for one single instant to the mind of Clive himself. Without cavalry, to abandon the field in which he had been beaten to a victorious enemy largely furnished with that arm, would be to court absolute destruction. And the destruction of Clive's army meant the fall of Trichinápalli, the permanent predominance of French influence throughout southern India. That was the stake fought for at Kávéripák!

No, there was no alternative. It was 10 o'clock. The fight had lasted four hours and his men were losing confidence. The grove fortress must be stormed—but how? If the enemy possessed a real commander, it was impossible. The experience of Clive in warfare against the combined forces of the nations then opposed to him had, however, led him to the conclusion that confidence often produced carelessness. What if the grove fortress could be entered from the open faces in its rear? It was just possible that, in the confidence inspired by having to meet an enemy advancing only from the front, the French might have left these unguarded. It was a chance, perhaps a desperate chance, but worthy at all events of trial. Thus thinking, Clive, selecting from the men about him an intelligent sergeant, well acquainted with the native language, sent him, accompanied by a few sepoys, to reconnoitre. After an interval which, though brief, seemed never-ending, the sergeant returned with the happy intelligence that the rear approaches to the mango-grove had been left unguarded. The incident which followed showed how completely Clive was the master-spring of the machinery. He had decided—should the report of the sergeant prove satisfactory—to take 200 of his best Europeans—that is considerably more than half, for by this time nearly forty of the 380 had been killed and more had been wounded—and 400 natives, and lead them, preceded by the sergeant as guide, on the desperate enterprise. He so far carried out this scheme that he withdrew the men, to the number and of the composition mentioned, from the watercourse, and marched stealthily in the direction indicated by the sergeant. But the departure of this considerable body, and above all, the departure of the leader himself, completed the dismay of the troops left behind in the watercourse. They suddenly ceased firing, and made every preparation for flight. Some of them even quitted the field. The sudden cessation of firing, revealed to Clive—when he had already proceeded half way on his expedition—that his presence was absolutely required on the spot he had recently quitted. He, therefore, made over the command of the detached party to the next senior officer, Lieutenant Keene, and returned to the watercourse. He arrived there in the very nick of time. His men, confused, dispirited, and disheartened, were running away. Fortunately the enemy had taken no advantage of their demoralised condition. Clive went amongst them, and succeeded, though with difficulty, in restoring order and in inducing them to renew their fire. To insure the success of the other movement, it was only necessary that they should impose on the enemy at this point. Influenced by the presence of Clive they did this, but it is doubtful whether they would, in their then state, have ventured, even under his leading, upon anything more daring. To induce them to act as they did act, it was absolutely necessary that Clive should remain with them.

Meanwhile Keene's detachment was proceeding on its perilous enterprise. Making a large circuit, that officer reached—at about half-past 10 o'clock—a position immediately opposite the rear of the grove, and about 300 yards from it. He then halted, and calling to him one of his officers who, fortunately, understood French perfectly (Ensign Symmonds), directed him to advance alone, and examine the dispositions made by the enemy. Symmonds had not proceeded far when he came to a deep trench, in which a large body, consisting of native soldiers—whose services had not been required in the watercourse—were sitting down to avoid the random shots of the fight. These men challenged Symmonds and prepared at first to shoot him, but deceived by his speaking French, they allowed him to pass. Symmonds then made his way to the grove and boldly entered it. The sight that met his gaze was eminently satisfactory. The guns were manned by men engaged in directing their fire against the English position on the high road. Supporting these guns and gunners were about a hundred French soldiers, whose attention was so entirely absorbed by the events in front of them that they paid no attention to their rear, which was entirely unguarded. It now became the object of Symmonds not only to return, but to return by a way which should avoid the sepoys in the ditch, as much to ensure his own safety as to find a clear road for his own countrymen. Fortune came to the aid of his calm and cool self-possession. Taking a direction to the right of that occupied by the sepoys in the ditch, he rejoined his party without meeting a single person. Success was now certain. Keene at once gave the order to advance. Proceeding by the path by which Symmonds had returned, he marched unperceived to within thirty yards of the enemy's Europeans. Halting here, he poured into them a volley. The effect was decisive. Many of the Frenchmen fell dead; the remainder were so astonished, that, without even attempting to return the fire, they turned and fled, abandoning guns and position; every man anxious only to save himself. In the heedlessness of sudden despair, many of them ran into a building at the further end of the grove which had served as a caravanserai for travellers. It was running into a trap, a trap moreover in which they were so crowded that they could not use their arms. The English followed them up closely, and, seeing their defenceless condition, offered them quarter on condition of surrender. These terms were joyfully accepted, and the Frenchmen coming out one by one delivered up their arms and, to the number of sixty, constituted themselves prisoners. Many of the sepoys escaped.

The battle was now gained, for though the troops in the water-course—ignorant of the events passing in the grove—continued their fire some time longer, the arrival of fugitives soon induced them to abandon their position and seek safety in flight. The field being thus cleared, Clive reunited his force, and halted on the field under arms till daybreak. Surveying the horizon by the light of the early morn not an enemy was to be seen. Fifty Frenchmen and 300 of their native soldiers lay dead on the field; besides these there were many wounded. He had captured nine field-pieces and three mortars, and he had sixty prisoners. On his own side he had lost in killed, mainly from the fire of the enemy's guns, forty Europeans and thirty sepoys. A great number of both were likewise wounded.

But the guns he had captured and the prisoners he had made constituted but an infinitesimal portion of the real advantages Clive had gained on this well-fought field. Sir John Malcolm attributes to the battle of Kávéripák the distinction "of restoring," or "rather," he says, "of founding the reputation of the British arms in India"; for before that "no event had occurred which could lead the natives to believe that the English, as soldiers, were equal to the French." That was most undoubtedly its moral effect. D'Esprémesnil's sortie from Madras, and the victory of Paradis at St. Thomé had revolutionised the relative positions of the natives and the French settlers. It had given the latter a moral preponderance, foreshadowing supremacy in Southern India. In that moral preponderance the English had, at first, a very light share. They had fallen back before the greater daring and energy of their European rivals. They had done little to impress, generally, the minds of the natives. The famous Marátha leader expressed the prevailing opinion of his countrymen when he stated that prior to Clive's heroic defence of Arkát, he had been convinced that the English could not fight. But even the favourable impression created by that brilliant feat of arms had been partly neutralised by the fact that another and a larger body of Englishmen had allowed themselves to be cooped up and besieged in Trichinápalli. Had the English lost the day at Kávéripák, there can be no doubt but that the favourable impression created by Arkát would have been replaced by the feelings which had preceded it, and the defence of that fortress would have been universally regarded as the exception which proved the rule. The moral effect of Clive's great victory, then, was greater even than to confirm the belief created at Arkát that the English could fight. It produced the conviction not only that they could fight, but that they could fight better than the French. It transferred to the English, in fact, the moral preponderance which D'Esprémesnil and Paradis had gained for the French at Madras and St. Thomé. In the history of decisive battles it becomes, then, the logical sequence of Paradis' victory. Its material results were not less important. On the mode in which it was decided depended the possibility of the relief of Trichinápalli by the English before that place should succumb by famine or by arms to its French besiegers. On the successful defence of Trichinápalli depended whether English influence or French influence was to predominate in Southern India. Had that place fallen, French influence would have been assured for ever. That nation virtually ruled the dominions now known as those of the Nizám, including the districts called the Northern Sirkárs. They only wanted Trichinápalli and Tanjúr to complete their control of Southern India, the independent kingdom of Maisúr alone excepted. Had Clive been defeated at Kávéripák it would have been impossible to relieve Trichinápalli. The French power would have received so great an accession of strength, moral and material, that the English would have found sufficient employment for their soldiers in the defence of their own possessions. Trichinápalli, even if it had not been attempted, would have been starved into surrender.

Materially, then, as well as morally, may the victory gained by Clive be classified amongst the decisive battles of India. It was a very decisive battle. Materially, as well as morally, it caused the transfer of preponderance in Southern India from the French to the English. It made possible the relief of Trichinápalli, and ensured the surrender of the largest French army which had till then fought in India. That surrender gave the English a position, which, though often assailed during the thirty years that followed, they never wholly lost, and which extending year by year its roots, can now never be eradicated.

In other respects the battle of Kávéripák is well worthy of study. The French lost that battle by their neglect to guard the weak points of their position. Had they possessed a commander who knew his business, they might have won it before Clive made his forlorn attempt against that point. With their immense superiority of artillery on their left, in a secure position there, they had but to advance their centre and right, strengthened with every available man, to have forced Clive from his position. Their numerous cavalry would have completed his discomfiture. Not possessing a daring leader, they waited in their grove fortress for the slower but apparently not less certain process, for the consequences certain, under ordinary circumstances, to result from a superior artillery fire, still having the cavalry handy to complete its effect. Adopting this slower process, knowing the character of the leader opposed to them, they should have guarded with more than ordinary care the weak points of their own position. Neglecting to do this, they gave that leader a chance which ruined them in the very hour of their triumph.

On the other side, this battle revealed, more than any of his previous encounters, the remarkable characteristics of Clive as a commander. Granted that he was surprised. On this point I will simply remark that a general unprovided with cavalry, pursuing an enemy well-furnished with horsemen, compelled by circumstances outside his own immediate sphere of action to strike boldly and to strike at once, can with difficulty avoid walking into a trap such as that laid for Clive at Kávéripák. But mark his readiness, his coolness, his decision, his nerve, his clear head, and his calm courage, when he found himself compromised. Without even the shadow of hesitation he acted as though he had no doubt as to the issue. Inspiring his men with a confidence in himself which may be termed absolute, he moved them as a player moves his pawns on a chess-board. Doubtless his death would have been followed by disaster. This became apparent when for a few moments he left the men in the watercourse to superintend the decisive movement to his right. But there is not a single great commander to whom the same remark might not apply. Deprived of its head, the body will always become inert. At Kávéripák, the disorder caused by the short absence of the leader from his accustomed place on the field, and the restoration of confidence produced by his return, proved very clearly how the spirits of the men rested on him, how without him their confidence would have vanished.

Victory is to the general who makes the fewest mistakes. Granted, as I have said, that Clive committed one great initial error by being led into a trap. That was his only error. He repaired it in a manner which deserves to be studied as an example to all commanders. But for the enemy who, having caught him, let him go!—for the want of enterprise displayed by their cavalry—for their supineness, their neglect of ordinary military precaution—for the marked absence of leadership on their side, the historian cannot find words too strong to express condemnation. They thoroughly deserved their defeat. It is a curious fact that the darkness, which in the outset seemed to favour their plans, ultimately gave opportunity for their overthrow. Clive could not have made his turning movement by daylight. So much the more worthy of condemnation is the carelessness which gave opportunities to a leader who had proved himself on other fields to be as enterprising and as daring as he was tenacious and fertile in expedients.

CHAPTER III.

PLASSEY.*

In the year 1644 there was a great commotion in the palace of the Great Mughul at Agra. The clothes of a favourite daughter of the reigning emperor, Sháh Jahán, had caught fire, and the princess had been severely burnt before the flames could be extinguished. In vain did native physicians of great learning and celebrity employ their skill and devote their time to effect a cure. To soothe the anxiety of the sorrowing father, some courtiers reminded him of the reputation which certain settlers from a distant country, carrying on their trade at Súrat, had acquired for proficiency in the healing art. Catching at the idea, Sháh Jahán despatched forthwith a messenger to the town on the Taptí, bearing a request that the foreign settlers would place at his disposal one of their most skilful practitioners.

* Long usage has, in this case, as in the cases of Calcutta, Pondichery, and Bombay, sanctioned an incorrect spelling. The proper rendering of the name of this place is Palási, from the palás tree (*Butea frondosa*), which used to abound in the vicinity. The *A'in-i-Akbari* makes special mention of the palás as the wood of which the balls for the game of *changán* (hockey) by night were made in the time of Akbar. "His Majesty also plays at *changán* on dark nights, which caused much astonishment, even among clever players. The balls which are used at night are set on fire. For this purpose *palás* wood is used, which is very light, and burns for a long time."—Blochmann's *A'in-i-Akbari*, page 298.

The settlers hastened to respond, and deputed Mr. Gabriel Boughton, surgeon of the East India Company's ship *Hopewell*, to attend the bidding of the ruler of India.

Mr. Boughton reached Agra, and succeeded in completely curing the princess. Asked to name his own reward, the patriotic Englishman allowed the opportunity of enriching himself to pass, and preferred to the Emperor the request that he would issue a firmán granting permission to the English to trade in Bengal free of all duties, and to establish factories in the province. The firmán was granted, and Mr. Boughton, taking it with him, set off at once to Rájmahal, where the Viceroy of Bengal. Sultán Shujá, second son of the Emperor, held his court.

Seven years before the event just recorded, the Súrat merchants had obtained a firmán which permitted them to trade in Bengal, but which restricted them to the port of Piplí, in the province of Orísá. The trade to this port had been opened, but the results had been so unsatisfactory that in 1643–4 the question whether the establishment at Piplí should be maintained or broken up was under the serious consideration of the Court of Directors.

The question was still pending when Mr. Boughton arrived with the revivifying firmán at Rájmahal. His good fortune accompanied him to that place also. One of the royal ladies of the zenana of Sultán Shujá was lying ill; in the opinion of the native physicians hopelessly ill. Boughton cured her. Thenceforth the gratitude of the prince was unbounded. It displayed itself during the twelve years that followed in the assistance afforded to the Englishman in carrying out his scheme for establishing the trade in Bengal on an efficient and a permanent basis. Under his protection factories were established at Hugli, and agencies at Patná and Kásimbázár, and a little later at Dhákah and Baleshwar (Balasore).

The privilege of free trade throughout the provinces of Bengal and Orísá was likewise granted for the annual nominal payment of Rs. 3,000.

The violent changes which occurred in the native dynasties during the forty years that followed did not practically affect the position thus secured to the English. But in the beginning of the year 1689, in consequence of the tyrannical conduct of Núwáb Sháista Khán, governor of the province for the Emperor Aurangzíb, the Company's Agent-in-Chief, Mr. Job Charnock, quitted Huglí with his subordinates, and sailed for Madras. Fortunately for English interests, Sháista Khán was succeeded during the same year by Ibráhím Khán. This man, known to our countrymen of that period as "the famously just and good Núwáb," invited the English to return. Mr. Charnock complied (July 1690), but instead of proceeding to his old quarters at Huglí, he established the English factory at the village of Chatánatí, north of the then existing town of Calcutta,* twenty-seven miles nearer to the sea than the station he abandoned. Mr. Charnock survived the removal only eighteen months.

At this time the English settlers had no permission to fortify Chatánatí, and their military establishment consisted of only 100 men. A rebellion against the Núwáb which broke out in Bengal in 1695 under the leadership of Súbah Singh, a Hindú zamindár of Bardhwán, forced them to solicit, and enabled them to obtain, permission to defend themselves. They proceeded at once to erect walls of masonry, with bastions or flanking towers at the angles, round their factory. The bastions were made

* Calcutta, or, as it was spelt by the natives, "Kálikáta," is mentioned in the *A'in-i-Akbarí* of Abul Fazl, written in 1596. The village of Chatánatí extended from the present mint to the Soba bazaar. For these and other details regarding the making of Calcutta, I would refer the reader to a very remarkable pamphlet, *Calcutta during the Last Century*, written and given as a lecture by the late Professor Blochmann, M.A., whose untimely death five years ago was a deadly blow to Oriental investigation. The little pamphlet, which ought to be preserved, was printed by Mr. Thomas Smith, City Press, Bentinck Street, Calcutta.

capable of bearing guns, but in order not to excite the suspicion of the Núwáb, the embrasures were built up on the exterior with a facing of wall, one brick thick. This was the origin of the old fort, also called Fort William. It covered the site of the localities now known as Fairlie Place, the Custom House, and Koilah Ghát Street. Before the walls had been quite completed an attack was made upon it by the insurgents, who had set fire to the villages in the neighbourhood, but they were repulsed.*

On account of the rebellion, Ibráhím Khán was removed by the Emperor, who, after a short interval, sent his grandson, Prince 'Azím u'sh Shán, to govern the province. From this prince, by means of a present of Rs. 16,000, the English obtained a grant of the three villages of Chatánatí, Gobindpúr, and Calcutta, with the lands adjacent to their fortified factory. As the wall of fortification occupied a portion of the ground appertaining to the village of Calcutta, that name was, for the first time, applied to the whole settlement (1699). The Company by this cession came to occupy the position of a zamindár, possessing administrative powers within the limits of the grant, and paying a yearly rental to the over-lord. In consequence of these acquisitions the Bengal settlement was raised to the rank of a Presidency, with a governor or, more correctly, a president in council, independent of Madras. The council of the new president was to consist of five members, inclusive of himself.†

In 1699 a new English company made a settlement at Huglí, in rivalry with the old company. The seven years which followed were principally marked by negotiations between the servants of the two companies. These terminated in 1706-7 by their fusion under the title of the United Company of Merchants of England trading to the East Indies. Huglí was

* Mr. Wheeler states that the rebels were "routed by fifty English soldiers in front of the factory at Chatánatí."—*Early Records of British India.*

† These were—the president, a vice-president and accomptant, a warehouse-keeper, a purser of marine, and a receiver of revenues and general manager.

abandoned, and the strength of the United Company was concentrated within the limits of the three villages I have mentioned. Thenceforth, and for the ten years which followed, the contention was between the English settlers and the native lords of Bengal, the former persistently striving to extend free commercial intercourse with Bengal and to strengthen their fortifications, the latter constantly endeavouring to exact larger revenues from the English zamindárs.

A circumstance, not dissimilar to that which had procured for the English the permission to establish factories and to trade freely in Bengal, came about this time to improve their fortunes and to extend their influence in the province. In 1713, the President of the Council despatched to the Court of Dihlí an embassy composed of two European gentlemen, an Armenian interpreter, and a surgeon. The name of the surgeon was William Hamilton.

When the embassy reached Dihlí, Farrakhsiyar, great grandson of Aurangzíb, had but recently, by the defeat at Agra of his uncle, Jahándár Sháh, obtained the throne of the Mughul. This prince had been suffering for some time from a complaint which had baffled all the skill of his physicians, and which compelled him to defer a marriage upon which he had set his heart, with a Hindú princess of Rájpútáná. Hamilton cured him. To show his gratitude, the Emperor, after the manner of Sháh Jahán, requested him to name his reward. Hamilton, as patriotic and as careless of self-interest as Boughton, asked that the privileges granted to his countrymen in Bengal might be extended, and that they might be relieved from the exactions and oppressions of the Governor of Bengal. The Emperor promised to comply, and, after some delay, issued (1717)* a firmán confirming all previous grants to the English company, authorising them to issue papers which, bearing the signature of the President of the Council, should exempt the goods

* Hamilton died that same year at Calcutta.

named therein from examination or duty, and bestowing upon them the grant of thirty-eight villages about and below Calcutta on both sides of the river, on payment of an annual ground-rent. He likewise placed the use of the mint at Murshidábád at their disposal.

These privileges and this grant greatly increased the prosperity of Calcutta. For the ten years that followed its progress was enormous. Its trade rapidly developed, the shipping belonging to the port increased to 10,000 tons, and, what was of very great importance, the town attracted the wealthy natives of Bengal. These, by degrees, built houses in and near to it, and brought the influence of their wealth to sustain and increase its prosperity. It should be added that the firm rule of the Núwáb of the province, Murshid Kulí Khán, contributed not a little to this result. Originally opposed to the new favours extended to the English settlers, especially to that portion of them which would have given them the command of both sides of the river, he had forced them to agree to a compromise which, whilst it did not interfere with their trade, prevented them from obtaining a position dangerous to the interests of the Mughul. He likewise insisted that the free passes should neither be transferable nor used for the purposes of inland trade, but should be strictly confined to the goods of the Company intended for export. These trade rules were insisted upon, not only by Murshíd Kulí Khán, but by his son-in-law, Shujá u'd dín Khán, who succeeded him on his death in 1725, and who administered the province for the fourteen years that followed. The firm hand of the Núwáb, and the strict compliance with his reasonable regulations on the part of the settlers, combined throughout this period to augment the influence and increase the wealth of the Company.

Shujá u'd dín Khán was succeeded in Bengal in 1739 by his son, Sarfaráz Khán, a debauchee. During his incumbency there occurred that terrible invasion of Nádir Sháh, which gave the most fatal blow to the stability of the rule of the Mughul. The subversive feeling, the result of this catastrophe, extended even to Bengal. Ali Vardi Khán, who had risen from the position of menial servant to the Núwáb of that province to be Deputy-Governor of Bihár, rose in revolt. The despotic conduct of Sarfaráz Khán had alienated the wealthy and respectable classes of the province. The great mercantile family of the Séths, the Rothschilds of Bengal, favoured the rebel. His very generals betrayed him. When he marched to crush Ali Vardi Khán with a force vastly superior, they arranged that the guns should be loaded with powder only. The consequences were such as might have been expected. When the decisive battle ensued at Ghíriah in January 1741, Sarfaráz Khán was slain, and his nobles and soldiers at once saluted Ali Vardi Khán as Núwáb of the three provinces of Bengal, Bihár, and Orísá.

The blow dealt by Nádir Sháh at Dihlí had so crushed the power of the Mughul that this revolution passed unnoticed. Ali Vardi Khán transmitted a handsome offering in money to the Emperor, Muhammad Sháh, and was confirmed as Núwáb of Bengal, Bihár, and Orísá, just as any other adventurer who might have supplanted him, and have forwarded a like sum of money, would have been equally confirmed. It was, in fact, the recognition of force—the same recognition which was claimed, and fairly claimed, by the people who afterwards, also by force, supplanted the successor of Ali Vardi Khán. This prince ruled the three provinces for fifteen years, from 1741 to 1756. His reign was a continued struggle. He had scarcely succeeded to the position gained on the field of Ghíriah when he was called upon to make head against a Marátha invasion. This invasion was the prelude to many others. They occurred every year from 1742 to 1750. They brought with them terror, desolation, often despair. Ali Vardi Khán resisted the invaders gallantly, and defeated them often. But in the end their numbers and their pertinacity wore him out; and when, in 1750, they had mastered a great portion of Orísá, he was glad to conclude with them a treaty whereby he yielded to them Katak, and agreed to pay a yearly tribute of twelve lakhs of rupees for Bengal and Bihár.

These invasions had not, however, interfered with the rising prosperity of the English settlement. Its security, in fact, invited more wealthy natives to take up their permanent abode within its bounds. Ali Vardi Khán, whilst continuing the privileges granted by his predecessors, had merely called upon the English, as he called upon all the zamindárs of Bengal, to contribute to the expenses of the defence of the province. But such was their prosperity, that in one instance, when the Núwáb was hard pressed, they had paid him without difficulty three lakhs of rupees. Not but that the alarm caused by the Marátha invasion did not reach even Calcutta. But the English, prescient in their policy, took advantage of the universal feeling to ask for permission to dig a ditch and throw up an intrenchment round their settlement. The permission was accorded and the work was begun; but when three miles of it had been completed, and there were no signs of the approach of the Maráthas, its further progress was discontinued. The work, some traces of which still remain, gave a permanent name to the locality, and to this day the slang term "the ditch" is often used to express the commercial capital of Bengal. Permission was granted at the same time to erect a wall of masonry, with bastions at the corners, round the agency at Kásimbázár.

From the peace with the Maráthas to 1756 nothing occurred to disturb the tranquillity of the English. On the 9th of April of that year, however, their protector, Núwáb Ali Vardi Khán died, and was succeeded by his favourite grandson, Siráju'd daulah.

This prince, who has been painted by historians in the blackest colours, was not worse than the majority of Eastern princes born in the purple. He was rather weak than vicious, unstable rather than tyrannical, had been petted and spoilt by his grandfather, had had but little education, and was still a minor. Without experience and without stability of character, suddenly called upon to administer the fairest provinces of India and to assume irresponsible power, what wonder that he should have inaugurated his accession by acts of folly?

Surrounded from his earliest youth by flatterers, he had been encouraged to imbibe a hatred towards the foreign settlers on the coast. Their rising prosperity and their wealth, increased largely by rumour, excited, there can be no doubt, the cupidity of these brainless flatterers, and these, in their turn, worked on the facile nature of the boy-ruler.

The result was that Siráju'd daulah determined to inaugurate his reign by the despoiling of the English settlers. Charging them with increasing their fortifications and with harbouring political offenders, he seized their factory at Kásimbázár, imprisoned the garrison, and plundered the property found there (4th June 1756). Five days later he began his march towards Calcutta with an army 50,000 strong, attacked that place on the 15th, and obtained possession of it on the 19th June.

I would willingly draw a veil over the horrors of the Black Hole. That terrible catastrophe was due, however, not to a love of cruelty on the part of Siráju'd daulah, but to the system which inspired the servants of an absolute ruler with a fetish-like awe for their master. There can be, I think, no doubt that the Núwáb did not desire the death of his English prisoners. Mr. Holwell himself acquits him of any such intention, and attributes the choice of the Black Hole as the place of confinement to the ill-will of the subordinates.* As to the

* "I had in all three interviews with him (the Núwáb), the last in Darbár before seven, when he repeated his assurances to me, *on the word of a soldier*, that no harm should come to us; and, indeed, I believe his orders were only

catastrophe itself, its cause was the refusal of the subordinates to awaken the Núwáb. That refusal might have been caused either by fear or by ill-will; but it was their refusal, not the refusal of the chief who was actually asleep. Thus much, but no more, may, in bare justice, be urged on behalf of Siráju'd daulah. For his conduct after the catastrophe not a word can be said. It is not upon record that he resented it. Most certainly those about him made him believe that the action had been planned with the best motives to draw from the English a confession as to the place where their wealth and treasures were hidden. His first act when he saw Mr. Holwell was to insist upon such confession being made. He expressed no regret, he extended to the captives no compassion, he spoke only of hidden treasures and their place of concealment. By his conduct he placed himself in the position of an accessory after the act.

The political result of the capture of Calcutta was the uprooting of the English settlements in Bengal. Of those who formed the garrison of Calcutta, some had been killed, others had been removed as prisoners to Murshidábád,* the remainder had taken refuge on board the English vessels which were waiting, at Faltá, the arrival from Madras of the troops who should avenge their wrongs and restore the fallen fortunes of the Company.

The news of the surrender of Kásimbázár reached Madras on the 15th July. Five days later a detachment of 230 European troops, commanded by Major Kilpatrick of the Company's service, sailed from Madras. They reached Faltá on the 2nd August. On the 5th of that month only did the story of the capture of Calcutta and its attendant consequences reach Fort St. George. Although the forces at the disposal of the Coast

general that for that night we should be secured; and that what followed was the result of revenge and resentment in the breasts of the lower jemadars to whose custody we were delivered, for the number of their order killed during the siege."—*Mr. Holwell's Narrative.*

* These were subsequently released, and joined the fleet at Faltá.

Presidency were not more than sufficient to meet the attack from the French which was believed inevitable—France and England being on the brink of a rupture—it was resolved, after some hesitation, to despatch with all convenient haste a fleet and army to restore British fortunes in Bengal. The discussions leading to this conclusion, and afterwards those relating to the choice of a commander, caused very great delay, and it was not till the 16th October that the fleet conveying the little army sailed. The first ship reached Faltá on the 11th December. All the others, two only excepted, arrived on or before the 20th. Of the two exceptions, one, the *Marlborough*, laden with stores, was so slow that she reached Calcutta only towards the end of January; the other, the *Cumberland*, grounding off Point Palmyras, was compelled to bear away to Vishákpatanam (Vizagapatam), and reached the river Huglí in the second week of March.

The commander of the military force was Robert Clive. The victory gained by this officer at Kávéripák had produced the most decisive results. It had enabled the English to relieve Trichinápalli, to force the surrender of the entire French army, to bestow the Núwábship of the Karnátak upon their own nominee: in fine, it had caused the transfer of the predominance in Southern India south of the river Krishna from the French to our countrymen. In January 1753, Clive put the seal to his victories by the capture of the fortresses of Kovilam and Chengalpatt. In the following month he sailed for England. There he was received and fêted as a hero. Of the same age as Bonaparte when Bonaparte made the marvellous campaign of 1796, he had acquired for his country advantages not less solid than those which the great Corsican was to gain in that campaign for France. After a sojourn of more than two years in his native country, Clive, holding the commission of lieutenant-colonel in the King's army, was sent to the Koromándal coast as Governor of Fort St. David. For a while his services were diverted to Western India, where, in conjunction with Admiral Watson, he attacked and reduced the piratical stronghold of Ghíriah. Thence he proceeded to Madras in time to be selected as the commander of the troops who were to conquer Bengal.

Clive's force, consisting, exclusive of the men in the *Cumberland*, of 800 Europeans, 1,200 native soldiers, and a due proportion of artillery, joined the remnants of Major Kilpatrick's detachment, which had been much reduced by disease, on the 20th December. Just seven days later the fleet ascended the Huglí. On the 29th, the enemy were dislodged from the fort of Bajbaj. The action which took place there, whilst in its details it reflects no credit on the generalship of Clive, was yet so far decisive in its result that it terrified the enemy's general into the abandonment of Calcutta. That place, left with a garrison of only 500 men, surrendered, without attempting a serious resistance, on the 2nd January. Prompt to strike, and anxious at once to terrify the Núwáb and to replenish the coffers of his countrymen, Clive, three days later, despatched a force to storm and sack Huglí, reputed to be the richest town within a reasonable distance of Calcutta. On the 9th the place was taken. The victors found, to their disappointment, that the more valuable of its stores had been, in anticipation of the attack, removed to the Dutch factory at Chinsurah.

But Siráju'd daulah had not yet been terrified. Raising an army said to have consisted of 18,000 horse, 15,000 foot, 10,000 armed followers, and forty guns, he marched on Calcutta. Clive, who was encamped at Kásipúr, observing, on the 2nd February, that advanced parties of the Nuwab's army were defiling upon the plain to the right of the Damdam road, and there taking up a position threatening Calcutta, made an ineffectual attempt to hinder them. The Nuwab arrived with his main body on the 3rd, and encamped just beyond the general line of the Marátha ditch. The following morning Fortune directed to the happiest results an action which seemed at first pregnant with destruction to the English. It had been the intention of Clive to surprise the Núwáb's army and to seize his person; but, misled by a thick fog he found himself at 8 o'clock in the morning in the middle of the enemy's camp and encompassed by his troops. He extricated himself by simply daring to move forwards. The intrepidity of the attempt so intimidated the Núwáb that he drew off his army, and on the 9th February signed a treaty, by which he restored to the English more than their former privileges, and promised the restoration of the property seized at the capture of Calcutta.

But Clive was not yet satisfied. War had been declared between France and England. His experience in Southern India had shown him how dangerous to English interests would be an active alliance between the French and a strong native power. In the Karnátak he had been able to balance one native force against another. In Bengal such a policy was impossible, for the Núwáb was supreme, and his great officers had not as yet shown themselves impressionable. Then, again, Clive's orders had been to return with his little army to Madras as soon as he should have reconquered Calcutta. But how, in the face of the possibility of an alliance between the Núwáb and the French, could he abandon Calcutta? To do so would be, he felt, to court for the English settlement permanent destruction. The French general, Bussy, was supreme at Haidarábád, possessed in real sovereignty the northern Sirkars, and rumour had even then pointed to the probability of his entering into negotiations with the Núwáb of Bengal. Under these circumstances the clear military eye of Clive saw but one course consistent with safety. In the presence of two enemies not yet united, but likely to be united, he must strike down one without delay. He would then be able to oppose to the other his undivided forces.

On this policy Clive acted. In spite of the prohibition of the Núwáb, he struck a blow at the French settlement of Chandranagar (Chandernagor), intimidated or bribed to idleness the Núwáb's general marching to its relief, and took the French fort (March 23rd).

This high-handed proceeding filled the mind of Síráju'd daulah with anger and fear. It is impossible for a fair-minded reader to examine the circumstances which surrounded this unfortunate Prince from the time when Clive frightened him into signing the treaty of the 9th February until he met his end after Plassey, without feeling for him deep commiseration. His attitude was that of a netted tiger surrounded by enemies whom he feared and hated, but could not crush. Imagine this boy, for he had not yet seen twenty summers, raised in the purple—for his birth was nearly contemporaneous with the accession of his grandfather to power—brought up in the lap of luxury, accustomed to the gratification of every whim, unendowed by nature with the strength of character which would counterbalance these grave disadvantages, invested with a power which he had been taught to regard as uncontrollable—imagine this boy set to play the game of empire against one of the coolest and most calculating warriors of the day, a man perfectly comprehending the end at which he was aiming, who had mastered the character of his rival and of the men by whom that rival was surrounded, who was restrained by no scruples, and who was as bold and decided as his rival was wavering and ready to proceed from one extreme to another. But this does not represent the whole situation. The boy so unevenly pitted against the Englishman was further handicapped by a constant dread of invasion by the Afgháns from the north and by the Maráthas from the west. He was afraid, therefore, to put out all his strength to crush the English, lest he should be assailed on his flank or on his rear. This dread added to his native uncertainty, and caused him alternately to cringe to or to threaten his rival. But he was more heavily handicapped still. I have said that his rival was restrained by no scruples. The truth of this remark is borne out by the fact that whilst the unhappy boy Núwáb was the sport of the passion to which the event of the moment gave mastery in his breast, the Englishman was engaged slowly, persistently, and continuously in undermining his position in his own Court, in seducing his generals, and in corrupting his courtiers. When the actual contest came, though individuals here and there were faithful, there was not a single great interest in Murshidábád which was not pledged to support the cause of the foreigner. The Núwáb had even been terrified into removing from his capital and dismissing to Bhágulpúr, a hundred miles distant, the one party which would have been able to render him effectual support, a body of Frenchmen commanded by M. Law!

The final crisis was precipitated by a curious accident. Whilst the wordy contest between the Calcutta Council and the Núwáb which marked every day of the three months which followed the capture of Chandranagar was progressing, Síráju'd daulah, always distrustful of the English, had located his army, nominally commanded in chief by his prime minister, Rájah Dúlab Rám, and supported by a considerable corps under Mír J'afar Khán—a high nobleman who had married his aunt—at Palási, a town in the island of Kásimbázár—called an island because whilst the base of the triangle which composed it was watered by the Ganges, the western side on which lies Palási is formed by the Bhágirathí, and the eastern by the Jalanghí. Palási is twenty-two miles from Murshidábád.

Clive and the Calcutta Council had taken great offence at the location of the Núwáb's army at Palási, and had affected to regard it as a sign of hostile intent towards themselves. When the relations between the two rival parties were in a state of great tension, a messenger arrived in Calcutta, the bearer of a letter purporting to come from the great Marátha chieftain of Birár, and containing a proposal that he should march with 120,000 men into Bengal and co-operate with the English against the Núwáb.

For once the clear brain of the director of the English policy was at fault. Clive could not feel quite sure that the letter might not be a device of the Núwáb to ascertain beyond a doubt the feelings of the English towards himself. Various circumstances seemed to favour this view. But if his vision was for a moment clouded, the political action of Clive was clear, prompt, decided, and correct. Treating the letter as though it were genuine, he sent it to Siráju'd daulah, ostensibly as a proof of his confidence, and as the ground for a request that he would no longer keep his army in the field. The plan succeeded. The letter was genuine. The Núwáb was completely taken in. He recalled his army to Murshidábád. For the first time since he had retreated from Calcutta he believed the friendly protestations of the English.

Never had he less cause to believe them. At that very time the Séths, the great financiers of Murshidábád, were committed against their Native ruler; Mír J'afar had been gained over by the English; the dewán, Rájah Dúlab Rám, was a party to the same compact. The bargain with the two latter had been drawn up, and only awaited signature.

The conduct of Siráju'd daulah himself gave the finishing touch to the conspiracy. Up to the moment of the receipt of the Marátha's letter his fear of the English had somewhat restrained the tyrannical instincts in which he had been wont to indulge at the expense of his own immediate surroundings. But the frankness of Clive in transmitting to him that letter had produced within him a great revulsion of feeling. That revulsion was accompanied by a corresponding change of conduct. Secure now, as he believed, of the friendship of the English, he began to threaten his nobles. Mír J'afar, the most powerful of them all, was the first intended victim. But this chief, quasi-independent, would not be crushed. Taking refuge in his palace, and summoning his friends and followers, he bade defiance to the Núwáb. Whilst thus acting towards his master, he urged upon Mr. Watts, the English agent at Murshidábád, to press that the English troops should take the field and commence operations at once.

The treaty by which Clive and the English Council had engaged to raise Mír J'afar Khán to the quasi-royal seat of his master, on condition of his co-operation in the field, and of his bestowal upon them of large sums of money, had by this time reached Calcutta, signed and sealed. Clive then had no further reason for temporising. He boldly then threw off the mask, and marched, on the 13th June, from Chandranagar.

The same day Clive dismissed from his camp two agents of the Núwáb, instructing them to notify to their master that he was marching on Murshidábád, with the object of referring the English complaints against him, which he enumerated, to a commission of five officers of his Government. He gave the names of those officers. They were the men who had conspired with him against their master.

Mr. Watts, the English agent, had received, previously, instructions to leave Murshidábád, the moment he should conceive the moment opportune. He and his subordinates fled from that place on the 13th June, and reached Clive's camp in safety. The evasion of Mr. Watts caused the scales to fall from the eyes of the unhappy Siráju'd daulah. He saw on the moment that the English were in league with Mír J'afar. Always in extremes, he was as anxious now to conciliate, as an hour earlier he had been eager to punish, his powerful vassal. His overtures caused Mír J'afar to make a show of submission, whilst he secretly warned Clive. The other conspirators made similar pretences. The Núwáb then ordered the army to march promptly to take up its former position at Palási. But here again he was met by unlooked-for opposition. When the leaders of an army are disaffected, indiscipline almost invariably permeates the rank and file. So it was now. Large arrears were owing to the men, and they had no great inclination to risk their lives for a personal cause. For it had come to this.

The cause did not present itself to their eyes as one in which the national interests were concerned, as one which involved the independence of Bengal. To the vast majority it seemed merely to balance one chieftain against another — Siráju'd daulah, the grandson of a usurper, against Mír J'afar, the most powerful noble of the province. It took three days to restore order among the soldiers, and this result was effected only by the distribution of large sums of money, and of promises. The delay was unfortunate, for the army did not reach its position at Palási till the 21st (June).

Meanwhile Clive, marching from Chandranagar on the 13th, arrived, on the 16th, at Palti, a town on the western bank of the Bhágirathí, about six miles above its junction with the Jalanghí. Hence he despatched, on the 17th, a force composed of 200 Europeans, 500 sepoys, with a field gun and a small howitzer, under Major Eyre Coote, of the 39th Foot, to gain possession of Katwá, a town and fort some twelve miles distant. The occupation of Katwá was important, for not only did the fort contain large supplies of grain and military stores, but its position, covered by the little river Ají, rendered it sufficiently strong to serve as a base whence Clive could operate against the island. The native commander at Katwá surrendered the place to Eyre Coote after only a show of resistance. Clive and the rest of the force arrived there the same evening, and at once occupied the huts and houses in the town and fort. It was a timely shelter, for the periodical rainy season opened with great violence the very next day.

A few miles of ground and the river Bhágirathí now lay between Clive and Siráju'd daulah. Since his departure from Chandranagar, the former had despatched daily missives to Mír J'afar, but up to the time of his arrival at Katwá he had received but one reply, dated the 16th, apprising him of his reconciliation with the Núwáb, and of his resolve to carry out the engagements he had made with the English. On the 20th, however, two communications, bearing a more doubtful significance, were received. The first was the report of a messenger returned from conveying a message to Mír J'afar. This man's report breathed so uncertain a sound that Clive wrote to the Select Committee in Calcutta for further orders, expressed his disinclination to risk his troops without the certainty of co-operation on the part of Mír J'afar, and his resolution, if that co-operation were wanting, to fortify himself at Katwá and await the cessation of the rainy season.

The second communication, received the evening of the same day, was in the form of a letter written by Mír J'afar himself the previous day, just as he was starting for Palási. In this he stated that he was on the point of setting out; that he was to be posted on one flank of the army; that on his arrival at Palási he would despatch more explicit information. That was positively all. The letter contained no suggestion as to concert between the two confederates.

This letter did not go very far to clear away the embarassment which the communication of the messenger had caused in the mind of the English leader. The questions "how to act," "whether to act at all," had to be solved, and solved without delay. Could he, dare he, with an army consisting, all told, of 3,000 men, of whom about one third only were Europeans, cross the Bhágirathí and attack an army of some 50,000 men, relying on the promises of the commander of less than one-third of those fifty thousand that he would betray his master and join him during the action? That was the question. Should he decide in the negative, two alternatives presented themselves: the one, to fortify himself at Katwá and await the cessation of the rains; the other, to return to Calcutta. But was either feasible? After having announced to all Bengal his intention to depose Siráju'd daulah—for his plans had been the talk of the bázárs and of the camp—could he, dare he, risk the loss of prestige which inaction or a retreat would involve? Could he, dare he, risk the cooling of his relations with his native confederates, their certain reconciliation with their master, a possible uprising in his rear? Advance without the co-operation of Mír J'afar seemed to be destruction; a halt at Katwá would be the middle course—so dear to prudent men—involving always a double danger; the third course, the retreat to Calcutta, meant an eternal farewell to the ambitious and mercenary hopes that had been aroused. Balancing the pros and cons in his mind, Clive, keenly alive to the importance of producing an impression upon the minds of the natives by display and by numbers, despatched that evening a pressing letter to the Rájah of Bardhwán, begging him to join him, if only with a thousand horsemen. He then summoned all the officers in his camp above the rank of subaltern to a council of war.

There came to that council, including Clive, twenty officers, some of them, such as Eyre Coote, of the 39th, and James Kilpatrick, of the Madras army, men of capacity and mental power. The question Clive put before them was whether, under existing circumstances, and without other assistance, the army should at once cross into the island of Kásimbázár, and at all events attack the Núwáb; or whether they should fortify themselves at Katwá and wait till the monsoon was over, trusting then to assistance from the Maráthas, or some other native power. Contrary to all custom, Clive gave his own vote first, and invited the others to follow his example in order of seniority. Clive voted against immediate action.

On the same side voted Major Kilpatrick, commanding the Company's troops, Major Archibald Grant, of the 39th, Captains Waggoner and Corneille, of the same regiment, Captain Fischer, Bengal Service, Captains Gaupp and Rumbold, Madras Service, Captains Palmer and Molitor, Bombay Service, Captain Jennings, commanding the Artillery, and Captain Parshaw, whose service I have been unable to ascertain. Major Eyre Coote took a view totally opposed to theirs. That gallant soldier showed the capacity for command which he possessed, and which he displayed throughout a long and distinguished military career, when he declared in favour of immediate advance, on the following grounds. First, he argued, they had met with nothing but success; the spirit of the troops was high, and that spirit would be damped by delay. Then he urged that delay would be prejudicial in another sense, inasmuch as it would allow time for the French leader, M. Law, who had been promptly summoned from Bhágalpúr to join the Núwáb, to arrive; that his arrival would not only greatly strengthen that ruler, but would impair the efficiency of the English force, because the French who had been enlisted into its ranks after the fall of Chandranagar would take the first opportunity to desert. Finally, he protested with all his force against the half measure of halting at Katwá. If, he declared, it were thought not advisable to come to immediate action—though he held a contrary opinion—it would be more proper to return to Calcutta at once. He dwelt, however, on the disgrace which such a measure would entail on the army, and the injury it would cause to the Company's interests. Major Eyre Coote was supported in his view by Captains Alexander Grant, Cudmore, Muir, and Carstairs, of the Bengal Service; by Captain Campbell, of the Madras, and by Captain Armstrong, of the Bombay Service. The majority against him, however, was thirteen to seven. By nearly two to one the council of war decided not to fight.

The members of the council separated, and Clive was left alone. The decision had not relieved the anxiety which pressed upon him. Strolling to a piece of ground shaded by a clump of trees, he sat down, and passed in review the arguments which had been urged on both sides. A thorough soldier himself, a man who had proved on more than one field that boldness was prudence, and that bastard-prudence carried within it the germs of destruction, he could not long resist the soundness of the views which had been so forcibly urged by Eyre Coote and his supporters. At the end of an hour's reflection, all doubt had disappeared. He was once more firm, self-reliant, and confident. Rising, he set out to return to his quarters. On his way thither he met Major Eyre Coote. Simply informing him that he had changed his mind, and intended to fight, Clive entered his quarters and dictated orders for the passage of the river the following morning.

Deducting the sick and a small guard left at Katwá, the army directed to march against the Núwáb consisted of 950* European infantry and 100 European artillery, 50 English sailors, a small detail of native lascars, and 2,100 native troops. The artillery train was composed of eight 6-pounders and two small howitzers. Obeying the orders issued the night before, this little force marched down the banks of the Bhágirathí at daybreak of the 22nd June, and began the crossing in the boats which had accompanied it from Chandranagar. It encountered no opposition, and by 4 o'clock the same afternoon it was securely planted on the left bank. Here Clive received another letter from Mír J'afar, informing him that the Núwáb had halted at Mankárah, a village six miles from Kásimbázár, and there intended to entrench himself. The Mír suggested that the English should march up the eastern side of the triangle which forms the island and surprise him.

Such an operation would have cut off Clive from his base, which was now the river Bhágirathí, and have entailed a march round the arc of a circle, whilst his enemy, traversing the chord, could sever him from all his communications. It was not very hopeful to receive such advice from a confederate, himself a soldier who had commanded in many a campaign. Clive met it in the direct and straightforward way calculated to force a decision. He sent back the messenger with the answer that he would march towards Palási without delay; that the next day he would march six miles further to Dáúdpúr; but that if,

* In these were included 200 men of mixed native and Portuguese blood.

reaching that village, Mír J'afar should not join him, he would make peace with the Núwáb.

The distance to Palási from the camp on the Bhágirathí, whence this message was despatched, was fifteen miles. To accomplish those fifteen miles the little army marched at sunset the same day, the 22nd, following the windings of the Bhágirathí, up the stream of which their boats, containing their supplies and auxiliary stores, were towed. After eight hours of extreme fatigue, the overflow of recent inundations causing the water to rise often up to their waists, whilst a deluge poured upon them from above, they reached, weary and worn out, at 1 o'clock in the morning of the 23rd, the village of Palási. Traversing this village, they halted and bivouacked in a large mango grove a short distance beyond it. Here, to their surprise, the sound of martial music reached their ears, plainly signifying that the Núwáb was within striking distance of them.

The mango grove which formed the bivouac of the English force was, in fact, little more than a mile from the Núwáb's encampment. It was 800 yards in length and 300 in breadth, and was surrounded by an earth-bank and ditch. In its length it was diagonal to the river, for whilst the Bhágirathí flowed about fifty yards from its north-west angle, four times that distance intervened between it and the south-western corner. The trees in it were, as is usual in India, planted in regular rows.* Just beyond the grove stood a hunting-box belonging to the Núwáb, surrounded by a masonry wall. Of this, Clive, as soon as the sounds of martial music to which I have adverted reached his ears, detached a small force to take possession. It is now time that I should explain how it was that such music came to be in his close vicinity.

The reader will recollect that in consequence of the mutiny of his troops at Murshidábád, the Núwáb had been forced to

* The last of these trees, Mr. Eastwick informs us, fell some years ago, and has been eaten by white ants.—*Murray's Handbook of Bengal*, 1882.

delay his march from that place till the 19th June. On that day he set out, but on that same day he heard of the arrival of the English army at Katwá. Judging from his knowledge of the character of their leader that they would cross the Bhágirathí and march on Palási without delay, he came to the conclusion that he had been forestalled at that place, and that it would be better for him to halt at Mankárah and watch thence the course of events. But when, on the 21st, he learned that Clive was still halting at Katwá, his resolution revived, and he marched at once to his old encampment at Palási about one mile to the north of the grove of which I have spoken. He had taken his post here twenty-six hours before the English reached the grove.

His army was strong in numbers. It consisted of 35,000 infantry of all sorts; men not trained in the European fashion, but of the stamp of those which may be seen in the present day in and about the chief towns of the territories of native princes of the second or third rank. They were, in fact, men imperfectly trained and imperfectly armed, and, in the rigid sense of the word, undisciplined. His cavalry, said to have amounted to about 15,000, were better. They were mostly Patáns from the north, the race of which the Indian irregular horse of the present day is formed, excellent light cavalry, well mounted, armed with swords or long spears. His artillery was better still. It consisted of fifty-three pieces, mostly of heavy calibres, 32, 24, and 18-pounders. But what constituted its greatest strength was the presence with that arm, to support the native gunners and to work and direct their own field-pieces, of forty to fifty Frenchmen—who had been allowed to remain when Law with the main body had been dismissed—commanded by M. St. Frais, formerly one of the Council of Chandranagar. These men were animated by a very bitter feeling against the Englishman who had despoiled their flourishing settlement.

This army thus strong in numbers occupied likewise a strong position. The intrenched works which covered it rested on the river, extended inland in a line perpendicular to it for about 200 yards, and then swept round to the north-east at an obtuse angle for about three miles. At this angle was a redoubt mounted with cannon. Three hundred yards east of this, and in front of the line of intrenchments, was a hillock covered with jungle, and about 800 yards to the south, nearer the grove occupied by the English was a tank, and 100 yards still nearer a larger tank. Both of these were surrounded by large mounds of earth at some distance from their margins. It is important to keep the mind fixed on these points when following the movements of the two armies.

At daybreak on the 23rd, the Núwáb's army marched out of its intrenchments and took up the following positions. The French, with four field-pieces, took post at the larger tank, nearest the English position, about half a mile from it. Between them and the river, and in a line with them, were placed two heavy guns under a native officer; behind them again, and supporting them, were the Núwáb's best troops, a body of 5,000 horse and 7,000 foot, commanded by his one faithful general, Mír Múdín Khán, by the side of whom served the prince's Hindú favourite, Mohan Lál. From the rearmost position of Mír Múdín, the rest of the army formed a curve in the direction of the village of Palási, the right resting on the hillock covered with jungle of which I have spoken, the left on a point covering the south-eastern angle of Clive's grove, at a distance of about 800 yards from it. The intervals were crammed with dense masses of horse and foot, artillery being interspersed between the masses or columns. The troops forming this curve, numbering about 45,000, were commanded by the traitor confederates, Rájah Dúlab Rám, Yár Lútf Khán, and Mír J'afar. The first was on the right, the second in the centre, Mír J'afar on the left nearest the English. The position was a strong one, for the English could not attack the point which barred their progress—that occupied by the French and Mír Múdín Khán—without exposing their right to a flank attack. In fact, they were almost surrounded, and, unless treason had played her part, they had been doomed.

From the roof of the hunting-box Clive watched the movements, as they gradually developed themselves, of the army of Síráju'd daulah. As Mír Múdín took up his position, as the corps of Mír J'afar, Yár Lútf, and Dúlab Rám poured out their myriads until the mango grove his men occupied was not only flanked, but the extreme end of the arc formed by those myriads threatened to even overlap its rear, he could not conceal his astonishment at the numbers against whom he was about to hurl his tiny band. "What if they should all be true to their master!" was a thought which must more than once have traversed his brain as he witnessed that long defiling. It was too late to think of that, however, and Clive, true to his military instinct, which in the time of danger was always sound, resolved to meet this bold display by a corresponding demonstration. Accordingly he ordered his men to advance from the grove, and drew them up in line in front of it, their left resting on the hunting-box, which was immediately on the river. In the centre of the line he placed his Europeans, flanked on both sides by three 6-pounders; on their right and left he posted the native troops in two equal divisions. He detached at the same time a small party with two 6-pounders and two howitzers to occupy some brick-kilns about 200 yards in front of the left (the native) division of his little army.

By 8 o'clock in the morning of this memorable day, the preparations on both sides were completed. The French under St. Frais opened the battle by firing one of their guns which, well directed, took effect on the British line. The discharge of this single gun was the signal for the opening of a heavy and continuous fire from the enemy's whole line, from the guns in

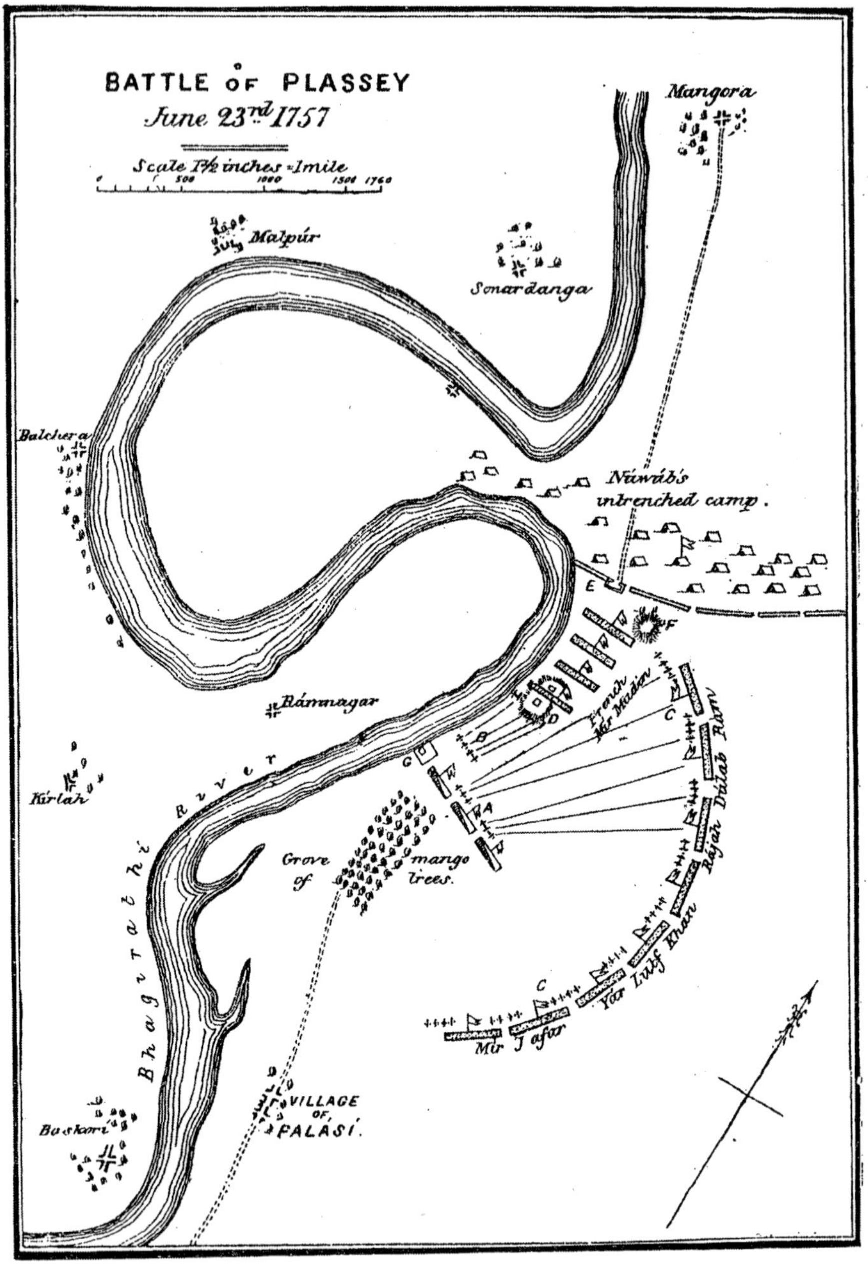

REFERENCE.

A—Position of the British army at 8 in the morning.
B—Guns advanced to check the fire of the French.
C—Náwáb's army in three divisions.
D—The bank occupied up to 3 p.m. by the French, supported in their rear by Mí dín Khán.
E F—The redoubt and mound taken at half-past four
G—The Náwáb's hunting box

front as well as from those in the curve. The English guns returned the fire with considerable effect. Still, however true might have been the aim of the English gunners, the disparity in numbers, in the weight of metal, and in guns was too great to allow the game to be continued long by the weaker party. Though ten of the enemy's men might fall to one of the English, the advantage would still be with the enemy. Clive was made to feel this when, at the end of the first half hour, thirty of his men had been placed *hors de combat.* He accordingly determined to give his troops the shelter which the grove and its bank would afford. Leaving still an advanced party at the brick-kilns, and another at the hunting-box, he effected this withdrawal movement in perfect order, though under the shouts and fire of the enemy. These were so elated that they advanced their guns much nearer and began to fire with greater vivacity. Clive, however, had now found the shelter he desired, and whilst the balls from the enemy's guns, cutting the air at too high a level, did great damage to the trees in the grove, he made the bulk of his men sit down under the bank, whilst small parties should bore holes to serve as embrasures for his field-pieces. From this new position his guns soon opened fire, and maintained it with so much vigour and in so true a direction that several of the enemy's gunners were killed or wounded, and every now and again explosions of their ammunition were heard. Protected by the bank, the proportion of the casualties of the English now lessened considerably, whilst there was no abatement of those of the masses opposed to them. Still, at the end of three hours, no great or decisive effect had been produced, the enemy's fire had shown no signs of diminishing, nor had their position varied. No symptoms of co-operation on the part of Mír J'afar were visible, nor, in the face of such enormous masses of men, who had it in their power, if true to their prince, to surround and overwhelm any party which should attempt the key of the position, held by

Mír Múdín Khán, did any mode of bettering the condition of affairs seem to offer. This was certainly the opinion of Clive when, at 11 o'clock, he summoned his principal officers to his side. Nor could he, after consultation with them, arrive at any other conclusion than this—that it was advisable to maintain the position till after nightfall, and at midnight try the effect of an attack on the enemy's camp.

The decision was sound under the circumstances, especially as it was subordinate to any incidents which might, in the long interval of twelve hours, occur to alter it. Such an incident did occur very soon after the conference. There fell then, and continued for an hour, one of those heavy pelting showers so common during the rainy season. The English had their tarpaulins ready to cover their ammunition, which in consequence sustained but little injury from the rain. The enemy took no such precautions, and their powder suffered accordingly. The result was soon shown by a general slacking of their fire. Believing that the English were in a similar plight, Mír Múdín Khán advanced with a body of horsemen towards the grove to take advantage of it. The English, however, received him with a heavy grape fire, which not only drove back his men, but mortally wounded their leader.

This was the crisis of the day. As long as Mír Múdín lived, the chances of Siráju'd daulah, surrounded though he was by traitors, were not quite desperate. The fidelity of that true and capable soldier might, under any circumstances, save him. But his death was a loss which could not be repaired. It is probable that some such conviction penetrated the heart of the unfortunate young prince when the news of the calamity reached him. He at once sent for Mír J'afar, and besought him in the most abject terms to be true to him and to defend him. He reminded him of the loyalty he had always displayed towards his grandfather, Ali Vardí Khán, of his relationship to himself; then taking off his turban, and casting it on the ground before him, he exclaimed, "J'afar, that turban thou must defend." Those who are acquainted with the manners of Eastern nations will realise that no more pathetic, no more heartrending, appeal could be made by a prince to a subject.

Mír J'afar Khán responded to it with apparent sincerity. Placing—in the respectful manner which indicates devotion—his crossed hands on his breast, and bowing over them, he promised to exert himself to the utmost. When he made that gesture and when he uttered those words he was lying. Never was he more firmly resolved than at that moment to betray his master. Quitting the presence of the Núwáb he galloped back to his troops, and despatched a letter to Clive, informing him of what had happened, and urging him to push on immediately; or, in no case to defer the attack beyond the night. That the messenger did not reach his destination till too late for Clive to profit by the letter, detracts not one whit from the baseness of the man who, fresh from such an interview, wrote and sent it!

But Mír J'afar was not the only traitor. The loss of his best officer, coinciding with the unfortunate damping of the ammunition, had completely unnerved Siráju'd daulah. Scarcely had Mír J'afar left him, than he turned to the commander of his right wing, Rájah Dúlab Rám, for support and consolation. The counsel which this man—likewise one of the conspirators—gave him, was of a most insidious character. Playing upon his fears, he continually urged him to issue orders to the army to retire behind the intrenchment; this order issued, he should quit the field, and leave the result in confidence to his generals. In an evil hour the wretched youth, incapable at such a moment of thinking soundly and clearly, followed the insidious advice, issued the order, and, mounting a camel, rode—followed by 2,000 horsemen—to Murshidábád.

The three traitorous generals were now masters of the position. Their object being to entice the English to come on, they began the retiring movement which the Núwáb had sanctioned. They had reckoned, however, without St. Frais and his Frenchmen. These gallant men remained true to their master in the hour of supreme peril, and declined to quit a position which, supported by the troops of Mír Múdín, they had maintained against the whole British force. But Mír Múdín had been killed, his troops were following the rest of the army, and St. Frais stood there almost without support. To understand what followed, I must ask the reader to accompany me to the grove.

I left Clive and his gallant soldiers repulsing the attack which cost the Núwáb his one faithful commander. The vital consequences of this repulse never presented themselves for a moment to the imagination of the English leader. It never occurred to him that it might lead to the flight of the Núwáb, and to the retirement of his troops from a position which they had held successfully, and from which they still threatened the grove. There can be no doubt but that, at this period of the action, Clive had made up his mind to hold the grove at all hazards till nightfall, and then, relying upon the co-operation of Mír J'afar and his friends, to make his supreme effort. Satisfied that this was the only course to be followed, he had entered the hunting-box and lain down to take some rest, giving orders that he should be roused if the enemy should make any change in their position. He had not been long absent when Major Kilpatrick noticed the retiring movement I have already described. He did not know, and probably did not care, to what cause to attribute it; he only saw that the French were being deserted, and that a splendid opportunity offered to carry their position at the tank, and cannonade thence the retiring enemy. Quick as the thought he moved rapidly from the grove towards the tank with about 250 Europeans and two field-pieces, sending an officer to Clive to explain his intentions and their reason.

It is said that the officer found Clive asleep. The message, however, completely roused him, and, angry that any officer should have dared to make an important movement without his orders, he ran to the detachment and severely reprimanded Kilpatrick. A glance at the situation, however, satisfied him that Kilpatrick had only done that which he himself would have ordered him to do had he been on the spot. He realised that the moment for decisive action had arrived. He sent back Kilpatrick, then, with orders to bring on the rest of the army, and continued the movement which that officer had initiated.

St. Frais, on his side, had recognised that the retreat of the Núwáb's army had compromised him, and that he was quite unable, with his handful, to resist the whole British force, which, a few minutes later, he saw issuing from the grove in his direction. Resolved, however, to dispute every inch of the ground, he fired a parting shot, then, limbering up, fell back in perfect order to the redoubt at the corner of the intrenchment. Here he planted his field-pieces ready to act again.

Meanwhile, two of the three divisions of the enemy's army were marching towards the intrenchment. It was observed, however, that the third division, that on the left, nearest to the grove, commanded by Mír J'afar, lingered behind the rest, and that when its rearmost file had reached a point in a line with the northern end of the grove, the whole division wheeled to the left and marched in that direction. Clive had no means of recognising that these were the troops of his confederate, but, believing that they had a design upon his baggage, he detached a party of Europeans with a field-piece to check them. The fire of the field-piece had its effect, in so far that it prevented a further advance in that direction. But the division continued to remain separate from the rest of the Núwáb's army.

Clive, himself, meanwhile, had reached the tank from which St. Frais had retreated, and had begun thence a vigorous cannonade of the enemy's position behind the intrenchment. What followed can be well understood, if it be borne in mind that whilst the leaders of the Núwáb's army had been gained over, the rank and file, and the vast majority of the officers, were faithful to their master. They had not been entrusted with the secret, and being soldiers and superior in numbers to the attacking party, they were in no mood to permit that party to cannonade them with impunity. No sooner, then, did the shot from the British cannon begin to take effect in their ranks, than they issued from the intrenchment—cavalry, infantry, and artillery—and opened a heavy fire upon the British force.

The real battle now began. Clive, seriously incommoded by this new move on the part of the enemy, quitted his position and advanced nearer to the intrenchment. Posting then half his infantry and half his artillery on the mound of the lesser tank, the greater part of the remaining moiety on a rising ground 200 yards to the left of it, and detaching 160 men, picked natives and Europeans, to lodge themselves behind a tank close to the intrenchment, he opened from the first and second positions a very heavy artillery fire, whilst from the third the musketry fire should be well sustained and well aimed. This masterly movement, well carried into execution, caused the enemy great loss, and threw the cattle attached to their guns into great confusion. In vain did St. Frais ply his guns from the redoubt, the matchlockmen pour in volley after volley from the hillock to the east of it, and from the intrenchments. In vain did their swarthy troopers make charge after charge. Masses without a leader were fighting against a man whose clearness of vision was never so marked, whose judgment was never so infallible, whose execution was never so decisive as when he was on the battlefield. What chance had they, brave as they were, in a battle which their leaders had sold? As they still fought, Clive noticed that the division of their troops which he had at first believed had designs on his baggage, still remained isolated from the rest, and took no part in the battle. Suddenly it dawned upon him that it must be the division of Mír J'afar. Immensely relieved by this discovery, inasmuch as it freed him from all apprehension of an attack on his flank or rear, he resolved to make a supreme effort to carry the redoubt held by St. Frais, and the hill to the east of it. With this object, he formed two strong detachments, and sent them simultaneously against the two points indicated, supporting them from the rear by the main body in the centre. The hill was first gained and carried without firing a shot. The movement against the redoubt was not less successful, for St. Frais, abandoned, isolated, and threatened, had no resource but to retire. The possession of this position decided the day. Thenceforward all resistance ceased. By 5 o'clock the English were in the possession of the whole intrenchment and camp. The victory of Plassey had been won! It had cost the victors seven European and sixteen native soldiers killed, thirteen European and thirty-six natives wounded.

Plassey was a very decisive battle. The effects of it are felt this day by more than two hundred and fifty millions of people. Whilst the empire founded by the Mughuls was rapidly decaying, that victory introduced into their richest province, in a commanding position, another foreign race, active, capable, and daring, bringing with them the new ideas, the new blood, the love of justice, of tolerance, of order, the capacity of enforcing these principles, which were necessary to infuse a new and a better life into the Hindústán of the last century. There never was a battle in which the consequences were so vast, so immediate, and so permanent. From the very morrow of the victory the English became virtual masters of Bengal, Bihár, and Orísá. During the century which followed, but one serious attempt was made, and that to be presently related, to cast off the yoke virtually imposed by Plassey, whilst from the base it gave them, a base resting on the sea and, with proper care, unassailable, they were able to extend their authority beyond the Indus, their influence amongst peoples of whose existence even Europe was at the time profoundly ignorant. It was Plassey which made England the greatest Muhammadan power in the world; Plassey which forced her to become one of the main factors in the settlement of the burning Eastern question; Plassey which necessitated the conquest and colonisation of the Cape of Good Hope, of the Mauritius, the protectorship over Egypt; Plassey which gave to the sons of her middle classes the finest field for the development of their talent and industry the world has ever known; to her aristocracy unrivalled opportunities for the display of administrative power; to her merchants and manufacturers customers whose enormous demands almost compensate for the hostile tariffs of her rivals, and, alas! even of her colonies; to the skilled artisan remunerative employment; to her people generally a noble feeling of pride in the greatness and glory of the empire of which a little island in the Atlantic is the parent stem, Hindústán the noblest branch; it was Plassey which, in its consequences, brought consolation to that little island for the loss of America, and which, whilst, in those consequences, it has concentrated upon it the envy of the other nations of Europe, has given to her children the sense of responsibility, of the necessity of maintaining a great position, the conviction of which underlies the thought of every true Englishman.

Yes! As a victory, Plassey was, in its consequences, perhaps the greatest ever gained. But as a battle it is not, in my opinion, a matter to be very proud of. In the first place, it was not a fair fight. Who can doubt that if the three principal generals of Síráju'd daulah had been faithful to their master Plassey would not have been won? Up to the time of the death of Mír Múdín Khán the English had made no progress; they had even been forced to retire. They could have made no impression on their enemy had the Núwáb's army, led by men loyal to their master, simply maintained their position. An advance against the French guns meant an exposure of their right flank to some 40,000 men. It was not to be thought of. It was only when treason had done her work, when treason had driven the Núwáb from the field, when treason had removed his army from its commanding position, that Clive was able to advance without the certainty of being annihilated. Plassey, then, though a decisive, can never be considered a great battle.

There was that about the events preceding it, occurring during its progress, and following it, which no honourable man can contemplate without disgust and repulsion. Not one actor in the drama was free from the stain which connection with dishonour always causes. The bargaining of Clive and the Calcutta Council with Mír J'afar and the other traitors, the episode with Amíchand, though they form no part of the military history of the battle, cannot be wholly ignored when considering its consequences. The greed for money, the ever increasing demand for the augmentation of the sum originally asked for, the dishonouring trick by which a confederate was to be baulked of his share in the spoil; these are actions, the contemplation of which makes, and will always make, the heart of an honest man burn with indignation. Then, to single out one, the chiefest of the conspirators, Mír J'afar Khán. This man had possessed honourable instincts. Ten years before Plassey had been fought, Alí Vardi Khán had removed him from his command because he had retreated before the Maráthas. The officer who replaced him advanced and defeated those warriors; then coming to Mír J'afar, offered to make him governor of Bihár if he would aid in deposing Ali Vardi. Mír J'afar refused then:—but in 1757 we see this man—then so loyal—conspiring with a foreign people, of whose power he was conscious, to seat himself on the throne—for virtually it was a throne—of his master. To accomplish this selfish personal end, he hesitates not to become a perjuror of the deepest dye; to doom to a violent death the nephew to whom he had sworn obedience, and to sacrifice the future of his country. If the people of India do indeed writhe under the sway of their foreign conquerors, they have to thank this Mír J'afar Khán, this man who sold their three richest provinces to the English that he might enjoy the mere pageantry of royalty.

It was indeed the merest pageantry. Soon was he made to learn that bitter truth that, by his own act, dominion in Bengal had departed from the Mughul. A tool, a cypher in the hands of the foreigners for whom he had betrayed his master, he was allowed to govern, never to rule. Well for him that he did not possess the power to dive into futurity and behold the representative of his name and office, an unhonoured pensioner of the people he had called in to subdue his country!

The name of Siráju'd daulah has been justly held up to obloquy in connection with the catastrophe of the Black Hole. Although, as I have shown, the Núwáb had not designed the death of our countrymen, still he made himself an accessory after the act, and must, therefore, bear the blame of the deed. Yet the hearts of those who condemn him most will scarcely steel themselves to the pity which the contemplation of his subsequent fate inspires. From the time when Clive beat up his quarters before Calcutta, to the hour of his death, the life of Siráju'd daulah was one of constant alarm and dread. He knew not whom to trust. He felt that he was betrayed, but he could not feel sure by whom. Confident one day that Clive was his enemy, believing the next that he was his friend—he could not resolve to offer him decided opposition, or to disarm in his presence. His vacillation, the child of uncertainty, completed his ruin. The body of Frenchmen whom, to please Clive, he had sent to Bhágalpúr, might have saved Plassey. When he could no longer resist the conviction that Clive was his bitter, his irreconcilable enemy, he called to his councils the very men who had sworn to betray him! Could there be a harder fate than this for a young boy suddenly raised to power, and not yet satiated with the follies of youth? At Plassey, again, he was betrayed; betrayed at a moment when, had he been loyally supported, he might have rid himself for ever of the hated English. Inexorable fate still pursued him. Fleeing from the field, he reached Murshidábád that night, only to learn in the early morn of the defeat of his army. Terrified by the prospect before him, he embarked that night accompanied by his favourite wife, on a boat prepared for him by one still faithful adherent, hoping to reach the French advancing under Law from Bhágalpúr. But at Rájmahal the strength of the rowers failed them, and he took refuge for the night in the buildings of a deserted garden. Here he was discovered and betrayed—again betrayed—and brought, bound like a common felon, into the presence of Mír J'afar. Trembling and weeping, he implored his life. It was a scene which recalls to the English reader another scene acted some seventy years previously, between Monmouth and James II. Mír J'afar was as inexorable as James. That night, by the express order of his son, Míran, Siráju'd daulah was stabbed to death in his cell.

He was more fortunate, and certainly less to be despised, than was Mír J'afar. Whatever may have been his faults, Siráju'd daulah had neither betrayed his master nor sold his country. Nay more, no unbiassed Englishman, sitting in judgment on the events which passed in the interval between the 9th February and the 23rd June, can deny that the name of Siráju'd daulah stands higher in the scale of honour than does the name of Clive. He was the only one of the principal actors in that tragic drama who did not attempt to deceive!

CHAPTER IV.

KONDUR AND MACHHLÍPATANAM.*

I HAVE already shown how the battle of Kávéripák virtually decided the fate of India south of the river Krishna. There still remained north of that river and south of the Vindhayan range the large territory belonging to the Súbahdár of the Dakhan, covering almost the entire northern portion of the peninsula, bounded on the west by the Western Ghâts, and on the east only by the sea. This important territory was then, and was likely to remain, under French influence, that influence being maintained by the presence at Haidarábád of a considerable body of French troops, commanded by an officer of rare intelligence and capacity, the Marquis de Bussy. It was soon made to rest on a basis still more solid. In 1753, an intrigue, set on foot by Sayud Lashkar, Minister of the Súbahdár, to rid his master of the French, had been completely defeated by the energy and resolution displayed by the

* The English of a hundred and thirty years ago chose to call this place, which is written and pronounced by the natives Machhlípatanam, or "the town of fish," Masúlipatam, a name which conveys no meaning whatever. The "Machhlí" was evidently first corrupted into "Maslí"; later on the "Maslí" became "Masúli." This barbarism has been continued to the present day.

French general. Marching on Aurangábád, where the court of the Súbahdár held high revelry at the time, Bussy had virtually dictated his own terms. These terms comprehended the cession, with zamíndári rights, to the French, of the provinces of Élúr, Shríkákolam (Chicacole), Kondapilli, and Murtazanagar,* the guardianship of the person of the Súbahdár, and the transfer to Bussy himself of an authority very similar to that now exercised by a British Resident at a native court. By this arrangement the French were relieved of the necessity of relying upon the favour of the Súbahdár—the cession of so important a territory made them practically independent.

The districts so ceded, inclusive of the territories in and about Machhlípatanam, previously granted in 1750, covered four hundred and seventy miles of sea-coast from the Chílká lake to the south bank of the Gundlakamma. It stretched inland to distances varying from thirty to a hundred miles, was watered by the Krishna, the Gundlakamma, and the Godávarí, and contained the important towns of Ganjám, Shríkákolam, Vijiyánagaram, Vishákpatanam (Vizagapatam), Koringa, Yanún, Machhlipatanam, Élúr, and Nizámpatanam. It possessed an area of about seventeen thousand geographical miles, and yielded an annual revenue of four hundred thousand pounds sterling. The forests within its limits abounded with teak. One of its districts was famous for its manufacture of cloths, another for its growth of rice. Nor was it wanting in capabilities of defence. Resting on the sea on the one side, it was covered on the other by a chain of mountains running at unequal distances nearly parallel with the coast. These mountains were covered with forests, then almost impenetrable, and traversed by three or four passes capable of being held by a very few men against an army. In

* The names of these districts underwent subsequently a partial revision. Shrikákolam was divided into Ganjám, Vishákpatanam, and Rajahmahéndri. Machhlipatanam absorbed Elúr and Kondapilli; Murtazanagar became Guntúr.

fine, to borrow the language of Mr. Orme, "these territories rendered the French masters of the greatest dominion, both in extent and value, that had ever been possessed in Hindústán by Europeans, not excepting the Portuguese at the height of their prosperity."

From December 1753 to July 1758 these territories were administered, under the general supervision of Bussy, by a French agent residing at Machhlípatanam, M. Moracin. At the disposal of this official Bussy placed a force of one hundred and fifty European and two thousand five hundred native troops. He farmed the revenues to Vijiyárám Ráji, Rájah of Vijiyánagaram, a man conspicuous for character and ability. Of the manner in which the country was administered under this high official, one of the greatest of the English authorities, the late Captain Grant Duff, wrote in terms of high praise. "The rent was moderate, enforced without rigour; accurate accounts were prepared, and most of the hereditary officers, if not those possessing rent-free lands, were confirmed in their property—facts which do Bussy and his nation great honour."

One of the first cares of Bussy, after obtaining possession of his new districts, had been to expel the few English from the places they had occupied in and near Machhlípatanam. This was a matter of policy for one who held it to be dangerous that a rival European interest should take root within the borders of Franco-Indian territory. During the four years and a half that followed nothing occurred to affect the stability of the French rule. In the various intrigues by which Bussy was occasionally hampered at Haidarábád, the possession of the northern Sirkárs proved to be of all the value he had anticipated. They became the seat of French power, from which Bussy was enabled on more than one occasion to turn the tables on his enemies. Never did the French hold upon them appear more secure than in the beginning of 1758. But never was the French hold upon them in greater danger than at that particular period. At the end of April of that year a considerable French force, commanded by the Count de Lally, had arrived at Pondichery with the avowed intention of expelling the English from Southern India. From the moment of his landing to the period of his embarkation as a prisoner on board an English vessel, Lally's movements were characterised by a rashness, by a contempt for the Indian experience of others which seem the peculiar property, even in the present day, of men possessing ability and reputation, but whom Nature has endowed with one-sided minds. An initial success did indeed attend his first movements. He expelled the English from Fort St. David. The next move he contemplated was against Tanjúr. But before he set out on this expedition he despatched an order to Bussy to repair at once to Arkát, leaving no French troops at the court of the Súbahdár, and only as many in the northern Sirkárs as would suffice to maintain them. The command of these and the general supervision of the province he directed Bussy to entrust to the Marquis de Conflans, an officer new to Indian affairs, but just arrived from Europe; and, as if still further to embarrass French interests in the province, he removed Moracin at the same time.

This letter of recall painfully affected alike Bussy and the Súbahdár. It called upon the former to renounce, for an uncertain issue, the work of the best years of his life, to leave the province he had won for France a certain prey to the victors in the struggle which was then beginning. Not so would he have acted had the supreme direction been entrusted to his hands. Whilst fighting for the Karnátak, he would never have relinquished his hold upon provinces the possession of which, combined with the influence over the Súbahdár which it assured, would have compensated for defeat even in the Karnátak. But, as he wrote to Lally, there was one thing which he had always known how to do better than anything else, and that was to obey. Five days after he received the order, after a painful parting with the

Súbahdár,* he set out from Haidarábád at the head of two hundred and fifty European and five hundred native troops. He reached Wáiúr on the north bank of the Krishna on the 3rd of August. Here he made over the charge of the northern Sirkárs to M. de Conflans. The next day he turned his back for ever on the provinces which he had gained for his country by the exercise of firmness, energy, intuition, and knowledge of native character such as have been rarely equalled, even in India.

His successor, M. de Conflans, younger brother of the general who commanded at the same period the French army of Germany, had, up to that time, placed on the record no achievement to illustrate his family name. A courtier in a corrupt court, he lacked the talents and the experience which were necessary to succeed in a task which had taxed all the great qualities of Bussy. From the moment of his taking charge, his difficulties began. At first he had to deal with a people to whom he was a stranger, who were strange to him, and always ready to test the qualities of a new administrator; a little later he had to meet the combined dangers of insurrection and invasion.

Very soon after Conflans had taken charge of the northern Sirkárs, a rumour reached those districts that the main French army, which was to reconquer southern India, had been compelled to beat an ignominious retreat from before the walls of Tanjúr. The rumour, promptly confirmed, gave birth to a conviction in the minds of one or two disaffected nobles that the time had arrived when an attempt to shake off the foreign yoke might be successfully made. Prominent amongst these nobles was Anandráz Gajapati, son and successor of the chief, Vijiyárám Ráji, who had administered the provinces with marked ability. The son had not, however, inherited the predilections

* Salábat Jang, writes Mr. Orme, "took leave of Bussy with the utmost despondency, called him the guardian angel of his life and fortune, and foreboded the unhappy fate to which he would be exposed by his departure."

of the father, and, dissatisfied at certain changes which Bussy had introduced on the death of Vijiyárám, he had from that moment become a conspirator. Before the departure of Bussy had even been contemplated, Anandráz had made overtures to the English in Madras, and when he became convinced that the paucity of their troops would not allow him to hope for any assistance from that quarter, he had transmitted similar proposals to Bengal. Before he could receive a reply, the discomfiture of the French army before Tanjúr, following on the departure of Bussy, induced him to strike a blow on his own account. Summoning all his retainers, and enlisting as many men as it was possible to attract to his standard—amounting in all to about three thousand—he suddenly (2nd September 1758) marched upon and took possession of Vishákpatanam, hauled down the French and planted the English flag, made prisoner the French chief, and plundered the French factory. Having done this, he despatched a second messenger to Calcutta, charged to inform the chief of the Bengal Presidency of all he had accomplished, to assure him that the native chiefs of the country were unanimous in their desire to be rid of the French rule; and that, with the assistance of a very small body of Englishmen, he would engage to drive them out of the country.

This messenger reached Calcutta early in October. The letters which he carried, and the message of which he was the bearer, were duly laid before the Calcutta Council. To every member of that Council, with one exception, his schemes seemed rash, chimerical, and dangerous. Bengal was threatened at the time by an invasion from the Sháhzádah, eldest son of the Great Mughul, and the feeling of the Murshidábád darbár was unmistakeably hostile. To denude the Presidency at such a conjuncture of a large body of troops, in order to support the revolt of a chief who had been able to muster only three thousand followers, seemed, in the eyes of the majority, to be little short of madness. The exception to these views was the Governor, Robert Clive. The experience in the Madras Presidency of this ruler of men induced in his mind the conclusion that, although the weakening of the British force in Bengal would entail some risks, yet the prospects opened out by the letters of Anandráz were so brilliant, and promised results so decisive, that sound policy counselled closing with his offers, and acting upon them without delay. Clive realised, in fact, that the success of an expedition sent from Bengal would transfer from the French to the English not only the valuable districts on the coast, but the predominant influence till then exercised with so much effect by the former at the court of the Súbahdár of the Dakhan. A diversion of this nature would likewise prevent the French in the northern Sirkárs from aiding Lally in the designs which, it was known, he was about to put in action against Madras. Whatever might be the result of the struggle then waging in the Karnátak, the transfer of those districts and of that influence would compensate for disaster or add enormously to the solidity of a victory.

It was impossible that he should go there. He must remain to ward off the evils threatening Bengal. But he had at hand an officer not second even to himself in capacity on the field of battle. This was Lieutenant-Colonel Forde, an officer who had risen to the rank of Major in the 39th Foot, and whom, by reason of the coolness and ability he had displayed under many trying circumstances, Clive had recently summoned from Madras to command the Company's troops in Bengal. It was a characteristic of Clive, that he was entirely devoid of military jealousy. He always sought out the best men he could find, and trusted them implicitly. He trusted Forde on this occasion. Having first carried his point in Council, he made over to him five hundred Europeans, two thousand native troops, six 6-pounders, and a small battering train, and bade him sail for Vishákpat-anam, disembark his troops, and drive the French from the northern Sirkárs. Forde sailed on the 12th, and arrived at Vishákpatanam on the 20th October.

Meanwhile Conflans had been doing little to re-establish his outraged authority. Having under his orders a force composed of five hundred seasoned European troops,—men trained by Bussy, and inspired by the recollection of many a victory—of four thousand native troops, and a brigade of artillery, he might by marching with all speed on Vishákpatanam, have crushed this rebellion in the bud. When the news of the revolt of Anandráz reached him, he was at Machhlípatanam, about a hundred and eighty miles from Vishákpatanam. An easy march of five days would have taken him to Rájahmahéndri; thence to Vishákpatanam, twelve days would have sufficed to march with ease and comfort. The rebellion had broken out on the 2nd September. Making every allowance, then, for difficulties, Conflans should have been able to reach Vishákpatanam some days before the English force under Forde had even sailed from Calcutta (12th October). But instead of using speed, the French leader displayed a hesitation which it is possible to explain only on the grounds that he believed himself to be face to face with a formidable insurrection, and that he feared to commit himself without assistance. Instead, then, of marching at all, he sent messenger after messenger to Lally, then straining every nerve to undertake the siege of Madras, begging him to send troops to strengthen him. It was only when he received an intimation from Lally, that he had directed Moracin to proceed with three hundred men to support him, but that meanwhile it behoved him to act with vigour, that he marched at all on Rájahmahéndri.

This delay had been of enormous advantage to Anandráz. One proof of the little vitality of his rebellion is to be traced in the fact that, notwithstanding all his endeavours, he had in six weeks been able to increase his force to a strength of five thousand men, and these for the most part a very miserable rabble. But few of them had fire-arms; the large majority only spears and bows and arrows. His main strength consisted in a body of forty Europeans, deserters and renegades of all nations, to whom he had entrusted four field-pieces. But neither these, nor the rabble with which they were associated, would have withstood for half an hour the force of Conflans had Conflans only chosen to advance.

His delay gave the English their opportunity. To herald the approach of Forde, these had despatched an agent with several assistants to Visháḱpatanam, alike to encourage the revolted Rájah, to re-establish their factory, and to prepare the place for the reception of an armed force. Forde arrived off the coast on the 20th October, and without delay disembarked his troops and stores. This operation and the provision of bullocks and means of transport took up some days, and it was not before the 1st of the following month that his army was able to move. Meanwhile the English agent was endeavouring to negotiate a treaty with the Rájah on the terms which he subsequently subscribed to. The main points of this treaty were that the Rájah should pay all the extra-expenses of the British force while it should co-operate with him; and, in the event of success, he should assign to the English all the country between Vishákpatanam and Machhlípatanam, whilst the territory inland belonging to native chiefs in the French interest should be transferred to himself.

Meanwhile Conflans—forced into action by letters from Lally—had reached Rájahmahéndri. The day after his arrival there, he learned that an English force had landed on the coast. Conscious that the opportunity of crushing the rebel Rájah had escaped him, he resolved to take up a commanding position, difficult to assail, if not impregnable, and to await in it the movement of the combined forces. For this purpose he selected a position about forty miles from Rájahmahéndri, within sight of the fort of Peddapúr, and commanding all the approaches from Vishákpatanam. Here he entrenched himself.

His force consisted of five hundred Europeans, six thousand native infantry, and about five hundred native cavalry; his artillery amounted to thirty pieces of sorts. He was still in this this position when on the 3rd December Forde, who had at length surmounted the many difficulties to which I have referred, came in sight of it. The numbers on both sides were about equal; for whilst Forde had under his own orders four hundred and seventy Europeans and one thousand nine hundred sepoys, with six guns, Anandráz accompanied him with his forty Europeans, his ragged rabble of five thousand men, five hundred horsemen, and four guns. Forde, after reconnoitring the French position, came to the opinion that it was too strong to be attacked. He, therefore, took possession of a village called Chámból, between three and four miles from the French camp, and almost as strong and commanding.

For four days the two armies remained watching each other; the leaders on both sides thinking the position of the other unassailable. On the 8th December, however, it occurred alike to Forde and Conflans, almost simultaneously, to make an attempt to place his enemy in a false position. The plan of Conflans was to send six guns, guarded by a respectable force, to occupy a small height which had been neglected by Forde, but which, Conflans had been assured by an intelligent deserter, commanded his camp. Of the confusion, which the sudden opening of a fire from these pieces would cause, Conflans would hold his army in readiness to take advantage. He fixed the night of the 8th for the carrying out of this project, so that the guns might open fire at daybreak on the 9th. Forde, on his part, designed another plan for the same morning. Tired of looking his enemy in the face without attacking him, he had arranged with Rájah Anandráz, also on the 8th, that the whole force should quit the encampment at Chámból, at a quarter past 4 o'clock the following morning, and move to a point whence it would be easy to reach, by a short cut, the main road leading to Rájahmahéndri. The march was to be a short one; only three miles, to the village of Kondúr.

It will be noticed that if the two rival plans had been carried out at the same moment, and with the same order and exactness, the English plan would have foiled the French plan. The French guns, in that case, would have reached the coveted eminence only to bombard a post which had been vacated. But, as it happened, of the three parties to the two transactions, one was unpunctual. This one was the Rájah. The French guns started for their destination at night, and reached it before daybreak. At daybreak their whole force was under arms, ready for any emergency. Forde marched in the direction of Kondúr at a quarter past 4 o'clock, but the Rájah and his troops had no thought of starting for two or three hours to come. It resulted from this delay, that a few minutes after daybreak he and his followers were unpleasantly aroused from their slumbers by the deadly messengers despatched by the six French guns which commanded their camp.

The fire of these guns was indeed most deadly and effective. The panic and confusion which it caused amongst the Rájah's half-armed followers is not to be described. Terrified out of his wits, the Rájah sent messenger after messenger to Forde, begging him to return. These met Forde—who had been equally surprised by the fire—hastening to the Rájah's rescue. The latter and his followers had meanwhile bestirred themselves to hurry on in the direction Forde had taken. The allied parties, therefore, met; then turning, they hurried on to Kondúr, which they reached in safety.

The partial success achieved by the French guns was fatal to Conflans. Ignorant of the exact state of affairs, he became confirmed in his belief of the truth of the story told him by the deserters, that the English force was composed of raw levies, and he was satisfied now that his guns had frightened them from their position at Chámból. He resolved to take instant advantage of their panic, as he believed it to be, and to act with his whole force.

About midway between the new position taken up by the English and the position occupied by the French, was a small village. Whilst the troops of Forde were entering Kondúr, those of Conflans were approaching this village, and taking up such a position that Forde could not advance without fighting, nor fall back without exposing himself at a disadvantage. Conflans, however, did not content himself with obtaining this good position. Still under the belief that the English force was composed of panic-stricken raw levies, he marched on towards Kondúr. Forde had not been half an hour in that place before he discovered first the enemy's native troops, and presently their whole line, at a distance of about a thousand yards from his left flank, moving on him in good order.

It was then half-past 8 o'clock. Forde instantly prepared for the inevitable battle. He placed the Rájah's troops, not yet recovered from the morning's panic, on the extreme right and left of his line; next to them he disposed his trained native soldiers, and in the centre, the English, including the Rájah's forty Europeans, with the guns equally divided on their flanks. He then advanced to take up a good position. Before, however, he had advanced far, the enemy's guns opened fire. Forde then halted his line in a position the centre of which was covered by a field of Indian corn which had grown so high as to conceal his Europeans entirely from the view of the advancing enemy. Connected with this fact was another, apparently of no moment whatever, but which combined with it to exercise a very decided influence on the battle about to ensue. This was, that whereas in the contests in Southern India between the French and English, the native troops in the service of both nations had been dressed in white, it had become the custom in the colder climate of Bengal to assimilate them in respect of clothing to their European comrades. The native soldiers, then, whom Forde had brought from Calcutta wore red coats. It was the first time that the French had met native soldiers so attired.

Conflans, meanwhile, had advanced in an oblique line towards the English with the intention, apparently, of turning their left flank. But when he noticed the movement in advance of which I have spoken, he halted, and directed his guns to open fire. This fire was very soon after replied to by the English, and was kept up on both sides for about forty minutes. At the end of that time Conflans, impatient for a more decisive result, ordered his army to renew its oblique advance, and to fall upon the troops on the left of the field of Indian corn, whom he believed to be Europeans. His orders were obeyed to the letter. His men advanced with great alacrity, and attacked the red-coated sipáhis simultaneously in front and on their flank with so much vigour that, notwithstanding all the exhortations of Forde, they broke in disorder, many of them, headed by the Rájah's followers, running for shelter as far as Chámból, pursued by the enemy's horse.

This easy success over an enemy who was not the enemy he was believed to be was fatal to the French. Believing that this first shock had won the battle for him, Conflans, with the impetuosity worthy of a Rupert, resolved that it should be decisive. Without stopping to inquire whether there might not be other enemies behind the field of Indian corn, he detached several platoons of his European force to join in the pursuit. These platoons started off, and were marching in haste without order, when they were suddenly confronted by the whole line of English troops, moving solidly to take up the position from which the red-coated sipáhís had been driven.

The positions of the two armies were at once reversed. Between the solid and compact array of the English, and the surprised and scattered platoons of the French, the contest could not be doubtful. In vain did the latter endeavour to re-form, to get together. Whilst they were still endeavouring, in the manner of men taken suddenly at a disadvantage, to bring about this result, the English line had opened a rolling fire, beginning from the left and reaching gradually to the right. The effect of this fire was so decisive, that before the last musket on the right had been discharged, the French had broken their ranks, and were running as fast as they could, without order or formation, to regain their guns, which were about half a mile in their rear.

Whilst matters had been thus progressing on the English left and centre, the French sipáhís on their left had been pressing the English right, and, for the moment, with some show of advantage. Forde, however, well aware that the contest in that quarter would be decided by the action of the Europeans in the centre, paid little heed to that part of the field, but, the moment he observed the French run in the manner I have described, he pressed on his Europeans, supported by the sipáhis who had just given away, but who had now rallied, in hot but orderly pursuit. This was the more necessary as the ground was open, the enemy's field guns were sufficiently numerous, counting thirteen, and, with a little time at their disposal, the French might yet have turned the fortunes of the day. He pressed on so vigorously, that although the French reached the shelter of their guns, they had time only to fire one or two rounds before his men, charging home, drove them from their pieces.

The day was thus virtually gained. The attack of the French had been repulsed, they had lost thirteen guns; the English were masters of the ground on which the battle had been fought. War has produced leaders who would have been satisfied with a result so brilliant. Not of such a school was Forde. He belonged to the class of men who believe that no satisfactory result has been achieved if anything yet remains to be accomplished. The French had been repulsed; they had not been thoroughly beaten. Forde resolved to improve his advantage by attacking their camp.

He halted till all his own sipáhís, and possibly the Rajáh's troops, should join him. Regarding the former, there was little delay. The native left wing had, we have seen, rallied after their first defeat and had rejoined him. The contest on his right had been decided in the manner he had anticipated; the French sipáhís had fallen back when they had seen their centre and right routed; their retreat enabled the English right wing to rejoin Forde. The Rájah's troops however, could not be induced to come on. To his cavalry, who, it was thought, might be useful in the pursuit which everyone now considered certain, message after message was sent, "but"—to use the language of the contemporary historian, Mr. Orme—"they could not be prevailed upon to quit the shelter of a large tank, at that time dry, in which they, his foot and himself"—Rájah Anandráz—"in the midst of them, had remained cowering from the beginning of the action."

Forde, however, cared little for the Rájah and his rabble. As soon as his own sipáhis had all joined, and he had made all his preparations, that is, about one hour after the capture of the French field-pieces, he advanced to attack the French camp; leaving, that nothing might retard his march, the field-pieces, which were drawn by bullocks, to follow.

A deep hollow way traversed the country leading to the French camp. Behind this all their troops had rallied, and their heavy guns had been planted so as to defend the passage of the hollow way. Several shots from these were fired as the English approached. These pressed on, however; and the defenders, not yet recovered from the effect of their defeat in the plain below, did not stay to meet them. As the English halted to give their fire, the French went suddenly to the right-about, abandoned their camp, and retreated, every man seemingly as he listed, in the utmost confusion, in the direction of Rájahmahéndri. The English then took possession of the camp with all its ordnance, ammunition, stores, tents, and camp equipage. The only things which the French succeeded in preserving from their hands were four small pieces and two camels laden with money and papers, which Conflans had despatched to Rájahmahéndri, there to await his orders, on the first repulse of his force. Conflans himself, accompanied by his commandant of artillery and staff, fled without making any attempt to rally his troops, and, riding hard, reached Rájahmahéndri before midnight. In the first and second divisions of the fight, and in the pursuit, he lost thirty-two pieces of cannon, and a hundred and fifty-six men, including officers, in killed, wounded, and prisoners, besides a number of native soldiers. The English loss amounted to forty-four Europeans, and five officers killed and wounded, in addition, likewise, to many sipáhís.*

Such was the battle of Kondúr, written then, incorrectly, as was the custom of our countrymen—one of those clinging customs which men find so difficult to shake off—Condore; a battle won solely by the genius and resolution of the English leader, Lieutenant-Colonel Forde. It was with design that that officer had placed his red-coated sipáhís in a position to attract the first attack of the French. Knowing the character of that nation, he had dared to risk the defeat of his left wing, in order that he might the more surely and with the greater effect smite the enemy when, scattered and careless, they would least expect him. He succeeded because he dared; he dared, because he had full reliance, first, on himself, on the coolness and calmness with which he could, in the storm of battle, direct a well thought-out movement; and, secondly, on the troops who had shown themselves during their service in Bengal thoroughly handy, amenable to the guidance of a skilful leader. Forde displayed, likewise, on that day a second quality, the possession of which is rarer than is generally supposed. He showed that he knew how to follow up a victory. Many a man would have been satisfied with the repulse of the first attack and the capture

* Cambridge's *War in India*, second edition, published in 1762.

of thirteen guns. On Forde the repulse of the first attack had the effect of bringing him to the resolution that within the limit of the northern Sirkárs there should never be a second; that he would turn this repulse into a defeat which should be decisive and irretrievable. Of such stuff are made the leaders of men who never know failure, and of such stuff was Forde.

The defeat was made irretrievable. The very same day Forde despatched a battalion of sipáhís under Captain Knox to follow up the enemy and to prevent their rallying. Knox pressed on so vigorously that he reached the vicinity of Rájahmahéndri on the evening of the 9th. He was reinforced during the night by two more native battalions. The fugitives had entered that town before him, but the spirit which had induced them to abandon their camp had entered with them. The sight of the red-coated sipáhís, undistinguishable from Europeans, deprived them of whatever nerve they had till then retained. Although Rajahmahéndri occupied an elevated position on the north bank of the Godávarí, and contained within its walls a mud fort in which were stored considerable supplies and some guns, the French had no thought of defending it. Their sole hope was to escape. The sight in the distance of the red-coats stimulated this hope. No sooner had darkness set in than they began to give vitality to it by evacuating the place. The Godávarí, however, presented great difficulties to the operation. This noble river, which at Rájahmahéndri has in the rainy season a width of nearly two miles, was in those days not crossed without much previous arrangement. Confusion, the child of panic, added on this occasion to the natural difficulties of the passage. The result was that when, at daybreak on the 10th, Knox forced his way into the town, he found fifteen Europeans hovering on the bank, eagerly expecting a return boat. He distinguished another party just landing on the southern bank, and about to disembark the guns and stores which their boat contained. His action was prompt and decisive. Making prisoners of the fifteen Frenchmen, he opened a fire from the guns in the fort on those who were landing on the opposite bank; and although it is certain that the missiles did not reach them, yet the booming of the guns and other demonstrations added so to the terror of the fugitives that they fled for dear life, leaving their guns behind them. These Knox at once secured. Forde, with the remainder of the force, reached Rájahmahéndri the following day. Conflans and his troops fled to Machhlípatanam.

But Forde was not yet satisfied. The large plan which had loomed before Clive, and which he had adopted—the plan which would secure for the English in the northern Sirkárs and in the councils of the Ṣúbahdár of the Dakhan the place which till then had been occupied by the French—could not be carried out so long as a single Frenchman remained in the former. Now the French still held Machhlípatanam and the districts adjoining. Machhlípatanam was by far the most important place in the province. Situated on the north side of the mouth of a branch of the river Krishna, on the western shore of the Bay of Bengal, it was in those days famous for the various branches of industry which it supported and encouraged. In its trade it rivalled Madras. Its cession to the French in 1750, and the subsequent expulsion from it of the English agents, had been regarded as a great misfortune. In fact, the possession by the French of Machhlípatanam and of the towns dependent on it, Kondapilli and Élúr, gave that nation a base whence it would be easy to move, on a convenient opportunity, to the recovery of the more northern districts. So long, then, as Machhlípatanam remained to the French, Forde's work was but half done. Forde was not the man to leave his work unfinished. But it was necessary for him to strike quickly. The state of affairs in Bengal and at Madras was such that at any moment he might be recalled.

His main difficulty was the provision of funds. He had no money; but before moving from Vishákpatanam the Rájah,

Anandráz, had promised to supply him. But in the flush of the success, towards which he had contributed nothing but intense personal fright, Anandráz would not only give no money, he even declined to refund twenty thousand rupees which Forde had in the earlier days advanced to him. It was only after six weeks' negotiation, under considerable pressure, on the giving of a solemn undertaking that all the sums advanced by the Rájah should be considered as loans, and that the revenues of all the districts south-west of Godávarí which might be reduced should be divided equally between the Company and the Rájah, that the latter at length relaxed his purse-strings. Much precious time, however, had been lost. In fact, the end of the third week of January had arrived before Forde—who, the better to bring his influence to bear on the Rájah, had fallen back to the fort of Peddapúr—could make arrangements for the forward movement he had so long contemplated.

But on the 28th of January he, though with great trouble, completed those arrangements and did move. Crossing the Godávarí, he marched on and occupied Élúr (6th February), an important provincial capital near the great Kolár lake. But here he was forced to make another halt. The Rájah, procrastinating according to his wont, had not yet brought the promised supplies. It was necessary to wait for the Rájah. Forde, however, was not the man to allow time to slip away unemployed if he could find the means of utilising it. He set to work, therefore, to ascertain how far he could disturb the preparations which the French had made to hinder his further progress.

Conflans, fleeing from the field of Kondúr, had reached Rájahmahéndri, and had as speedily left that place without making any attempt to rally his forces, without even paying any heed as to their fate. He did not deem himself safe, in fact, till he reached Machhlípatanam. When, however, he found that Forde did not follow him across the Godávarí, that he had even fallen back on Peddapúr, he recovered part of his courage, and turned his attention to the defence of the country that still remained to him. He was by no means destitute of resources. Notwithstanding his losses at Kondúr he still had under his own personal orders upwards of seven hundred men, the gaps made by those losses having been more than replenished by the garrisons he had left behind him; he had the certainty that Moracin, at the head of three hundred men, was coming by sea to his assistance; and, in consequence of his urgent entreaties, Salábat Jang, Súbahdár of the Dakhan, was marching with an army to support him. Regarded from the point of numbers, then, the prospects of the French were very promising. They required but one thing to make success for them an absolute certainty—that was the possession of a man to command them. Unfortunately for them, in Conflans they had a leader who could not lead, a man whose lack of mental capacity was only equalled by his deficiency in the lower quality of personal courage.

The crisis which was now approaching offered to a man possessing any pretensíons to capacity a rare opportunity. The chiefs of the country south of the Godávarí were still French in their sympathies, the country abounded in places capable of offering stubborn resistance to an invader, armed assistance was approaching. To throw every possible difficulty in the progress of the invader till that assistance should arrive, or—what was of scarcely less importance—till Anandráz should grow tired of furnishing him with supplies, was the course which would have recommended itself to a man of even average intelligence.

But Conflans possessed neither average intelligence nor average courage. He ordered Élúr, which possessed a very strong mud fort, and was in other respects advantageously situated, to be abandoned. He remained himself shut up within Machhlípatanam. The utmost of which he was capable was to send into the field, under the command of an officer named du Rocher, a force which he called "an army of observation," composed of two hundred European and two thousand native troops, with four field-pieces, to watch the strong places in which he had allowed garrisons to remain. One of these strong places was Narsipúr, twenty miles south-east of Élúr. This place was garrisoned by one hundred European and about three hundred native troops, under the command of M. Panneau, chief of the French factory there.

To understand clearly the position, the reader will bear in mind that Élúr, in which Forde and his army were halting, waiting for Rájah Anandráz, lies forty-eight miles due north of Machhlípatanam, held by Conflans; that Narsipur lies twenty miles south-west of Elúr, on the north bank of the mouth of the Godávarí; whilst du Rocher's "army of observation" had taken up a position nearly due west of Élúr, and thirty miles distant from it, with the object, apparently, of giving a hand to the army of the Súbahdár. Narsipúr, then, was isolated, more distant from Conflans and du Rocher than from Forde. Noting this, Forde resolved to take it before it could be relieved.

With this object, taking first the precaution to secure, by a threat of destruction in case of refusal, the neutrality of the zamíndár of the district, Forde despatched, a day or two after his arrival at Élúr, a battalion of sipáhís, under his best officer, Captain Knox. Panneau appears to have been a man formed in the mould of Conflans. The moment he heard that the English sipáhís were marching against him, and that the zamíndár of the district had been "got at," he caused to be sunk or destroyed all the ammunition he could not carry away, abandoned Narsipúr, and marched off to join the army of observation. Knox found in the place only a few old guns.

At length Rájah Anandráz arrived, and Forde was able (1st March) to march. Crossing the great Kolár lake, which was then nearly dry, he arrived on the 3rd in the vicinity of a small but strong fort, called Konkál, garrisoned by thirteen Frenchmen and two companies of sipáhís, commanded by a sergeant. This sergeant was a man of a higher natural stamp than either Conflans or Panneau. He had received the day previous a letter from du Rocher, requiring him to defend the fort to the last extremity, and promising to march to his relief. The sergeant did defend the place to the last extremity, repulsed two attacks, and only gave way when the gates were battered in and the English rushed in in overwhelming numbers. The small relieving party sent by du Rocher, learning in time of the disaster, fell back to rejoin him. Forde pushed on from Konkál, and on the 6th March arrived before Machhlípatanam. Conflans up to that day had occupied a very advantageous position in the town, about two miles from the fort of Machhlípatanam. He had here five hundred Europeans and two thousand sipáhís, whilst close at hand was du Rocher's army of observation, which hitherto had observed nothing. It was important to the French to maintain their position in the town, as it contained an abundant supply of water, whereas there was none in the fort, except a certain amount hoarded up in cisterns. The position would have been difficult to attack, and a retreat from it, had a retreat been necessary, would have been covered by the guns in the fort. But Conflans had not forgotten Kondúr; he would not risk a second action. When Forde approached he retired behind the defences of the fort.

That fort was well capable of offering a prolonged defence. An irregular parallelogram, with an average length of about eight hundred yards, and a breadth of from five to six hundred, it stood nearly a mile and a half from the sea-shore, on the edge of a sound or inlet of the sea, upwards of five hundred yards in breadth, and was surrounded on the three other sides by a morass of considerable extent. This morass varied in depth in different parts, from three to eighteen feet. The outline of the works consisted of eleven bastions of various sizes and shapes, connected by long curtains; round the whole was a palisadoed berm and a wet ditch, but no glacis; the escarp and the counterscarp were of earth faced with masonry.

The reader will not fail to observe that the face of the fort, which rested on the inlet of the sea—the southern face—was practically unassailable. Nor did the three other faces fail to offer extraordinary difficulties. A range of sand-hills extended on the western and eastern sides of the fort to about half a mile inland. On the eastern side they approached to within eight hundred yards of the fort, and—the morass lying between them and it and a creek running between the two—they formed here the nearest point whence the place could be assailed. The town, which Conflans had evacuated, lay nearly two miles to the north-west of the fort, and was also surrounded by the morass. The mode of communication between the two was by means of a narrow raised causeway, about two thousand yards in length, leading to the north-west bastion of the fort, in which was the only gateway. The last hundred and twenty yards of this causeway was formed into a long *caponnière*, which, at the part furthest from the fort, terminated in a strong ravelin.

On the 7th March, Forde invested this strong place with a force inferior in Europeans to that which defended it. Regular approaches being out of the question, he took up a position on the sand-banks I have described as being within eight hundred yards of the eastern face of the fort. Here he began to erect his batteries.

From the 7th to the 25th March, Forde was engaged in erecting these batteries. During this period he was exposed to difficulties and obstacles sufficient to madden any man. Scarcely had he sat down before Machhlípatanam when du Rocher's army of observation woke into sudden life and acted on his communications. Du Rocher's movements towards Rájahmahéndri, and the threats, which he took care should be reported, that he would make a raid upon the ancestral domains of Rájah

Anandráz, so terrified the latter, that he closed his hands, and refused to advance money to his allies, or to pledge his credit on their behalf. The effect of this, coming at a moment when the British treasure-chest was empty, and when Forde depended for its replenishment on supplies known to have arrived at Rájahmahéndri, or, failing them, on Anandráz, was most disastrous. To add to his troubles, certain intelligence reached him that the Súbahdár of the Dakhan, the ally of the French, with an army of forty thousand strong, was approaching.

Was it possible for a position to be apparently more hopeless than that of Forde at this conjuncture (18th March)? He was besieging an enemy who, strong in their superior numbers and the mud walls behind which they fought, literally laughed at him. His communications were cut off, and the supply of money on which he depended to pay his troops was threatened by the enemy; his native ally was abject with terror, and ready to betray him; the overlord of the country was marching at the head of an army forty thousand strong to force him to raise the siege. That was his position on the 18th March—a position full of despair, not offering one ray of hope. But his cup of troubles was not yet full.

Up to that date Forde had managed to subsist his army by using the prize money gained by the troops, but not yet distributed, by expending all his own private funds, the private funds of his officers, and the money which otherwise would have gone to pay his soldiers. One consequence of this was that his troops were several months in arrears of pay. This alone was a hardship; but when they saw, for they could not help seeing, that their hard-earned prize money had disappeared, that nothing was left, that their food was bad and insufficient, that they were engaged on an impossible enterprise—they, too, lost heart. On the 19th the European troops broke into open mutiny, and, turning out with their arms, threatened to march way. Forde, by a mixture of firmness and tact, succeeded in quieting them, and, assuring them that their money was on its way from Bengal, persuaded them to return to their duty. Four days later the money, which had reached Rájahmahéndri, was, to preserve it from the French, hurriedly shipped on board boats to be conveyed to the coast town of Kákináda, and was thus lost for the time to the English. The next day du Rocher entered Rájahmahéndri, and made as though he would march on Vishákpatanam. The day following, 25th March, the English batteries were sufficiently completed to enable Forde to open fire. The bombardment which then began continued to the 6th April, without any substantial result. It is true that it demolished many houses in the fort and made many breaches in the bastions. But not only were the breaches made by day repaired by night, but the French, erecting a battery on the unapproached side of the inlet, poured in during this time a fire which, taking the English batteries in flank, caused considerable damage. To add to Forde's embarrassment, the day after his batteries had opened, the Súbahdár of the Dakhan, Salábat Jang, arrived at Baizwárá, forty-four miles from Machhlípatanam, and sent an express to Rájah Anandráz ordering him to quit the English camp and to join his standard.

These items of intelligence reached the English camp on one and the same day. They appeared to bring the misfortunes of Forde to a climax. Rájah Anandráz showed his appreciation of their importance by marching off the next morning, without notice, in the direction of his territories. When, however, it was pointed out to him that between himself and his territories there was du Rocher, and that his only chance of prosperity, perhaps even of existence, lay in contributing as far as he could to the success of the English, he returned. Meanwhile, Forde himself opened out negotiations with Salábat Jang. The result was a ray of light. Salábat Jang consented to receive an English envoy in his camp, and, meanwhile, to remain at Baizwárá.

But this ray of light was soon succeeded by a darkness blacker even than that which had heralded its appearance. On the 5th April there fell heavy rain, which added greatly to the swampy nature of the morass. The following day intelligence arrived that Salábat Jang had broken up his camp at Baizwárá, and was marching on Machhlípatanam, and that du Rocher, retracing his steps from Rájahmahéndri, was hurrying to effect a junction with him. That morning the senior artillery officer reported to Forde that not more ammunition than was sufficient for two days' service of the batteries remained in store!

The issue had now greatly narrowed itself. It had become a battle to the death between two men, Forde and Conflans, with every advantage on the side of the latter. However greatly though Forde might dare, Conflans had only to remain firm to baffle him. Let him but display ordinary intelligence, ordinary courage, ordinary forethought, and he had him safe and secure in the hollow of his hand. According to every rule of war Forde, in fact, was lost. With fewer than four hundred Europeans and about fourteen hundred sipáhís, he had before him a fortress which defied him, behind him an army which he could not beat; his ammunition, his supplies, his funds were alike exhausted. Never was a commander, not even Wellington before Talavera, in a position so radically false. He was in a trap, apparently lost.

If Forde had been Conflans he had been lost indeed, without redemption. It is too much to say, looking at the record of the men who were his contemporaries, of men such as Clive, as Eyre Coote, as Caillaud, as Munro, and as Adams, that if he had not been Forde he had been lost. But this, at least, may be asserted, that if he had not held a double first-class degree in the university of nature, if he had not possessed to a supreme extent the qualities which mark men amongst their fellow-men, and if, it must in fairness be added, he had not been opposed to a leader who in all qualities, soldierly or other, ranked as much below the ordinary humanity of the age as Forde ranked above it, he could not have emerged from the crisis in which he found himself with success, or even with credit. As it was, his conduct stands out a brilliant example to all men beset by difficulties. He faced them with coolness, he met them with a calm determination to conquer them.

No sooner had Forde become aware that the avenues behind him were closing up, and that he had but two days' ammunition left, than he determined to bring matters to an issue by attempting to storm Machhlípatanam. Success there would be success everywhere. Defeat there would be no greater calamity than the calamity which stared him in the face on the sand-hills on which he stood.

Resolved, then, to make a supreme effort to conquer—to venture all to obtain all—Forde, on the morning of the 7th April, opened a fire from his batteries so fierce, so continued and so concentrated, as to surpass all his previous efforts. Calculating that the tide would be at its ebb about midnight, that then the depth of the water in the ditch of the fort would not exceed three feet, he ordered the whole of his force to be under arms at 10 o'clock. To mislead the enemy as to the intended point of attack, he directed the fire equally upon all the bastions, and, to prevent their repair, he continued it to the latest moment. He had resolved to make the real attack on the bastion mounting ten guns at the north-east angle of the fort, but—again to mislead the enemy—he ordered that Captain Knox should distract them by making a demonstration, to be converted, if necessary, into a real attack, against its south-west angle, between the bastion resting on the sound, and that to the north of it. At this point the broad swamp, bounded externally by a small rivulet, served the purpose of a ditch, and rendered the face apparently impregnable; but Forde had discovered, on the night of the 6th, that the passage through the swamp, though difficult, was practicable. In a desperate attempt, desperate efforts must be resorted to, and it was considered possible that this point, considered impregnable, might be left comparatively unguarded. Still further to distract the attention of the garrison, it was arranged that Rájah Anandráz, with all his following, should proceed along the causeway and make an attack upon the ravelin covering the caponnière.

At 10 o'clock that night the various attacking parties were under arms, awaiting the signal. As the party led by Captain Knox, comprised entirely of sipáhís, seven hundred in number, destined to wade through the swamp and attack the south-west angle, had a longer distance to traverse, they started first.

The main attack, formed in three divisions, and composed of three hundred and twelve European infantry, thirty gunners, thirty sailors, and seven hundred sipáhís, was to set out about half an hour later, but some time was lost in waiting for the officer appointed to command it, Captain Callender, and eventually the party started without him. The camp was then left in charge of Rájah Anandráz. It was arranged that he and his followers should remain halted there till they should hear the sound of attack from one or the other quarter—it having been settled that neither attack should begin before midnight, but that each party was free to act the moment the gongs of the fort should strike twelve—and that then they should advance to the attack of the ravelin.

Precisely at 12 o'clock the sound of firing from the direction of the southern face of the fort, proved that Knox had begun operations. Rájah Anandráz at once sent his men along the causeway, whence they opened a musketry fire on the ravelin, which served at least to distract the attention of the defenders. Leaving them at this task, I propose to follow the main attack. Setting out a good half hour late, this party—led by Captain Fischer—proceeded across the morass from a point opposite the bastion they intended to storm. Notwithstanding all their efforts, the unfortunate delay in starting interfered with the symmetry of the projected assault, for before they could reach the ditch they heard the fire indicating that Knox had begun his task. Rendered more eager by this sound they marched on as fast as they could, up to their knees in mire, across the swamp, and up to the middle in water and mud in crossing the ditch. The first division had just waded through the latter, and were engaged in tearing up the palisades on the berm, when the French, who had discovered them only just before they had reached the palisades, gathered on the breach, whilst other of their troops opened an artillery and musketry fire from the next bastions on their right and left. This opposition, however, only increased the ardour of the assailants; and whilst the first division, composed of Europeans and sipáhís, led by Captain Fischer, attacked the breach; the second, composed only of sipáhís, under Captain Maclean, replied to the fire from the bastion on their right; and the third, composed only of Europeans, led by Captain Yorke, answered that pouring on them from the left. Several men were killed, however, before Fischer succeeded in gaining the breach; but no sooner had he accomplished this feat than Yorke's men, clambering up, joined him, and the united parties, turning to the left, seized the bastion whence Maclean had been fired upon. This left a clear way to Maclean's party. But before his men could clamber up, Fischer turned along the ramparts to the right to secure the bastions in that direction. Leaving him for a moment, I must follow the fortunes of Yorke.

Fischer had but just set off when it was reported to Yorke that one of the guns was on the bastion he had gained, ready loaded. Yorke at once brought it to bear along the southern face of the rampart, and was preparing to follow in the same direction, when he beheld a body of French sipáhís advancing between the foot of the rampart and the buildings of the town, with the object of reinforcing the Frenchmen on the bastion, of the capture of which they were evidently not aware. With rare courage and presence of mind Yorke ran down to the detachment, and, seizing the French officer who commanded it, bade him order his men to lay down their arms, as the defences of the place had been gained. Surprised and half stupefied, the officer obeyed; his men laid down their arms and were sent as prisoners to the conquered bastion. Yorke, observing that the way below the bastion was free from interruption, and broader than the rampart, then brought his men down and pushed along it parallel to the rampart. He had successfully reduced and secured two out of the three bastions which still remained on that face, when an event occurred which had almost marred the success of the whole plan.

Yorke's men had followed him at first with alacrity, but as they pressed on in the darkness, separated from their comrades, towards unknown dangers, their leader had discovered, not only that their alacrity had vanished, but that it was difficult to urge them on. This difficulty became more marked after the second bastion, counting from that by which the stormers had entered, had been gained. Many of them held back when Yorke, after securing his prisoners, urged them to advance. They had yielded, however, to his threats and persuasions, when suddenly they came upon a small building close to the rampart. It was simply an expense magazine; but some of the men, who had stopped from curiosity to examine it, discovering that it contained gunpowder, called out "a mine, a mine!" The words had scarcely been uttered before the whole division ran back panic-stricken, leaving Yorke, who was marching at their head, alone, with two native drummer-boys, who continued to beat the Grenadiers' march. In vain did they beat; not only would not the men advance, they ran back to the bastion by which they had entered, and, disregarding their officers who tried to rally them, began to debate whether they should not leave the fort. They were discussing this question when Yorke, whose patience had been exhausted, appeared amongst them. Infuriated at what he heard, he jumped to the breach and threatened to kill the first man who should offer to come near it. Yorke was an old 39th officer, and there were some men in the grenadier company he was leading who had served in that regiment. These, ashamed of their previous behaviour, at once sided with him; their example became contagious, and in a minute Yorke found thirty-six devoted men ready to follow him. At the head of these, and leaving the others to follow as soon as their officers could bring them round, Yorke started off, always with the two native drummers at his side, to resume his task.

But the delay caused by this blind panic had given the enemy time to rally. The officer who commanded the third and last bastion, towards which Yorke had been advancing when his men recoiled in the manner I have described, had brought down a gun loaded with grape and pointed it towards the roadway along which the English were advancing. When they arrived within a few yards of it he fired it. The effect was most disastrous. Yorke himself, always in front of his men, was struck down with a ball through each thigh; the two native drummers were killed at his side; several of the men were killed, and sixteen were wounded. The survivors, carrying with them their wounded captain, fell back to the breach and to the two bastions beyond it, where Forde was with a small reserve. There they awaited the result of the movements of Fischer.

I have already recorded that when, on gaining the breach, Yorke had moved along the rampart to the left, Fischer had moved to the right. He gained without difficulty two bastions in that direction. The third was connected with the caponnière covered by the ravelin which Rájah Anandráz was feebly assailing. But feeble as was his assault, the effect on the French garrison was just as great as if it had been made with vigour. The French officer who commanded at the ravelin, losing all thought of the common danger, and treating as serious an attack which the slightest perception would have shown him to be a simple demonstration, allowed himself and the hundred men with him to be isolated—to be kept from the important part of the field of action; for Fischer, advancing from the second bastion, and taking in at once, as he approached the third, the position of affairs, promptly closed the gate leading to the ravelin. Just as he had done this, Captain Callender, whose want of punctuality had, it will be remembered, delayed the advance for more than half an hour, appeared on the scene and assumed command; as the party, however, advanced to the fourth bastion, a stray shot from that post killed him, and Fischer resumed it.

Whilst matters were thus progressing to the right and left of the breach, where was Conflans? Roused from his slumbers by the musketry discharge of Knox's false attack, that officer had not quitted his house, but had increased the general confusion of the garrison by sending to the various posts repeated and contradictory orders, based on the exaggerated reports which reached him every minute. Never very strong in his head, he was driven wild by the fact that the attack was made on four different faces of the fort, and he had not the sense to distinguish the feigned from the real. First, Knox's attack had alarmed him. He had met that by sending to his southern face the greater part of his reserves, when a very few only would have been sufficient, for Knox had been unable to cross the swamp, and his men had no ammunition beyond that which they carried in their pouches. Then, Rájah Anandráz, as powerless to cause him evil as was Knox, had disquieted his nerves. It would have been easy for him, on the first alarm, to send to the ravelin, and ascertaining how feeble was the attack, and how easily the position could be held by twenty men, to have drawn off the remainder to meet the only assault which was really formidable; but he did nothing of the sort, and thus another hundred men were isolated. Again, when the breach was stormed, the fact that the rampart was assailed on the right and left simultaneously, completed his mental prostration. A few reserves well in hand might yet have retrieved the day, might have converted the repulse of Yorke's men into a defeat, and might have checked the advance of Fischer. But, as I have said, the double attack of the storming party, combined with the continued rattle of musketry from the assailants of the southern face, and of the ravelin, finished him. Believing that all was lost, he sent a messenger to Forde to propose to capitulate on honourable terms. This happened just at the moment when the ammunition of Knox's party was all but exhausted, when Yorke's men, repulsed, were bearing their wounded leader back to the breach whence they had started, when Callender, dropping from the clouds, had been shot dead. Forde, who had joined Maclean's men on the rampart, was eagerly watching Fischer's advance, upon the progress of which the fate of the fort seemed to depend, when he received the offer of capitulation. He answered it in a manner becoming one who felt it necessary to complete the discouragement of his foe. The surrender, he replied, must be a surrender at discretion: the garrison must instantly lay down their arms, and constitute themselves prisoners. Conflans acceded—and the contest ceased. The garrison laid down their arms. The most important stronghold of the French fell into the hands of our countrymen.

Mr. Orme has well remarked that "the improbability of the attempt" on Machhlípatanam "was the principal cause of its success, for its garrison from the beginning had regarded the siege with mockery, and, being in daily expectation of the arrival of a body of troops which were coming by sea from Pondichery, had concerted that the army of observation, joined by this reinforcement, and a great detachment if not the whole of Salábat Jang's army, should then surround and attack the English army." Yes—but admitting that mockery, the result, but for the incapacity of their leader, would undoubtedly have corresponded to their anticipations. It would have been so if a Forde had occupied the place of Conflans; it would have been so if a man of ordinary intelligence had occupied the position of the French leader.

After all, the work was the work of one man. It was the consequence of a display of daring, of calm courage, of cool calculation, not surpassed in the history of the world. Imagine once more the position of Forde, his gun ammunition reduced to a supply barely sufficient for two days, facing a fortress garrisoned by an army superior to his own, cut off from his resources, two armies behind him, and another expected daily on the coast. All way of retreat for him by land was cut off; to remain where he was was impossible. He might, it is true, have embarked his troops on board the ships which were on the coast, but such a course he rejected as dishonourable. In whichever direction he might attack, he must meet a superior force. In a moment of supreme danger Forde chose the straight, direct, and simple course, which, not in war only but in every other circumstance of life, it becomes a man to follow. He followed it, and won!

At the storming of Machhlípatanam, Forde lost twenty-two Europeans killed and sixty-two wounded, among the former two officers. Of the sipáhís, who vied with the Europeans in courage, fifty were killed and a hundred and fifty wounded. He captured a hundred and twenty pieces of cannon, besides many military and other stores. The garrison which surrendered numbered five hundred Europeans and two thousand five hundred and thirty-seven natives, the latter all capable of bearing arms, but of whom only a proportion were trained sipáhís.

When he stormed the place the army of Salábat Jang was within fifteen miles of it; du Rocher's army of observation was still nearer. A week later ships conveying a corps of three hundred Frenchmen under Moracin appeared off the coast. Had he failed, then, Forde would have left few traces of his enterprise behind him.

His success, well earned, gained for England the five districts which had constituted the most valuable possession of France in Hindústán—the districts constituting the province of the Northern Sirkárs, and including those now known as Ganjám, Vishákpatanam, Rájahmahéndri, Machhlípatanam, and Guntúr. Salábat Jang, after a little bluster, signed, on the 14th May, a treaty conferring upon the English, as a free gift, the whole sirkár of Machhlípatanam with eight districts, as well as the sirkár of Nizámpatanam, and the districts of Kondávid and Wakalmannar.

Three years after this date, Nizám Alí, who had succeeded Salábat Jang, offered the whole of the Sirkárs, with the exception of Guntúr, to the English, on condition of their aiding him with troops. They declined, but four years subsequently the grant of the whole, made at the instance of Clive by the Court of Dihlí, was confirmed by the Súbahdár, then and ever subsequently known as the Nizám. The right of the English to those Sirkárs has never since been questioned.

But the cession of the Northern Sirkárs was not the most important result obtained by the storming of Machhlípatanam. From the date of that capture the paramount influence at the Court of Haidarábád was transferred from the French to the English. By the treaty made by Salábat Jang on the 14th May, the French were not only expelled, they were forbidden to have a settlement in that country. The corps of Moracin which had landed at Ganjám was, after a few fruitless efforts to disturb the new arrangements, completely dispersed. Du Rocher, it is true, lingered some time longer. But the fiat had gone forth. The victory of Forde laid the foundation of that predominance at the Court of the Nizám which, placed some forty years later on a definite basis by Marquess Wellesley, exists at the present day.

Rightly, then, may Kondúr and Machhlıpatanam rank among the decisive battles of India. Few battles have produced more brilliant results. If Kávéripák was the turning-point in the contest between the French and English for the possession of Southern India south of the Krishna, the capture of Machhlípatanam most assuredly secured for them the authority tney now command and the influence they now exercise in the provinces lying between that river and the Vindhayan range.

One word regarding the man who gained for his country that splendid position. Forde had been recommended by Clive to the Court of Directors for the command of the Company's troops in Bengal. The recommendation was not listened to. Nor, though immediately after his expulsion of the French from the Northern Sirkárs, Forde proceeded to Calcutta to gain, in the vicinity of Chinsurah, another victory over another European enemy of superior force, did he receive any proof of the gratitude of the corporation he had served so well. In spite of this neglect his name has descended to this generation, and it will descend to posterity, as the name of a great Englishman, of one who nobly upheld the honour of his country, and who, by the display of a calm and cool courage, aided most materially in laying the foundation of the British Empire in India.

CHAPTER V.

BIDERRA.

Of the five great maritime powers of the sixteenth and seventeenth centuries, Holland was the second to enter into commercial communication with India. Not less the spirit of adventure, than the desire to snatch for their country the trade and to injure the resources of her Iberian enemies, animated her children in this great enterprise. Spain was her first enemy, but in 1580 Portugal had been united to Spain. From that date all the efforts of Holland, in the East, were directed to transfer to herself the position and the influence which had been acquired in that part of the world by the latest component portion of the empire of her mortal foe.

She succeeded almost beyond her hopes. In the Chinese seas, in the Malay peninsula, in Java, in Sumatra, in Ceylon, in India, her troops gradually prevailed. The hostility, once excited, survived the severance of Portugal from Spain. In 1646 Holland had planted an agency at Chinsurah on the river Huglí, twenty miles north of Calcutta. But, fourteen years later, in one year, she expelled the Portuguese from their possessions south of Goa on the western coast, and from Nágapatanam,* and all the others on the eastern.

* "The city of snakes," so called from "Nâga" (a snake), and "patanam" (city). With their usual carelessness regarding the correct rendering of Indian

The general affairs of the Dutch in the East were not, however, directed from the soil of India. In 1619 they had built in Japan a city which they called Batavia, and which they destined to be the capital and head-quarters of all their possessions in that quarter of the globe. Gradually, as they settled in Bengal, as they seized the possessions of the Portuguese, and established themselves in Ceylon, in Sumatra, and in the Malay peninsula, this plan assumed consistency. In the beginning of the eighteenth century Batavia had become the recognised capital of all the Dutch establishments in the East. There resided the Governor-General and the Council of the Dutch Indies, and to them all the other possessions, great and small, were subordinate. These possessions were ranked in grades, some being ruled by a governor, some by a chief or director; some by a commandant, some simply by an agent. On the Malabár coast of India, Kochin, properly called Kuchí, was the head-quarters of the government. On the eastern coast, Nágapatanam first, afterwards Palikát, occupied a similar position. In Bengal, Chinsurah was the head-quarters of a director presiding over all the other factories on that side of India.

This arrangement was in force at the time when Sirája'd daulah sacked Calcutta in 1756. The Dutch and the French at Chinsurah and at Chandranagar had purchased immunity from a similar catastrophe, by the payment each of a large sum.* They had no idea at the time, that, from the misfortune of their rivals there would be a rebound which, in its course, would likewise overwhelm them.

proper names, the English of a century and a half ago transmuted this singularly expressive name into Negapatam—placing the accent on the last syllable—a name utterly meaningless. The barbarism continues at the present day.

* The Dutch paid 450,000 rupees; the French, 350,000. The difference in favour of the latter being a consequence of their having furnished the Núwáb with two hundred and fifty chests of gunpowder.

How the English repaid the Núwáb for his attack on Calcutta, and how the rebound affected the French at Chandranagar, has been already related. We have seen how Mír J'afar succeeded Siráju'd daulah. From that date English influence, gradually but steadily progressing, became paramount throughout the three provinces. In vain did Mír J'afar struggle against the yoke he had imposed upon himself. He could not shake it off. To purchase English aid he had mortgaged the resources of the State. The assessments which were imposed to pay off that mortgage alienated many of his most influential followers, and turned against him the hearts of his people. In spite of himself, he was forced, on every emergency, to call in the aid of the English. He had to invoke that aid first against his people, then against some of his nobles, and finally against an attack from the north. Of course he had to pay for it. New trading advantages, new concessions, new transfers of land followed each transaction. He felt that he was more and more involving himself in a net from which there was little hope of extrication; that his allies were becoming every day more and more his masters. But what was he to do? In his secret council-chamber, conferring with his son and his intimates, he bewailed the fatal necessity which forced him to be the suppliant of the race to which he owed his throne, and implored them to suggest a remedy. For long, not even the astutest among them could point to one. Suddenly, however, a faint wail from the Huglí was wafted to his ears. At first it attracted no attention, but as it increased in volume and persistency, and, changing its tone, finally resolved itself into a suggestion, he turned to it with increasing eagerness, until he became satisfied that he had at last discovered the plan which would rid him of his foes.

The wail came from the Dutch at Chinsurah. The concessions granted by Mír J'afar to the English, more especially the monopoly of the saltpetre trade, the right given to them to search all the Dutch vessels coming up the Huglí, and to prevent the employment of other than English pilots, had caused great exasperation in the Dutch colony. Their trade, likewise, had been seriously affected. That of the English, on the other hand, fostered by the Núwáb, had at the same time proportionally increased.

The position may thus be described. The English, in virtue of the consequences of Plassey, were prospering to an extraordinary degree; the Dutch, in virtue of the same consequences, were declining in influence and wealth; the Núwáb was anxious to shake off the yoke imposed upon him by the English. It was not long before the feeling of resentment entertained by the two last produced a firm understanding against the first. The Núwáb first listened to the remonstrances of the Dutch against the privileges he had, to their detriment, granted to their rivals. In return he questioned them about their power, their resources, their ability to carry out a great plan. This exchange of questions led to confidence, and a secret agreement was arrived at in virtue of which the Dutch promised to procure from Batavia a force sufficient, in men and ships, to expel their rivals from Bengal; whilst the Núwáb, concealing his complicity, should secretly prepare his army to co-operate with them at the opportune moment. The arrangement embodying this plan was arrived at in November 1758. The time for action seemed to the contracting parties to be singularly favourable, for in the preceding month Clive had despatched a great number of his available troops, under Forde, to the northern Sirkárs. For the defence of Calcutta and the British factories in Bengal, and to assert the British influence at the court of Mír J'afar, there remained, then, in Calcutta, little more than three hundred English, and two weak battalions of native troops. It is true that Clive was there as governor, but Clive was so little suspicious of danger, so confident in himself, and so bent on using all his resources to aid in the defeat of the French, then threatening Southern India, that he was despatching all the reinforcements from England, as fast as they arrived, to Madras.

No moment, then, could be more opportune for the conspirators. Conscious of this, the Dutch war-party at Chinsurah, which then enjoyed an ascendency in the councils of the director, pressed their plans on the Supreme Government at Batavia, and urged immediate action. In the meanwhile, and before Batavia could respond, Mír J'afar had been forced, sorely against his will, to appeal once again to the protecting arm of Clive. Threatened by an invasion from the north, led by the rebellious son of the Emperor of Dihlí, Mír J'afar, doubtful of his own followers, had invoked the assistance of the English. Clive had speedily repelled the invasion. As a reward, the Núwáb had bestowed upon him a large personal jaghír, and in the month of June following (1759), had accompanied him to Calcutta. Whilst there, he received from the Dutch a private intimation that their plans were approaching maturity. Mír J'afar stayed then but a short time in Calcutta; but he returned to that place in the October following, professedly again to visit Clive, really to be near at hand when the expected crisis should occur. Meanwhile, as far back as August, rumour had spoken of the expected arrival of a large Dutch force. During that month, in fact, a Dutch vessel, having on board a considerable number of Malayan soldiers, had arrived at the mouth of the Huglí. Clive at once informed the Núwáb of the event, whilst he took precautions to prevent alike the passage of the ship up the river and the landing of the soldiers. The Dutch authorities, called upon to explain, declared that the vessel was really bound for Nágapatanam, and had been driven to the Huglí by stress of weather; that as soon as she could provide herself with water and provisions she would resume her voyage. She did so, eventually, although a clandestine attempt of the Dutch master-attendant to convey eighteen of the Malayan soldiers to

Chinsurah in his official barge—an attempt discovered and frustrated—threw some doubt on the explanation.

But, in the October following, whilst Mír J'afar was in Calcutta, the real attempt was made. In that month seven armed ships, full of troops, European and Malayan, arrived at the mouth of the Huglí. Clive hastened to inform the Núwáb of this invasion. The Núwáb, forewarned, affected to treat the matter lightly, and announced his intention of proceeding at once to his own town of Huglí, to summon thither from Chinsurah the Dutch authorities, and to insist upon their at once dismissing their ships, or, in case of their refusal, of chastising them and driving them out of Bengal. Mír J'afar did proceed to Huglí; he did summon to his presence the Dutch authorities. What actually passed in secret conference cannot be known, but the historian has the authority of Clive himself for asserting that Mír J'afar "received them in a most gracious manner, more like friends and allies than enemies to him and to his country." A few days later the Núwáb wrote to Clive to inform him that he had granted the Dutch some indulgences with respect to their trade, and that they had engaged to leave the river with their ships and troops as soon as the season would permit.

The occasion was one of those which brought into the strongest light all the higher qualities of Clive. In the presence of danger his intellect was always clear, his judgment always unerring, his action always prompt and resolute. Not for a moment was he taken in by the specious letter of the Núwáb. Reading between its lines he saw not only that the Dutch had no intention of sending away their ships, but that they had obtained the Núwáb's assent to bring them up to Chinsurah. He at once resolved, to use his own emphatic words, that they "should not" bring them up. The events of the few days immediately following came to justify his prescience. Certain information reached him that the Dutch ships had weighed anchor, and were moving upwards, that Dutch agents were actively engaged at Chinsurah, at Kásimbázár, and at Patná, in raising troops, and that at these acts the Núwáb was conniving.

The position was such as would have driven an ordinary man to despair. On board the Dutch vessels in the river were seven hundred Europeans and eight hundred Malay troops, well-armed and equipped; at Chinsurah were a hundred and fifty Dutch soldiers, and native levies daily increasing in number; behind the Dutch was the Núwáb, as ready now to act as he had been at Plassey, the moment fortune should seem to declare in their favour. To meet this enemy Clive had at Calcutta three hundred and thirty Europeans and twelve hundred sipáhís. It is true that he had other detachments scattered over the province, but the nearest of them was too distant to be available at the crisis then impending. But in this hour of danger Clive was cool, calm, self-reliant, even confident. He took at once every possible precaution. He sent special messengers to summon all available men from the outposts; he called out, to defend the fort and the town, the militia, amounting to three hundred men, five-sixths of whom were Europeans; he formed half a troop of horse of some twenty to thirty volunteers, and enlisted as infantry nearly a similar number of men who could not ride. Of the four English vessels then in the Huglí, he despatched one, the smallest, with an express to Admiral Cornish, then cruising on the Arakan coast, asking for immediate aid; the three others he ordered up to aid in the defence of the town. The batteries which commanded the most important passages of the river near the town, Tannah fort and Charnock's battery,* were greatly strengthened: heavy cannon were mounted at each, as well as on the face of the new fort, Fort William, commanding the river. Just at this moment Colonel Forde, fresh from the storming of Machhlípatanam,

* The fort of Tannah was five miles below Calcutta, on the right bank of the river; Charnock's battery was nearly opposite to it.

arrived, accompanied by Captain Knox. To the first Clive assigned the command of the whole available force; to the latter that of the parties at Tannah fort and Charnock's battery.

These preparations were made not a moment too soon. In the second week of November, the Dutch, finding further delay would not screen them, threw off the mask, and forwarded to Calcutta a long remonstrance, recapitulating all their grievances, and threatening vengeance and reprisals unless the English should renounce their claim of the right of search and all opposition to the free progress of their ships and their vessels. Clive replied, with a specious audacity, that the English had offered no insult to the colours, had not attacked the property, and had infringed no privilege of the Dutch; that if their boats had been stopped and searched, and the advance of their troops opposed, it had been by the express direction of the Núwáb, acting with the authority of the Emperor. He concluded by referring them to the Núwáb, and by offering his services as a mediator on the occasion. Notwithstanding the tone of this reply, Clive—as he records himself—was not a little embarrassed as to the course he should adopt in case the Dutch, continuing to advance, should pass the batteries below Calcutta. The responsibility of commencing hostilities against an ally of England was very great, and Clive and the Council felt grave doubts as to whether the Court of Directors would hold him justified in incurring it.

From further anxiety on this head he was saved by the conduct of the Dutch. The reply of Clive, containing, as it did, expressions which, though true in the letter, were the reverse of true in their plain signification,* exasperated them to a degree

* Though Clive had the authority of the Núwáb for the acts complained of by the Dutch, it was an authority which he had himself solicited for the protection of British interests; and the Núwáb, who had given him that authority, had encouraged and even implored the Dutch to pay no regard to it, as having been extracted from his necessities, and being therefore void.

beyond endurance. Without attempting further diplomatic intercourse, they attacked and captured seven small English vessels, lying off Faltá, tore down the English colours, and transferred the guns and stores they carried to their own ships. Amongst the captured vessels was the despatch-boat carrying Clive's letter to Admiral Cornish asking for assistance. At the same time landing troops at Faltá and Riápúr, they burned the houses and effects of the English agents stationed there. Their ships then stood up the river. Having no pilots, however, their progress was necessarily slow. This action on the part of the Dutch reassured Clive. He at once sent a despatch to the Núwáb, apprising him of the acts of violence which had been committed, and stating his wish that as the quarrel lay only between the Dutch and the English, it might be fought out between those two nations alone. Whilst, however, asking no direct assistance, he added that the Núwáb would convince him of his sincerity and attachment if he would "directly surround their (the Dutch) subordinates, and distress them in the country to the utmost." Whilst thus writing to the Núwáb, Clive directed Forde to take possession of Bárnagar (Barnagore); to cross then the river with his troops and four field-pieces to Shirírámpúr (Serampore); and to march thence on Chandranagar; the object being not only to strike terror into Chinsurah, but to be ready to intercept the Dutch troops in case they should endeavour to gain that place by land. I shall describe in its proper place the manner in which these instructions were executed.

Meanwhile the Dutch ships were moving upwards. On the 21st they anchored in Sankrál reach, just below the point of the fire of the English batteries. The next day they landed their troops—seven hundred Europeans and eight hundred Malays—on the right bank of the river, with directions to march to Chinsurah. They then dropped down to Melancholy Point.

This action cleared the ground for Clive. He had now two distinct objects before him, each to be met on its own ground.

The landing of the Dutch troops had severed them from their base, the ships which had conveyed them. To attack and overthrow these troops before they could gain a new base—that at Chinsurah being the only possible one—and at the same time to attack and destroy the old base—the Dutch ships—these were the clear and definite objects at which he aimed. Sending information to Forde of the landing and march of the Dutch troops, and directing Captain Knox, with the parties at the batteries, to join that officer with all possible expedition, he proceeded to deal with the Dutch ships.

I have stated in a previous page * that before the commencement of hostilities Clive had but three ships of any size at his disposal, and that he had directed these to come up close to Calcutta, so as to aid in the defences of the town. They were three Indiamen—the *Duke of Dorset*, 544 tons, Captain Forrester; the *Calcutta*, 761 tons, Captain Wilson; the *Hardwicke*, 573 tons, Captain Sampson. They all carried guns. When the senior officer, Captain Wilson, who acted as commodore, received the order to bring his ships nearer to Calcutta, the Dutch squadron had already passed him. He had therefore followed it up steadily, anchoring some distance below it. But when, on the 23rd, the Dutch squadron, after having landed its troops, fell back to Melancholy point, Wilson made as though he, in his turn, would pass them; but the Dutch commodore noticing his intention, sent him a message to the effect that if he persisted in the attempt he would be fired upon. Wilson, having no orders to engage, at once desisted, but sent a report to Clive. Clive's answer was clear and determined. He directed Commodore Wilson to send at once a despatch to the Dutch commodore, demanding immediate restitution of the vessels, property, and British subjects he had seized, a full apology to the English flag, and his immediate departure from the river.

* Page 114

If these terms were not complied with, Wilson was directed to attack the Dutch squadron.

To understand the nature of the task which Clive had imposed upon this brave sailor, I may mention that whereas Wilson had at his disposal only three vessels, each capable of carrying at the most thirty guns, the Dutch squadron was composed of four ships, the *Vlissingen*, the *Bleiswyk*, the *Welgeleegen*, and the *Princess of Orange*, each carrying thirty-six; of two, the *Elizabeth Dorothea* and the *Waereld*, each carrying twenty-six; and of one, the *Mossel*, carrying sixteen guns. It was a force which exceeded his own by nearly two to one.

On the 24th Commodore Wilson transmitted his demand. It was promptly refused. Upon this Wilson weighed anchor and stood for the Dutch squadron. Captain Forrester, in the *Duke of Dorset*, the best sailer of the three, took the lead, and soon laid his ship alongside the *Vlissingen*, which bore the flag of the Dutch commodore. He had scarcely taken up this position when the wind changed, and his consorts were unable for some time to come near him. With great gallantry, however, Forrester attacked his antagonist, and though the mark himself for the first half-hour of other ships in the Dutch squadron, he stuck to her, and, after a contest which lasted two hours, forced her to strike. But before this had happened the *Hardwicke* and the *Calcutta* had succeeded in approaching the other ships. So well were they managed, and so hot was the fire they maintained, that in a very short time two of their smaller adversaries cut their cables and fled, whilst a third was driven on shore. The other ships maintained the contest till the *Vlissingen* had struck, when, with one exception, they followed her example. The exception was the *Bleiswyk*, the captain of which made his way to Kálpí, the English ships being too crippled to follow him. He was not, however, destined to escape. At Kálpí he met two English ships, the *Oxford* and the *Royal George*, which had arrived at the mouth of the Huglí two days before, and were now hastening upwards. They made an easy capture of the last of the Dutchmen.

In this most brilliant action the loss of the English in killed was very slight. The *Duke of Dorset*, though riddled through and through, though ninety shot were in her hull and her rigging was cut to pieces, and though many of her crew were wounded, did not lose a single man. The Dutch lost, in killed and wounded, upwards of a hundred men. On the *Vlissingen* alone thirty were killed and more than double that number wounded. It was an action worthy to be compared with the best achievements of the British navy.

Thus successfully had been carried out one of the two clear and distinct objects which Clive had determined to accomplish. I turn now to record the manner in which he dealt with the other. The reader has seen that Clive had no sooner heard of the debarkation of the Dutch troops and of their march towards Chinsurah, than he sent information to Forde, and directed Captain Knox to join him with the troops manning the two river batteries. I proceed now to examine the manner in which those two officers improved their opportunities.

Obeying the first orders transmitted to him on the 19th November, Forde, at the head of a hundred Europeans, four hundred native troops, and four guns, had the following day attacked and captured the Dutch factory of Bárnagar. Crossing the river to Shirírámpúr, he marched thence towards Chandranagar, and encamped, on the night of the 23rd, in the French gardens south of the fort. It had been his intention to march the next morning and take up a position nearer Chinsurah, which lies only three miles north of Chandranagar. But the Dutch had not noticed in vain the advantage which taking the initiative gives to fighting men. They did not take into consideration the fact that about fifteen hundred of their own troops were marching on Forde's rear, and that if they could only hold their own in Chinsurah till their arrival they would place Forde between two fires. They resolved to anticipate them. They therefore sent their whole available force, amounting to a hundred and twenty Europeans and three hundred native soldiers, from Chinsurah on the evening of the 23rd, and bade them take up a position in the ruins of Chandranagar, and hinder the further progress of the English. In that position, supported by four field-pieces, Forde found and attacked them on the morning of the 24th. The numbers were about equal on both sides, but on that of the English the soldiers, native and European, had been inured to Indian warfare. The result was never doubtful. Forde drove the Dutch from their position up to the very walls of Chinsurah, and captured their guns. That evening he was joined by Knox. This junction raised his numbers to three hundred and twenty Europeans and eight hundred native infantry and fifty European volunteer cavalry. The Núwáb had also placed about one hundred horsemen at his disposal, not to fight, but to spy.

From the prisoners he had taken, and from other sources, Forde learned that same evening that the Dutch force landed from the ships would certainly arrive the following day. He at once sent off an express to Clive, stating that he thought he had a fair prospect of destroying the enemy, but that he required explicit instructions as to the course he should pursue. Clive was engaging in playing whist when this note reached him. He read it; then, without quitting the table, he wrote on the back of it in pencil, "Dear Forde—Fight them immediately. I will send you the Order in Council to-morrow," and dismissed the messenger.

Armed with this authority Forde, early on the morning of the 25th, took up at Biderra, about midway between Chandranagar and Chinsurah, a position commanding the road to the latter place. His right rested on the village of Biderra, his left on a mango-grove, both of which he occupied; his front was covered by a broad and deep ditch. Securely planted behind this, his guns commanded the treeless plain in front of it. It was the very best position that could have been taken, for whilst very defensive, it commanded all the approaches. At about 10 o'clock in the morning, the Dutch force, led by Colonel Roussel, a French soldier of fortune, was seen advancing across the plain. As soon as the enemy arrived within range, the four guns of the English opened fire; but, notwithstanding the gaps they made, the Dutch pressed on. At last they reached the ditch. This obstacle, of the existence of which they were ignorant, stopped them. The halt caused great confusion, as the men in the rear, ignorant of its cause, continued to press on. This confusion, and the exposure, at the same time, to a concentrated fire of small arms from their enemies, some posted in the village, some in the grove, were fatal to the Dutch. After many gallant endeavours to surmount the difficulty, they fairly turned. Forde used the first moment of their wavering to launch at them his English cavalry. The small number of these was not at the moment apparent to the enemy, and the charge, made at an opportune moment, forced their masses back in disorder. Seeing the effect produced, that the Dutch were fairly beaten, the cavalry of the Núwáb, who had not responded to the invitation to accompany their European comrades in the first charge, dashed forward and completed the defeat. The Dutch and Malays, fresh from the confinement of shipboard, the latter unused to fight cavalry, were ridden over in their efforts to escape. No victory was ever more decisive. Of the seven hundred Europeans and eight hundred Malays comprising the Dutch force, a hundred and twenty of the former and two hundred of the latter were left dead on the field; three hundred in about equal proportions of both were wounded; whilst M. Roussel, fourteen of his officers, three hundred and fifty Dutch, and two hundred Malays were made prisoners.* Some sixty Dutchmen, and two hundred and

* I have followed, in the main, the account of this contest given by the Dutch East India Company. *Vide* Grose's *Voyage to the East Indies*, vol. ii page 376.

fifty Malays escaped, and of the former only fourteen eventually succeeded in finding their way to Chinsurah.

In this brilliant manner did Forde carry out the second distinct object aimed at by Clive. The policy of the latter had been carried out to the letter. By vigour, decision, and daring, a danger, greater than any which since January 1757 had threatened the British settlement in Bengal, had been encountered and overthrown. Of the secret understanding between the Dutch and the Núwáb, there can be no doubt whatever. Clive entertained none. The Núwáb, in fact, groaning under the restraints imposed upon him by the British connection, was anxious to substitute for a foreign master a foreign ally. His troops were ready for action. Had the Dutch squadron beaten the three English ships in the river, and had Forde been vanquished at Biderra, these troops would have joined the Dutch in an attack upon Calcutta. If that attack had succeeded, the Núwáb, grown wise by experience, would have imposed upon the Dutch terms far less galling to himself than those which had made him little more than a pageant sovereign guided by English counsels.

This conspiracy had been defeated by the calm decision of Clive, by the gallantry, skill, and daring of Forde and of the officers and men, sailors as well as soldiers, who were engaged. The victory on the Huglí, and the victory at Biderra, brought the Dutch, hitherto so threatening, to the feet of the English governor; not only for mercy, but for protection. They sorely needed the latter. Three days after the battle, Míran, the son and heir of the Núwáb, arrived from Murshidábád with six thousand horse. Up to that moment the great opponent of the English alliance, the secret instigator of the intrigues with the Dutch, Míran had come down in the hope of dictating his own terms, if, as he hoped, the English had been beaten. But finding them victorious on all points, the Dutch broken—almost annihilated,—he, with characteristic versatility, at once changed his tone. The yoke of the English must still be borne. His policy must be to ingratiate, not to offend. In this view he spoke of nothing less than the extermination of the Dutch, of expelling the remnant of them from Bengal. To protect themselves from the consequences of these threats, the Dutch implored the aid of the enemy whom they had so gratuitously provoked. Clive displayed a mastery of statesmanship, the greater inasmuch as it bore the appearance of signal generosity. After the victory of Biderra, he had responded to the submission of the Dutch by ordering Forde to cease all hostilities. He now proceeded to Chinsurah, and succeeded in effecting an accommodation between the Dutch and the Núwáb. But the terms of the accommodation bore the impress of the practical mind of a man who was resolved that no opportunity should ever again be afforded to the Dutch to wage war against the English in Bengal. For, whilst he persuaded the Núwáb to confirm all the trading privileges previously accorded to that people, and gave them permission to maintain a hundred and twenty-five soldiers for the protection of their factories at Chinsurah, at Kásimbázár, at Patna, and at Baleshwar (Balasore), he compelled them to send away their squadron with those prisoners recently taken by the English, who would not serve the conqueror; to discharge all the native soldiers whom they had raised; and to agree never to carry on hostilities, to enlist or introduce troops, or to erect fortifications, within the limits of the three provinces.

The other terms of the accommodation were not less satisfactory. The Dutch agreed to disavow the conduct of their fleet, to acknowledge themselves as the aggressors, and to pay three lakhs of rupees to cover all the losses sustained by the English, and the expenses of the war. This decision was subsequently approved by special commissioners of the two nations appointed in Europe to examine into the whole question. The conduct of Clive was declared, by this impartial tribunal, to have been marked by a prudence, a judgment, and a generosity such as to entitle him to unqualified commendation.

For us—judges after an interval of more than a hundred and twenty years—there remains something more than a mere confirmation of this verdict. We have to render justice to the hand as well as to the head, to the scholar as well as to the master. Without detracting for one instant from the supreme qualities manifested by Clive at this crisis, we must not fail to render homage to the man who, fresh from the storming of Machhlípatanam, decisively foiled, with a force inferior in numbers, the attempt to establish an Indo-Batavian empire, on the field of Biderra

CHAPTER VI.

ÚNDWAH NÁLÁ.

THE secret alliance of Mír J'afar with the Dutch had been one of the consequences of Plassey. That battle had given the new Núwáb, bound hand and foot, into the hands of the English. They were thenceforth his masters. Mír J'afar was in all external affairs but a pageant ruler. To satisfy the demand of his allies he had pledged his credit and oppressed his people. The alliance with the Dutch was an attempt to shake off a galling yoke. How, thanks to the prescience of Clive and the skill and valour of Forde, it failed, I have described. Thenceforward Mír J'afar gave up the secret struggle. He resigned himself to his fate.

Very soon after the attempt of the Dutch to replace the English in Bengal had been foiled at Biderra Clive quitted India. For the moment he made over charge of his government to Mr. Holwell; but a few months later the real successor, Mr. Vansittart, selected by Clive himself, came round from Madras and assumed the reins of office. A very few days after his arrival Mr. Vansittart was called upon to decide in Council an important question vitally affecting the immediate future of Bengal. The decision at which the Council arrived, and the policy which followed that decision, imperilled, and went very far towards undoing, the great work of Clive.

Almost immediately after Clive had quitted India the provinces ruled by Mír J'afar were assailed by a formidable army under the prince who had previously invaded it as Sháhzádah, but who had just become, by the death of his father, King of Dihlí and titular Emperor of India. This change in the position of the invader made the attempt far more formidable than that which had preceded it. The Núwábs of Tirhut and of Púrniá, and many lesser nobles, discontented with the existing rule, declared in his favour; and, to add to the danger, a considerable body of Maráthá horsemen joined him.

But, formidable as seemed this invasion, the skill and decision of the English officers, Major Caillaud, Captain Knox (distinguished at Machhlípatanam and Biderra), and others, and the valour of their men, sipáhís as well as soldiers, completely foiled it. Hostilities were begun in February 1760. Before the end of July the Emperor and his allies had been twice defeated on the field, whilst an attempt made by the former to take Patná by storm, though aided by a body of Frenchmen under M. Law, had been decisively repulsed. The campaign would have been still more fruitful of results but for the supineness and refusal to advance displayed by the young Núwáb, Míran, only son and declared heir of Mír J'afar, who commanded the Bengal forces on the occasion. Towards its close it had become evident that Míran was in communication with the Emperor, and a strong opinion prevailed that he was awaiting only a favourable opportunity to betray his allies.

For him the opportunity never came. On the night of the 2nd July 1760, a day following many in which the young Núwáb and his followers had shown extreme reluctance to follow up the retreating enemy, Míran was struck dead by lightning. His death raised primarily the question of the succession. Mír J'afar had other sons, but they were illegitimate and of tender age. The opening of the question of the succession led, it will be seen, to the consideration of another question, still more fruitful in consequences.

Three weeks after the death of Míran, Mr. Vansittart arrived in Calcutta to assume the government of Bengal. The gravity of the crisis, which had been minuted upon by his acting predecessor, Mr. Holwell, and by his colleagues in Council, forcibly impressed him. He at once summoned Major, now Colonel, Caillaud from the army to add the weight of his advice as to the proper course to be followed.

In the discussion which followed the arrival of Colonel Caillaud opinions were divided. That officer supported the policy recommended by Mr. Holwell, to the effect that the opportunity should now be seized to reduce the Núwáb of Bengal, Bihár, and Orísá from his quasi-independent position to his proper status of Súbahdár, subordinate to the Court of Dihlí; that the Company should become the Díwán of the Emperor with complete financial control; that the monetary transactions between Calcutta and Murshidábád should be settled, the Company receiving certain districts in lieu of the money due; and that the Núwáb should be made to discharge the large rabble army which consumed his revenues. This opinion was not without its recommendations in the eyes of the Council, and, but for the opportune arrival of an envoy from the Núwáb, a man of great tact and ability, charged to congratulate the new governor, it might have prevailed. The envoy from Murshidábád, admitted to the secret deliberations of the Council, managed, however, to bring its members to a decision beneficial alike to his own private interests and to their own.

The new envoy was Mír Muhammad Kásim Khán, generally called Mír Kásim, son-in-law of Mír J'afar. Mír Kásim had become, by the death of Míran, the most prominent personage in the three provinces. The Núwáb had not seen more than sixty summers, but he was older than his years, for the worries of the preceding four years had told upon a constitution which since his accession to power, had been tried by dissipation. His eldest surviving son had seen scarcely thirteen summers. Under these circumstances Mír Kásim, forty years old, a man of iron will, quick decision, large views, and free from scruples, stepped naturally into the place to which his relationship to the Núwáb entitled him. Once in that place, he determined to use it to his own advantage.

Mír Kásim had, in common with many other nobles of Murshidábád, recognised with intense dissatisfaction the fact that the battle of Plassey had bound the Núwáb, hand and foot, to the English alliance, and that the English alliance meant the transference to Calcutta of the secret rule over the three provinces. Every transaction since Plassey—the suppression of the risings within, the repulse of the two invasions from without, the crushing of the Dutch—had confirmed and strengthened the predominance of the English. Mír J'afar had become simply a tool in their hands, an unwilling tool, it is true, but a tool whom the circumstances of every year forced to be more submissive. Against the position the whole soul of Mír Kásim had revolted. But up to the time of the death of Míran he had been powerless. The jealousy of his weak, vicious, and dissolute brother-in-law had excluded him, latterly, from all influence. A thunderbolt, however, had removed that obstacle from his path, and Mír Kásim, on the steps of the throne, without a rival, resolved at once to stretch out his hand to clutch the sceptre falling from the grasp of his enfeebled father-in-law, and, having secured it, to take such measures as, in a short space of time, would restore the lost power of the Núwábs, and make him, in very deed, ruler as well as governor of the best portions of the three provinces.

Such was the man who, in September 1760, came to Calcutta to congratulate Mr. Vansittart on his assumption of the office of governor. Admitted to the deliberations of the English councillors, Mír Kásim, feeling his way carefully, soon came to the conclusion that there was not one amongst them who could not be bought. His father-in-law had bought their predecessors: he would ascertain their price and buy them. Bringing, then, to bear on the discussions the arguments, at once skilful and temperate, of an accomplished man of the world; admitting and condemning the laxity displayed by Mír J'afar with regard to his monetary engagements; insinuating, gradually even asserting, how, by the pursuance of a different method, it would be easy for a ruler of the three provinces to carry out engagements still more onerous, and to gratify to the full any personal aspirations, Mír Kásim at length won over the Calcutta Council. They came at last to the conclusion to discard the scheme propounded by Major Caillaud, and to accept in its stead one which had been shadowed out in the course of the discussions by the clear-headed but unscrupulous envoy of Mír J'afar. On the 27th September they signed with that envoy a treaty in virtue of which it was arranged that all the real power in Murshidábád should be transferred at once to Mír Kásim, the title and its honours, with a considerable income, being secured, during his lifetime, to Mír J'afar; that a firm friendship should exist between the English and Mír Kásim, his enemies being their enemies, and his friends their friends; that, whenever required, the English would be ready to support Mír Kásim in the management of his affairs, with troops; that for all the charges of the Company, of their army, and of provisions in the field, Mír Kásim should assign them the districts of Bardhwán, Midnapúr, and Chátgáon (Chittagong), and should grant sanads for the same; that certain advantages in the purchase of chunam in the Silhat district should be secured to the English; that the jewels pledged by Mír J'afar should be redeemed by cash payment; and that no agreement should be made with the Sháhzádah (then titular Emperor) without the joint counsels of the contracting parties, those counsels to be directed to the point of preventing him from gaining a footing in the three provinces. Such were the open stipulations. Those of a private nature were advantageous only to the members of the Calcutta Council. In fact, as the price of the foregoing treaty, Mír Kásim had promised to pay, as soon as possible after his installation, the following sums:—To Mr. Vansittart five hundred thousand rupees; to Mr. Holwell, two hundred and seventy thousand; to Messrs. Sumner and MacGuire each two hundred and fifty-five thousand; to Colonel Caillaud, two hundred thousand;* to Mr. Culling Smith and to Captain Yorke, one hundred and thirty-four thousand each. He pledged himself likewise to advance five hundred thousand rupees on loan to the Company for the expenses of the war on the coast. Three days after the signature of this treaty Mír Kásim set out for Murshidábád to prepare for the part which would soon devolve upon him. Mr. Vansittart followed two days later to break the decision to Mír J'afar.

In the interviews which took place on Mr. Vansittart's arrival at Murshidábád, 15th, 16th, and 18th September, Mír J'afar showed a not unaccountable disinclination to relinquish any portion of his authority, and to accept Mír Kásim as chief minister. Mír J'afar was, in fact, in the hands of the Hindú financiers, and these, divining the ambitious schemes of his son-in-law, had resolved at all hazards to baffle them. Mr. Vansittart appears to have been touched by the pleadings of the old Núwáb, and under their influence to have been more than half inclined to leave matters as he had found them. But Mír Kásim was at his elbow to remind him that he had gone too far to be able to retrace his steps, to insinuate that the promise of the stipulated *douceurs* was based upon the performance of a

* It is but just to the memory of Colonel Caillaud to state that he had adhered to his own proposal, had voted against the treaty with Mír Kásim, and had left India before he was aware that any sum had been stipulated for on his behalf. The money was paid to Mr. Vansittart, and Colonel Caillaud first learned from his agents in England that a sum to that amount was standing at his credit. It may be presumed that he then accepted it.

defined contract, and to declare that if there were any alteration in the scheme which was to invest him with absolute power, he must withdraw from Murshidábád to provide for his own safety. These considerations decided Mr. Vansittart to adhere to the compact.

Mír J'afar had been, on the 18th, granted only twenty-four hours to consider the proposals which the English governor had made him, to constitute Mír Kásim as virtually mayor of the palace. When, on the expiration of that period, Mír J'afar had vouchsafed no reply whatever, the English troops and the division commanded by Mír Kásim surrounded his residence. Well, indeed, on that eventful morning, might the thoughts of the old man have carried him back to a period little more than three years distant, when, on the field of Plassey, he too, in secret compact with these same English, had betrayed his kinsman and master to obtain the seat which another kinsman was now by similar means wresting from him. What to him had been the power thus basely and dishonourably obtained? All the agonies of the preceding fifty-eight years of his life paled before those which he had suffered during the three years he had ruled as Núwáb in the usurped palace of Siráju'd daulah. He could not but contrast his position, threatened by the men to whom he had sold his country, with that which he would have occupied if, at Plassey, he had been loyal to the boy relative who had, in the most touching terms, implored him to defend his turban. With the prestige of having been the main factor in the destruction of the insolent foreigners who had since dictated to him, and who now threatened to dethrone him, he would have wielded a real power; his name would have been honoured; his country would have been secure. But now:—a glance from the window of his palace showed him the redcoated English soldiers rallying round the standard of his kinsman in revolt against himself. Would Mír Kásim show him more mercy than he had shown to Siraju'd daulah? The recollection of the fate to which he had abandoned his kinsman and master must have passed through his mind when, after having first threatened to resist, he declared to the English Commissioners who waited upon him, that under no circumstances would he place his life in the power of Mír Kásim. As the only possible alternative he declared his readiness to resign the administration entirely, and to retire to live, as a private gentleman, in the territory of the Company. The alternative was at once agreed to. Declaring that he would not trust himself to Mír Kásim for a single night, the Núwáb then and there placed himself under the protection of a European guard, and started the following morning for Calcutta.*

Mír Kásim had now attained the height of his ambition. He was ruler of Bengal, Bihár, and Orísá. But he had not enjoyed his new authority many days before he, too, experienced the enormous difficulty of having to satisfy from an empty exchequer the demands of a grasping ally. Mír Kásim found the treasury of Murshidábád exhausted; the accounts in a state of inextricable confusion. The demands upon him were at the same time most pressing. He had, above all things, to satisfy his own army, then greatly in arrear; to pay the English troops engaged, at Patná, in showing front to the Emperor; to furnish the English with at least a portion of the promised loan. It must be admitted that he displayed, under these circumstances, considerable energy and a great force of character. He made the Hindú financiers, who had fattened on the absence of control in the time of his predecessor, disgorge their gains; and he introduced a simple and rigorous system into the treasury department. By these means he was able, in a very brief period, to pay his own and the English troops, and to remit to Calcutta half the promised subsidy.

Into the details of the contest which followed between the

* Here he took up his residence at Chitpúr, two houses in that suburb having been provided for himself and his suite by the Company.

allied troops of the English and the Núwáb and those of the Emperor, and which terminated by the peaceful investiture of Mír Kásim by Sháh Âlam at Patná as Núwáb of the three provinces (March 1761), and by his subsequent withdrawal to Dihlí, I do not propose to enter. It will suffice to say that the brunt of the fighting fell upon the English, and that the conduct of his own troops whenever they were brought under fire convinced Mír Kásim of the necessity of a reform in his army as stringent as that which he had introduced into his treasury.

Mír Kásim was a man of a stamp very different to that of his father-in-law. The pliant disposition which had caused the latter to bend on every decisive occasion to the will of his European masters, did not belong to his nature. He had from the very first resolved to be master in his own house. He had used the English to procure him power; but he never trusted them as Mír J'afar had trusted them. In a short time he came to hate them with all the intensity of bitter and brooding hatred. He had full reason to do so, for the annals of no nation contain records of conduct more unworthy, more mean, and more disgraceful, than that which characterised the English Government of Calcutta during the three years which followed the removal of Mír J'afar. That conduct is attributable to one cause, the basest and meanest of all, the desire for personal gain by any means and at any cost. It was the same longing which has animated the robber of the northern clime, the pirate of the southern sea, which has stimulated individuals to robbery, even to murder. In point of morality, the members of the governing clique of Calcutta from 1761 to 1763, Mr. Vansittart and Mr. Warren Hastings excepted, were not one whit better than the perpetrators of such deeds.

On the 20th October 1759, Colonel Clive, writing to Mr. Vansittart, then his destined successor, used the following words: "The expected reinforcements will, in my opinion, put Bengal out of all danger but that of venality and corruption." Clive had reason to write thus. After his departure, a venality and corruption such as he, even, had never dreamt of, came almost to destroy the work which he had founded. I will briefly state how.

I have already mentioned that Mír Kásim had covenanted to pay certain sums to the members of the Calcutta Council to support his ambitious plans. Mír Kásim performed his covenant. But he had scarcely done so when the majority of the members of Council whom he had bought either retired or were removed, and their places were filled by men greedy of gain, careless how they obtained it, and deeming that the shortest road to their end lay in compassing the ruin of Mír Kásim, in order to make a market of his successor.* These men were at the end of 1761 in a majority in the Council, and controlled its policy. Mr. Vansittart had but one steadfast supporter, Mr. Warren Hastings. The policy which led to the crisis I am about to describe was not the policy of those two gentlemen.

Before describing that policy I must trace in a few words the earlier measures taken by Mír Kásim. His first resolution was to be master in his own domains. As soon, then, as peace had been concluded with the Emperor, he removed Rámnarain, Governor of Patná, a staunch adherent of the English, but who had amassed enormous wealth by plunder and peculation. Then, to strengthen his own position, and to be further from the English, he removed his capital to Mungér,† a place on the right bank of the Ganges, three hundred and seventy-one miles by the river route from Calcutta, and containing a fort regarded in those days as of great strength. To this strength Mír Kásim made additions. His next task was to pay off all his obligations to the English, the failure to do which had, he well knew, proved the bane of his predecessor. This, by strict financial control, by insisting upon regular payments, and,

* This actually was done in 1763 and again in 1765.

† Incorrectly spelt "Monghyr" by many Englishmen, though whence they derive the letter "h" it is hard to say. The superfluous introduction of this letter is, however, a common failing with some classes of our countrymen.

as I have already stated, by compelling those to disgorge who had taken advantage of the disorder of the State to fill their pockets, he accomplished. At the close of 1762, he had not only paid off all the debts of the State, but his revenue returns showed an excess of income over expenditure. Free on this point, he next turned his attention to the formation of an army on the European model. He had witnessed the point of excellence to which it was possible to bring the sipáhís by submitting them to the European system and the European discipline, and he well knew that without such training no native army would ever stand against the English. To bring about such a result amongst his own troops, he set to work to re-form a large portion of his army on the model which had excited his admiration. He sought out everywhere European adventurers, especially Frenchmen and foreigners whose dislike to the English he could not doubt. To these adventurers he entrusted the remaking of his army. He bestowed upon them high grades, and assigned to them large salaries. Amongst the wandering outcasts, eager for service and adventure, came the Alsatian Reinhard, better known as Sombre or Samrú, and the Armenian, Markar; both of them men of ability, but in both of whose natures the love of life and the love of gain had quenched every noble aspiration. For the moment, however, these men and their associates applied themselves to their task with an assiduity which promised the best results. Before the close of 1762 Mír Kásim had, ready for action, armed, trained, and disciplined in the European fashion, a force of twenty-five thousand infantry, and a regiment of excellent artillery-men. Provident in all things, he had during the training of these men set up a large foundry for casting cannon, and this foundry had provided him with guns as serviceable as any which could be brought against him.

These preparations, his move to Mungér, his repairing and strengthening of the fortifications of that place, the reform of his revenue system, had been inspired by one motive—distrust of the English. Good reason had Míí Kásim for that distrust. Less than two years after the departure of Clive, the Council of Calcutta had become a hot-bed of "venality and corruption." Those two kindred vices, which Clive had with prophetic insight denounced as the only two evils which could undermine the British edifice in Bengal, reigned there supreme, unchecked by all save by Vansittart and Warren Hastings, and checked inadequately for all practical results even by them. The cheek of every honest Englishman must burn with shame as he reads the account of the policy adopted by the leading men amongst their countrymen in India a hundred and twenty years ago, towards the native ruler who had bought from the Calcutta Council his position, and whose only subsequent fault in their eyes was his endeavour to protect his subjects from European extortion. The sad story may be summarised in a few words.

To enrich themselves and the Company the Council of Calcutta had passed an enactment in virtue of which country goods supplied with European passes should be allowed to descend the river free of transit duty, whilst goods unprovided with such passes should pay a heavy tax. The English flag flying over a boat or a fleet of boats, and the appearance on board of natives dressed as English sipáhís, were sufficient to exempt the boats from the search.

This system, originally intended to enrich a few high-placed Englishmen, had been so abused that the whole system of trade had become disorganised. It had been bad enough when the civil servants of the Company had practically in their own hands the monopoly of the trade. But, in course of time, these sold their rights to others, until matters had arrived at such a point that it was impossible to discover who had, or who had not, the right to use the British flag and employ men dressed as English sipáhís. Whenever the revenue officers of the Núwáb made an attempt to stop the traffic, however illegal it might be, they were seized by the nearest English agent and punished. The results of this shameful and oppressive system were that the respectable class of native merchants were ruined, whole districts became impoverished, the entire native trade became disorganised, and the Núwáb's revenues from that source suffered a steady and increasing declension. In vain did Mír Kásim represent, again and again, these evils on the Calcutta Council. In vain did Mr. Vansittart press upon that Council the necessity of reform. Supported only by one member, he was powerless to repress the rapacious instincts, already whetted by enjoyment, of his colleagues. The evil at length reached a height when it was necessary to do something. After many stormy discussions it was agreed that Vansittart should visit the Núwáb at Mungér, and agree to a compromise which should meet the views of both parties.

Armed, as he believed, with full powers, Vansittart visited the Núwáb at Mungér. It should be borne in mind that although the conference which ensued took place between two men both honest in their intentions, both convinced of the radical vices of the existing system, and both anxious to arrive at a compromise which should at least contain the elements of fairness and equity, yet that one, the Englishman, was heavily handicapped by the knowledge that the views of the majority of his Council went far beyond his own. It is not, under these circumstances, surprising, that the compromise which was arrived at contained provisions not only greatly, but unduly, favourable to the English. The high contracting parties, after much discussion, agreed to terms, beyond which Mr. Vansittart would not—possibly, with the knowledge of the Council behind him, could not—yield. They agreed that whilst the English should pay nine, the natives should pay twenty-five per cent. on all goods passing the borders of the Núwáb's dominions; that, to prevent abuses, the English passes should be signed by the English agent and countersigned by the revenue officer of the Núwáb through whose circle the goods should pass. It is but fair to add that the Núwáb acceded to this compromise with great reluctance. He considered its provisions quite inadequate to check the evils. At the earnest request of Vansittart, however, he promised to give it a fair trial, warning him, at the same time, that if it should fail he would have no choice but to throw the whole trade open and give his own subjects an equal chance with the servants of the Company.

But the Council of Calcutta would not allow the scheme even a fair trial. Greedy of gain, careless of the public interests, they refused to ratify the agreement, insisting that the trade carried on by and for the English should—the article of salt alone excepted—be subjected to no duty whatever. Upon salt they expressed their willingness to pay a duty of two and a half per cent., but they declared that in all disputes which might occur between their own people and the Núwáb's officers the English agents should hear and decide. Mír Kásim, incensed at the nature of the English demands, well aware that compliance with them would bring ruin upon his own subjects, replied by a decree which put into action the alternative of which he had warned Vansittart. He abolished all import duties whatever, and established free trade throughout his territories.

This bold and prudent measure—for, even if judged by the result, defeat and ruin in a righteous cause were preferable to the lingering torture to which the policy of the Calcutta Council would have subjected Mír Kásim—roused all the worst passions of the corrupt clique ruling in the English capital. Declaring that their own trade was affected by the edict, and that the action of the Núwáb was tantamount to a declaration of war, they made preparations to resist it.

Prominent in urging a decided course, in treating the Núwáb as though he had no more title to a fair consideration than an underling caught in an act of flagrant disobedience, was Mr. Ellis, one of the new members of Council, a man of violent passions, who had recently been appointed to the agency of Patná. But if Mr. Ellis took the lead, other members of Council—Mr. Amyatt, Mr. Hay, Mr. Smith, and Mr. Verelst—were not slow to follow. These, one and all, had come to the conclusion that when an independent Núwáb of Bengal should dare to move in a direction contrary to that which had been urged upon him from Calcutta, there was but one remedy, and that remedy was force.

For the moment, however, it was determined, in deference to the strong representations of Vansittart and Warren Hastings, to endeavour, in the first instance, to persuade. A deputation, composed of Messrs. Hay and Amyatt, proceeded accordingly from Calcutta to wait on the Núwáb. They found him, whilst firmly resolved to adhere to the policy which he declared with the most perfect truth was the only policy capable of saving the industrial classes of his dominions from absolute ruin, yet anxious, almost painfully anxious, to avoid hostilities.

Whilst negotiations were yet pending, information reached the Núwáb that Mr. Ellis was making preparations to seize his city of Patná, and that a fleet of boats laden with ammunition and other stores to enable him to effect that purpose was just then touching at Mungér. Under these circumstances Mír Kásim pursued the only course which, in his position as Viceroy of the three provinces, under no bond of service to the English, was open to him. He refused to allow the hostile convoy to proceed; he required that the two English members of Council should not leave Mungér; and he sent an envoy to Calcutta requesting the Governor to disavow the conduct of Mr. Ellis, and to direct the removal of the detachment of English troops and sipáhís from Patná to Mungér, at which place, in the presence of his own army, they would not be prepared to commit any sudden act of hostility.

The Council at Calcutta not only refused to comply with this request—they treated the making it as an act of hostility.

They sent instructions to Messrs. Hay and Amyatt to leave Mungér forthwith, and either to return to Calcutta or to proceed to Patná, as they might find practicable. They decided, further, that as soon as the safety of these gentlemen had been assured they would employ their only remedy.

But, before these instructions had reached Mungér, Mír Kásim, still anxious for peace at any price short of sacrificing his own independence and the happiness of his people, had requested Mr. Amyatt to proceed to Calcutta to represent to the Council the cruel position in which the open and undisguised warlike preparations of Mr. Ellis had placed him; that he was still anxious for peace, but that if war were forced upon him he must defend himself and his people. Pending the return of Mr. Amyatt, Mr. Hay and the subordinate members were detained as hostages for the safety of the officers of the Núwáb then in Calcutta. They were treated with great civility and respect.

Before, however, Mr. Amyatt could reach Calcutta, Mr. Ellis had precipitated the crisis. Believing that Messrs. Hay and Amyatt had left Mungér, and inferring that their departure permitted him to avail himself of the permission to take aggressive measures should he find the Núwáb bent upon making war, that gentleman marched from the English factory with all the British troops he could collect, early on the morning of the 25th June, hoping to surprise the city of Patná before the reinforcements, which he knew to have been sent from Mungér, could reach it, and whilst its people and its garrison were sleeping the sleep of profound trust and confidence. He so far succeeded that he gained possession of the city, with the exception of a large building, built of stone, within it, and of the citadel. The English troops, flushed with their easy success dispersed to plunder, whilst Mr. Ellis, equally delighted, returned to his camp to breakfast, and to pen the usual magniloquent despatch, announcing a great victory over men who had not fought.

Far differently did those whom by his action he had made enemies employ their time. Whilst some of the Núwáb's troops, recovering from their surprise, were using every means to strengthen their position, their leader, Mír Mehdí Khán, hastened towards Mungér to represent in person to the Núwáb the outrage to which his city had been subjected. On his way thither Mír Mehdí met, at Fatwá, the advanced-guard of his master's troops, of the trained brigade, in fact, commanded by Markar, the Armenian, to whom I have already made allusion. Fatwá lies only eight miles from Patná, and Markar, learning that the two strong places in the city still held out, and that the English had dispersed to plunder, determined to hasten up his men, then to push forward and recover the city. He carried out his plan with great gallantry, charged and captured the English guns posted at the gate of the city and bearing on the road by which he advanced, drove his panic-stricken enemy out of the city, and, pursuing his advantage, laid siege to the English factory. Mr. Ellis and the officer commanding the troops, Colonel Carstairs, finding, after a few days' experience, that it would be impossible to defend the factory against a determined enemy, evacuated it on the night of the 29th June, and, crossing the Ganges, commenced a movement towards Chaprá in the hope to gain Awadh (Oudh). They had defended the factory, however, just long enough to render their escape impossible. The Núwáb had no sooner heard of the re-capture of Patná by Markar, than he had despatched his other trained brigade, under Samrú, to Baksar, to cut off retreat in case the English should retire. With an enemy in front pursuing—for Markar followed them on the 30th—and another enemy barring their retreat, the case of the English force, harassed moreover by the severe rainy season, was desperate. The resources to which they might have trusted with any hope of success, those of daring and energy, appear to have been conspicuous by their absence. They had but one chance of escape—that was to make a daring onslaught on one or other of the divisions of the enemy's army. Looking at the subsequent events of the campaign, it is not too much to say that such an attack, ably planned and energetically carried out, must have succeeded. The detachment, however, preferred to await the attack of the enemy. The result was never doubtful. Though, on this occasion (1st July 1763), the men individually displayed their wonted bravery, they fought without plan and without cohesion, and when their commander, Colonel Carstairs, and eight other officers had fallen, the survivors, hopeless of a successful resistance, laid down their arms.* They were conveyed by the victors prisoners to Patná.

In anticipation of the capture or defeat of the English party, the Núwáb had prepared a protest, dated 28th June, the accusing character of which was the more galling because the allegations it contained were absolutely true, against the conduct of Mr. Ellis. This protest, as soon as his anticipations were realised, he forwarded to Calcutta. In it Mír Kásim charged Mr. Ellis with having attacked his city of Patná like a robber in the night; with having plundered the bazaars, robbed the merchants, and slain the unoffending citizens. For this—sarcastically observed the Núwáb—Mr. Ellis himself had personally given him satisfaction by supplying him with the arms and ammunition of which he stood in need. But that satisfaction still left the Company his debtor. From it the Núwáb demanded a reparation similar to that which Calcutta had claimed for the treatment accorded to it in 1756. Passing from that single action, he next reviewed the policy of the

* Colonel Broome, in his *History of the Bengal Army*, states that "judging from two official returns of the force shortly prior to its destruction, it appears that nearly three hundred Europeans and upwards of two thousand five hundred natives must have been killed or surrendered on this occasion, and that seven officers of artillery and twenty-nine officers of infantry were slain on the field, died of their wounds, or were made prisoners, or subsequently perished."

Company, as represented by the Calcutta Council, towards himself. He charged upon that Council that, after having made with him a treaty, "to which they had pledged the name of Jesus Christ," by virtue of which he had made over to them three districts for the avowed purpose of paying the expenses of an army which should support him and promote his affairs, they had used that force for his destruction. He called upon them, therefore, to return to him the three years' rents which they had misapplied, to restore the three districts, and to make compensation, likewise, for the violences and oppressions exercised during the same time by the English agents within his territories.

This letter reached Calcutta on the 7th of July. A day or two prior to its arrival the air had been filled with rumours to the effect that a great disaster had befallen the British arms. Mír Kásim's allusion to the fate of Mr. Ellis went far to confirm those rumours. The Calcutta Council then proceeded to put into action the arrangements which they had been, during the few days preceding, been negotiating with the late Núwáb, Mír J'afar Khán.

The terms upon which Mír Kásim had bought the Súbahdárí of the three provinces from the Company's agents have been stated in a preceding page. It was his misfortune that some of the members of Council who had profited so largely from his liberality and punctual payment had left the country some twelve months after he had been installed, and had been succeeded by men whose love of gain had been whetted by the sight, almost, of transactions in which they had had no share. These men looking about for plunder, and gauging the character of Mír Kásim, had clearly seen that the only chance which could possibly occur to gratify their ravenous instincts during his lifetime was to provoke him in such a manner as to afford them the opportunity of selling his office to another. This was the instinct which had animated them from the very first. It was to provoke a contest which could only have such a result that Mr. Ellis had attacked Patná. It was to attain it that the Calcutta Council had refused to ratify the liberal concessions which the Núwáb had made to Mr. Vansittart. One strong proof of these assertions is to be found in these two facts; one, that in the middle of the preceding April they had given instructions to the commander of their forces how to act under certain circumstances, all connected with hostilities against the Núwáb; the other, that so far back as that date, when the only question between the Company and Mír Kásim was the question of commercial duties, which Messrs. Amyatt and Hay were then discussing at Mungér, they had begun to enter into negotiations with Mír J'afar.

That veteran intriguer was found to be ready once again to betray his country. The three years' miserable experience he had had of office without authority had not sickened him. He had still children, and for them, in his eyes, a degraded inheritance—also probably to be purchased—offered greater attractions than the repose of an every-day life. Mír J'afar, then, clutched at the offers which were made him. He agreed to confirm the cession of the three districts made by Mír Kásim; to levy the ancient duties on all but the English traders, who were to be free of all duties excepting one of two and a half per cent. upon salt; to maintain a force of twelve thousand horse and twelve thousand foot, and pay thirty lakhs of rupees for the expenses of the war; further, to make a donation of twenty-five lakhs to the army and half that sum to the navy; and, finally, to indemnify private individuals for all losses they had suffered.*

* It was stated at the time this clause was agreed to that the amount would not exceed five lakhs of rupees. Eventually it amounted to fifty-three lakhs. "So strong," writes Colonel Broome, "was the prevalence of personal interest over public duty, that although" (at the conclusion of the war) "the claims of the Company were still undischarged, more than half these amounts for compensation were extorted from the Núwáb, and the money immediately lent to

Having obtained from the low ambition of Mír J'afar the advantages which the patriotism of Mír Kásim had refused to them, the Calcutta Council on the 7th July—the date on which they received the protest I have referred to—issued a declaration of war against Mír Kásim, and invited all his subjects to return to their allegiance to Mír J'afar. From that date it was a war for existence between Mír Kásim and the English. Victorious, he would extend to them neither mercy nor consideration; defeated, he knew he could expect neither. Let us pause for a moment to consider the chances of the combatants.

On the one side was Mír Kásim, wielding the resources of three rich provinces, possessing a well-stocked treasury, an army forty thousand strong, trained to a great extent on the European system, and large supplies of ammunition and *matériel.* He was ready for war, his troops were flushed with the first victory gained in the open field in Bengal by purely native troops over Europeans. Added to this, he was a man of a clear head and strong character, who thoroughly understood his position, who knew full well that not to be victorious was to be beaten, and that defeat meant utter and absolute ruin. On the other side the English began the war under a demoralised Government; a Government each component part of which cared a great deal for itself, very little for the general weal. Thus, whilst the senior members of the Government were rich, the Government treasury was empty. When the war broke out, it was found difficult to furnish the military chest even with the insignificant sum of ten thousand rupees. Though the army had been placed on a war footing the preceding April, the force ready to take the

Government at 8 per cent. interest by their own servants, who—however regardful of private advantage—were rapidly sinking the pecuniary affairs of the Company into a state of ruin. According to Mr. Scrafton, the Núwáb was in fact no more than a banker for the Company's servants, who could draw upon him as often and to as great an amount as they pleased."—*History of the Bengal Army*, page 497.

field in July did not number more than eight hundred and fifty Europeans and fifteen hundred natives. Though it possessed abundant supplies of ammunition and small arms, yet in guns it was far inferior to the enemy. It will be seen, then, that whilst the force with which the English began this campaign was smaller than that which fought at Plassey,* that of the enemy was far stronger, far better trained, and far more united, than that which had succumbed, less to English arms than to treason, at that memorable fight.

The comparison between the rival combatants would not be complete if I were to omit from consideration the generals on both sides. Here the English had an advantage which compensated for every other deficiency. Mír Kásim Khán, clear-headed though he was on the political scene, had no genius for leading an army. Some writers have even questioned his personal courage. Others,† again, have recorded their opinion that policy dictated his leaving the command to his generals. If that were the case, I cannot help thinking it was a mistaken policy. In more than one contest in the war, the presence on the field of a great personage would have produced a unity of action, the want of which was fatal. After a careful study of all the evidence, I dismiss as utterly unworthy of credit the charge of want of courage. Having regard to the great talents and clearness of vision of Mír Kásim, I cannot think that any consideration would have kept him from the place where he believed his presence would be useful. I am forced, then, to the conclusion that, like many other men of supreme ability in the cabinet, he had no genius for war, and felt that his presence on the field of battle

* At Plassey, the English had nine hundred and fifty European and two thousand one hundred native troops.

† The able writer of *Transactions in India from 1756 to 1783*, himself a contemporary, states that Mír Kásim was inured to the hardships of the field, "that he united the gallantry of the soldier with the sagacity of the statesman," but that "he did not hazard his own person in any engagement where his officers might have made a merit of their treachery in betraying him."

would interfere with the independent action of his generals. It was a misfortune—as the result proved, a fatal misfortune.

The leader of the English army, Major John Adams, was, on the other hand, a man possessing supreme capacity as a leader. Trained in the school of Clive, Adams had succeeded to the command of the united forces of the Crown and the Company in Bengal on the departure of Major Caillaud (1762). No one could have been more fitted for the position. To calmness and coolness on the field of battle, Adams united great decision of character, a clearness of vision not to be surpassed, a power of impressing his own will upon others. He could plan a campaign and lead an army. He knew how to maintain the strictest discipline and to win the love of his men. It is not too much to say that never has the British army produced a soldier more capable in all respects. Had he lived he would undoubtedly have risen to the greatest distinction. In the few years of his active life he illustrated the art of war by a campaign which has been placed by a military writer* on a level with the most famous campaigns of antiquity, and which will not lose from comparison with any in the world.

Such were the leaders under whom the war began. On the 5th July, acting under orders from the Council, Major Adams had directed the detachments forming the component parts of the force I have enumerated to march from their several cantonments in the Mednipúr and Bardhwán districts, so as to form a junction at or near Murshidábád. But long before they could reach that city, Mír Kásim's irregular troops had forced the English troops occupying the factory there to surrender. The victorious army, reinforced immediately afterwards by a trained brigade which had marched upwards from Bírbhúm under the command of Muhammad Takí Khán, one of Mír Kásim's best generals, had marched then on the village of Palási, and had taken up a position there with the view of intercepting the detachments of

* The late Colonel Arthur Broome, *History of the Bengal Army.*

the English force as they should arrive, or, if need were, of the entire English force.

Major Adams, meanwhile, marching slowly, reached Katwá —famous in the story of Clive's march six years before—with the bulk of his force, on the 16th July. The next morning he crossed the Bhágirathí, and took post at the village of Agardíp. There, on the 17th, whilst waiting for a convoy under Lieutenant Glenn, he was joined by the newly re-installed Núwáb, Mir J'afar.

On the same day, the first encounter, subsequent to the declaration of war, took place. Glenn's detachment, which was escorting a convoy of cattle, grain, and treasure, and which was composed of a battalion of native troops and six guns, was attacked on the morning of the 17th, near the banks of the Ají river, by a large force of irregular troops, mostly cavalry, despatched for that purpose by Muhammad Takí Khán. Contemporary historians* rate the number of the attacking party at seventeen thousand men. Fortunately, they had no guns. Glenn, who, besides his European sergeants and a small detail of gunners, had no Europeans, offered to this attack a most determined resistance. Again and again did the enemy, eager for the plunder, charge home. The ground was not favourable for them, and his sipáhís behaved with the most splendid courage. Three times, however, did the enemy capture the guns and treasure, but three times did the sipáhís, returning to the charge, force them to let go their hold. At length, after a fight which lasted four hours, the enemy drew off, repulsed and baffled. Glenn's loss had been severe, but theirs had been enormous. Glenn did not content himself with merely repulsing the enemy. He marched straight from the field of battle on Katwá, only to find the town evacuated by Adams and the fort occupied by Mír Kásim's troops. Without the smallest hesitation he attacked and carried the latter, the garrison making only a feeble resist-

* Caraccioli's *Life of Clive*; the *Sayar-ul-Muta'akhkhirín.*

ance. The next day he joined the main force, bringing with him not only the convoy he had escorted, not only grain and cattle found in the fort of Katwá, but the prestige of the first victory.

Meanwhile, Muhammad Takí Khán had advanced from Palási towards Agardíp, and had taken up a position on the left bank of the Bhágirathí, nearly opposite Katwá, barring the road to Adams. Owing to some jealousy on the part of their commanders, the irregular troops, which had been so maltreated by Glenn on the 17th, refused to join him, but took up a position in rear of his left flank, too far off to render him support. Major Adams, on the morning of the 19th, advanced to attack him. The battle which followed was one of the bloodiest and best-contested of the whole war. Muhammad Takí himself and the Rohílahs and Afgháns, of whom he had formed a chosen corps, behaved with unsurpassed courage. Long the issue was doubtful. At one time it seemed as though the English were about to succumb. Muhammad Takí, who possessed just those qualities in which Mír Kásim was deficient, perceived, or thought he perceived, a wavering in their ranks, and, to confirm it, charged their flank with his chosen horse. At the very point selected, however, Major Adams had placed a party in ambuscade. A timely volley from the men so placed, just as the hostile leader was making a charge which he believed would give him victory, decided that day. That volley laid low, with a bullet through his brain, the gallant Muhummadan leader and many of the brave band which followed him. Victory was then assured to Adams. He captured the enemy's camp, all their guns, their cattle, and their stores. He bivouacked that night on the field of battle, within sight of the shooting-box so famous in the story of the battle of Plassey. The irregular horsemen, who had fought Glenn the day before, and who might have decided the victory, and with it the war, in favour of Mír Kásim, took no part in the action, and retired after it had been decided. The history of India abounds in instances of such unpatriotic conduct. Indeed, it may be affirmed that few things have more contributed to the success of the English than the action of jealousy of each other of the native princes and leaders of India.

Adams halted for three days on the field of Katwá—for such was the name given to the battle—then, following the route which Clive had pursued in 1757, marched on Murshidábád. The remnants of the beaten army had, however, taken up a strong position two miles south of that city, their front covered by a large tank called Motijhíl. But, well posted as they were for defence, the troops of Mír Kásim were still under the influence of the defeats on the A'ji, and of Katwá. When vigorously attacked they gave way, and hastened to join the army which, comprehending the brigades trained so carefully on the European model, Mír Kásim had caused to assemble at Sútí. The day following Adams escorted Mír J'afar, more than ever a pageant Núwáb, in triumph into Murshidábád.

The town of Súti lies thirty-seven miles from Murshidábád, on the direct road from that place to Dánápúr. It was at this place that Mír Kásim had resolved to fight his decisive battle —a battle which should drive the English into the sea, or be the certain precursor of his ruin. The position had been extremely well chosen. Strong by nature, it had been rendered still stronger by art. Intrenchments covered his whole front, whilst the nature of the country guarded it from being easily turned. To it Mír Kásim had sent his best troops. The brigades Samrú and Markar were there; the trained cavalry of Assad'ullah was there; the rocket-men of Mír Nasír Khán, fresh from the recovery of Patná, were there; the survivors of the men who had fought so bravely at Katwá were there, eager now to wipe out the recollection of their defeat. Altogether, there were assembled in that camp of Sútí twenty-eight thousand fighting men of a good stamp, eight thousand of whom were infantry.* This force was supported by a powerful artillery, manned in a great measure by Europeans and Eurasians. It wanted but one man, a skilful leader, such a man as the Muhammad Takí Khán, whom they had lost at Katwá, to make success, humanly speaking, absolutely certain. It had not that man; it was not even inspired by the presence of the prince for whom it was fighting. Mír Kásim, who might have calmed the jealousies of rival commanders, and have directed a decisive movement on the field of battle, remained, throughout this important part of the campaign, at Mungér.

Perhaps it was owing to the absence of Mír Kásim, perhaps to the confidence of his generals, who wished, probably, to engage on a plain in which the enemy might not only be repulsed, but annihilated, that the decisive battle was not fought at Sútí. The English army, strengthened to a thousand European and nearly four thousand native troops had, marching northwards, just crossed the Bánslí, near the point where that river joins the Bhágirathí (2nd August), when it found itself in face of Mír Kásim's troops drawn up to oppose them. The position chosen by the latter betokened alike over-confidence and stern resolution to achieve a decided result. For whilst it allowed the English the advantage of having their flanks covered by the two streams, it ensured their destruction in case of defeat. The streams which guarded their flanks would equally bar their flight. This, doubtless, was the reason which decided the enemy to quit the intrenched camp; from that they might have repulsed the enemy, here they hoped to annihilate him.

The position taken up by the Bengal army barred the road to the English. In the centre were the trained brigades of Samrú and Markar; on the right was Mír Assad'ullah Khán with his trained cavalry and twelve thousand irregular infantry; the rocket-men were on the left of the trained brigades, and on

* Many writers have placed the number higher, but the contemporary evidence of the author of *Transactions in India* seems decisive on the point.

their left again was a small brigade commanded by Shír Alí Khán, flanked on his left by the river. The village of Ghériah, about a mile distant from the scene of action, gave its name to the plain.

Major Adams had no sooner recognised the presence of the enemy in force, than he formed his line of battle and advanced. He placed his Europeans, composed of the 84th and Bengal European Regiment,* in the centre, with three battalions of sipáhís on each flank, the guns in the intervals, and one battalion of sipáhis as a reserve. The action began with a discharge of artillery from both sides. Under cover of this, the infantry advanced, and the European troops in the centre were soon engaged with the trained brigades of Samrú and Markar, slightly, at first, to the advantage of the former. No sooner, however, had Mír Assad'ullah observed the battle joined in the centre, than he hurled his cavalry against the left wing of the English. So well-directed was the charge, so impetuous the onslaught, that the English wing was rolled up and broken. Their sipáhis fought well, but the force of the shock had been too great; the wing was forced back, and the men of the left portion of it were cut to pieces, or driven into the Bánslí. Major Adams had noticed the charge and its result without being able to avert the evil which he foresaw. He had hastened, however, to take measures to repair the mischief by ordering to the spot the reserve and two guns, under Major Carnac. But before this reinforcement could arrive, the leading division of the enemy's cavalry, led by a very gallant officer, Badru'dín Khán, had, pursuing its victorious career, made an intervention to favour Samrú and Markar, by attacking in the rear the troops with whom they were maintaining an almost equal combat. Charging with the same impetuosity as when they broke the left wing, the enemy's horsemen captured two of the English guns, and caused great confusion in their ranks—a confusion which was augmented

* Now the 101st Fusiliers.

by a simultaneous attack made on their front by the rocket-men of Mír Nasír Khán. Although, whilst this was happening in the centre, Carnac had, with the reserve, succeeded in rallying some of the remnants of the broken left wing, and in restoring the semblance of order, the position of the English was now extremely critical. Their left wing was virtually gone, their centre was in extreme danger, their reserves were exhausted. One vigorous attack on their right, and all was over with them. Fortunately for them, however, the commander of Mír Kásim's left wing, Shír Alí Khán, possessed neither the dash, the intuition, or the knowledge when to strike, which had characterised the other leaders of the army. He made his attack so cautiously and so feebly, that Adams, divining how he could be dealt with, left half a battalion to oppose him, and moved the remainder of his right wing, with great rapidity, to support the endangered centre. This timely aid, and an opportune movement made simultaneously by the rapidly-recovering left, enabled the 84th and the Company's regiment to disengage themselves. In a timely charge they recovered the two guns, wounded Badru'dín, and so imposed upon Assad'ullah Khán, who was advancing, as he believed, to complete his victory, that he wavered and fell back. Major Adams took advantage of the first retrogade step which this leader took to order an advance of his whole line. This charge decided the day. The enemy's cavalry fell back before it with increased rapidity. In vain did Mír Nasír Khán, placing his rocket-men in the bed of a small nálá, attempt to check the progress of the pursuers; he was driven from his position. Samrú and Markar, the leaders of the trained brigades, had fought fairly well as long as victory seemed inclined to shine upon them; but they were evidently deeply imbued with the principle that it was better to live to fight another day than to sacrifice themselves and their men, for, as soon as the English centre had shown a disposition to rally, they had begun to withdraw from the field. They withdrew, however, in good order, and their attitude imposed a check on the ardour of the pursuers.

The victory, however, was gained. Seventeen guns and a hundred and fifty boats laden with stores fell into the hands of the conquerors. They bought their triumph dearly. Their actual loss in numbers I have not been able to ascertain, but it is stated to have been greater than on any previous encounter between the Europeans and the natives of India. Certainly, never was a battle more fiercely contested; never at one period of its duration did defeat seem more assured; never were native cavalry better led; never did men show greater courage. The coolness of Adams and the steadfastness of the Europeans combined with the want of vigour of Shír Alí Khán and the selfish instincts of Samrú and Markar to snatch victory out of the fire.

The battle of Ghériah was a battle which well deserves to be remembered. It inflicted a blow, a very heavy blow, on the enemies of England. But it was not decisive. The enemy quitted the field, but not in disorder; they quitted it to take up a stronger position, well prepared to receive them, and already occupied by men whose numbers would do more than fill the gaps already made in their ranks.

This position was called the U'ndwah Nálá, a small stream giving its name to a strong pass leading into the hilly districts of Rájmahal. In the plan of campaign he had drawn up, Mír Kásim, whilst calculating on the preponderating chances of a decisive victory at or near Palási in the first instance, or, in case of a reverse there, at Sútí, had not forgotten that the chances of the field of battle were uncertain, and that it might be necessary, for a third time, to grapple with his foes. But regarding the issue of the third contest there should, he was resolved, be no doubt whatever. He had, then, carefully selected a position of amazing strength, which could be held by a few against many, which could not be turned, and which it would be necessary for his enemy to attack in front. U'ndwah Nálá offered such a position. The rivulet, which at that season of the year, July and August, was swollen to the dimensions of a river, drained a deep morass to the right and left of the road, which formed a sort of narrow causeway across it. This road was entirely commanded by the pass. In the view of a possibility of a defeat at Sútí, Mír Kásim had fortified this pass in a manner so as to render it all but impregnable. In front of the rivulet and on the extreme left of the position, he had thrown up an intrenchment, which, resting on the Ganges, and running thence in a south-westerly direction for about a mile, abutted upon a steep isolated hill which he had likewise strongly fortified; from this point the intrenchment branched in a more southerly direction across the road and round the main spur which formed the right side of the pass, and terminated amid ravines and scarped precipices far beyond it. He had made the ramparts of this intrenchment sixty feet high and ten feet thick; he had surmounted them by a parapet eighteen feet high and seven feet thick, and along the entire front on the plain he had caused to be dug a ditch sixty feet wide and twelve feet deep. To reach this ditch the morass had still to be traversed. Under his instructions batteries had been erected at convenient intervals, and upon them he had mounted more than a hundred pieces of cannon. Some distance to the rear of this intrenchment was the old line of works—which it had in a measure superseded—and the U'ndwah Nálá, the steep banks and swollen waters of which formed a natural defence. This nálá was crossed on the line of the road by a stone bridge, to guard which a strong detachment had been told off. Such was the position, between the rivulet and the new intrenchment, to which Mír Kásim, on learning the result of the battle of Ghériah, had ordered his reserves, composed of a brigade four thousand strong, trained in the European fashion, commanded by an Armenian named Aratoon, and three irregular brigades, mustering in all about twelve thousand men, infantry, cavalry, and artillery, commanded by the best officers who still remained to him, Mír Najaf Khán, Mír Himmat Alí, and Mír Médhí Khán. As a measure of security, and to be ready for every emergency, he despatched his family and treasures to the strong fortress of Rotásgarh, on the Són, but he himself still remained at Mungér.

Ghériah had been in a certain sense a surprise to Mír Kásim. He had fully counted upon victory; but the battle, fought in the open and in a position more favourable to the English than to his own troops, had only just been lost. At U'ndwah Nálá he could oppose to them a stronger position, a greater number of troops, and a far more numerous artillery. There did not seem a single flaw in his arrangements. If the small body of English and English-trained natives could force that pass in the face of the forty thousand men who, on the arrival of the army beaten at Ghériah, would be there to defend it, no strong places, no opposition, no army in the world could stop them. On the other hand, repulse to them would mean destruction. On the battle about to ensue, then, he deliberately placed the issue whether the three provinces should belong to a Núwáb ruling independently of the English, or to the English. If he were beaten he could offer no resistance that could possibly avail; if the English were beaten the result of Plassey was undone, the labours of Clive were rendered fruitless.

Two days after the battle of Ghériah, the beaten army of the Núwáb joined, behind the intrenchments of U'ndwah Nálá, the reinforcements he had sent thither from Mungér. Meanwhile Adams, indulging his troops with a two days' halt, marched on the 4th, and on the 11th arrived at Palkipúr, a small village about four miles from the enemy's position. In front of that village, and in a line nearly parallel to that position, Adams formed his camp. Here he remained about three weeks, busily engaged in constructing fascines and gabions, in erecting batteries, in landing heavy guns, and in repulsing the harassing attacks of the enemy. Even when, on the twenty-fourth day, he opened fire from the three batteries he had constructed, the nearest of which was about three hundred yards from the enemy's intrenchment, he found, that though manned with siege guns, the fire produced little or no impression on the massive ramparts which Mír Kásim had thrown up. A very small breach had, indeed, been effected close to the gateway near the river, but it was very imperfect. Nearer he could not advance his guns, nor on the other face could he move his infantry, for the morass, saturated at that time of the year, covered the position. The difficulties which presented themselves on all sides were, indeed, sufficient to make the bravest despair. Not even Masséna, before the lines of Torres Vedras, felt more acutely than did, on this occasion, the English leader, the hopelessness of his position.

But a chance, denied to the Prince of Essling, was granted to Adams. In the brilliant novel of *Coningsby*, Sidonia lays down the aphorism that an individual, even against a vast public opinion, is divine. The aphorism is true, although the conditions under which it operates are sometimes startling. It was the act of a single individual which converted the despair of the English into confidence; it was the consequence of that act which changed the confidence of Mír Kásim's army into despair.

The individual who on this occasion performed the divine function for the English army was a repentant deserter. This man, originally in the service of the Company, had, for some unknown reason, deserted to Mír Kásim, and now, either from a desire to reingratiate himself with his old masters, or from a love of treachery for its own sake, he prepared to betray him. Creeping out of the defensive position on the night of the 4th September, he made his way to the English camp and offered, on condition of pardon, to point out a ford in the morass by which the troops might cross and attack the rampart defending the isolated hill which commanded the enemy's position. Adams, persuaded that the representations made by the deserter were correct, resolved to take advantage of them without delay, and fixed the following morning for the purpose. That night he made the necessary preparations, told off the assaulting parties, arranged the signals to be made under all eventualities, and prepared for every possible misadventure. Three hours before daybreak the storming party, composed of the grenadiers of the 84th and the Company's European regiment, and of two battalions of sipáhís, the whole commanded by Captain Irving, set out to cross the morass; at the same time the bulk of the remaining force, led by Captain Moran, moved into the trenches for the purpose of distracting the enemy by a false attack, to be converted, if necessary, into a real one. Another portion of it, formed into a reserve, under Major Carnac, was held in readiness to move rapidly on any point where its presence might seem desirable, whilst a fourth, and much smaller party, was left to guard the camp. I propose first to follow Captain Irving and the stormers.

The deserter had correctly represented that the morass might be forded, but neither he nor the English leader had sufficiently appreciated the difficulties which fighting-men carrying their muskets and ammunition would experience in the operation. So deep was the ford that the men, moving through it with difficulty, were compelled to carry their muskets and pouches on their heads, whilst the scaling-ladders necessary to effect their purpose were similarly conveyed by the native followers. Had but one of the defenders been on the alert, the entire storming-party must have been destroyed. Fortunately for those who composed it, not a sign of life appeared in the enemy's works, and the storming-party succeeded in reaching the base of the rampart without being discovered. Irving had given strict orders to move as silently as possible, and to use only the bayonet. A few of the enemy were found asleep under the parapet. To despatch these with the bayonet, to plant the ladders, to begin the ascent, was the work of a few seconds. Before, however, the leading files could reach the summit the alarm had been given, and the enemy rushed in confusion to ascertain the cause of the disturbance. But before they could collect their ideas the stormers had gained the rampart, and, driving the enemy before them, had taken possession of the stockade on the summit of the isolated hill! The history of war cannot show an achievement more ably planned, more effectively carried out!

The light of a torch suddenly kindled and held aloft in the centre of the most important position of the enemy gave the signal to Moran in the trenches that the first act in the drama had been successfully played. It was for him now to make his attack a real one. Preluding it with a heavy fire from the guns in the advance battery, Moran, under the cover of its smoke, moved as rapidly as possible towards the imperfect breach of which I have spoken. At length he reached, and with great difficulty crossed, the ditch. Even then he seemed at first to have gained little, for the breach was found to be very steep, and wide enough only for one person. Had the enemy displayed the smallest conduct, or the faintest courage, the attack on this point must have failed. But it is a peculiarity of the Oriental nature that surprises, sudden attacks, and attacks made in the night, so completely discompose it, so interfere with the power of thought, that for a long time after the shock one instinct, and one only—that of self-preservation—is able to assert itself. On this occasion the combined suddenness and daring of the shock added to the mental confusion which the sight of the burning torch on the summit of the isolated hill had caused. The enemy were in no real danger had they kept their heads. But utterly distracted, they allowed the English, baffled at the breach, to plant scaling-ladders against the rampart. By these a few men entered and opened the gate to their comrades. Then all was over; Moran's party, feeling to the right, gave their hand to Irving's party descending from the hill, and the two, combining, swept all before them with irresistible fury. The enemy's troops were incapable, by circumstances, of flight; by mental paralysis and confusion from making an effective resistance. Flight was denied them, because a guard of their best troops, posted on the bridge crossing the nálá (stream), had received positive instructions to fire upon any troops who should attempt to cross it. This order, issued with the design of forcing the native troops to fight to the last, was carried out to the letter. The result was most disastrous to Mír Kásim's army. Attacked in front by the British, fired upon from the rear by their own men, and suffering, as I have said, from moral and mental paralysis, his troops were shot down in hundreds. The passages which might have served as an issue were speedily blocked up by the dead. In despair many threw themselves into the river and were drowned. Some tried to cross the U'ndwah, but the steepness of its banks barred their flight. Many threw down their arms and begged for a quarter which was not refused them. But the loss of life was terrible. It was computed at the time that fifteen thousand men perished either during the attack or from its consequences. Those who did escape from the assailed points stole away in twos and threes, skirting the hills and hiding in caverns. The reserve in the old lines, composed of Samrú's and Markar's brigades, attempted a show of resistance, but it was only a show. They soon sought safety in flight, the only portion of the splendid army of the previous day that was not absolutely broken!

Such was the battle of the U'ndwah Nálá—one of the most glorious, one of the most daring and most successful feat of arms ever achieved. It was, in every sense of the word, a most decisive battle. Adams did not merely defeat the army of Mír Kásim, he destroyed it. The blow had been so great that a rally thenceforth was impossible. In one morning, with an army five thousand strong, of whom one fifth only were Europeans, Adams had stormed a position of enormous strength, defeated forty thousand and destroyed fifteen thousand men, captured upwards of a hundred pieces of cannon, and so impressed his power on the enemy that they had no thought but flight. They made no attempt to stop at Rájmahal, which was fortified, or to defend the passes of Síkrigalí and Tiríahgalí, both of which were naturally as strong and as defensible as that from which they had been driven. Mír Kásim, on whom adversity had the effect of developing the cruel side of his nature, had shown his resentment at the result of the battle of Ghériah by consigning to death the native noblemen whom he held in confinement. He displayed his passionate rage at the total defeat of U'ndwah Nálá by threatening the slaughter of the English prisoners he still retained at Patna. He carried out this threat as soon as he heard of the surrender of Mungér.

A few lines yet to show how decisive had been that morning's achievement. Marching from the field of battle, Adams captured Rájmahal on the 6th September, occupied Mungér, which, though strongly fortified, made no resistance, on the 1st October, and recovered Patná on the 6th November. On the fall of Patná Mír Kásim quitted Bihár, and proceeded, with the followers who still remained to him—the most important had submitted to the English—to implore the protection of the Núwáb of Awadh (Oudh).

One word more with respect to the hero of the war. In little more than four months Major Adams had begun and brought to conclusion a campaign which did more than confirm the advantages which Clive had gained for his country by the victory of Plassey. Contending with a comparatively small force against a prince whose soldiers had been drilled after the European fashion, who was served for the most part by officers of tried ability, who was well furnished with cannon manned by

Europeans, and with supplies; who, moreover, was supported by the sympathy and affection of his people—Adams, in the short period I have stated, defeated him in three pitched battles, drove him from his dominions, virtually reconquered Bengal and Bihár, the capital of which he stormed, captured four hundred pieces of cannon, and carried the Company's arms to the banks of the Karamnásá. Regarded as a military achievement it can compare with any in the history of the world. It was possible only on the condition of the display of military conduct of the highest order, of gallantry, devotion, and tenacity on the part of the troops. All these qualities were displayed to a degree which never has been surpassed. Whether we look at the genius of Adams, the tenacity of Glenn, the conduct of Knox, who again greatly distinguished himself, of Irving, of Moran, and the other officers, and of the men who served under them, we fail to find a flaw; we can see only that which is worthy of admiration.

Nor were the political results less important. If Plassey made the Súbahdár of the three provinces a pageant ruler under the influence of Clive, the campaign of Major Adams gave those provinces to the English. Thenceforward there was only a titular ruler possessing no real power—a prince who, until he was still further to be despoiled, was, to repeat the expressive language of Mr. Scrafton, "no more than a banker for the Company's servants, who could draw upon him as often and to as great an amount as they pleased." The campaign concluded by Adams at the Karamnásá, subsequently continued by Carnac, and victoriously concluded by Munro against the Náwáb-Vazír of Awadh, assured more than the predominance, it assured the absolute supremacy, of the English.

It is painful to add that the great soldier who had produced the results I have recorded did not live to return to his native land. The climate, the fatigues and anxieties of the campaign, had so told upon him that after the expulsion of Mír Kásim from the three provinces he made over his command to Major Carnac, and proceeded to Calcutta. He died, unhappily, just as he was about to embark for England, 16th January 1764, leaving behind an unsurpassed reputation as a soldier. Those who may study the history of his great achievements will, I am confident, endorse and confirm this verdict of his contemporaries.

CHAPTER VII.

Baksar.

How the battle of U'ndwa Nálá completely destroyed the power of Mír Kásim; how, skilfully and promptly followed up, it forced him to evacuate Patná, and, crossing the frontier of Bihár, to throw himself into the arms of the Núwáb-Vazír of Awadh (Oudh); how the most influential nobles of the country then submitted to the British: has been already told. By his great victory Major Adams had brought the British standards to the Karamnásá; but in bringing them to that border-line of Bihár, and in forcing the defeated ruler of the three provinces to cross it, to receive a hearty welcome from the powerful satrap of the Mughul Empire whose dominions he would then enter, Major Adams had come upon a new enemy, an enemy not at all disinclined to look him in the face, to dispute with him the possession of the three provinces, to conquer which from Mír Kásim had required three pitched battles, several minor combats, and a siege.

The province of Awadh (Oudh) had not escaped the great Muhammadan invasion of the twelfth century. The decisive victory gained in 1194 by Sháhab'u'dín Muhammad over Jaichand Rai, the Hindú sovereign of Kanój, had been followed by the complete conquest of the neighbouring provinces. Thenceforth Awadh had become an integral portion of the empire ruled by the sovereign of Dihlí. When, then, in the last quarter of the sixteenth century, the illustrious Akbar welded into one compact whole the provinces which had been conquered by Muhammadan invaders of various races, Awadh came naturally into the general system. It was reckoned as one of his most important provinces, for it virtually included all the districts watered by the river Ganges, from Sháhjahánpúr to the Karamnásá.

In the disruption of the Mughul empire which followed the death of Aurangzíb, in 1707, the powerful nobles, each fighting for his own hand, had sought to secure for their respective families, in permanent possession, provinces or districts which they might claim as their own. Whilst one family appropriated the large territory known as the Dakhan, another the Karnátak, a third Bengal and Bihár, the representative of a fourth looked with longing eyes upon Awadh. This was Saadat Khán, an adventurer of a Khorasáni family of traders who had but recently come to Dihlí, at the Court of which he struggled for paramount influence with the famous Chin Killich Khán. In 1722 Saadat Khán, then Vazír of the empire, procured his own nomination to the government of the province he had coveted, under the title of Núwáb-Vazír. He began immediately to employ all the means in his power to render the office hereditary in his family. He succeeded. On his death in 1739, his nephew and heir, Abdu'l Mansur, better known under the name of Safdar Jang, succeeded him in both offices; and on Safdar Jang's death, seventeen years later, his son, Shuja'u'd daulah, assumed his title and position without a murmur from any quarter.

The accession of Shuja'u'd daulah to the rule over Awadh, in 1756, was contemporaneous with the accession of Siráju'd daulah to the Súbahdárí of Bengal. The new ruler of Awadh had not been an inattentive observer of the events which had followed, in that province, the proceedings of its young and inexperienced Núwáb. He had noticed how he had run his head against a race of foreigners from beyond the sea, and how that race of foreigners had in return deposed him. For the moment he was too much occupied with his own affairs to give very much attention to the events passing outside his own domains. But when the death of the Emperor Alamgír II., in 1759, had enabled him to achieve the project contemplated by his great-uncle, of establishing himself, on a basis secure and permanent, in the province over which he ruled as Núwáb-Vazír, Shuja'u'd daulah began to inquire more narrowly into the events which were passing in the provinces adjoining his own dominions. There did not then (1760) seem very much to disturb him. The foreigners from beyond the sea appeared to acquiesce in the rule of the Núwáb of their own making. But an ambitious Muhammadan ruler is always glad to foment disturbances in the dominions of a neighbour. When, therefore, the war broke out between Mír Kásim and the foreigners, the attention of Shuja'u'd daulah, till then spasmodic, became fixed. Ideas of aggrandisement for himself began to flit through his brain. Whichever of the two rivals might conquer, the victor must be weakened: then would come his turn. It would be no slight achievement, after having secured his own independence in Awadh, to add three fertile provinces to his dominions. Full of these ideas, Shuja'u'd daulah levied an army at Lakhnao, and summoned his vassal, Balwant Singh, Rájah of Banáras, whose dominions adjoined Bihár, to prepare for the campaign which he declared to be impending.

The result of the battle of U'ndwa Nálá had made it clear to Shuja'u'd daulah that it was with the English, and not with Mír Kásim, that he would have to fight for Bengal. He made preparations accordingly. He deemed it of especial importance to have Mír Kásim in his camp, not only because he represented, from a Muhammadan point of view, the cause of national independence, nor even, although that was of no little importance because he disposed still of the trained battalions of Samrú and Madoc—but because he had still money. The treasures which, after the battle of Ghériah, Mír Kásim had despatched to the strong fortress of Rotás, were still at Rotás. Between Rotás and the northern bank of the Karamnásá the communications were as yet uninterrupted. But they might not be so for long. It was of the greatest importance to act with vigour and promptitude. The fall of Patná rendered the situation still more difficult. Mír Kásim had, in anticipation of that event, sent to Rotás for his family and for his treasures. Any delay in their arrival would be fatal. Fortunately for the common cause, no such delay occurred. When the convoy from Rotás reached Mír Kásim, the English were still two days' march in his rear. Mír Kásim mounted his retinue and his property on camels, and started for the Karamnásá. Just before reaching its banks, an opportune letter, despatched by the Núwáb-Vazír, reached him. In that letter, and in the fly-leaves of the copy of the Korán which accompanied it, Shuja'u'd daulah promised him protection and support. The receipt of an invitation so solemn decided Mír Kásim, against the advice of many of his friends, to throw himself into the arms of the Núwáb-Vazír. He accordingly crossed the Karamnásá.

Meanwhile, however, events had happened in North-Western India and in Bundelkhand which had modified, if they had not altogether changed, the intentions of the Núwáb-Vazír. Although by the death of Alamgír II., Sháh A'lam had become titular King of Dihlí and Emperor of India, he had not, up to this time, been able to seat himself on the throne of his ancestors. His capital was still occupied by some of the Afghán victors of Pánipat, and an attempt made by Sháh A'lam, about this very time, to recover it, had resulted in signal failure. His army had, in consequence, gradually so dwindled down that it could only be regarded as a body of followers, without discipline, without proper arms, without organisation. Of all the sections of his subjects, the Rohílahs alone had remained faithful to him. This anomalous condition of affairs—the capital occupied by foreigners, and the King a wanderer—had stimulated the ambition of many a powerful noble to follow the example which had been set by the rulers of the Dakhan, of the Karnátak, of Awadh, and of Bengal, to create for his own family an independent kingdom from the now separating portions of the Mughul empire. Amongst the first to adopt this course was the Rájah of Bundelkhand.

Bundelkhand, the country of the Bundelá Rájpúts, was separated solely by the river Jamná from the dominions of the Núwáb-Vazír of Awadh. The independent action of the Rájah of that country would, under any circumstances, have affected him. It affected him very considerably indeed, when the Rájah, not content with independence, proceeded to aggression; when, at the head of an army deemed by himself to be irresistible, he crossed the Jamná and began to overrun the districts of his neighbour. It became, then, a matter of very serious consideration with the Núwáb-Vazír whether he should not renounce his designs upon Bengal, and march, rather, against the invader from Bundelkhand. Whilst he was yet pondering over the he course should adopt, he was visited at Lakhnao by the fugitive Emperor, Sháh A'lam, who, bestowing upon him the flattering title of Protector of the Empire, earnestly besought him to espouse his cause. Nothing was further from the mind of the Núwáb-Vazír than to render to the Emperor the only assistance he really wished for—the assistance of an army to recover Dihlí; but the ruler of Awadh was far too sensible of the advantages which would accrue to himself from the presence in his capital, and in his camp, of the representative of the authority of the Mughul, to reject his advances. He welcomed Sháh A'lam, therefore, with great respect and heartiness, and persuaded him to accompany him on the march he was then about to undertake to Alláhábád.

Before quitting Lakhnao, the Núwáb-Vazír had despatched to

Mír Kásim the letter and the Korán of which I have already spoken. A little later, however, there came to give him grave cause for reflection, first, the news of the invasion of the Rájah of Bundelkhand, and, secondly, letters from Mír J'afar informing him of the collapse of Mír Kásim and his party, and most earnestly beseeching his friendship and alliance. The consideration that the friendship of the last would enable him to deal effectually with the first, caused the Núwáb-Vazír to repent that he had given so pressing an invitation, accompanied by a safe-conduct, to Mír Kásim. However, his preparations had been made, and he set out for Alláhábád.

But when he arrived at that city, he found that Mír Kásim had preceded him thither. It was necessary that he should pay his guest the first visit. Accordingly, with great ceremony, and escorted by ten thousand horsemen, the Núwáb-Vazír, the very day of his arrival, proceeded to the camp of Mír Kásim. As he entered the camp he saw, drawn up to do him honour, the battalions and the artillery of the trained brigades of Samru and Madoc, the men well set-up, well armed, uniformly dressed —the gunners smartly arrayed after the manner of the English. The Núwáb-Vazír had never seen European troops. The sight, then, of sipáhís clothed and drilled according to their fashion, and presenting a striking contrast to the soldiers of his experience, made a deep impression upon him. He had entered Mír Kásim's camp all but resolved to dismiss him from his dominions; he left it, after the interview, all but resolved to use him for his own purpose.

His mind, however, was not absolutely made up. In concert with the Núwáb Vazír, and with his entire concurrence, the Emperor had already despatched a letter of congratulation and of friendship, with a dress of honour to Mír J'afar. This friendly missive had persuaded the latter that he had nothing to fear from his rival, that Mír Kásim would enter the dominions of the Núwáb Vazír only to be expelled from them, and he had persuaded the English that it was unnecessary to challenge the enmity of an independent prince by pursuing their defeated enemy across the Karamnásá. But Mír J'afar had not given sufficient weight to the consummate ability of his son-in-law. We have already noticed the impression which the skilful array of his troops produced upon the mind of the Núwáb Vazír. Mír Kásim hastened to confirm and strengthen this impression. We have seen how, three years' before, he had bought the members of the Calcutta Council. He still had plenty of money. With that money he now bought the ministers and favourites of the Núwáb-Vazír and of the Emperor. He did even more. Setting forth, in a plain unvarnished statement, the proceedings of the foreigners from beyond the sea; showing the Núwáb-Vazír how, in six years, they had risen from the position of humble and dependent traders to be masters of the three richest provinces of the Empire; and reminding him that, according to the ideas of an aggressive race, the process of absorption never is complete so long as anything remains to be absorbed; that the frontier of the foreigners now touched the domains of his vassal, the Rájah of Banáras, and that, therefore, he himself would most certainly be the next victim: he induced Shuja'u'd daulah to return to his earlier idea—that which had for its aim the conquest of Bengal, the expulsion of these foreigners.

But one difficulty remained to bar the full acceptance of this policy; and that was the invasion of the Rájah of Bundelkhand. Mír Kásim was equal to the occasion. He offered to proceed at once, with his own troops only, against the Rájah of Bundelkhand, provided that on his return successful from the enterprise the Núwáb-Vazír would at once invade Bihár. Shuja'u 'd daulah closed immediately with the offer.

Mír Kásim promptly marched to the banks of the Jamná and attacked the army of the Bundelkhand rájah. The enormous relative superiority of soldiers disciplined after the European fashion to the irregular armies of the native princes at once asserted itself. We have seen how in their desperate struggle for the three provinces the soldiers of Mír Kásim had succumbed to the English. The very same soldiers gained an easy victory over the Rájpút warriors of Bundelkhand. The campaign was short but decisive. Beaten in two pitched battles, the invading Rájah hastened to retreat within his own borders; nor did Mír Kásim relax his hold until he had rendered his enemy incapable of pursuing further the contest, and had forced from him a renunciation of all his ambitious plans. Mír Kásim then returned to Alláhábád, to find the Núwáb-Vazír dazzled by his exploits and eager now to afford him the assistance which he desired.

The terms of the co-operation were speedily settled. Mír Kásim, whose wealth was far from being exhausted, agreed to pay his powerful ally eleven lakhs of rupees a month, from the day that his army should cross the Ganges. In return he received a promise that as soon as the English had been beaten, Mír Kásim should be restored to the Súbahdárí, on the condition of paying a yearly tribute to the Emperor and of maintaining a body of disciplined troops ready always to aid the Núwáb-Vazír. It was further arranged that the treasures and property of the English and of Mír J'afar should be divided between the contracting parties.

There were no more delays. The combined armies set out at once, reached Banáras on the 7th March (1764), and immediately made preparations for throwing a bridge of boats across the Ganges. Whilst they are engaged in that operation I propose to trace the movements of the enemy they were marching to encounter.

Various causes combined to offer to the enterprise of the Núwáb-Vazír and Mír Kásim many chances of success. The first of these was the change in the English command. After driving his enemy across the Karamnásá, Major Adams, whose abilities had so much contributed to the success of the campaign, had been forced by the state of his health to proceed to Calcutta. He had been succeeded for the moment by Major Knox, one of the heroes of Machhlípatanam and Biderra; but the fatigues and exposure of the campaign had told upon Knox, and he was forced in a very few weeks to resign the command to Captain Jennings. Jennings was an artillery officer who had served through the Plassey campaign. He possessed considerable merit, but he laboured under the disadvantage of knowing that he held the chief command only till his successor should be appointed. This knowledge rendered him unwilling to assume any unforeseen responsibility.

Jennings was the less disposed to cross the Karamnásá in pursuit of Mír Kásim, because of the hopes entertained by Mír J'afar, and communicated by him to the Calcutta Council, that his rival would receive no assistance from the Núwáb-Vazír. The interchange of compliments and assurances between the courts of Lakhnao and of Murshidábád fully justified Mír J'afar, veteran intriguer as he was, in entertaining such a belief. He could offer more than could Mír Kásim, he could offer peace and alliance whilst the Núwáb-Vazír should march against the Bundelás; he never dreamt that Mír Kásim would render a service which could bind the Núwáb-Vazír to him by the ties of confidence. This illusion constituted the second cause which gave to the projected invasion its greatest chance of success.

The third cause arose from the undermining process adopted by the agents of Mír Kásim. That Núwáb had left in the provinces he had quitted a large number of partisans—men who preferred an independent prince of their choice to a ruler dependent upon, under the control of, and upheld by, the foreigner. Amongst these partisans were men of great ability, who, seeing the collapse of force, endeavoured to obtain their end by ruse and intrigue. They submitted, then, to the inevitable, acknowledged Mír J'afar, and then proceeded to work in the dark for the restoration of his rival. The great obstacle in their way was that army of Englishmen and of English-trained sipáhís which had driven Mír Kásim across the border. But the English portion of that army contained not only some Englishmen who were discontented; it contained likewise many foreigners, some the remnants of the Dutch beaten at Biderra, others Frenchmen driven from Chandranagar, and others, adventurers from other parts of Europe. Upon the lower stratum of the natures of these men, and upon the sipáhís, the conspirators set instantly to work.

After Mír Kásim had crossed the Karamnásá, the English field force remained for some time encamped at and near Sáwant, a small town on the river Dúrgawatí.* Here, on the 26th January, it was joined by a reinforcement from Bardhwán, commanded by Captain Maclean. With this reinforcement there came also two French companies from Madras, who had formed part of the expedition sent from that presidency against the Manillas, and who had there displayed many symptoms of indiscipline. On arriving at the camp on the Dúrgawatí, these two companies were broken up and re-formed into three.

A long halt in a country which offered no field for employment; the presence in the camp of an unusually large number of foreigners—for, in addition to the three French companies, to the Dutch, the Germans, and other adventurers, there was a fourth French company, commanded by Lieutenant Claude Martine, subsequently the founder and endower of the Martinière in Lakhnao—afforded to the friends of Mír Kásim the opportunity for which they had been waiting. They had, a few weeks earlier, made proof that the English soldiers were not above temptation, for, just before Major Knox resigned his command, they had induced three of them to quit their colours. These men had, indeed, been recaptured, but, owing to the confusion resulting from a change of command, they had

* The Dúrgawatí joins the Karamnásá about twenty-seven miles above the point where the latter empties itself into the Ganges.

escaped the punishment they had merited. Their good fortune was not likely to act as a deterrent to others. The conspirators now set to work on a more systematic principle.

They were immensely aided at this crisis by the conduct of the English Government. In the earlier days of the campaign, when everything depended upon the devotion, the valour, the endurance of the English soldiers and their native comrades, Mír J'afar had promised the men of the Bengal army that, should they emerge victorious from the campaign, they should receive a handsome donation. This promise had, with the sanction of the Calcutta Council, been communicated officially to the army. Yet when the campaign was over, when the devotion, the valour, and the endurance of the English and the English-trained sipáhís had won for Mír J'afar all that he had demanded, the Calcutta Council withheld the promised reward. Mír J'afar was ready enough to pay it, but his finances were under the virtual control of the Calcutta Council, and its members, always ready to help themselves, closed their ears to the just demands of their soldiers.

The first manifestation of the ill-feeling caused and nurtured in the manner I have described, took place on the 30th January (1764), when the European troops, assembled under arms on the parade-ground, refused to obey the word of command. Captain Jennings, who then commanded, was told on the spot by one of their ringleaders that the conduct of the men was prompted by the want of faith of the Government in the matter of the donation promised by the Núwáb; that they had performed their allotted task, had, after a campaign of extraordinary severity, seated Mír J'afar on the masnad; that two months had since elapsed, spent in idleness on the banks of the Dúrgawatí; that they saw no signs of the payment of the promised reward; that, considering themselves aggrieved and defrauded, they had resolved to refuse further service until their wrongs should be redressed.

For the moment Jennings pacified the men, and induced them to return to their duty by promising to write to Calcutta and support their claims, and by assuring them that, to his knowledge, a sum of money was then on its way to the camp, and that from this he would pay an instalment of the promised donation. And, in fact, on the day following, he issued an order, in which, whilst exhorting the men to emulate by their good conduct in camp their gallantry in the field, he pledged his word of honour that the verbal assurances he had given them should be carried out as soon as possible. Three days later Jennings endeavoured to check the spread of the mutinous feeling by detaching the companies in which it had chiefly manifested itself on command to the Karamnásá.

But the evil had taken too deep a root to be eradicated either by smooth words or by paltry expedients. It should always be borne in mind that amongst the Europeans now remaining in camp the foreign element was largely represented. Foreigners, indeed, represented two-thirds of the entire number, and these foreigners had been worked upon by the agents of Mír Kásim! When, then, after the lapse of twelve days, the promised payment had not been made, these men persuaded their comrades to act. At their suggestion the entire European infantry turned out, and electing from their own ranks a commander bearing the name of Straw, with the title of Major, compelled the lascars to draw out six field-pieces and place them in position on the flanks of the battalion. It was only by extraordinary exertions on the part of their officers that the sipáhís were induced to refrain from joining their European comrades in this movement. Jennings acted on this occasion with promptitude and vigour. Riding up to Straw, he seized him by the collar, and announced his intention of carrying him to the quarter-guard as the ringleader of the mutiny. The mutineers forced him, however, to let go his hold, and declared their intention, as they saw no prospect of receiving their money by remaining where they were, of marching to Patná, taking up on their way their comrades who had been detached to the Karamnásá. A long parley followed, Jennings using all his efforts to pacify the men, and even promising to raise a portion of the money from the private funds of the officers. To his advice and promises they paid, however, no regard; finally, to end the matter, Straw gave the order to march to the Karamnásá. The men set out at once in that direction; but, to reach their destination, they had to pass through the camp of the Núwáb. Mír J'afar, forewarned of all that was going on, met the mutineers as they were entering his camp, and promised to pay them a lakh of rupees on the spot, the balance before 1 o'clock of the following day, if they would return to their duty. At this crisis, however, the influence of the foreigners and of the men whom Mír Kásim had bought, came into play. These persuaded their comrades to disregard the offer of Mír J'afar and to carry out their original intention. The mutineers, therefore, pushed on for the Karamnásá.

But Jennings did not yet despair of bringing them to reason. Ordering the officers and the non-commissioned officers to follow the mutineers and to reason with them, he galloped across country to the camp on the Karamnásá, and detaching thence the Europeans encamped there in a direction nearly opposite to that by which their comrades were approaching, turned out the two battalions of sipáhís with the two 6-pounders in the camp.

Meanwhile, however, events were happening in the ranks of the mutineers which gave a new colour to the transaction. Obeying the orders of Captain Jennings, the officers and non-commissioned officers had followed the men, and, mingling with them, had all but persuaded the English portion of them to listen to reason. This was far from suiting the purpose of the foreigners. They threatened to drive the officers from their midst, and at length induced their English comrades to persevere in their design. Upon this some of the officers desisted; others, however, continued to persevere. Amongst the latter was a French lieutenant, to whom I have already made allusion, Claude Martine. As Martine continued to exhort his countrymen, one of the mutineers, likewise a Frenchman, took him aside, and told him that his exhortations were useless, that the men had made up their minds, that the plea of the money and of the march to Patná was only a blind, that they had pledged themselves to the Núwáb-Vazír of Awadh, and were now on their way to cross the Karamnásá and enter his dominions. He concluded by assuring Martine that if he would put himself at their head, he should be their general!

Astounded at this revelation, Martine gave an evasive reply, and made his way back to the camp in search of Jennings. Not finding him there, he took the same way across country which that officer had followed, reached the Karamnásá before the mutineers, and communicated the information he had received. He had hardly done so when the mutineers arrived, and, seeing that the sipáhís had no serious intention of opposing them, took possession of the two field-pieces.

Again did Jennings harangue them; this time with fuller knowledge of their real intentions. His serious tone, his exposure of the real aims of the men who were misleading them, produced a marked effect upon the English portion of his listeners. Straw himself, the whilom commandant of the band, was one of the first to recognise that he had been duped. Not only did he admit his fault, but he exerted himself to his utmost to induce his comrades to return to their duty. The consequence of Jennings's exhortations, of a promise of free pardon, and of the exertions of repentant sinners like Straw, was soon visible. By twos and threes the English came over to stand or fall by their commander. Impatient at this, the foreigners, fearful of further desertions, broke off the conference, and, giving the order to advance, to the number of three hundred crossed the Karamnásá. They were accompanied by about six hundred sipáhís, amongst whose battalions, whilst Jennings was haranguing the Europeans, the Mughul horsemen, devoted to a man to Mír Kásim, had been extremely busy.

But the English officers had not abandoned the task of persuasion. Some seven or eight of them followed the mutineers, and, mixing in their ranks, induced about eighty Europeans and three hundred sipáhís to return. Conspicuous in these efforts, so long as the English officers were present, was a Sergeant Delamarr, a man born in London of French parents, and who, as a sergeant of the 84th, had so greatly distinguished himself during the recent campaign that Major Adams had promised him a commission. Major Adams had died, and the promise had not been kept. Delamarr had seen other non-commissioned officers who had rendered far inferior services promoted and provided for, whilst he was still kept in the background. Dissimulating his resentment, he, under the cover of zealous sympathy with his officers, became the soul of the mutiny. So much did the officers trust him, that on this critical occasion one of them had lent him a horse to follow and use his persuasions with the men. Delamarr did follow with the seven or eight officers to whom I have referred, but when they had left with their repentant following, he put himself at the head of the remainder, and declared he would show them the way to fortune and glory.

If the Núwáb-Vazír had been close at hand to receive and to encourage the malcontents as they crossed the Karamnásá, the situation would have been serious indeed. But the march into an unknown country, where no welcome awaited them, acted upon a large number of the mutinous soldiers as a plunge into a cold bath acts upon a drunken man. It completely sobered them. The further they advanced the more did their confidence vanish. The cautious German element was especially affected by considerations which grew stronger every moment. By degrees every man of that nationality fell out and retraced his steps. Of the whole force, there finally joined the Núwáb-Vazír at Alláhábád a hundred and seventy-three deserters, of whom only three were Englishmen. The remainder were almost all Frenchmen. The majority of them joined the brigades of Samrú and Madoc. The more intelligent were received into the special service of the Núwáb-Vazír, and were subsequently entrusted with subordinate commands.

Meanwhile, with the return of the repentant deserters, order had been restored in the British force. The receipt of a lakh of rupees from Mír J'afar enabled Captain Jennings to make a timely distribution of a part of the promised donation, and his men, touched by this liberality, and free from the pressure of their French comrades, evinced not only shame for their conduct, but a desire to atone for it by some striking act of service.

An opportunity soon presented itself. In his distribution of the Núwáb's money Jennings had paid the European soldier more than six times the amount he had allowed to the sipáhí.* The gross unfairness of the proportion produced a marked effect upon the minds of the men who had to a very great extent resisted the pressure put upon them by their European comrades and by their co-religionists to desert. To them it appeared in the light of a premium upon revolt. They resolved, therefore, to obtain their rights by the means which in the case of their European comrades had proved so successful. Accordingly, on the morning of the 13th February, the day after the issue of the order directing the distribution, the sipáhís turned out in tumultuous order on their parade-grounds. Jennings at once ordered the European battalions and the artillery under arms. He had no need to incite them to do their duty. He found them only too eager to wipe out, by an attack

* The proportions were—to all sergeants, and to corporals and bombardiers of the artillery, 80 rupees each; to corporals of infantry and gunners, 60 rupees each; to private soldiers and drummers, 40 rupees each; to havildárs (native sergeants), 12 rupees each; to náiks (native corporals), 9 rupees each; to sipáhís 6 rupees each.

upon the men who had presumed to follow their example, all recollection of their contumacy. An extraordinary scene followed. The Europeans occupied a position which cut off one native battalion from the other. For a time no movement was made by either party. Suddenly, however, the sipáhí battalion on the extreme left advanced in a tumultuous manner towards the Europeans. Rightly conjecturing that the object of the sipáhís was not to make an assault but to effect a junction with their comrades, and especially anxious to avoid a contest which, however it might terminate, could not fail to prove fatal to English interests, Jennings, with great presence of mind, controlled his troops so far as to force them to refrain from drawing a trigger. The moment was very critical, for the discharge of a single piece must have precipitated a conflict. The sipáhís came on in tumultuous order, passed through the Europeans, and joined their comrades on the other flank. Two of the native battalions then marched towards the Karamnásá; of the other two present, one, though clamorous and excited, was restrained by its officers; the fourth showed no disposition to mutiny; a fifth, on duty in the camp of the Núwáb, was kept under control; two others were on detached duty on the Karamnásá; and it was to join these, which had already displayed disaffection, that the two revolted battalions now marched.

Jennings and his officers followed them, and by promising them the same concessions which had been accepted by the other battalions, he succeeded in inducing them to return to their duty. Similar concessions ensured the loyalty of the two battalions on the Karamnásá. The concessions were that the share of the native rank and file should be increased from less than one-sixth to one-half of that awarded to their European comrades.

It is strange that a revolt, which, in the cases alike of the Europeans and the sipáhís, might have been attended with the most serious consequences, should have been precipitated by the conduct of the authorities, and that, in both instances, it required the breaking of the bonds of discipline to force those authorities to consent to an act of simple justice. The delay in carrying out a solemn obligation in the one case, and the insult offered to the sipáhís in the other, imperilled without necessity the British hold upon Bengal.

Captain Jennings, hoping that a change of quarters might have the effect of effacing the recollection of the scenes of the previous fortnight, marched, as soon as order had been restored, to Sahasrám (Sasseram). Here he remained for a fortnight and then moved to Hariganj on the Són. On the 5th March Major Carnac arrived at that place to take command.

Major Carnac was not one of the glorious illustrations of the old Indian army. He possessed few of the qualities which are required in a general. Careful of his own comfort, absorbed by a love of the acquisition of money, then very prevalent amongst the high officials in India, he displayed neither energy nor enterprise. With far greater means at his disposal than had been possessed by Major Adams, he accomplished much less. He paid but little attention to the comfort of his troops, who, however, disliked him less on that account than for the distrust he evinced on many occasions of their capacity to beat the enemy. The intense dislike felt towards him by his officers and men, and which can be traced in all the correspondence of the time, was increased by the semi-regal state with which, whilst careless for others, he shrouded himself. It was his delight to pitch his camp at some distance in the rear of that of his army, and, whilst living in it a life of luxury and ease, to leave the details of his command to subordinates. That his officers and men gauged his military capacity aright was shown some years later, when his conduct in the campaign against the Maráthás imperilled Western India.*

* I allude to the conduct which led to the shameful convention of Wargáon.

The first act of Major Carnac after assuming command gave evidence of the want of enterprise which was his besetting fault as a general. I have already described how, after the fall of Patná, Mír Kásim had proceeded to the fort of Rotás, and, mounting the members of his family and all his portable treasure upon camels, had succeeded in escorting both across the Karamnásá. But many valuables, not to be transported in that easy manner, had been left at Rotás. To secure these likewise, Mír Kásim had dispatched in February, from Alláhábád, one of his ablest officers, Shekh Ishmáil Bey, with a chosen body of troops and a supply of cattle. The enterprise had not been so secretly conducted but that it came to the knowledge of Mír J'afar. Mír J'afar communicated the information to Jennings, and Jennings, on the 2nd March, had despatched a party to intercept the convoy, and, if possible, to take possession of Rotás.

Three days later Carnac assumed the command. His first act was to recall the intercepting party, at that time within a few miles of its destination.

Carnac had found ready to his hand a force consisting, in spite of the recent desertions, of seven hundred and fifty European infantry, a hundred and fifty artillery-men, about seventy cavalry, some three or four hundred native cavalry and seven battalions of native infantry, a total strength of about six thousand men. He knew well, moreover, that reinforcements of both races were on their way to join him, and that the Europeans would arrive some time in April. Without counting these, he had an army larger than that with which Clive had fought at Plassey, numerically stronger than that other at the head of which Adams had conquered at Katwá, at Ghériah, and at U'ndwah Nálá, and he was, moreover, supported by the army, twelve thousand strong, of Mír J'afar. His own men were especially eager for the fray. They were tired of inaction, and they greatly longed for an opportunity to wipe out, by gallantry in the field, every recollection of their insubordination on the banks of the Dúrgawatí.

Their hopes in this respect were, however, soon dispelled. Although, on his way to join, Carnac had received precise information regarding the movements of the Núwáb-Vazír and Mír Kásim, knew that they had quitted Alláhábád, and had calculated that they would reach Banáras a day or two after his assumption of the command of the British force, he remained for some days unaccountably idle. In another way he pursued a line of conduct not less irritating to his troops. As though he distrusted them, he ordered his own tent to be pitched, not in camp of his army, but in the camp of his ally, Mír J'afar, separated from that of his army by the river Dúrgawatí. To lessen the inconveniences which might arise from such a course, he—two days after his arrival—issued an order directing that all reports were to be made to his second in command, Major Champion, "who, when there is anything extraordinary, will report to the Commander-in-Chief."

This conduct, and the apparent determination of Carnac not to move, caused considerable discontent, and for a moment there appeared symptoms of the renewal of the disturbances which had only recently been subdued. Prompt measures—amongst them the despatch to Calcutta of Claude Martine's French company, and the disbursement of the remainder of the Núwáb's donation—checked these for the moment, and the brooding discontent was further dissipated by the issue, on the 12th, of an order to move forward. On the 17th the army reached Baksar.

The delay of more than a week, however, had given the enemy —who had, we have seen, reached Banáras on the 7th—time to prepare and throw across the Ganges a bridge of boats. If we may form a conclusion from his correspondence, Carnac had never intended to anticipate them at that place. He had formed a resolution to halt at Baksar; to await there the negotiations which Mír J'afar was carrying on with the Rájah of Banáras, and which, according to the calculations of those days, were likely to be pecuniarily more profitable even than a successful campaign, and it was with a feeling of relief that, two days after his arrival at that place, and when the tracing of the intrenchments with which he designed to cover his camp had been begun, he learned that the enemy had successfully placed their bridge of boats, and were engaged in crossing the Ganges. He resolved to await them where he was.

This Fabian conduct by no means corresponded to the views of the Calcutta Council. Whatever opinion we may form of the moral character of the gentlemen who formed that Council, we are bound to do justice to their political foresight. These men, the colleagues of Clive and of Adams, had, though not soldiers themselves, gleaned from the action of those leaders a very clear view of the manner in which a war with a native prince ought to be conducted. They had noticed that, alike in Southern India and in Bengal, Clive had been successful because he had attacked. Adams had followed the same system. What faith, then, could they place in a plan, the principle of which was entirely opposed to that with which unbroken success had made them familiar? If Carnac was right, they argued, Clive and Adams had been wrong. To argue that Clive and Adams had been wrong was an absurdity; therefore it was the new system which was defective, and must be abandoned. Full of this conviction, the Council sent orders to Carnac to cross the Karamnásá and proceed to act against the enemy.

Carnac received these orders on the 24th. He at once despatched an officer to arrange for throwing a bridge across the Karamnásá, and wrote to the Council that their orders would be obeyed as soon as he should have collected a sufficient supply of grain. This collection of grain, however, was a mere excuse to evade the orders he had received. For the next twelve days he remained encamped at Baksar, and when on the 3rd April he received another despatch from the Council urging more decisive measures, he called a council of war.

A council of war never fights. Carnac forced a decision favourable to his own views by proving that the army had not a supply of provisions sufficient to permit them to advance. He did not tell them that the army might have had a sufficient supply of provisions if he had made serious efforts to obtain it. Some of the members of the council did not shrink from expressing that opinion. But it was now too late, and, although the enemy's army was marching upon them, the council decided to retreat on Patná.

On the following day, the 4th, the army fell back, and on the 13th reached Dánápúr. On the 14th the European reinforcements, augmenting the army by nearly two hundred Europeans and as many sipáhís, reached Patná. The Europeans at once joined the army in the field.

At Dánápúr, Carnac halted five days. The murmur of his troops, and certain information that the enemy were approaching the Són—a river most difficult to cross in the face of an enemy—induced him to announce his intention of marching to prevent them. But again he was too late. The very day after he had set out he had a rough proof that the enemy had been beforehand with him; for his own tent, pitched as usual at a distance from the camp, was threatened by a detachment of their cavalry, and he himself was roused from the occupation of a game of whist to run for refuge amongst his own sipáhís. This adventure, which reflected little credit on the intelligence department,* had the effect of inducing Carnac to abandon the unmilitary habit of encamping at a distance from his men.

Certain now of the proximity of the enemy, Carnac despatched his European cavalry—consisting of about seventy men inclusive

* For secret-service money, attendance, and table-money, Major Carnac drew the unprecedentedly large allowance of Rs. 11,291.8.0 per mensem, a sum greatly exceeding those drawn by his predecessor and successor for similar purposes.

of officers—under Captain Hay, with instructions to engage them, then suddenly to retire and draw them into an ambuscade. Hay had not even set out when Carnac changed his mind, without, however, informing Hay of the change. The consequence may be imagined. Hay obeyed orders literally; engaged the enemy at so great an advantage, that the latter sent forward considerable bodies of troops to support their broken advance-guard; then fell back, drawing the enemy's masses after him to the grove, to which the infantry intended for the ambuscade should have been sent. To his amazement, not a man was to be seen, and Hay, recklessly abandoned to his fate, had great difficulty in extricating himself from his false position.

The near approach of the enemy forced the British army, two days later, to fall back on Patná. After a harassing and disorderly march, it reached that place on the 25th and took up an intrenched position, part of which was already occupied by the army of Mír J'afar. The left of this position rested on the Ganges, then made a sweep round the eastern side and a portion of the southern side of the city, then receding, ran parallel to its western side. It was thus covered for three parts of its extent by the guns mounted on the city walls. Its front was defended to the same extent by a low rampart and a deep ditch. Mír J'afar's army occupied the left portion of the intrenchment, the extremity of which rested on the Ganges; the English sipáhís, the part covered by the south-west bastions of the city wall, and protected by the intrenchment; the Europeans, the most vulnerable portion of the line, running parallel to the western side of the city, not covered by the rampart guns, and open towards the front. The force occupying this intrenchment numbered—including Mír J'afar's army of twelve thousand men and about a thousand Europeans and English sipáhís within the city—nineteen thousand men. It was the largest force ever, till then, put into the field against an enemy in Bengal; it was certainly the first that had allowed itself to be beleaguered.

Leaving their commander, Major Carnac, engaged in completing his preparations for its defence, I propose to return to the Núwáb Vazír and Mír Kásim.

We left those potentates entering Banáras on the 7th March, and we have heard of them quitting that city by the bridge of boats they had thrown over the Ganges on the 17th. The object being to reach Patná, the direct route led the army to Baksar, a distance of sixty-two miles. The passage of the Ganges proved, however, to be an operation far longer than had been anticipated; indeed, had Major Carnac displayed the smallest enterprise, it might have proved fatal to the invaders. When rather less than one half of the force had crossed to the opposite side, the bridge suddenly gave way. What an opportunity for Carnac! At this very time he was frittering away his energies at Baksar! Some days elapsed before the bridge could be repaired, and it was not till the 2nd April that the enemy's army, reunited on the southern bank, was in a position to march towards Baksar. The information that it had marched compelled Carnac, as we have seen, to make a hasty retreat towards Patná (4th April).

The Núwáb Vazír reached Baksar on the 9th April, and, learning the somewhat erratic movements of Carnac, resolved to make an effort to cut him off from Patná. He pushed on, therefore, with all speed, crossed the Són, unopposed, on the 17th and 18th, and sent to the front the reconnoitring party which, as we have seen, surprised and almost captured Carnac on the 20th. Whilst Carnac was planning the counter-attack which he failed to support, the Núwáb Vazír detached on the 21st, a considerable body of troops to cut off his army from Patná. This operation, which, if carried out in its entirety, might have produced serious results, was frustrated only by an accident. Carnac being in want of provisions, had ordered a battalion of sipáhís and three guns, to escort, on the 22nd, a convoy from Patná to his camp. Captain Smith, who commanded this escort, happened to receive information during his march, of the approach of the enemy's detachment. He was on the line by which the enemy must advance, and close to an extremely strong position formed of the bed of a tank with mud embankments on every side. He promptly took possession of this natural fortress, and when the enemy approached, gave them a reception so unexpected and so warm, that, imagining their purpose had been discovered, they renounced the enterprise and rejoined the main army.

How Carnac fell back before that army, and after a somewhat disorderly retreat, took up a strong position under the walls of Patná, has been already told. The next day the armies of the Emperor, the Núwáb-Vazír, and Mír Kásim, about forty thousand strong, of whom, however, not more than twelve thousand were regular troops, and the larger proportion of the remainder cavalry, took up a position fronting him. The Emperor, Sháh A'lam, was on the right opposed to Mír J'afar; Mír Kásim, with his trained brigades, and having his head-quarters at Bánkípúr, opposed the right wing of Mír J'afar and the left wing of the English; the Núwáb Vazír, with his head-quarters at Lohannapúr, occupied the ground facing the south wall of the city, and opposed the right wing of the English.

It was altogether a new position for the contending parties; an English force nineteen thousand strong, thus bearded in their camp by an enemy whose troops, though exceeding them in number by nearly two to one, were, for the most part, of a quality greatly inferior. But prestige—the prestige gained at Plassey, at Katwá, at Ghériah, and at U'ndwa Nálá—still fought for the English. That prestige had so impressed their enemies with their prowess, that for a week they hesitated to attack. During that period the English and their allies remained passive behind the trenches.

On the 2nd May, however, information reached the Núwáb Vazír which forced a decision of some kind. He learned that a detachment of English troops, between two and three hundred strong, commanded by Captain Wemyss, was approaching Patná. It was already too late, even had it been possible, to send a force to crush them; Patná, and the army under its walls, barred his way; he resolved, therefore, to attempt to crush that army before the reinforcement should arrive.

At daybreak of the following day (May 3rd), he made the attempt. The English being the most formidable of his enemies, and the most exposed, he formed up his line of battle so as, if possible, to overwhelm them, whilst, by a feigned attack, he should prevent Mír J'afar from detaching troops to their aid. The English, it will be recollected, occupied the right of the line parallel to the southern face of the city, their left touching the troops of Mír J'afar under the south-western bastions of the city. It should be added that their strongest point was a slight eminence close to, and under the fire of, the south-west bastion.

Leaving the troops of the Emperor to amuse Mír J'afar, the Núwáb-Vazír ranged his own army in the following order. On his right, nearly opposite the mound of which I have spoken, he placed his own choicest soldiers, supported by three thousand Rohílah horse; immediately to the left of these, the divisions of his Minister, Behní Bahádur, and of the Rájah, Balwant Singh, of Banáras; to their left again, a body of five thousand fanatics, all perfectly naked, and covered with paint and ashes. Formed next to these troops, and facing the English line, where it receded and ran parallel to the western face of the city, were the troops of Mír Kásim. Samrú occupied, with his Europeans and five battalions of regular sipáhís and sixteen guns, the post of honour on the right, touching the five thousand fanatics. Next to Samrú were the cavalry and irregular infantry, flanked by the rocket-men of Mír Kásim. The Núwáb was in the rear with the reserve.

A distant cannonade naturally preluded the attack. Under

cover of its fire the Núwáb-Vazír advanced, and, sheltered by some buildings which served as intrenchments, opened and maintained for some time a musketry-fire on the enemy. The task allotted to Samrú was more difficult. His men had no cover, and they were called upon to beard the British troops in the open. They advanced with great precision, but no sooner had they come within range than they were received with so hot a fire, that after several attempts to induce them to press on, Samrú drew them off to the protection of a hollow way, nearly half-a-mile from the intrenchment. On the enemy's left, affairs had not progressed much better. It is true that Mír Kásim's horsemen made several gallant charges, and, supported by their infantry, did their utmost to storm the eminence in advance of the English line, held by Captain Wilding with a company of sipáhís; whilst at the same time his rocket-men used every effort to turn the extreme right of their line. Though they did not succeed, their attack produced the effect of occupying the attention of a large portion of the English force, and thus gave an opportunity to the enemy's leader to concentrate all his efforts on another part of the line.

The Núwáb-Vazír, in fact, noticing how thoroughly Mír Kásim's troops were occupying the English on their left, resolved to make one determined effort to crush their right. For this purpose he brought up his guns close to the intrenchment, and opened a very heavy fire, sending word to Mír Kásim to send either Samrú or his reserves to support him. The fire was continued for some time with great vigour, but the Núwáb-Vázír looked in vain for the support he had solicited from Mír Kásim. Irritated at last beyond measure, he despatched a peremptory message to his ally. But Mír Kásim, great in council, had no head on the battle-field. There he was incapable of even issuing an order. In vain did the message reach him; he neither sent his own troops nor gave an order to Samrú. Compelled to rest solely on his own resources, the gallant ruler of Awadh ordered then the five thousand naked fanatics to attack the angle of the intrenchment —a point where it was defended solely by Europeans. The fanatics rushed forward with great impetuosity with wild shrieks and gestures, presenting a very formidable appearance; but the English received them with a volley so well directed, that many of them were laid low and the remainder scattered in disorder. They had scarcely cleared the way, however, when the Rohílah horsemen galloped at full speed to accomplish the allotted task. These gallant men met, however, no better success. The solid musketry-fire from the unbroken line of unconquered Englishmen emptied many a saddle, and compelled the survivors to fall back to rally.

It was now half-past two. The attack, begun at noon, had been foiled at all points. Still the Núwáb-Vazír did not despair. He had fought with great vigour; the cavalry and the rocket-men on his right had displayed signal courage, but the rest of the army had scarcely fought at all. Neither from Samrú, from Behní Bahádur, nor from the Rájah of Banáras, had he received any support. As for Mír Kásim's reserves, the English artillery-fire, passing over the hollow in which Samrú lay ensconced, had put them to flight long before. The Núwáb-Vazír, then, did not feel himself beaten because his first attack had failed. He resolved to make one more bid for victory. Forming up in line his own troops and those of his immediate dependents, he made a gallant advance, still unsupported either by Samrú or Mír Kásim, against the British line. So gallantly did his troops charge home, that, for a moment, it seemed as though victory were about to crown his efforts. The English line wavered, a part of the intrenchment was forced, and some prisoners were made. One effort more, and victory! A similar thought crossed the minds of the English. With calm determination they closed their ranks and presented a new front to the advancing foe, this time not to be broken. Just at this moment, too, the guns from the south-west bastions of the city opened fire with great effect on the enemy's line. The soldiers of the Núwáb-Vazír displayed, notwithstanding, prodigies of valour. They did not retire until thè battle had gone irretrievably against them.

Beaten but not disgraced, the Núwáb-Vazír fell back, sending, as he did so, a contemptuous message to Mír Kásim, to the effect that he should renew the action the following day with troops more to be depended upon than those led by himself and by Samrú. The English were anxious to pursue him, to turn the repulse into a complete defeat, but were withheld, to their great indignation, by Carnac. The victory, then, was almost barren. The Núwáb-Vazír carried off all his guns, left no prisoners, and returned to the position he had occupied before the fight. The losses on both sides were never certainly stated; but there can be no doubt but that the enemy suffered far more than the English.

Though the reinforcements commanded by Captain Wemyss safely reached Patná, Carnac still remained on the defensive. He sent, indeed, parties, one to put down insurgents, into the Sáran district, and ventured upon one or two skirmishes; but, judging from the reasons he himself assigned, he dreaded, though at the head of the largest force till then employed by the English in Bengal, to attack the enemy in their intrenchments, lest the attack should fail. Possibly his inaction was due to the fact that whilst the armies faced one another before Patná, he himself was carrying on negotiations with the Núwáb-Vazír and the Emperor, and that, as the result showed, a year later,* he found negotiating more profitable than fighting.

The approach of the rains at last forced the Núwáb-Vazir to retreat. On the 30th May he broke up his camp, and, not

* In 1765, when again at the head of the army, Carnac wrung from the impoverished Emperor a donation, for himself individually, of two lakhs of rupees.

pursued by Carnac, though Carnac was at a very early hour made acquainted with the movement, fell back upon Baksar, where, with fertile provinces behind him, and resting upon the river, he resolved to await in an intrenched position the approach of the English army. Leaving him there, I return to relate the very important measures which now began to affect that army.

On the 28th June, Major Carnac was, by an order of the Court of Directors, removed from the Company's service. His removal was due to causes which bore no reference whatever to his conduct of the campaign, at that time unknown in England. But it was, nevertheless, a great satisfaction to the Calcutta Council, who had lost all confidence in him, and an intense relief to the officers under his command.

His successor was Major Hector Munro. Munro, who belonged to the 89th Foot, was on the point of embarking for England with the officers and men of his regiment, who had not volunteered for the Company's service, when he received the intimation that his services were required to command the army in Bengal. Taking with him the remnant of his own regiment and of the 90th, he proceeded to Calcutta, and arrived there at the end of May. He remained there a short time at the request of the Council; acquainted himself, as far as he could, with the views of its members, and with the state of affairs generally; had interviews with Major Carnac and with Mír J'afar, who had likewise quitted the field; then started off and joined the army, strengthened by the arrival of fresh troops, on the 13th August.

Munro was the very opposite of Carnac. Not a great tactician, he was a daring, dashing warrior, always on the alert, ready for any enterprise, however foolhardy it would appear. He disdained the ceremonious pomp and stately ceremony in which Carnac had delighted. To him, danger, privations, difficulties, were as nothing. To set out stealthily with a lightly equipped force, and dash without warning upon an enemy, was a warfare after his heart. Time was to show him, in another part of India, that such tactics might be turned against himself by a resolute and watchful enemy; but in Bengal, the prestige acquired by the English allowed them to dare greatly with impunity.

But Munro had his difficulties likewise. Scarcely had he joined when the sipáhí battalions displayed, in a worse form, those mutinous symptoms which had with difficulty been repressed, a few months previously, on the Dúrgawatí and the Karamnásá. After some less important manifestations, repressed without difficulty, the men of Captain Galliez's battalion, the oldest corps in the service, rose at Mánjí, imprisoned their officers, and declared their intention of serving no longer, as the promises made to them had not been kept. A battalion stationed at Chaprá, the 6th, commanded by Captain Trevannion, was at once despatched to Mánjí to bring the mutineers to reason. The 6th proved, as Captain Trevannion believed they would prove, loyal to their colours; and the mutineers, taken by surprise, surrendered themselves as prisoners to their native comrades. They were at once embarked upon rafts and conveyed to Chaprá.

Munro was awaiting their arrival at that place. Having received information of the date and of the hour on which he might expect them—8 o'clock on the morning of the 13th—he had assembled the troops of the station, European and native, on the parade-ground. The prisoners were at once landed and drawn up in front of their loyal comrades. Their own commanding officer then, at Munro's request, selected fifty of the ringleaders. From these fifty he again picked out twenty-four, and these Munro brought at once before a general court-martial on capital charges of mutiny and desertion. The court found them guilty, and sentenced them to be blown away from guns.

Munro was a humane man, averse from bloodshedding unless

in cases of absolute necessity. But the times were critical. Misplaced leniency would, he felt, endanger the whole fabric of British dominion in Bengal. The easy condonation of the events on the Karamnásá had alone rendered possible the mutiny of Mánjí. He accordingly directed that the sentence of the court should be carried into effect.

The sentence was about to be executed—four of the condemned mutineers were being tied to loaded guns, when four of their comrades stepped forward and declared that, as they belonged to the grenadier company, and had occupied the post of honour on the field of battle, they claimed their right to it on the present occasion. The request of these gallant men was complied with; they were tied to the guns and blown away!

The action of these men, the calmness with which they met their fate, their tragic end, produced an immense effect upon the spectators. There was scarcely a dry eye on the parade-ground. Detestation for the crime had been effaced by admiration for the romantic heroism of the criminals. On the loyal sipáhís the effect was different. They could not bear to assist at the slaughter of men of their own blood—sent to that slaughter for a cause with which in their hearts they sympathised. The murmurs in their ranks became irrepressible, and their commanding officers, stepping forward, interpreted those murmurs by declaring to Munro that their men would not allow the execution to proceed.

Again was the moment critical. Any faltering on the part of Munro would have made the sipáhís masters of the situation. Fortunately he was equal to the occasion. Directing the officers of the artillery to load their guns with grape, he drew up the marines on one side of them and the European grenadiers on the other; dismissed the commandants to their regiments, and gave orders to the sipáhís to ground their arms. Instinctively they obeyed him. Firmness and decision are qualities which can always command Asiatics! The execution then proceeded. Sixteen of the remaining men were blown away; the remaining four were sent to Moniah and executed in a similar manner in the presence of the two battalions there stationed, who had recently evinced a disposition to mutiny.

Having, by this decided conduct, weeded his army of the "perilous stuff" which might have ruined it and him, and having reorganised his force, Munro issued, on the 6th October, the welcome order to advance. Bearing in mind the great superiority in cavalry possessed by his opponent, he resolved to leave a considerable body of men to protect Bihár, whilst with a select and lightly-equipped force he should execute his favourite manœuvre of beating up the enemy. The force he selected for this purpose consisted of nearly nine hundred Europeans—artillery and infantry—eight battalions of sipáhís, and the Mughul horse, now increased to a thousand men. Of this force two sipáhí battalions and about a hundred Europeans were at Chaprá. Whilst he himself, then, should advance from Bánkípúr by the direct route, Munro directed that the Chaprá force should set out from that place under Major Champion, and form a junction with him at Kalvarghát on the Són, on the 10th. At the same time a ninth sipáhí battalion (Captain Goddard's), was ordered to surprise Rotás, and then join the main body at the same point.

These arrangements having been completed, Munro set out on the 9th October from Bánkípúr. He reached Kalvarghát on the 10th, only to find the opposite bank of the Són occupied by the enemy. A passage which might have been extremely difficult was rendered easy by the timely arrival of Major Champion. That officer was more than true to his appointment, for he had marched up the west bank of the Són, and was therefore in a position to take in flank the enemy sent to oppose the advance of Munro. The enemy, not liking the new position, resolved to reserve their energies for another day, and, after a demonstration against Champion, fell back in the direction of A'rah. The British force then crossed and halted. The following day it was joined by Goddard.

The army being completed by this arrival, Munro divided it into three divisions, assigning them to Majors Champion, Pemble, and Stibbert. On the 13th he again advanced. He found A'rah evacuated; but as he pressed on, his advanced guard, commanded by Champion, came upon a body of the enemy's horse drawn up on the further bank of the Bonás nálá, close to the spot where, ninety-three years later, Vincent Eyre gained his ever-memorable victory. Champion easily dispersed the horsemen, but, following them up too quickly, was led, about a mile beyond the nálá, into a village in which the enemy had planted an ambuscade. The leading files, suddenly assailed from the houses, turned rein and galloped back, pursued by the enemy, who emerged not only from the village but from the groves in the neighbourhood. Following up their advantage, the enemy charged and put to flight the Mughul horse, notwithstanding the efforts of their European officers. They then dashed across the bridge, sabring all who came in their way; but noticing, a few hundred yards beyond it, two companies of sipáhís drawn up to receive them, they fell back, contented with their morning's work. They had killed or severely wounded seventy-two of their adversaries. They themselves, though not unscathed, suffered far less.

This surprise caused a greater exhibition of caution on the part of the English. Thenceforth they strengthened the advance-guard by the addition of two companies of Europeans and two guns. On arriving at their ground every day they were practised likewise in the order of battle to be observed in the event of being attacked in camp or on the march. Their further progress continued to be harassed by cavalry attacks, but the presence of the guns prevented a recurrence of the disaster of the bridge over the Bonás nálá.

At length, on the 22nd October, Munro reached the plain of Baksar, and beheld the enemy's army drawn up in front of their intrenchments. The two armies remained in presence for a short time, neither prepared to attack. At the end of an hour, the Núwáb Vazír withdrew his troops within their lines, whereupon Munro moved into the position marked out for his men, and convened a council of war. While they are deliberating, I propose to record the events which had occurred in the camp of the Núwáb-Vazír, subsequent to his arrival at Baksar.

The army which had fought against the English at Patná, and which, repulsed before that place, had retreated on Baksar, had had three nominal leaders, but only one directing head. The Emperor was virtually a state prisoner, lending only to the cause the halo of the imperial title. Mír Kásim had held an independent command in the attack on Patná. But his conduct in that engagement had brought the Núwáb-Vazír to the resolution to rid himself of him altogether. He acted to this end with the cunning which, in an oriental nature, occupies the place of prudence. Mír Kásim still had money; he still possessed a certain amount of influence. Until that money should be spent and that influence be dissipated, the Núwáb-Vazír would seek, by the means dear to an Asiatic, to prepare to become possessor of his property and to inherit that influence. The day at last arrived when, whilst they were in the intrenchment at Baksar, Mír Kásim's treasures became exhausted. Then, in conformity with his plan, the Núwáb-Vazír treated him with marked and studied insolence. After some bye-play, the whole truth burst upon Mír Kásim. He discovered that his troops, the trained brigades of Samrú, his Europeans, had been secretly bought by his ally; that all his friends except one solitary attendant were prepared to desert him. The very same day he was robbed, by the Núwáb-Vazír's orders, of the few valuables that remained to him, confined as a prisoner, and, the day after the appearance of the English force at Baksar, placed upon a lame elephant, and dismissed, as one who brought bad luck to any cause, from the camp.*

Undisputed master, now, of the legions, possessing courage and no inconsiderable military skill, Shuja'u'd daulah might fairly hope to give a good account of the comparatively small force which was about to assail him in his intrenchments. He could still dispose of some forty thousand men, one-third at least of whom were trained warriors, and this time they would not be assailing men behind intrenchments covered by a fortress—they themselves would have the advantage of the cover. His position was really a strong one, the left flank covered by the Ganges, the right by the Torah nálá, and the whole front covered by earthworks. Well might he calculate that, before his right flank could be turned or his centre forced, the weight of his greatly superior numbers would tell.

There is an impulse, however, in the nature of the Latin and the Oriental races which makes it impatient of delay, which upsets all the calculations of prudence. At Dettingen, at Talavera, and on many other fields, the French have voluntarily flung to the winds the natural advantages which would have secured to them victory. We have seen how, at Ghériah, Mír Kásim's army, leaving its strong intrenchments, marched into the open to meet the English. And now, at Baksar, the Núwáb-Vazír pursued the same course. He had sighted the English army on the morning of the 22nd. He had waited for them in his intrenchments all that day. As they did not attack him, he resolved to attack them on the following morning. At daybreak he moved out of his intrenchments accordingly.

We left Munro, meanwhile, presiding at the council of war which he had summoned after dismissing his troops on the

* The story is told in detail in the *Sayar il Muta'akkhirin*. Mír Kásim eventually found his way to Rohilkhand, where, after many vicissitudes, he became a pesioner of the upright and virtuous Najíb-u'd daulah. Left by his death without a protector, he eventually died in Dilhí in extreme poverty, his last shawl being sold to pay for his winding sheet.—*Asiatic Annual Register*

morning of the 22nd. There were officers present who, during the stay of the army at Baksar under Carnac, had gained a thorough knowledge of the ground; two, even, who had surveyed the position now occupied by the enemy. After a brief consultation it was resolved to give the main body of the troops a rest on the 23rd, and to attack the intrenchment on the 24th, that a strong detachment should endeavour, then, to turn the right of the position, whilst the main body should assail it in front; that, meanwhile, trenches and false batteries should be thrown up on the 23rd opposite the enemy's left, so as to delude them with the idea that the English intended to proceed by regular approaches.

The Núwáb-Vazír disconcerted all these arrangements by boldly challenging a combat on the 23rd. His army was discovered, soon after daybreak, marching in battle array towards the English camp by Major Champion, who had been detached with a party to prepare the false approaches of which I have spoken. Champion at once sent word to Munro, and Munro, after galloping to the front to reconnoitre, ordered his men to form up in the order of battle in which he had practised them during the line of march, and which would enable them, if threatened by cavalry, to form, on the moment, an oblong square.

That order was in two lines. In the front line the Royal troops, composed of the Marines, and details of the 84th, 89th, and 90th Regiments, commanded by Captain Wemyss, occupied the right centre; four companies of the Company's European troops—two belonging to Bombay, and two to Bengal—commanded by Captain Macpherson, the left centre. Flanking these two centres, on the right and on the left, were two battalions of sipáhís. In the intervals between these four battalions were two six-pounders; in the intervals between the Royal and the Company's Europeans were four six-pounders; on the extreme flanks were one twelve-pounder and two six-pounders.

In the second line, about two hundred of the Bengal European Battalion occupied the centre, with two battalions of sipáhís on either flank, two six-pounders filling up the spaces between the Europeans and the natives, and two being posted on either flank. The cavalry was divided into two divisions. One of these, supported by four companies of sipáhís taken from the battalions in the second line, was posted at a village to protect the baggage; the other, commanded by Captain Hay, occupied a position fifty paces behind the centre of the front line, supported by a reserve composed of the European grenadiers. The force numbered, exclusive of officers and sergeants, eight hundred and fifty-seven Europeans, of whom seventy-one were artillerymen, and forty cavalry; five thousand two hundred and ninety-seven sipáhís, and nine hundred and eighteen native cavalry (Mughul Horse); or a total of seven thousand and seventy-two. It had twenty-eight guns. The right wing of the front line was commanded by Major Champion, and the left by Major Hibbert. Major Pemble commanded the second line; Captain Hay, as I have said, the cavalry, with the reserve; and Lieutenant Vertue the cavalry and sipáhís guarding the baggage.

It remains only to describe the position. To the left and in front of the left wing was an extensive morass, and beyond that a village; in front of the right wing a large grove, between which and the village on the left the space was clear; to the right of the grove, beyond the extreme right of the line, was another village. These points, the villages and the grove, had been occupied by the enemy before the English line could be formed.

The Núwáb-Vazír had been allowed, indeed, plenty of time to consider the ground upon which he now resolved to fight; and it must be allowed that in his choice he had displayed considerable skill. His position was, indeed, formidable. His left, which, resting on the Ganges, occupied the fort and village of Baksar, was composed of the division of Behni Bahádur, several native battalions officered by the foreigners who had deserted from the Karamanásá in the preceding February, supported by a chosen body of horsemen raised by the Núwáb-Vazír in Awadh, and known as the Shekhzádí,* commanded by Shekh Gulám Khádar. In the centre were the trained brigades of Samrú and Madoc, consisting of eight battalions of sipáhís and eight field-pieces worked by Europeans, and supported by a mixed body of horse and foot, six thousand strong, commanded by Shujá Kuli Khán. In this centre, on either flank of the trained battalions, were powerful batteries of heavy guns, worked by trained native gunners under European superintendence. The right wing was composed of the division of the Rájah of Banáras, a large body of Rohílahs, horse and foot, and five thousand Afghán cavalry, known as the Duráni horse, from the fact that the majority of them had served under Ahmad Sháh Duráni at Pánípat. The reserve, composed mainly of cavalry, was posted in the rear. The Núwáb-Vazír, though he commanded the whole army, took especial direction of the right wing.

The Núwáb Vazír advanced slowly towards the English force until, judging himself within range, he halted and opened fire from his heavy guns in the centre. He had judged correctly, and Munro, finding that his own guns were not of sufficient calibre to reach the enemy's line, whilst his own men were a target for theirs, gave the order to advance. This forward movement was especially trying, as the morass in front of the left wing was unfordable and had to be turned, and this under a heavy fire from the enemy's guns and rockets. But never did British troops behave more steadily than on this trying occasion. Calmly and deliberately as on the parade ground they accomplished the manœuvre. Meanwhile, as they advanced within range, the guns of their centre and of their right wing opened fire, with a better aim than that of the enemy. The

* Literally, the sons of the Shekh.

morass at length cleared, the line was re-formed, and the advance continued. Just at this moment the Duráni Horse, galloping up, threatened the left flank. Again, as on parade, the two British lines executed the manœuvre to which they had been accustomed, and promptly forming into an oblong square, poured in a fire of grape and musketry so galling that the Duránis recoiled. An attempt by the same horsemen made immediately afterwards, in conjunction with the Shekzádís, on the baggage, was more successful. The whole of this fell into their hands.

Flushed with this success, the two bodies of horsemen charged impetuously the rear-line of the British. The charge, though repelled, was repeated and repeated, the enemy behaving with the greatest gallantry, many of their men falling in hand-to-hand contest in the very ranks of the assailed. Amongst these was their heroic leader. Not even his loss, however, checked their ardour, nor did the survivors retire until the heaped-up bodies of their comrades, dead and dying, convinced them of the impossibility of breaking down the solid British wall before them.

Whilst his cavalry were thus maintaining their reputation on the rear of the British lines, the infantry of the Núwáb Vazír were, under his own personal directions, using every endeavour to gain the victory which should make him master of the three provinces. A battery of heavy guns had been moved to the village overlapping the right of the British line, beyond the grove immediately in their front, and the fire from it had already produced something like a wavering in their right wing as it advanced. Munro, perceiving this, recognised that the critical moment had arrived when, if he did not wish to allow the conviction to steal over his men that they were overmatched, he must achieve some striking success. He accordingly ordered a battalion of sipáhís to charge the village. This feat was performed with great gallantry and skill by Lieutenant Nicoll, Adjutant-General of the sipáhís. This officer, making a detour, surprised the enemy, and drove them out at the point of the bayonet. No sooner had this been accomplished than Munro, sending another battalion to support Nicoll, directed him to carry his success further, and attack the grove. The enemy, however, were by this time on the alert, and they received Nicoll with so much resolution, and with numbers so superior, that they forced him back. An opportune charge of cavalry completed his discomfiture.

A decisive moment had now arrived. If the enemy could maintain themselves in the grove, the ultimate victory must be with them. Samrú and Madoc were at least holding their own in the centre; on the right the Núwáb-Vazír had not lost an inch of ground. Could he repulse the English once more from the grove, and then overwhelm them with a charge of cavalry, the day would be his own. No one recognised the position more clearly than Munro. He felt that unless he could carry the grove he was beaten. He resolved, therefore, to carry it at all hazards.

That there might be no mistake this time, Munro supported the battalions already in advance, and which he further strengthened, with his entire right wing, and directing them to trust only to the bayonet, sent them forward. Had the enemy only shown resolution, the contest might have been doubtful; but the pertinacity of the English daunted them; they could not view with firmness the sight of the dark masses advancing against them. As soon, therefore, as the English entered the grove the enemy gave way, leaving twenty-seven guns behind them. A volley from the victors hastened their retreat, but they formed up again on the left of the line, and presented there an unbroken front.

Still the battle, though more favourable to the English, was not yet decided. A mistake made by the commander of the mixed horse and foot, Shujá Kúli Khán, who was supporting the brigades of Samrú and Madoc, came, however, opportunely to give the final touch to the impending catastrophe. This officer had no sooner heard the volley which the English had poured upon the infantry retreating from the grove, than, elated as he was with the promising aspect of affairs, he came to the unfortunate conclusion that they were the troops of the Núwáb-Vazír who had fired it—the retreating English who had received it. The moment, then, had arrived, he thought, to complete the victory. Without communicating with anyone, then, he moved round the skirts of the morass, and charged the English left wing in front and in flank. But here again English steadiness, never more conspicuously displayed than on this memorable day, baffled the gallantry of the enemy. The men of the left wing, Natives and Europeans, repulsed charge after charge, and at length compelled the baffled survivors of the enemy, who had lost their gallant leader, to retire broken and in disorder. That leader had paid more than his life for his mistake. His discomfiture was the signal for the retreat of the whole line!

Munro at once gave orders for a general advance. Riding to the head of his troops he thanked them for their conduct, told them that the victory was now in their hands, and, taking off his hat, gave three cheers, to which the men responded. The battalions then broke into column, and pushed on to improve their success.

Fortune again favoured them. The Núwáb-Vazír, who was formed of a good fighting material, and who had not spared himself during the battle, had, on seeing the victory on which he had counted escape from his grasp, taken up a new position to check pursuit and, if possible, to restore the battle. He would probably have succeeded in doing the first. But, unfortunately for him, Behní Bahádur, who had occupied the fort and village of Baksar, had not heard of the defeat of the main body. Himself dismounted and his men in loose order—

chatting, probably, regarding the victory they believed had been gained—they were surprised by the sudden apparition in their midst of the English soldiers. To mount, to flee, all in disorder, was the simultaneous thought of several thousands of men. The consequent rush of terrified fugitives was fatal to the new dispositions taken up by the Núwáb-Vazír.

Thenceforward all was over. There was nothing for it but flight—or pillage. The Duránî horse, true to their Afghán instincts, chose the latter alternative, and set to work with a good will to plunder the camp of the master for whom they had fought. The Núwáb-Vazír himself succeeded in crossing the Torah nálá with his regular brigades, his moneys, and his jewels; but no sooner had he seen them on the opposite bank than, like Napoleon after Leipsic, he ordered the bridge of boats to be destroyed. The rear of the force and all the camp-followers were thus exposed to destruction. Still they pushed on; some into the stream, elephants, camels, horses, men, and bullocks all mixed together, the same animal instinct inspiring them all. The result was terrible. In this struggle for life, writes the native chronicler, so many perished that at last a bridge, three hundred yards long, was formed of their bodies, over which the survivors escaped! It need scarcely be added that across that bridge the victors did not follow them.

Such was the battle of Baksar! a battle in all respects a test battle, won by courage, endurance, and, above all, by discipline and steadiness. If we may say that the English were fortunate in possessing as a leader a man so cool, so enterprising, and yet so firm and decided as Hector Munro, we must also admit that never before had they encountered an enemy in all respects so formidable. Shuja'u'd daulah, Núwáb-Vazír of Awadh, was the most skilled native leader of soldiers in India. Contemporary writers declare that if he had lived in the palmy days of the Mughuls, his force of character, his astuteness, and, above all, his qualities as a general, would have placed him in the very front rank. The same writers proceed, whilst lamenting the fortune which brought him, at a critical period, in contact with a race physically superior and which had attained a higher standard in the practice of arms, to point to the statesmanlike wisdom which admitted defeat, recognised that the conqueror was not to be withstood, and eventually bound him towards himself and his family by ties of friendship. Such a leader was no unworthy opponent even of Munro; and the most critical will admit that he fought the battle with skill and resolution. He cannot be held responsible for the mistakes of Shuja Kúlí Khán and of Behní Bahádur—mistakes, the first of which ensured his defeat, and the second made of the defeat a rout. Again, his men, especially his cavalry, fought most bravely. Witness the charges on the second line of the English, the first defence of the grove, the firm attitude of the disciplined brigades. But for the wonderful steadiness of the English those charges would have brought them victory. It was that steadiness, as conspicuous here as it was on the hill of Albuera and on the field of Waterloo, which not only saved Bengal, but gained for our countrymen the north-west provinces of India.

For those were the stakes. The English risked the three provinces of Bengal, Bihár, and Orísá, the Núwáb-Vazír the north-western provinces from Sháhjahánpúr to the Karamnásá. They fought to decide to whom both should belong. That was the practical issue. Had the English been badly beaten—and defeat would have meant annihilation—Shuja'u'd daulah would not have stopped short of Calcutta. What were the consequences of his defeat? Baksar was fought on the 23rd October 1764. By the following February the English had subdued the country as far as Alláhábád, including Banáras and Chunár; in March they had overrun Awadh, occupied Faizábád and Lakhnao, beaten the enemy at Karrah, again at Kalpí on the Jamná, and finally forced the Núwáb-Vazír—a "houseless wanderer"—to throw himself upon their generosity. The extent of the territory conquered alone prevented the English from, at the time, taking the fullest advantage of their victory. From motives of policy they restored to its owner the greater part of the stake, all of which, nevertheless, the victory of Baksar, well followed up, had won for them. Clive, who arrived from England in time to negotiate the treaty, would have given back nearly the whole of it. But circumstances were too strong for him. The victory of Baksar advanced the English frontier practically to Allháhábád.*

That victory cost the English eight hundred and forty-seven in killed and wounded; of these a hundred and one were Europeans, and nine of these, again, were officers. The enemy's loss was more severe. Upwards of two thousand men lay dead on the field, and many more were wounded. The victors captured a hundred and thirty-three pieces of artillery, the standing camp, and all the personal effects of the enemy. Exclusive of the number of articles plundered, the booty, when sold, realised upwards of twelve lakhs of rupees!

Whether regarded as a duel between the foreigner and the native, or as an event pregnant with vast permanent consequences, Baksar takes rank amongst the most decisive battles ever fought. Not only did the victory of the English save Bengal, not only did it advance the British frontier to Alláhábád, but it bound the rulers of Awadh to the conqueror by ties of admiration, of gratitude, of absolute reliance and trust, ties which made them for the ninety-four years that followed the friends of his friends and the enemies of his enemies. For that constancy of friendship England repaid them in 1855–6!

* The English held that place nominally for the Emperor till 1771, when they sold it to the Núwáb of Awadh for fifty lakhs of rupees. They continued, nevertheless, to garrison it. It was formally transferred to the English in 1801.

CHAPTER VIII.

Porto Novo.

The present kingdom of Maisúr* (Mysore) is bounded on the north-west by Dhárwár, in the Bombay Presidency, and by the Portuguese territory of Goa; on the north-east and east by the districts of Ballári, Kadapá, and Karnúl; on the south-west by the province of Kurg; on the south-east by Arkát; and on the south by the Nílgiris. At the time when the genius of its Muhammadan ruler made its name formidable to the English, Maisúr comprehended an extent of territory far greater. Not only did it include southern India as far as Travankúr, but its ruler held likewise a portion of south and north Arkát, and made his influence felt sometimes even to the very walls of Madras. For a moment it seemed even possible that Madras itself might be swallowed up. It is of the campaign which forced him to relax the firm grip he had taken of the Karnátak, and which so far as related to the danger of the predominance of Haidar Alí in southern India was decisive, that I propose now to write.

Very little is known of the early history of Maisúr. Accord-

* The name Maisúr is abbreviated from "Mahesh A'sur"—the buffalo-headed monster—said to have been slain by the goddess Káli, who, under the title of Chamúndi—the discomforter of enemies—is an object of special worship in the country.

ing to the preserved tradition two young men of the tribe of Yádava left the court of Vijayanagar in search of adventure, at a time when the influence of the Rájahs of Vijayanagar extended over nearly the whole of southern India; reached the little fort of Hadava, a few miles from the site of the present town of Maisúr, and rescued from a marriage which would have disgraced her the only daughter and heiress of the petty lord of the soil. The elder of the two then married her, and became the founder of the Hindú dynasty which still governs the province.

Such is the tradition. The little domain acquired by the marriage enjoyed for many years that followed the inestimable advantage of attracting no notice from its larger neighbours. It is known, however, that in 1524 a descendant of the Yádava intruder, Kám Ráj by name, moved the capital from Hadava to Maisúr, and that in 1571 another successor, Hirá Kám Ráj, not only refused to pay tribute to Vijayanagar, but took possession of Shrirangapatam, and greatly enlarged his borders. From the date of his rule the enlargement became progressive. In the course of a few years (1638), the hero of the race, Kánti Réva Narsi Ráj, whose exploits are to this day, far more than those of the Muhammadan Haidar Ali, the favourite themes of the bards and story-tellers of Maisúr, and whose stone bed is still preserved in the royal palace, came to increase further the ancestral territories. In the reign of his successor, Dúd Deo Ráj, those dominions assumed the dimensions of a kingdom. It was this rájah who set on the hill overlooking Maisúr, popularly known as the hill of Chamúndí, the colossal figure of Shiva's bull, which, for the beauty of its design and the skill with which it has been executed, commands to this day admiration.

By this time the kingdom had become sufficiently large to attract the notice and the jealousy of the neighbouring potentates. We hear of one rájah levying tribute from Trichinápallí; of another attacking Madura, of the son of another defeating the Maráthás in a pitched battle. It was on the strength of this victory that the descendant of the Yádava adventurer, Chik Déo Ráj, felt emboldened to send an embassy to the great Aurangzíb. The Mughul emperor rejoiced to welcome as a friend one who had been able to defeat his bitterest enemies, received the embassy with great cordiality (1700), conferred upon the rájah many titles of honour, and conceded to him the right of sitting upon an ivory throne.

The descendants of Chik Déo failed, however, to maintain by force of arms the position which that sovereign prince had acquired. We find his grandson, Dúd Kishen Ráj, compelled, in 1724, to buy off, by the payment of a million sterling, the attack made upon him by the Núwábs of Karnúl, Kadapa, and Savanúr, and the Maráthá chief of Gutti. Two years later the Maráthás extorted a similar price for their forbearance; and, although the money expenditure was to a large extent made good by the capture, in 1728, of Savendrug, the accumulated treasures of which fell into the hands of the Maisúr Rájah, still the Hindú dynasty never recovered from the blow which the payment of the money for release from the demands of a conqueror always inflicts.

It was about this time that the power of the Rájahs of Maisúr glided from their hands into the hands of their hereditary ministers, the Dalwais. It was a custom not unknown to Hindú races. It had prevailed in the great Maráthá dynasty enthroned in western India. Whilst the descendant of Siváji was a pageant sovereign, the Peshwás descending in a hereditary line exercised all the power. And now the principle took root in Maisúr. The Dalwais were said by tradition to be descended from the younger of the two Yádava adventurers who had laid the foundation of the kingdom. The same tradition affirms that the right to hold in perpetuity the office of prime minister had been made, at that early period, hereditary in their family. It was only, however, when the royal dynasty began to show signs of decrepitude and decay that the right was offensively asserted. In 1736 the representative of the Dalwai family, Déo Ráj, was a man of remarkable ability. The reigning prince being distinguished for his vices, Déo Ráj deposed him, placed on the throne a distant relative to exercise the ornamental functions of royalty, whilst he himself, as mayor of the palace, should really govern.

This Dalwai, Déo Ráj, restored the fortunes of Maisúr by defeating in a pitched battle the army of Dost Alí, Núwáb of the Karnátak. When he felt his strength begin to decay, he made over his power to his brother, Nanjíráj, a man whose abilities were but little inferior to his own. Under the command of Nanjíráj, the Maisúrians stormed the stronghold of Deonhalli, and took a prominent part in the contest, nominally between Chanda Sáhib and Muhammad Ali, really between the French and the English, for supremacy in the Karnátak. Alike in the storming of Deonhalli, and in the contests which followed, Nanjíráj was greatly assisted by the skill, the valour, and the enterprise displayed on every occasion by a Muhammadan soldier of fortune whom he had enlisted under his banners, and to whom, after a time, he entrusted very high commands.

The name of this soldier of fortune was Haidar Alí. Haidar Alí was the second son of Fateh Muhammad, a náik or commander of peons, or irregularly-armed infantry, in the service of the Núwáb of Sera. Fateh Muhammad, after a career which might be termed successful, for he had been able to attach to his name the coveted title of "Khán," and to receive the jaghir of Budikóta, was slain in one of those sanguinary contests which followed the attempt of the Súbahdár of the Dakhan to found an independent principality in southern India. At that time his elder son, Shábáz, was nine years old; the younger, Haidar, was seven. The death of the father obliterated the recollection of his services. Under the pretext that some moneys had not been accounted for by the deceased náik, the son of the man for whom that náik had given his blood demanded payment from the widow and her children, and, when compliance with the demand was evaded, he did not hesitate to apply torture, in its most cruel and ignominious form, to the two boys, and probably, it is said, to their mother. Young as he was, Haidar neither forgot nor forgave the indignity; nor did he fail to avenge it.

The death of his father and the subsequent misfortunes of his family deprived Haidar Ali of the advantages of education. To the end of his life he had never mastered even the faculty to read and write. His character as a young man was peculiar. He was always in extremes. Impatient of restraint, he would absent himself for weeks from his family, and pass his time in voluptuous riot; then, suddenly awaking, would proceed to the opposite extreme of abstinence and excessive exertion. The political disorders of the age at length forced him to take a decided part. His brother, Shábáz Sáhib, had, some time previously, through the kind offices of a Hindú officer of rank, obtained a position as a subordinate officer of peons in the service of the Dalwai. By good conduct he had gradually risen to the command of two hundred horse and a thousand peons, and at their head he formed part of the army which, in 1749, was besieging Deonhalli. Haidar, tired of an aimless life, joined that body of men as a volunteer.

His service at this siege settled his future career. Daring, cool, and resolute, Haidar distinguished himself as the first on the field of danger, the foremost in every fray. He did more than that. It was Haidar who suggested the plan by which the enemy was to be baffled, the manœuvre which was to prelude success. He attracted the attention of the all-powerful Nanjíráj; and Nanjíráj, always eager to attach talent to himself, appointed him, on the fall of Deonhalli, to command a body then consisting of fifty horsemen and two hundred footmen, gave him orders to recruit and augment it, and placed him in charge of the principal gate of the conquered fortress.

From this time the rise of Haidar was assured. We find him

in the following year combating the Maráthás, and, by a visit to Pondichery, laying the foundation of that regard for the French which lasted to the end of his days. In 1751–52 we hear of him, his corps augmented to a thousand, fighting before Trichinápalli, and distinguishing himself in every encounter. The following year he was appointed by Nanjíráj to take charge of the important fortress of Dindigal, ceded by Muhammad Alí. At this time his command was increased to fifteen hundred horsemen, three thousand regular infantry, and two thousand armed footmen, with four guns. It is generally believed that at this period of his life his mind first conceived those ambitious designs which he afterwards so effectually carried out.

It would take too long, and it would be foreign to the purpose of this work, to narrate the means by which Haidar Alí gradually built up for himself an enduring position in the Maisúr State. It must suffice to state that his wonderful knowledge of men, and the address which was born of that knowledge, soon made him the most popular man in southern India; that, aided by a confederate, Kandé Ráo, whom he placed at Maisúr to watch the proceedings of the court, to furnish him with information, and to support his demands, he made himself in a very short time necessary to the Dalwai; that when, in 1758, the Dalwai, Déo Ráj, died, and the Maisúr army mutinied to obtain its arrears of pay, Haidar Alí, by means peculiarly his own, settled their claims; that having thus assumed the character of a general benefactor of the State, he took care that his troops should take all the guards of the fortress of Shrirangapatam; that he then compelled the Maráthás who had invaded Maisúr to quit the country and to renounce their claims on the territories previously ceded to them in pledge; that, on his return, he was received by the pageant Rájah, and now, by his means, the almost pageant Dalwai, in full darbár, and greeted with the title of Bahádur, or hero, which was ever afterwards affixed to his name; that, having felt his power, he then, acting under the shadow of the name of the Rájah, turned all his influence against his original benefactor, the Dalwai, Nanjíráj, forced him to relinquish all his appointments, to proceed in forced retirement to Kunnúr, some twenty-five miles west from Máisúr, and appointed his own adherent, Kandé Ráo, under the name of Díwán, to fill the vacated post; that Kandé Ráo having a little later, in collusion with the Rájah, turned against him, and even defeated him in the field, Haidar, by an artifice which did great credit to his imaginative powers, crushed his enemy and more than recovered his position; that, as a consequence, he assumed charge of the whole country, assigning three lakhs of rupees for the personal expenses of the Rájah, and one lakh for those of Nanjíráj; that he then increased the dominions of Maisúr, by the defeat of Murári Ráo, the conquest of Bednúr, of Bellári, the submission of many independendent chiefs, the extension of his territories to the Malabar coast; more than doubling the extent and more than quadrupling the resources of the kingdom, which was now virtually his own. In 1766, the pageant Rájah having died, Haidar, after a mock installation of his successor, resumed the grant of three lakhs, plundered the palace of its jewels, and confined the Rájah within its four walls. Thenceforth he was supreme.

In the course of these events, of which I have given the briefest possible summary, Haidar Alí had never come in contact as a principal with the English. He had met them in the field before Trichinápalli, and that was all. The time was now approaching when his experience of them was to be more varied. The English, after the position gained by their decisive victory over the French in southern India had been confirmed and established by the peace of Paris (10th February 1763), had proceeded on lines widely different from those on which they had travelled in Bengal. There they had effectually asserted themselves, had controlled the policy of the puppet they had set up. But in southern India they had been content with playing "the secondary part in politics, the first in the field." They allowed, in fact, the puppet whom they had placed on the semi-regal throne of the Karnátak to pursue his own foreign policy, and they were content blindly, and without inquiry, to fight for that policy. Now, Muhammad Alí, whom British efforts alone had placed in a position of power, had entertained a great jealousy of the rising power of Haidar, and he had formed an alliance to crush him with Nizám Alí, Súbahdár of the Dakhan, and with the Maráthás. In the campaign which they contemplated, both Muhammad Alí and the Súbahdár designed to place the English in the front line of battle. The English, no longer under the direction of a guiding mind, were not unwilling. They were content—to use the words of the contemporary historian, Colonel Wilks—"to engage in the contest in the exclusive character of dupes."

Haidar Alí was equal to the occasion. He possessed one great advantage, that he fought for one hand, and that hand his own. His enemies were animated by four interests, all really opposed the one to the other. By the payment of thirty-five lakhs of rupees, and the cession—intended only to endure until he was able to re-occupy it—of some territory, he bought off the Maráthás. He then cajoled the Súbahdár, Nizám Alí, to renounce his alliance with Muhammad Alí, and, conjointly with himself, to invade the Karnátak. Entering that country, Haidar fought —3rd September 1767—with the English at Changámah a battle, which, whilst it was so far a victory for that people, inasmuch as they repulsed every attack, was followed, two hours later, by their retreat to Trinomalli from the position which they had victoriously maintained. To Trinomalli Haidar and his ally followed them. He might then have starved them into a surrender, for his own position before it was unassailable. Pressed by his ally, however, he again tried the fortune of war, and on the 26th September moved into the plain to attack his enemy, led, as on previous occasions, by Colonel Joseph Smith; attacked him; and was defeated with great loss of men and of material. One result of this defeat was recrimination between the two allies, each casting the blame of the mishap on the other. The formidable character, up to this point, however, of the invasion may be realised from the consideration of the fact that, whilst the battle was being fought, Típú (Tippoo), then a boy of seventeen, undergoing for the first time "the baptism of fire," was engaged, under the guidance of an experienced officer, Ghází Khán, in plundering the country houses of the Members of the Council of Madras.*

The defeat of Trinomalli was a blow, but it was not a decisive blow. It warded off for a time Haidar's meditated attack upon Madras. For a month after its occurrence Haidar remained encamped at Kallimodu, in the district known as Baramahal, watching the movements of the English army. He soon ascertained that the English leader was adopting a system of which he would be able to take advantage, the system of cantoning his army in three places, each at a great distance from the other—Kánchipuram, Wandiwásh, and Trichinápalli. The moment he ascertained that the distribution had been completed, Haidar broke up his camp, captured Tripátúr and Vaniambadi, and laid siege to Ambúr (15th November).

Ambúr was a strong place, situated on the summit of a mountain of pure granite, accessible only on one face, terminating the valley of Baramahal, on the north, and overlooking the fertile valley which, forming a right angle with Baramahal, extends to the eastward down to Vélúr and Arkát. It is about a hundred and ten miles from Madras. When Haidar approached it, it was garrisoned partly by the troops of the native Kiladár, or commandant, partly by a small body of English troops under Captain Calvert.

Again did British skill and British valour baffle Haidar.

* The houses on the Adyar and in other localities outside the fort.

Calvert, despite of the discovered treachery of his native ally, the Kiladár, made an excellent defence, and kept Haidar before the place a time sufficiently long to enable Colonel Smith to re-collect his scattered forces and advance to his relief. Then came the turn of Haidar to fall back. He effected this operation with considerable skill; covered with his own army the retreat of the more disorganised forces of his ally, the Súbahdár; risked a skirmish, to gain this object, with the English at Vaniambadi; then, abandoning that place and Tripátúr, fell back on the previously prepared and strongly fortified position of Kávérípatam.

The fortifications of Kávérípatam were so formidable that Smith, who had closely followed up Haidar, would not, under the circumstances, have ventured to attempt them. But the discord, the divisions, the perplexities, which reigned in the camp of the allies, came soon to relieve him from all anxiety. Haidar maintained a bold front only until his own heavy guns and baggage, and the greater portion of the army of Nizám Alí, with Nizám Ali himself, had had time to re-ascend the gháts leading to the elevated plateau of Bangalor. As soon as he heard that this ascent had been safely accomplished, he followed himself, leaving behind him only a strong division, chiefly cavalry, to watch the English. Again, unwittingly, had he lost an opportunity. He had lost the chance which comes always to those who know how to wait. For the two days previous to his retirement the English army had been without food! His retreat alone enabled them to fall back, in security, to search for it!

The campaign effectually detached Nizám Alí from Haidar. That potentate returned to his alliance with the English. It had further the result of giving birth to a hope of independence amongst the recently subdued chiefs on the Malabár coast. To crush this nascent feeling, Haidar, with great skill and promptitude, transported his army by forced marches before Mangalúr

(May 1768); compelled the bulk of the English garrison* who had been sent to feed the insurrection, to take refuge in their boats; the remainder, consisting of the sick and wounded, to surrender. Having, by this vigorous action, crushed every spark of rebellion on the coast, Haidar re-ascended the gháts, and prepared on the Maisúr plateau for the campaign he intended to inaugurate on the cessation of the rainy season.

Meanwhile the English army, divided into two divisions, led respectively by Colonels Smith and Wood, had been engaged, preparatory to an ascent of the plateau, in driving the garrisons of Haidar from the strong places occupied below the passes, from Vaniambadi on the north to Dindigal and Pálghát on the south-east and south-west. On the 8th June, an advanced division, commanded by Colonel Donald Campbell, ascended the pass to Budikóta, reduced Venkatagadi, and thence opened out the pass leading to the vale of Vélúr. Campbell next bribed the Kiladár of the strong fort of Malwágal, one of the strongest in the country, and with the connivance of that traitor took possession of it. Colonel Smith's main division then advanced, and, joined by Colonel Campbell, took Bághír on the 28th June, and Hussúr (Ossoor) on the 11th July. At this place the army halted, waiting partly for the recovery from sickness of Muhammad Alí, Núwáb of the Karnâtak, who was with it, partly for the appearance of Colonel Wood on the south-western surface of the plateau, and the junction of Murári Rao, from whom a promise of co-operation had been obtained. Murári Rao joined with three thousand horse and two thousand irregular footmen on the 4th August. The very same day saw Haidar Alí, returning from his victorious expedition to the western coast, march into Bangalor.

The two principals in the contest were now within striking

* These who thus embarked consisted of two hundred and forty-one Europeans and twelve hundred sipáhís. The sick and wounded amounted to eighty Europeans and one hundred and eighty sipáhis.

distance—for Hussúr is but twenty-four miles from Bangalor—nor did any great length of time elapse before their troops came in contact. Having assertained that Murári Rao was encamped about half a mile to the right of the English position, Haidar, on the night of the 22nd August, made an attempt to beat him up. The attack failed. Haidar then, having made sufficient provision for the safety of Bangalor, resolved, with the instincts of a great commander, to move with great rapidity to the eastward and overwhelm Wood before that officer could have notice of his approach.

Meanwhile Wood, having completed the conquest of the strong places to the south-west, had returned to Baramahal, and, unsuspicious of danger, was marching through a long defile to Budikóta. Haidar, endeavouring to conceal his movements from Smith, and believing that that officer would be content to await Wood's arrival at Malúr, two marches short of Budikóta, had taken up a position whence he could open an enfilading fire on Wood's men as they should emerge from the defile. He had not calculated, however, on the energy of Colonel Smith. That officer, divining Haidar's plans, far from halting at Malúr, had marched not only to Budikóta, but beyond it, and had taken up, unknown to his enemy, a position on the other side of the defile. Haidar, then, was effectually baffled. Indeed, but for the ill-advised action of Colonel Wood,* which informed him of the vicinity of Smith, and enabled him to make a precipitate retreat, he could scarcely have escaped a great disaster.

The English, after the junction, marched to Kolár, whilst Haidar made a circuitous march at once to recruit his army, and to overawe the vassals whom his ill-success had incited to acts bordering on rebellion. At length he, too, considerably

* On emerging from the defile Wood, who had just received private intimation of the close vicinity of Smith, halted to fire a *feu-de-joie*. This gave the alarm to Haidar and enabled him to escape. Smith so severely reprimanded Wood, that the latter resigned his command. He was replaced by Colonel Lang.

reinforced, approached Kolár. He was not very eager for combat. In every encounter in the field with the English he had been worsted. But something he must attempt. One half of his territories and a large number of his strong places were in the possession of the enemy. Those territories and strong places he must recover. But how?

The answer was not very clear at the moment. Still in the prime of life, he never questioned the possibility of success. But many things made him anxious for a speedy settlement, and, influenced by the hope to obtain one, he made advances to the English. He proposed to pay ten lakhs for the expenses of the war, and to cede to them the country below the passes, known as Baramahal—the country intervening between the passes and the dominions of Muhammad Alí*—between Vaniambadi and Pálghát. The English, however, flushed with victory, and eager for money, pressed upon Haidar the necessity of his paying the entire expenses of the war, calculated at a very extravagant rate, of his yielding tribute to Muhammad Alí, of making concessions to Murári Ráo, and of surrendering a territory very much larger than Baramahal. Haidar, indignant at these demands, broke off the negotiation, and appealed to the God of armies.

The appeal was not made in vain. Rarely have rapacity and extortion met with a prompter punishment. Driven to bay, the wild and untutored genius asserted itself. I have already told how, corrupting the Kiládár, Colonel Campbell had by a stratagem mastered the strong mountain fortress of Malwágal. Adopting the same process of corruption, Haidar now recovered it. Knowing that the English would not permit such an important place to remain in his hands, Haidar then, selecting his choicest troops, moved at their head, unperceived, into a position from which he could operate on an advancing enemy in such a manner as, humanly speaking, to ensure their destruction. His first

* Now constituting the northern portion of the Shélam (Salem) district.

anticipations were realised. The English, eager to recover Malwágal, detached a force under Colonel Wood, now restored to command, to retake it. From his lair Haidar watched his enemy engage himself in the difficult ascent, capture the lower fort, and attempt in vain the stronghold on the summit. The next morning he sent a small and apparently isolated party to skirmish near the English position, with orders to fall back if they should be pursued. Wood fell into the snare, followed the light horsemen who challenged him, until suddenly Haidar was upon him. Never did the soldiers of Maisúr behave better. Emboldened by a confidence which their numbers, their splendid position, the isolation of their enemy, gave them, their infantry charged home with the bayonet—and with effect. They carried point after point, drove the English from one position to another, and were on the very verge of consummating their triumph, when, suddenly, an act of heroism—a stratagem inspired by genius—baffled them. On the English side all was lost, when Captain Brooke, who had been left, wounded, to guard with four weak companies the baggage, the sick, wounded, and followers, in the lower fort, noticing the impending disaster, conceived a plan which, carried out with spirit and vigour, might avert it. He had observed a flat-surfaced rock, rising at the edge of the jungle on the left flank of the enemy. To this rock he moved silently through the jungle with every man who could crawl, and two guns. Unperceived, he mounted the two guns, loaded with grape, on its summit. Then, suddenly, discharging them on the dense masses of the enemy, he showed his detachment, the men waving their caps with joy, and shouting "Smith! Smith!" each shout followed by a hurrah. Haidar's troops, to whom the name of the commander-in-chief of the English army was familiar, seeing the shouting soldiers, rushed to the conclusion that the main army had come up to relieve their comrades. Wood's men drew the same conclusion. The result was a sudden pause in the till then victorious attack on the one side, a return of confidence on the other. Wood drew his men together, took up a stronger position, and opposed a new front to the enemy. Haidar, who had soon discovered the stratagem, was unable to recover the advantages of which its exercise had deprived him. The moral superiority which surprise had given him had vanished. After some more desperate efforts to break the English, he gave up the attack. He had lost, it was surmised, about a thousand men; but he had killed eight officers and two hundred and twenty-nine of his enemy, and had captured two guns. Both sides had expended nearly the whole of their ammunition.

Though he had not succeeded in destroying Wood, Haidar drew good augury from the events of the day. He had numbers on his side, numbers which the resources of the country enabled him to maintain, and he felt that a few more such battles as that of Malwágal would place him in a position to dictate rather than to ask for terms. He maintained his position, then, until fresh supplies of ammunition should reach him.

Meanwhile the conduct of the English was marked by the vacillation which accompanies a divided command. The presence with the army of the Núwáb of the Karnátak, and the position which he assumed as supreme director of the operations, in which the English were to play the part of allies subordinate to himself, had greatly embarrassed Colonel Smith. The embarrassment now reached so great a height that that officer wrote to represent to the Council at Madras the impossibility of carrying on successful operations on such a system. The result was that Muhammad Alí was invited to Madras, avowedly to consult with the Council regarding the plan of the campaign. To deprive the invitation of its real significance, Colonel Smith was asked to accompany him. The command of the army was thus left (14th November) with Colonel Wood, who, being a fair specimen of the class which succeeds, on the strength of vigorous self-assertion and small successes, in establishing a great reputation, was believed by the Council to be their only general.

Meanwhile Haidar, taking advantage of the inactivity which these changes had caused in the English camp, had, after one or two demonstrations, marched rapidly on Hossúr and besieged it. Wood, now commander-in-chief, proceeded at the head of about four thousand men, of whom seven hundred were Europeans, with the usual proportion of artillery and two brass 18-pounders, to relieve the place. He reached Báglúr, about four miles short of it, on the 17th. Leaving in this walled town all his baggage, his stores, his camp-equipage, and the two brass 18-pounders, he set out the same night with the intention of surprising the enemy's camp. But Haidar had been a close observer of his movements. Learning or divining his adversary's expectations, he had withdrawn his troops from the siege, and taken up a position to the north-west of Hossúr. No sooner did he notice that Wood's advanced guard was entering that place, than, masking his operations by a cloud of cavalry, he interposed his whole army between the main body of the English and Báglúr, and, still covered by his cavalry, dashed against that place.

Báglúr was styled a walled town. But its walls, made of mud, were from fifteen to twenty feet high, and but eighteen inches thick at the summit. It was garrisoned by one of Muhammad Alí's best native regiments, commanded by Captain Alexander, and encumbered with the baggage, not yet arranged, which had been left behind by Colonel Wood. Against it, thus in a state of disorder, Haidar dashed with the full strength of his artillery and infantry. He did not dash in vain. The two brass 18-pounders, left outside because the gate was too narrow to admit them, fell first into his hands; the town and the greater part of the baggage followed. Alexander and his regiment had but just time to make their way into the fort. Haidar made no attempt upon that. All his care was directed to see that the captured guns and the spoils were promptly despatched on the road to Bangalor. This done, he followed, knowing well that Colonel Wood, on discovering the ruse to which he had been a victim, would promptly retrace his steps.

It was so, indeed. Some hours elapsed before Wood had ascertained the direction taken by Haidar's infantry and artillery, but the moment the conviction flashed upon him he returned to Báglúr. He arrived there to see in the extreme distance Haidar's army *en route* to Bangalor, driving before it his two heavy guns, some two thousand of his draught bullocks, and nearly the whole of his stores, baggage, and camp equipage. He could not follow him. Uncertain how to act, he threw the stores and ammunition that remained to him into Hossúr and then marched—the evening of the 21st—to Alyá, on the road to Kolár, where there was a small further supply. On his march thither, Haidar, who had safely disposed of his trophes, suddenly attacked him. Wood, whose dash and energy up to this point had led him into misfortune, now tried opposite tactics, and, when a vigorous charge might have forced a passage for himself and his men, contended himself with a defensive attitude—an attitude which, without bettering his position, cost him before nightfall seven officers, twenty Europeans, and two hundred sipáhís. But Haidar had not finished with him. Knowing the real character of the man, he, as soon as the shades of evening fell, made a show of retreating to a distant position. Wood, deceived as to his real intentions, thought the moment opportune to complete the movement he had begun in the afternoon. Accordingly, about 10 o'clock at night, he gave the order to advance. Scarcely, however, had he cleared the ground on which he had fought, than Haidar was upon him. All night long was he engaged in repulsing attacks on his rear and on his flank. When day broke a fresh column of the enemy appeared in his front. Wood was now compelled to halt and place his men amongst the rocks, with which the country abounded, their faces to the enemy. Here for several hours they offered a gallant and successful resistance. About noon, however, their ammunition all but exhausted, utterly worn out, they were on the point of succumbing, when Haidar, apparently to them without cause, drew off his troops. Good cause, however, had Haidar. A relieving force, gallantly led by Major Fitzgerald, appeared on his flank. Leaving his work unfinished, he drew off his troops, and returned towards Báglúr.

Fitzgerald's movement was one of those brilliant deeds which stamp an officer. It was entirely spontaneous. Rumour had brought to him, at Venkatagadi, where he was posted with a small force, intelligence of the surprise at Báglúr. Deeming that Wood's position might be critical, he called in all his detachments and marched in the direction he thought it likely he would take. The firing on the morning of the 22nd fixed that direction beyond a doubt. He pushed on, and arrived just in time to save the British force from destruction.

The events of those four days had completely shattered the only general of the Madras Council. On the representation by Fitzgerald of the state of the army, Wood was removed from command, and was replaced by Colonel Lang. Haidar, who was kept well informed of all the movements in the British camp, no sooner learned that an officer other than Smith* had succeeded Wood, than he prepared to execute the plan he had long meditated, the plan which of all others commended itself to his natural genius, that of carrying the war into the enemy's country.

Most effectually did he pursue that plan. Remaining for the moment himself on the plateau of Maisúr, he despatched his best general, Fazal úllah Khán, with instructions to burst upon the lowland country by the gateway of Koimbatúr (Coim-

* Haidar was in the habit of saying that he would always avoid, if possible, fighting with Smith, but that he would fight Wood wherever he might meet him.

batore). That officer, feeling his way, set out in November at the head of a well-organised party of seven thousand infantry and cavalry, well provided with guns, forced the passes of Kávéripúram and Gujalhati, occupied Koimbatúr on the 4th December, and, pushing on south-eastwards to Dárapuram, drove the sipáhí garrison, commanded by Captain Johnson, from that place to the very gates of Trichinápalli. Haidar himself, on learning from his lieutenant that Koimbatúr had been secured, descended eastward by the passes of Pállikód and Tapúr into Baramahal. He was preceded by crowds of emissaries, who spread the information far and wide that he had destroyed the British army, and was now marching to the conquest of Madras. The ruse completely discouraged the garrisons, consisting mostly of the Núwáb's sipáhís, of the strong places, and these fell before him with a rapidity scarcely surpassed by that which characterised the yielding of the garrisons of the strong places of Prussia after the defeats of Jena and Auerstadt. Lang, as soon as he had received information of the movement, had despatched Fitzgerald with a well-equipped corps of five thousand men, of whom one-fifth were Europeans, to follow the daring ruler of Maisúr. Fitzgerald, notwithstanding his rapid marches, could for a long time only trace the course of Haidar by the places which had surrendered to him. At one time he arrived almost within striking distance of him; but Haidar, by a skilful movement, induced his adversary to march to Trichinápalli, in the belief that he himself was about to attack that stronghold; then, profiting by his adversary's error, he took possession of the considerable town of Kárúr, and pressed forward thence to invest the more strongly garrisoned Yiród (Erode).

Then occurred an event previously unparalleled in the history of English wars in India. On his march to Yiród, Haidar intercepted, attacked, and completely destroyed a detachment of fifty Europeans and two hundred sipáhís, sent from that place to procure supplies from Kárúr. Flushed with his victory, he pressed on to Yiród, and, displaying a flag of truce, demanded the services of an English surgeon. The surgeon came, dressed the wounded, and returned. Haidar then, again under a flag of truce, requested that Captain Orton, the commandant, would come out to confer with him regarding the capitulation of the place, promising him that he might return if terms were not agreed to. Orton, who, it is said, had dined, complied. At the interview which followed, Haidar pointed out to Orton that the officer second to him in command, Captain Robinson, had violated his parole, by carrying arms against him after having given his word not to serve during the remainder of the war; and added that the dereliction in this respect of Robinson absolved him from the maintenance of his own promise. He therefore required Orton to write an order to Robinson for the surrender of the place, engaging in that case for the safe conduct of the whole garrison to Trichinápalli. Orton resisted for twenty-four hours, but in the end he yielded to pressure, and Yiród surrendered.

Having thus, by his daring march, recovered, in the space of six weeks, the whole of the country which it had taken the English two campaigns to wrest from him, two untenable places excepted, Haidar despatched the corps of Fazal Ullah to operate from Dindigal upon the provinces of Madura and Tinnevéli, whilst, crossing the Kávérí, he directed his own march to the eastward, along the northern bank of that river. It was whilst he was engaged in this march (January 1769) that the Madras Government, bitterly regretting the insanity which had prompted them to refuse the fair terms pressed upon them by Haidar in the month of August preceding, made advances for an accommodation.

Negociations followed. Captain Brooke, an officer of high character and ability, was deputed to the camp of the great warrior, and was at once accorded an interview. The conversation which followed was of a most interesting character. Haidar, who could be frank and straightforward when it suited his purpose, opened his whole soul to his visitor. He told him plainly that their ally, the Núwáb of the Karnátak, had been alike the cause of the war, the cause of the rejection of his offers in August, and that he would be the cause of its continuance; that he had ever wished and tried to be on terms of solid friendship with the English, but that Muhammad Alí had always baffled his efforts. Proving his case by references to facts which could not be denied, he expressed his willingness still to make peace with the English, if they would exclude Muhammad Alí from their councils, negotiate for their own interests only, and send Colonel Smith, or a Member of Council, with full powers to treat. He added that the moment was especially critical; that the Maráthás were at the very moment contemplating an invasion of southern India; that he would much prefer to ally himself with the English against that marauding people; but that he could not consent to be the victim of both; if the English refused his alliance, he was bound to accept that of the Maráthás. Captain Brooke found it difficult to gainsay any of these assertions; but he had no power to treat on so broad a basis. He could only forward to Madras a detailed account of the conversation, and await instructions. The result, after a vain attempt to induce Haidar to accept terms falling far short of his own proposals, was the despatch to the British camp of Colonel Smith and Mr. Andrews, the former to assume command of the army, the latter to proceed to Haidar's camp to negotiate. After some tedious delays, Mr. Andrews agreed to convey personally to Madras the terms beyond which Haidar would not give way, and a truce of twelve days was agreed upon to await the reply of the Council. That reply proved unfavourable, and hostilities were resumed on the 6th March.

Haidar was equal to the occasion. Knowing that the Madras Council, alarmed for the safety of Madras, had, in the manner of the Aulic Council, invested Colonel Smith with very restricted powers, he resolved to strike a blow which they should feel. After some manœuvres designed to puzzle the enemy, he marched with his whole army southward, to draw away the English. Smith, believing it to be Haidar's intention to march southward, then to turn suddenly and pounce upon Madras by the route followed by Paradis in 1746, felt bound to follow his army. No sooner had the rival forces reached a point nearly a hundred and forty miles south of Madras, than Haidar struck his blow. Directing his main body to retire through the pass of Ahtúr, as if marching westward, he, with a select body of six thousand horsemen and two hundred of his choicest infantry,* dashed suddenly at the Presidency town. Marching a hundred and thirty miles in three days and a half, he found himself with his cavalry, on the 29th March, within five miles of Madras.† He at once despatched a letter to the Governor, stating that he had come for peace, and requesting that Mr. Dupré, whose character he esteemed, might be sent to him to negotiate. The Governor complied, and Mr. Dupré was sent to St. Thomas's Mount, where Haidar had his quarters. Orders were at the same time transmitted to Colonel Smith to abstain from hostilities, and to halt at a fixed distance—in excess of thirty miles—from Haidar's main army.

Haidar, in fact, was master of the situation. The native town and the private houses of Madras were at his mercy. In the panic which his arrival had caused, the fort itself might have fallen. He was in a position to dictate his own terms, and, virtually, he did dictate them.

The main provisions of this treaty were as follow:—1st, That all hostilities should cease between the contracting parties and their allies; 2nd, That in case of either of the contracting

* Formed of men such as are now in the Maisúr palace who can run their ten miles in the hour.

† The infantry arrived the following morning.

parties being attacked, they should, from their respective countries, mutually assist each other to drive the enemy out; 3rd, That the treaty should include the Presidency of Bombay; 4th, That all prisoners taken on both sides should be promptly released; 5th, That all conquests made on both sides should be restored, except the fort of Kárúr and its districts, which would be held by Haidar. With the Núwáb of the Karnátak, Muhammad Alí, Haidar persistently refused to negotiate. The difficulty was solved by the English negotiating in their own name, for their own possessions and the Karnátak—Muhammad Alí agreeing officially to signify his consent to the procedure—a promise which, by the way, he did not keep.

I must pass lightly over the next eleven years. In their course, Haidar was invaded by the Maráthás; invoked, and was refused, the assistance of the English; made, after a bad defeat, a disadvantageous peace with the invaders; then conquered and annexed Kúrg (Coorg); then avenged himself on the Maráthás, and recovered more than he had lost; seized the Ballári districts and Gutti; extended his dominions southwards; discussed with the Maráthás a scheme for a general alliance against the English, but, his clear vision recognising the certain ascendancy of that people, offered to them an alliance whereby, yielding to them on the east, for a sum of twenty lakhs of rupees, the lowland districts of Baramahal, of Shélam (Salem), and of Ahtúr, he should keep for ever the Maisúr plateau, and the country to the coast on the west. The rejection of these terms made him resolve to drive the British from southern India. With this view he turned his earnest attention to the French—now recovering their influence—and between whom and the English hostilities were now impending.

In 1778 the expected war between the rival European nations broke out in India. Before Haidar was ready to intervene, Pondichery, beleaguered on the 8th August, had fallen (18th

October). Flushed with their victory, the English sent their fleet to attack Mahé.

The conquest by the English of a town such as Pondichery, on the eastern coast, separated by large tracts of territory from his own possessions, had only caused to Haidar the regret which is naturally produced in the mind of a man by the strengthening of his enemies and the weakening of his friends. But the case of Mahé was far different. On the western coast, contiguous to his own dominions, the possession of Mahé by the English would be a standing threat to himself. It would give them an eye to see, a base whence to strike at his very heart. When, therefore, the Governor of Madras intimated to Haidar his intention of sending an expedition to reduce Mahé, the ruler of Maisúr replied explicitly that he should regard such an attack as a breach of the understanding which had placed the possessions of the European powers on the western coast virtually under his protection, and that in the event of the Governor carrying out his intention he should retaliate by detaching a body of troops to lay waste the province of Arkát. Undeterred by this declaration the Governor of Madras persisted in his determination. The English fleet sailed, and, in spite of the fact that Haidar displayed the Maisúr standard on the walls of Mahé, took possession of the place (March 1779). As soon as Mahé had fallen, the Governor, to still the resentment of Haidar, despatched an envoy to offer explanations and excuses. The envoy selected was Mr. Gray, formerly of the Bengal Civil Service. Whilst in his selection of that gentleman no fault can be found with the Governor and Council of Madras, it must be admitted that the offerings with which he was charged were of a nature to convey at once insult and contempt. To the powerful prince, accustomed to receive handsome presents, the Madras Government sent only a saddle and a gun; the former not only made of pigskin, and therefore totally unsuited as a present to a Muhammadan, but of such a shape that to ride upon it would have been a trial. Nor was the gun much better. It was made to load at the breech; but the ammunition sent with it could only be used, and used ineffectually, in the ordinary manner. Haidar, who, in his reception of Mr. Gray, had displayed considerable temper, returned these valuable presents. In the interview which followed,* he plainly told the British envoy that he had satisfied himself that the English were a people whom no treaties could bind; that in 1769 he had come to terms with them, and that they had promised to aid him in case he should be attacked; but that when, the following year, he was attacked by the Maráthás and demanded the promised aid, it was refused him; that, since then, the English had conquered Tanjúr, though that place had been guaranteed by treaty; on various occasions had afforded aid to his rebellious subjects; and, with respect to Mahé, had deliberately chosen a course which they knew must lead to war. Haidar concluded with these significant words: "Formerly I was of opinion that the English excelled all other nations in sincerity and good faith; but, from late experience, I am convinced that they have no longer any pretensions to those virtues." Mr. Gray was dismissed without further audience.

Once resolved on war, Haidar determined it should be war with a vengeance—a war which should exterminate his enemies. He assembled at Bangalor an army, eighty-three thousand strong, extremely efficient in all its departments, attached to it a corps of four hundred Frenchmen, and in June set forth on his expedition. Of all the wars undertaken against the foreigner in southern India, this was the most popular. For its success, fervent prayers were offered alike in the mosques of the Muhammadans and the temples of the Hindús. The in-

* It was not, properly speaking, an interview, for Haidar declined to see Gray. A confidant of Haidar's conveyed to Haidar the envoy's explanations and to the envoy the replies which Haidar dictated.

habitants of the villages through which his army passed turned out to help the national leader, to invoke for him the protection of heaven. In the person of Haidar were concentrated the hopes of the populations of southern India.

Descending the passes, and marching through the territories below them, Haidar maintained the most perfect order and discipline. It was only when he entered the country which formed the semicircle of which Madras was the centre—the country peculiarly British—that he marked his advance by merciless desolation, by the burning of towns and villages, and the deportation of the population. The English, so bold in their action regarding Mahé, had made no preparations to meet the war, of the breaking out of which—if they should persist in that action—Haidar had fairly warned them. Almost before they had made a single movement in their defence, Haidar had established his head-quarters at Kánchipuram (Conjeveram), forty-two miles from Madras.

Information that Haidar, with his centre and part of his right wing, was at Kánchipuram; that his left wing, commanded by his son, Típú Sáhib, was proceeding by forced marches towards Guntúr; that a portion of his right wing, under his second son, Karím Sáhib, had penetrated to Porto Novo, some twenty-five miles from Fort St. David, reached Madras on the 24th July. At that date the forces at the disposal of the Government at Madras and in its immediate vicinity, consisted of the 73rd Highlanders, the Madras European Regiment, four regiments of sipáhís, and some artillerymen, in all five thousand two hundred and nine men. But at Guntúr, two hundred and twenty-five miles from Madras, Colonel Baillie was stationed with a corps amounting, of all arms, to two thousand eight hundred and thirteen men, and, on the first news of the outbreak of hostilities, orders had been transmitted to him to march with all haste to Kánchipuram, at which place he would be joined by the whole available English force from Madras. Yet, so dilatory had been the proceedings of the English, and so rapidly had Haidar moved, that the latter had occupied the place appointed for the junction, Kánchipuram, before Baillie had set out from Guntúr, whilst Típú Sáhib was on his way to that place, and before an English soldier had moved from St. Thomas's Mount!

Here was a dilemma! Who were the men at Madras capable of meeting it?

The Commander-in-Chief of the Madras army was the Hector Munro whom we have seen so daring, so eager to court danger, so ready in resources, so calm and cool under fire, when combating the Núwáb-Vazír of Awadh at Baksar. When I introduced him on that occasion to the reader, I stated that the daring tactics which were admirably adapted to the occasion then under record, might be turned against himself by a resolute and watchful enemy. The occasion had now arrived for Munro to show whether to the brilliant qualities of the dashing leader he added the cautious skill of the tactician, whether acting with vigour he could act also without passion.

It so happened that the then existing law required that the Commander-in-Chief should remain at Madras itself, to complete the complement of the Members of Council. Were that law to be enforced, the command of the troops in the field would devolve upon Lord M'Leod, an officer who had just arrived from England in command of the 73rd; and, in fact, this officer did receive the order to proceed to Kánchipuram, to effect there the designed junction with Baillie. But Lord M'Leod was far too clear-headed a man to carry out, without remonstrance, a military movement which, in his opinion, would involve the English force in a destruction extending possibly to Madras itself. In a remarkably able and judicious letter he pointed out the inevitable consequences to Baillie of still insisting upon the junction at Kánchipuram, and urged that that officer should be at once directed to change his course to Madras. This opinion so nettled the Commander-in-Chief that he resolved to assume the command himself, and to prove practically that his own opinion was correct. An illegal arrangement was made to complete the quorum in Council, and Sir Hector Munro assumed the command of the army in the field. Before setting out, he directed Colonel Braithwaite, who commanded at Pondichery, to move with his force of fifteen hundred men of all arms to Chengalpatt, and thence to Madras; and Colonel Cosby, who was at Trichinápalli, to march with his force of two thousand sipáhís, two regiments of the Núwáb's native infantry, and two guns, from the north bank of the Kolrún, to act on the enemy's communications. We shall see that the dispositions of Haidar rendered it impossible for either of these officers to carry out their orders. Having issued them, and equipped his force, Munro set out, on 25th August, for Kánchipuram.

Meanwhile, Haidar had not been idle. Leaving Kánchipuram he had, on the 12th August, invested Wandiwásh, a town to the south-west of Madras and Chengalpatt, distant from the former seventy-two miles, and from Arkât thirty-eight. Its central position thus invested it with a vast importance, and Haidar was so sensible of its value that he had purchased its native commandant, who had agreed to deliver it up on the appearance of Haidar's army before it.

But, this time, the presence of mind and daring of a single Englishman baffled Haidar. The record is remarkable, though happily not unique, in the history of our country. Colonel Braithwaite, who, we have seen, had received orders to march from Pondichery to Chengalpatt, was well aware that the occupation of Wandiwásh by the enemy would checkmate him, and that the only chance he had—a slender chance at the best—of preventing that occupation was to detach an officer, upon whom he could depend, to replace the Kiladár in the command. He selected for this purpose Lieutenant Flint, an officer whose name betokened his resolute and daring character. Flint, accompanied by a hundred sipáhís, made a rapid and fatiguing march across unfrequented paths, successfully avoided the enemy's army, then hovering round the place, and reached the vicinity of Wandiwásh the forenoon of the 11th August. He at once sent a message to the Kiladár announcing his approach, and demanding admission. The Kiladár, already bought by Haidar, returned for reply that he would be fired upon if he should attempt to come within range of the fort's guns, and sent a party to stop him at the verge of the esplanade. Flint, however, advanced, and meeting the party, used the influence which prestige had already secured for the European in India to persuade the officer in command of it that he had mistaken his orders. He continued to advance pending a reply to the reference made to the Kiladár; again, when that reply was unsatisfactory, pending an answer to a second, until he had arrived within musket-shot of the ramparts, which were lined with troops; the gates, also, were shut. Flint then halted, and sent a message to the Kiladár to the effect that he had a letter from the Núwáb, his master, which he was authorised to deliver into his hands only. The Kiladár, after some hesitation, agreed to receive the letter in the space between the gate and the barrier of the sortie. To this space Flint was admitted with four attendants; men whom he had fully instructed as to his intentions. He found the Kiladár seated on a carpet, attended by his officers, thirty swordsmen, and a guard of a hundred men. After the usual compliments, Flint admitted that he had no letter from the Núwáb, but merely the order of his own Government written in communication with Muhammad Alí, which was fully equivalent to a letter; and that the order directed him to assume command of the place. The Kiladár treated the pretension with derision, and, angry at having been, as he perceived, duped into a conference, ordered Flint to return whence he came.

But Flint was equal to the occasion. As the Kiladár, his

wrath rapidly increasing, was in the act of rising to his feet, Flint suddenly seized him, and declared that he would kill anyone who dared to wag a finger on his behalf. The four sipáhís backed the movement by bringing their bayonets to the charge. The suddenness of the action, its daring, the surprise it caused, and, above all, the prestige of the European, paralysed the followers of the Kiladár. Before they could recover from that paralysis, the English sipáhís admitted their comrades, and the fort was won!

No single act in the war contributed so much to save southern India as this act of Lieutenant Flint. Had Wandiwásh then fallen, it had gone hard, after the events I am about to describe, with Madras. For Flint, on the eve of the investment of the place, not only seized it; he, the only Englishman behind its walls, held it for seventy-eight days—from the 12th August 1780 to the 12th February 1781—against the flower of Haidar Alí's army. He found it in a ruinous state, with many guns, indeed, but with no carriages and little gunpowder, and without one artilleryman. His energy supplied every want; he repaired the works, constructed carriages, manufactured gunpowder, trained gunners, raised a corps of cavalry for exterior enterprise, and not only fed his own garrison, but procured supplies and intelligence for the main British army. Flint effected for Wandiwásh what Eldred Pottinger effected for Herát in 1839. His work was, practically, even more beneficial to the interests of England, inasmuch as Wandiwásh was nearer the heart of her possessions. It was the shield whith protected Madras.*

Haidar, baffled by this gallant Englishman, left the flower of

* Colonel Wilks, who is my principal authority for the details on the text states that for the immensely important service rendered by Lieutenant Flint —a service which in these modern days, if one may judge by the rewards showered upon men for doing their simple duty, would obtain crosses and distinctions without number—that officer had the barren glory of receiving letters, written with his own hand, from Sir Eyre Coote, full of affectionate attachment and admiration. The Court of Directors refused even to bestow upon him a brevet!

his troops to prosecute the siege of Wandiwásh, and proceeded with the remainder to Arkát. This place he invested on the 21st August. He was still engaged before it when he received intelligence which determined him to strike a blow such as would make the English reel.

Somewhat uncertain as to the route which Baillie would take from Guntúr, and never anticipating that so experienced a commander as Sir Hector Munro would leave him without support, Haidar had recalled to the main body the corps under Típú Sáhib, and that corps, composed mainly of the *élite* of his cavalry, was with him before Arkát. On the 29th, however, information reached him that whilst Munro was marching on Kánchipuram, and would probably reach that place that very day, he had held out no hand to Baillie, but had directed him, when he had arrived six miles south of Gumadipundi, almost under cover of Madras—within twenty-seven miles of it in fact, and two easy marches from his own camping ground—to proceed by a circuitous route, a route covering upwards of fifty miles, and which would sever him entirely from the main army, to Kánchipuram. There were no advantages, speculative or other, to be gained by this deviation. The only explanation that has ever been offered for it is that Sir Hector Munro had declared that a junction at Kánchipuram was feasible; that to demonstrate that proposition he had placed himself, *ultra vires*, at the head of the army; and that he was resolved that the junction should take place at Kánchipuram, and nowhere else. In the presence of a skilful tactician like Haidar, it was playing with edged tools, and Haidar soon made him feel it.

The very instant he heard it, Haidar, exclaiming, "At last I have them!" broke up his camp, and detaching his son Típú, at the head of five thousand regular infantry, six thousand horse, twelve light and six heavy guns, to intercept Baillie, moved with his main body to Kánchipuram, and on the 3rd September encamped within six miles of Munro's army, which he thus held in check. Munro, in fact, had exhausted his supplies, and the Núwáb's agent having refused to procure any for him, he was in a manner chained to the vicinity of Kánchipuram.

Haidar maintained his position before the English army for nearly two days. On the afternoon of the second day a despatch from Típú reached him, to the effect that on the following morning, the 6th, he should attack Baillie. Haidar then broke up his camp, and, with the view of interposing his main army between Munro and the combatants, made as though he intended to turn the English right. Munro, completely deceived, refused his right wing, and thus allowed Haidar, without striking a blow, to interpose his whole army between himself and his lieutenant.

Meanwhile Baillie, obeying the orders he had received from Munro, had quitted his encampment near Gumadipundi on the 25th, and marched nearly eleven miles to the river Kortelaur. The bed of this river being nearly dry and little more than three hundred yards wide, Baillie might easily have crossed it. But deeming that to be always feasible which at the moment was easy, he carelessly pitched his camp on the left or northern bank. Rightly was he punished. During the night a storm arose, the rains of the north-eastern monsoon fell with more than their wonted force, and, when the day broke, the bed which had been nearly dry the previous evening was covered by a roaring torrent. For ten days Baillie was chained by this torrent to the northern bank. On the 4th September he crossed, and on the morning of the 6th reached Parmbákam, fourteen miles from Munro's position at Kánchipuram.

The reader will understand the position. The left of the English force at Kanchipuram; its right at Parmbákam, with Haidar between the two, ready to fall upon the left the moment it should show the smallest indication to assist the right, round which Típú Sáhib was hovering. Haidar had, in fact, executed one of those manœuvres which twenty-four years later were to characterise the first campaign of the greatest general the world has ever seen!

Meanwhile Típú, covered by a cloud of cavalry, had followed the movements of Baillie from the banks of the Kortelaur, waiting only for a favourable moment to attack him. On the 5th he wrote to his father that the English would encamp the day following at Parmbákam, and that as the ground there offered peculiar facilities for the movements of cavalry he would attack him. At 11 o'clock that day he kept his word.

Had Típú attacked with the vigour and energy displayed invariably by his father, there had been an end, then and there, of Baillie's detachment. But, it is strange, just as the bigoted Aurangzíb has left a far deeper and more lasting recollection in the minds of the Muhammadans of northern India than his infinitely greater ancestor—the wise and liberal Akbar—so in southern India the memory of the cruel, narrow-minded, and bigoted Típú Sáhib is revered much more than the memory of his able and liberal-minded father. The reason is not far to seek. Akbar and Haidar were very lax in their religious exercises. The descendant of the one and the son of the other were narrow-minded bigots. Bigotry rules the Muhammadan world. And though the bigots lost the empires which their far-sighted and liberal ancestors had won, the Muhammadan world has pardoned the temporal loss, and, whilst it pays no heed to the qualities of the founders, still venerates the piety of those who undid the founders' work!

Típú, cruel and vulgarly ambitious, possessed none of the great qualities of his father. He was a poor soldier; never, as had been the wont of Haidar, inspiring his soldiers by personal leading. He did not lead, he sent his soldiers to the attack.

On this occasion, at Parmbákam, he fought as though he dreaded a hand-to-hand encounter. His cavalry charged and charged, but did not charge home. They charged, expecting that the English would give way. But when, after three hours' fighting, they did not give way; when to every charge they replied with a volley; Típú renounced the attack, and sent to his father to say he could do nothing without reinforcements, that he had lost from two to three hundred men and had made no impression. The position of Baillie was scarcely improved. He had, it is true, repulsed the attack; but he had lost about a hundred men; he could not move in the face of the overwhelming cavalry force of Típú. He wrote at once to this effect to Munro, and begged him to march to his assistance.

Now, this was just the one thing which Munro conceived he could not do. Haidar barred the way with an army enormously superior. That army he could not attack with any chance of success. Besides, he could not move without sacrificing his heavy guns and the supplies he had stored in the pagoda of Kánchipuram, and for which he had not sufficient carriage. But he could not leave Baillie to his fate. Whilst, therefore, he opposed a bold front to Haidar, he detached—on the evening of the day on which the letter was received, the 8th September —four companies of Europeans and eleven of sipáhís, in all a thousand and seven men, under the command of Colonel Fletcher, to effect a junction with Baillie. He hoped that this movement would escape the vigilance of Haidar.

Haidar, well served by his spies, knew that Fletcher's detachment was about to set out long before it had left the camp; he knew to a man its strength and its composition; and he had taken care to provide for it guides upon whom he could depend. He allowed it, then, to march, without making any corresponding movement, feeling sure that his own guides would lead it into a position in which he could overwhelm and destroy it. He had calculated every eventuality, save one: he had not taken into account the natural intelligence of the British officer. The critics of modern days have said some very hard things against the officers of the unreformed British army. But history has never recorded actions displaying greater intelligence, greater devotion, and greater courage, than those which in India and on the continent of Europe secured for those officers an eternal renown.

Colonel Fletcher was a fair type of the officers of the unreformed army. Before setting out, he had reconnoitred the position held by Haidar; had noted in his mind the bearings of the country. Riding in front with the guides he observed that, after a time, they took a road which, he felt sure, must lead him into the heart of the enemy's camp. Divining at once the treachery intended to be practised, he took upon himself to change the route, then, making a detour, passed unperceived the outlying parties of the enemy, and reached Baillie's camp early on the morning of the 9th. It was no slight feat thus to have outwitted Haidar!

This reinforcement raised Baillie's force to three thousand seven hundred and twenty men, and inspired Baillie himself with the fullest confidence. He allowed the new arrivals to rest during that day, whilst he made preparations to march an hour after sunset, so as to accomplish the fourteen miles which separated him from his chief before daybreak. Whilst he is making those preparations, I propose to return to Haidar.

That veteran soldier recognised very soon that Fletcher had outwitted him. Although furious at his disappointment, he did not allow the circumstance to disturb him. Again did he review his position. In front of him was the weakened force of Munro, now less than ever capable of fighting him. Fourteen miles away to his left was the augmented force of Baillie, watched by Típú's horsemen. But Típú had proved unequal to Baillie before the latter had been reinforced, and it seemed to Haidar probable that if he himself should attempt to crush Munro, Baillie, beating aside Típú, might be upon him before he had succeeded. On the other hand, should he send his infantry to reinforce Típú, Munro, informed of their departure, might attack him. Under these circumstances he endeavoured, by various means, to fathom the intentions of Munro. Soon there accumulated in his mind evidence sufficient to convince him that Munro had no intention of separating himself from his heavy guns and supplies in Kánchipuram. This conviction decided him. That night (the 9th) he detached the bulk of his infantry to reinforce Típú. At 4 o'clock in the morning, noticing that Munro had not taken the alarm, he followed himself.

The very same hour which saw his infantry set out, witnessed the departure of Baillie from Parmbákam, harassed and cannonaded, but not closely attacked, by Típú. Baillie had already covered six miles out of the fourteen, when, suddenly, without any reason, and in opposition to the earnest and repeated advice of his second in command, Colonel Fletcher, he gave the order to halt for the night. It has been conjectured that this order was prompted by Baillie's desire to exhibit his troops fresh, and with all their equipments, at Kánchipuram in the morning; that, judging from the manner in which he had baffled the opposition offered during the first six miles, he felt he need entertain no apprehension regarding the remainder. He reckoned, however, without Haidar. Scarcely had his men piled their arms, when the trained infantry despatched by the latter, joined Típú. Típú spent the remainder of the night in concerting with the commander of these troops, with the senior French officers M. de Lally and M. Pinorin, and, by means of messengers, with Haidar himself, the mode of attack for the morrow.

The plan they adopted was as follows:—To occupy in force a strong position about two miles in front of the English position, and commanding the road which they must traverse. That road lay through an avenue of trees on to a plain, three quarters of a mile beyond which was a village. They proceeded further, then, to place the main body of their infantry in that village, whilst they erected batteries to command the road leading from the avenue across the plain. Ignorant of these preparations, Baillie marched from his bivouac at daybreak, traversed the avenue, and debouched on to the plain. Scarcely had his columns emerged when, for the first time that morning, an artillery-fire opened upon them. Baillie, instead of pressing on to the village, which might have yielded to a charge, halted his troops, and returned the fire with his guns. Finding, however, very quickly, that the enemy's fire was superior to his own, he sent to the front ten companies of sipáhís to storm the battery which specially annoyed him. This feat the sipáhís, led by their English officers, performed with great gallantry and success. They stormed the battery and had spiked three of the guns, when the Maisúr cavalry, dashing from the flank and threatening to cut off their retreat, forced them to fall back. The English troops, forming into an oblong square, as it is styled, then made a forward movement. They had proceeded but a short distance, however, when, covered by the cavalry, the Maisúr infantry and artillery advanced, and, after a short interval, from three sides—from the front, from the right, and from the rear—poured upon them a deadly fire of all arms. The fierceness of the attack proved that Haidar himself had joined his son.

Still the English square—the sick, the baggage, and the ammunition in the centre—moved slowly on; its human walls repelling every assault. Its behaviour compelled the admiration of the Frenchmen who fought with Típú.* So stern was the resistance, that Haidar, dreading every moment

* One of the French officers present thus recorded his opinion:—"In the whole of this trying day the English preserved a coolness of manœuvre which would have done honour to any troops in the world. Raked by the fire of an immense artillery, the greatest part of the action within grape-shot distance; attacked on all sides by not less than twenty-five thousand horse, and thirty battalions of sipáhis, besides Haidar's European troops, the English column stood firm, and repulsed every attack with great slaughter; the horse driven back on the infantry, the right of our line began to give way, though composed of the best troops in the Maisúr army."

lest Munro should appear on his rear, resolved to retreat, and sent orders to his cavalry to cover the movement.

But just at this moment two events happened which induced him to recall the order. The first of these was the blowing up of two tumbrils in the English square; the second, the almost instantaneous charge, on the face most affected by the explosion, of a thousand Maráthá horse, led by a man to whom Haidar had attributed the blame of Colonel Fletcher's escape, and who was determined to retrieve his good name or perish. That charge, though fatal to its leader, was decisive. It broke the face of the square.* The remainder of the enemy's cavalry followed it up in so decisive a manner as to render all rallying impossible. The Europeans, indeed, closing their ranks, attempted for some time longer to resist. But the attempt was vain. After a time, Colonel Baillie, seeing further resistance fruitless, ordered his men to lay down their arms, and surrendered.

The loss of the English had been very great. Of the entire force of five hundred Europeans, two hundred only remained alive, and many of these were wounded. The sipáhís suffered in at least equal proportion. Of eighty-six officers, thirty-six were killed and thirty-four were wounded. But the loss in killed and wounded was insignificant when compared with the loss of prestige.

Whilst this desperate fighting was going on, where was Munro?

We have seen that Munro had remained quiet during the whole day and night of the 9th. Soon after daybreak on the 10th, he perceived that Haidar had given him the slip. He at once broke up his camp and took the road to Parmbákam. After marching two or three miles he saw in the distance the smoke of the battle; about a mile further, a still greater smoke,

* A large painting of this stage of the fight, done by his own express orders, adorns, to the present day, one of the walls of Típú's summer palace, close to Shrirangapatam.

evidently that caused by the explosion of the tumbrils. Munro was then about three miles distant from the battle-field. Obviously, he should have pushed on with all speed. We have seen that that was the very movement which Haidar most of all dreaded. Munro was at first inclined to pursue this course, but almost immediately afterwards he was sensible of a lull in the artillery-fire, succeeded by desultory discharges of musketry. At this conjuncture he would seem to have lost his head. Coming to the somewhat arbitrary conclusion that the sounds which reached him betokened a victory on the part of Baillie, he checked his forward march, and moved in every direction but the right one, until, when it was too late to alter the result, he learned the truth from a wounded sipáhí. Then—to use the words of his own despatch—"for the security of the army, he retired to Kánchipuram," having spent his day very much in the same unsatisfactory manner in which, in the next century, Count d'Erlon was to spend his, on the 16th June 1815, and with the same unsatisfactory result. Munro reached Kánchipuram at 6 o'clock in the evening.

But he did not deem himself safe at Kánchipuram. Having spent the day in fruitless marching and counter-marching, he passed the night in throwing his heavy guns, his military stores, and the supplies he could not carry away, into a deep tank. Early the following morning, the 11th, he set out in the direction of Chengalpatt, where, annoyed and harassed by Haidar's light troops on the march, and forced, in consequence, to sacrifice the greater part of the stores still remaining to him, he arrived on the morning of the 12th. He was cheered there by the sight of Colonel Cosby's detachment, which, having been unable to execute the orders given to it to act upon the enemy's communications, had cut its way to the same place. This happy junction saved Madras. Munro felt strong enough now to march to St. Thomas's Mount. He arrived there on the 14th, and moved the next day to the securer position of Mámillamma (Marmalong), where, with a river covering his front, he deemed himself safe from all attack.

Haidar, on the 11th September, had Madras at his mercy. The direct road to it lay open, and there was not a soldier in the place. He was only forty-two miles distant from it. He knew the line of Munro's retreat, and he could easily so interpose his cavalry as to hinder, if not absolutely to prevent, that officer's march from Chengalpatt, thirty-six miles south-west of Madras. But one thing prevented him from making this decisive movement, and that was the holding out of Wandiwásh. The flower of his army was still detained before that place, and he hesitated to make the decisive movement till it had fallen. His reasoning would not have commended itself to a really great captain. A master of the art of war would have told him that the greater contains the less; that the surest way of compelling the fall of Wandiwásh was to make a dash—before it could be covered, before the panic caused by his victory over Baillie had subsided—upon Madras. But age was beginning to tell upon Haidar. Shrinking from a course at which ten years before he would have clutched, he proceeded to invest Arkát.

Arkát, invested on the 19th September, fell—though garrisoned by English troops—on the 3rd November; Ambúr surrendered on the 13th January: the sieges of Vélúr, of Parmakol, of Chengalpatt, and of Wandiwásh, were vigorously prosecuted, when on the 18th, Haidar heard that on the previous morning the English army, commanded now by Sir Eyre Coote, had quitted Madras.

The Madras Government, in fact, on learning Baillie's defeat, had despatched a swift vessel to Bengal, with letters stating their misfortunes and their pressing need of immediate succour. Fortunately for them, Bengal was then ruled by an administrator whose guiding principle was, above all things, the maintenance of the honour and greatness of his country. Though embarrassed by the financial pressure resulting from

Maráthá wars, from the necessity of providing for the defence of the British possessions in Bengal and Bombay, Warren Hastings at once raised the money sufficient to meet the emergency; called upon Sir Eyre Coote once again to place himself at the head of an army, and despatched him with every available soldier to Madras. Not content with doing things by halves, Warren Hastings suspended the Governor of Madras, Mr. Whitehill, appointed a more vigorous administrator in his place, and entrusted to Sir Eyre Coote complete and independent charge of the military operations.

Coote reached Madras on the 5th November, only to find the resources of the Presidency so exhausted that ten weeks were required to equip his army for the field. It was not till the 17th January that he was able to set out. His design was, to march southward, relieve the places besieged in that direction by Haidar, and then to advance on Pondichery—which the French had re-occupied—drawing Haidar after him.

Coote's first efforts were successful. On the early morn of the 21st, a detachment of his army stormed the strong fortress of Karungalli; on the 23rd he raised the siege of Wandiwásh, and on the 25th began his march for Parmakol. On that day he heard of the presence of a French fleet off the coast. Being indifferently provided with provisions, Coote's first idea was to return to Madras; but the desirability of recovering Pondichery and of destroying the boats which might aid in the landing of French troops, decided him to push on towards the French capital.

Haidar, meanwhile, had watched, with eager and searching eyes, every movement of his enemy. As soon as he heard of the direction his army had taken, he raised the siege of Vélúr, and, acting in concert with the French authorities at Pondichery, massed his army, and followed him. On the 25th January he, too, learned that a French fleet, commanded by the Chevalier d'Orves, had been sighted near Gúdalúr (Cuddalore). This event raised his hopes to the highest degree. Whilst he should sever Coote's communications with Madras, the fleet would blockade the coast; and Coote, shut out from the grain-producing country, would be starved into surrender.

Whilst Haidar and his French allies were carrying out this plan with great skill, Coote was marching further and further into the trap. On the 8th February, Haidar having made as though he would attempt Gúdalúr, Coote, thoroughly taken in, moved with his whole army to cover that important place. This movement enabled Haidar to seize a strong position which quite severed his enemy from Madras. In Gúdalúr itself there were but three days' supply of food. Both the rival leaders could see the French fleet, unthreatened, guarding the coast. In vain did Coote offer battle to the Maisúr chief. Haidar was content to occupy an unassailable position which barred Coote from the grain-producing country.

Coote himself recognised all the danger of his position, the fault he had committed in allowing himself to be severed from his base. Unless supplies could reach him, he knew that he was lost. But as long as Haidar and the French should maintain their respective positions, no supplies could reach him.

Haidar maintained his. But from some cause, to this day unexplained, d'Orves was false alike to his reputation and to his country. In another work* I have dwelt at some length on the crime perpetrated by a Government which commits the command of its fleets to men deficient in decision and nerve. Never had France such an opportunity of revenging herself for the defeats of Dupleix and Lally. There was no doubt about the issue. D'Orves had only to remain off the coast to see the last army possessed by the English starved into surrender. Haidar, in constant communication with him, pressed him to remain, if only for a week longer; or, at all events, to land the one French regiment he had on board. D'Orves would do neither.

* *Final French Struggles in India.*

On the 15th February, to the intense relief of Sir Eyre Coote, and to the indignation of Haidar, he bore away for the islands. The English at once obtained supplies from Madras.

Five weary months then elapsed; Coote, to a certain extent blockaded at Gúdalúr, forced to look to the sea for his supplies: Haidar watching him, and whilst watching him, obtaining the surrender of many of the strong places behind him. At last, on the 16th June, Coote, realising that the only possible mode of retrieving his position was to force an action on his wary enemy, quitted Gúdalúr, crossed the river Vallár on the 18th, and that night attempted to surprise and storm the strongly-fortified pagoda of Chelambram. Haidar's garrison, however, composed of nearly three thousand good troops, repulsed the English sipáhís with serious loss, and even captured one of their guns. Baffled in this quarter, Coote drew off his army in the night, and, after a hesitation which lasted four days, recrossed the Vallár, and encamped near Porto Novo, a village on its northern bank, close to the sea, and only seven miles from Chelambram, which place he at once made preparations, in concert with Admiral Hughes, to besiege.

Perhaps it would have been as well if Haidar had been content to reinforce the garrison of Chelambram, to strengthen its defences, then to count upon the action of the monsoon on the fleet, and of his army on the besiegers. But the repulse of the English before that pagoda, the details of which were conveyed to him in a greatly exaggerated form, had so elated him, that, believing the English army would prove now an easy prey, he resolved to strike a decisive blow. Quickly collecting his forces, then, he crossed the Kolrún; moved rapidly to the north, then making a sweep to the eastward, interposed his whole army between Gúdalúr and the English, having marched a hundred miles in two days and a half. On the 27th June, when Coote had all but completed his arrangements for an attack on Chelambram, he was suddenly informed that Haidar, with his whole army, was fortifying a position within three miles of him.

Coote called a council of war. The issues which he put before that council were simply these:—The declining of a battle meant the conducting of military operations at a great disadvantage, the incurring of a liability to be attacked suddenly, when one part of the force should be already occupied; an unsuccessful battle meant destruction, for it would entail the loss of Madras and, with it, of southern India; a successful battle, on the other hand, meant relief from all difficulties; and, not until they had compelled Haidar to move off, would they be in so good a position, with regard to numbers, to fight a successful battle. The council with one voice voted for fighting.

At 7 o'clock, then, on the morning of the 1st July, Coote marched towards the enemy—his army formed in two lines. His whole force consisted of 8,476 men, of whom 2,070 were Europeans. It was difficult to reconnoitre the enemy's position, as Haidar, with his usual craft, had covered it with swarms of cavalry, whilst Coote was deficient in that arm. We, however, who are behind the scenes, may state that the position selected by Haidar was a very strong one. His army numbered forty thousand men, and these occupied three villages, and were spread over a line which, crossing the road to Gúdalúr, extended from commanding grounds on the right to a point on the left which rested on a range of sand-hills following the line of the seashore. The ground on his front and on his right flank was intersected in every direction by deep ditches and watercourses. Embrasures for his heavy artillery had been cut in mounds of earth formed from the hollowing of ditches. These batteries protected at once the front and the right flank.

It was not until Coote had marched a mile and a half that he was able to gain a view of this formidable position. He halted, and spent an hour in minutely examining every point of it, exposed throughout that time to an incessant cannonade from guns advanced from the front of the enemy's position, and from their left flank. His own guns, to economise their limited supply of ammunition, made no reply.

At 9 o'clock the English general had made his decision. He recognised that the weak point of Haidar's position was his left, for the sand-hills had not been fortified, and could be turned. He directed, then, General Stuart, who commanded his second line, to move by columns, under cover—first, of the front line, and afterwards of the sand-hills on the coast—to a point beyond those sand-hills, and, turning them, to march on till he should reach an opening which would enable them to take the enemy in flank. Whilst Stuart was engaged in this operation, Coote himself would make a strong demonstration against the enemy's front, taking care not to commit himself to a serious attack until the success of Stuart's movement should be assured.

Rarely has a planned military manœuvre been carried out with greater precision than was this. Haidar, bent on making his right and centre proof against attack, had deferred fortifying the sand-hills, especially as he deemed it to the last degree improbable that an enemy would, as it were, cut his army in two to attempt to turn him on that flank. No longer the active man whom we have known, seizing victory or staving off defeat by personal prowess, he was compelled, in these days, to watch, motionless, the movements of the rival forces. On this occasion he sat, cross-legged, on a stool which had been placed for him on an eminence, immediately behind his centre. From this point he commanded the field. As soon as he caught sight of Stuart's manœuvre, recognising its importance, he despatched some of his best troops to strengthen his left, and sent orders to his cavalry to hold themselves in readiness to take advantage of the smallest check given to the enemy. Before these orders could be received Stuart, marching with great rapidity, had turned the position of the enemy, discovered a road made between two sand-hills, and led his men to gain it. But Haidar's troops, well on the alert, repulsed a first attack, and a second. Just at this period Haidar's orders reached the commanders of the two wings of cavalry. He of the right wing, deeming the moment opportune, charged the first line led by Coote, and was repulsed only after a most desperate encounter. But it was upon the action of the commander of the left wing that everything depended. Could he fall successfully upon the twice-repulsed troops of Stuart the battle was over. But in this quarter fortune frowned on Haidar. The commander, Mír Sáhib, one of Haidar's best officers, was about to give the order to charge, when he was cut in two by a round shot. Almost at the same moment a broadside from an English schooner, which had been worked close to the shore, made terrible havoc amongst the drawn-up squadrons. A panic ensued; the charge was never made. Availing himself of the panic, Stuart promptly made his third attempt on the gap, and succeeded.

The simultaneous advance of the first line, whilst the second, though still strongly opposed, was working steadily from the left flank towards the centre, convinced those about Haidar that the day was lost. Haidar himself, however, refused to believe that the fruit of exertions so earnest, so well thought out, had been lost by one mistake and one freak of fortune. He refused to quit the field, constantly uttering regrets that he could no longer by his own exertions retrieve mishap. At last, about 4 o'clock in the afternoon, the danger had become so imminent that a favourite groom seized his legs, put on his slippers, and with the words, "We will beat them to-morrow, meanwhile mount," helped him on to his horse. The whole army followed in full retreat, taking with them all their guns. They had lost many men, how many can never be known. The English had lost three hundred and six, and had gained only the ground on which they had fought.

Such was the battle of Porto Novo, called also the battle of Chelambram; assuredly one of the most decisive battles ever ought in southern India. To the English, defeat would have meant not only expulsion from Madras, but the absorption of the Karnátak by the ruler of Maisúr. The English had but that one army. To provide that army, Bengal had been exhausted. Bombay was fighting for her own hand. A few months later the arrival of Suffren deprived the English of supremacy in the Indian seas. To fight under the circumstances was a desperate remedy; but it was the only possible, and, as it proved, a successful remedy.

Haidar, it is true, fought some more desperate battles with the English, and even gained some partial successes; but the spell was broken. The battle of Porto Novo had decided not only the fate of Madras, it had given a death-blow to the exterminating projects of Haidar. It might be said, indeed, that it did more. Mushroom kingdoms, like that of Haidar Alí, depend for their vitality on the constant activity of their ruler. When that ruler ceases to conquer, his power and his influence alike wane. In this sense Porto Novo was a check from which the dynasty of Haidar Alí never recovered.

It is true, as I have said, that Haidar fought again. After Porto Novo, Coote marched northward along the coast to meet reinforcements which had been sent from Bengal. But so demoralised was Haidar, that though many opportunities offered he never attacked his enemy, but allowed a junction—which added one-third to that enemy's strength—to take place at Palikát without striking a blow to prevent it (2nd August). On the 22nd of the same month, he had the mortification of witnessing the storming of Tripasor, in the presence of his whole army. On the 27th, Coote, at the head of twelve thousand men, attacked his forces, raised now to seventy thousand men, and strongly posted on the acclivities of a range of hills near Parmbákam; after a desperate conflict, stormed the plateau on the left, gained a position which was the key to the right of his defence, and thus compelled Haidar to abandon the field, and to retreat to Kánchipuram during the night. One result of this action was the re-victualling of Vélúr, and the recovery of the fort of Chittúr, by the English.

A transient gleam of sunshine played over the fortunes of Haidar when, on the 18th February 1783, his son, Típú Sáhib, compelled the surrender, after a three days' contest, of an English detachment commanded by Colonel Braithwaite; when, also, on the 8th June following, he enticed into an ambuscade and nearly destroyed, in the presence of Sir Eyre Coote, a body of English horse. But none of his smaller triumphs made up for the defeat of Porto Novo. That battle was his Leipsic. Thenceforth he ceased to be an aggressor; he endeavoured only to retain the places he had gained.

It is due to him to add that, in his later operations, Haidar was much hampered by his French allies. These, badly led, displayed a caution and backwardness as foreign to the character of their nation as it was uncongenial to the nature of Haidar.

Six months after his last successful skirmish with the English (the 7th December 1783), Haidar Alí—become prematurely old, for he was but sixty-five—passed away. The war languished after his death; continued with varying fortunes* for fifteen months, when it was concluded by the Treaty of Mangalúr (11th March 1784), which stipulated for the restitution of all places, and the liberation of all prisoners, taken by both parties during its continuance.

It has ever been the misfortune of Eastern dynasties that an Amurath can never secure that he shall be succeeded by an Amurath. Haidar Alí, a man of genius, of energy, a born warrior, was succeeded in the vast territories he had made a kingdom, by a passionate and narrow-minded bigot; a man who, in fact, had inherited all the passions of his father without

* An account of those varying fortunes has been given by the Author in a book entitled *Final French Struggles in India* (1878). Towards its close, those of the English were at a very low ebb indeed.

one scintilla of his genius. The consequences were such as might have been predicted. Típú Sáhib lost all that Haidar Alí had gained. Notwithstanding the peace of Mangalúr, he did not cease to molest his neighbours. At last he had the temerity to attack a protected ally of the English, the Rájah of Travankúr. War followed (1790). Bangalor fell into the hands of the English. Shrírangapatam was invested; Típú in despair sued for peace. He was able to obtain it only by the sacrifice of one half of his dominions, and the payment of upwards of £3,030,000 (19th March 1792).

To recover the lost moiety of his territories, Típú, six years later, intrigued with the French republic. When, informed of his conduct, the Marquess Wellesley demanded of him securities for his good behaviour, Típú treated the demand with contempt. The Governor-General then declared war, and, in alliance with the Nizám and the Maráthás, sent an army, under General Harris, into Maisúr. The strong places, no longer defended by the genius of Haidar, fell in quick succession. On the 3rd April, General Harris invested Shrírangapatam; on the 4th May he stormed it. In defending it, Típú Sáhib was killed, and the remnant of Maisúr—for some slices of it were taken to satisfy the English and their allies—was restored to the Hindú dynasty which Haidar Alí had dispossessed.

That this result was possible was a consequence, though a later consequence, of the battle of Porto Novo. Had Haidar Alí won that battle, he would have expelled the English from Madras, and would, for a season, have been master of southern India. That he would have retained it is scarcely probable. But that the danger was great, that the fear which existed was widespread, is shown by all the contemporary records of the period. The terror survived his death, survived the campaign, survived even the first defeat of Típú Sáhib. It was the recollection of the danger which the Muhammadan dynasty of Maisúr had brought home to the English which was a main factor in the policy by which Marquess Wellesley was actuated in dealing with Típú. To the battle fought near Porto Novo, then, no Englishman can look back without a feeling of pride. That battle crushed the aggressive schemes of Haidar, forced him to act on the defensive, and paved the way, after his death, to the destruction of the mighty power he had created. Under his rule Maisúr had become a robber's stronghold, a stronghold the existence of which was only possible when the paramount power was inert. The British never effected a work more truly beneficial to the people of India than when they destroyed that stronghold, and, expelling the dynasty of the robber, substituted the mild sway of the Hindú ruler for the empire of the sword!

CHAPTER IX.

ASSAYE.

MADHAJÍ Sindia was the greatest man India produced in the last century. He towered above his contemporaries. He was a greater warrior and a more far-sighted statesman than Haidar Alí of Maisúr; he possessed none of the cruelty or the habitual and senseless perfidy of Nizám Alí of Haidarábád; amongst the Maráthás not a single man equalled him in intellectual power. Alone amongst his countrymen he detected the necessities of the English position, the alternative of further conquest or annihilation which lay before them, the life struggle which must ensue between them and the princes of India. To prepare for that life struggle, to avoid internecine national quarrels, to effect a union amongst all castes and races against the ever-encroaching foreigner, had been for many years the aim of his policy, the darling desire of his life. At one time he had contemplated the bringing of Haidar Alí and the Nizám within the confederacy. He had been forced to wait, however, tlll his own position should be consolidated, his own influence in Western India supreme, before he could give the final touch to the scheme. Before that time arrived Haidar had died, after a vain attempt to accomplish, single-handed, that which a combined effort on the part of all the races of India might have secured; and Tipú, foiled in another unsupported effort, had been shorn of half his dominions. But in June 1793, Madhají had attained the summit of his wishes. He swayed the destinies of Central India, and, as far as and including Alígarh, of North-western India; his troops, trained and commanded by Frenchmen and other Europeans, occupied the strong places from Ujjén to Agra and Dihlí; his only possible rival in Central India, Tukaji Holkar, was at his feet; and at Púnah, the capital of the Peshwá, he was rapidly gaining a supreme influence. He wanted but a few short years to work out his dream. He had not seen quite sixty summers, and had lived a temperate and active life. The expectation that a brief time might yet be granted to him was not extravagant. It proved, however, to be fallacious. When yet on the last step of the pedestal he had spent the preceding thirty years to attain, he was struck down by fever, and died. With him perished the last hope of unity of action against the foreigner.

The direction of the fabric which Madhají Sindia had raised with much patience, so much skill, and so much forethought, devolved upon a boy of fifteen—a boy possessing a character, which, if still unformed, had displayed waywardness, indecision, and a dislike of control.

This boy was Daolat Ráo Sindia. He succeeded very suddenly to a position which demanded all the qualities of a ripened statesman. The influence he had inherited was predominant at Púnah, and events very shortly happened which called upon him to exercise it. Unhappily he was too young or too wilful to take up the large scheme bequeathed to him by Mádhají; and when events convinced him of its wisdom and forced its principle upon him, he had descended many steps from the height to which Mádhají had attained.

The first great event which demanded his prompt action was the sudden death of the Peshwá. On the 25th October 1795, Mahádeo Ráo Náráyan, the last but one who bore that title, threw himself, in a fit of profound melancholy, from a terrace of his palace, and two days later died from the effects of the injuries he then received. When this event happened, Daolat Ráo, marching at the head of his army towards Gwaliár, had reached Jamgaon. Recognising the importance of the situation he promptly replied to the invitation sent him by the minister of the late Peshwá, and returned to Púnah, arbiter, if his capacity had been equal to his power, of the destinies of Western India.

His capacity was not, however, equal to his power. He allowed himself to be hoodwinked, deceived, and led in leading-strings by a man who, at the age of twenty-one, had gained the reputation of being the most consummate intriguer of the day—a man at that time under surveillance in his own camp—the cousin of the late Peshwá—the notorious Báji Ráo Raghunáth. By the influence he managed to exercise upon Daolát Ráo, Báji Ráo became Peshwá. He immediately began to intrigue for the departure of his too powerful patron.

In the hands of the new Peshwá Daolat Ráo was a mere child. By degrees Bájí Ráo undermined his influence, raised enemies against him even in his own household, stirred up Holkar to attack him, until at last, Daolat Rao, wearied and disgusted, saw himself forced to quit Púnah to defend his own dominions from attack (November 1800).

He was but just in time. Before he could muster his forces in full strength Jeswant Ráo Holkar had inflicted two successive defeats on detachments he had sent for the protection of Ujjén (June 1801). The following month his great park of artillery was saved from falling into the hands of the same daring rival, by the gallantry of an Englishman in his service, named Brownrigg. But in October he was ready, and on the 14th of that month he inflicted upon Holkar a crushing defeat in front of his capital, Indúr, which, as a consequence, fell into his hands. Had Daolat Ráo followed up his victory there had been an end for ever to the career of Jeswant Ráo. But not recognising the importance of the situation he preferred to negotiate. Again was he duped. Jeswant Ráo, whose intellect was subtle and whose insight was keen—who was, in fact, an intriguer of intriguers—amused Daolat Rao till, with the marvellous recuperative power always displayed by the Maráthás, he had recruited his army. He then suddenly broke off, renewed hostilities in Khándésh, and defeated Sindia's army, led by his general, Sheo daséo Ráò, near Púnah (25th October 1802).

This defeat was productive of the most disastrous consequences to the Maráthás. It broke up for ever the Maráthá confederacy. It was one of those incidents which, slight in themselves, yet suffice to change the course of events. The defeat of one Maráthá power by another Maráthá power brought upon the scene, in a manner as marvellous as it was unexpected, the power which was destined to control them all. The result was due mainly to the obstinacy and shortsightedness of Daolat Ráo.

The defeat of Sindia's army near Púnah on the 25th October 1802 caused the Peshwá, Bájí Ráo, to flee in trepidation from his capital. From Suwarnadurg (Severndrúg), where he took refuge, Bají Ráo addressed pressing solicitations to Sindia, then in camp at Ujjén, to come to his aid. It is not too much to say that the fate of India was, at that moment, in the hands of Daolat Ráo Sindia. Had he marched to the aid of his suzerain he would have regained by force of arms the position he had lost by intrigue; there would have been no treaty of Bassein; the Maráthá confederacy would have presented an unbroken front to the foreigner.

But Dáolat Ráo had not yet grasped the full conception of his astute predecessor. He cast away the opportunity never to recur, and declined to march to the assistance of the Peshwá. The Peshwa in despair threw himself on the protection of the British. The result was the treaty of Bassein.

The Treaty of Bassein was the greatest diplomatic triumph which the world has ever witnessed. On the eve of a contest, impending, which could not have been long delayed, between the Maráthá Confederacy and the British, it broke up the Maráthá Confederacy: it relieved the English of the danger which had long threatened them of having to face at one and the same time the united power of a league whose territories comprehended the north-west provinces of India, Central India, and the greater part of western India; and allowed them to meet and to conquer each section of that league singly. Above all, it paralysed the vast influence which attached to the name and to the authority of the Peshwá.

By the Treaty of Bassein, negotiated under the orders of Marquess Wellesley by Sir Barry Close, the Peshwá engaged to admit the thin end of the wedge of British protection, that wedge always fatal to the independence of a native dynasty. He engaged to receive from the British a subsidiary force of six battalions, with guns, and to cede certain districts for their payment; to refer to the British Government all his disputes with the Nizám and his claims against the Gaíkwár. The British, on their part, undertook to restore the Peshwá to his dominions, to defend him against all hostility or aggression whatsoever "in the same manner as the rights and territories of the Honourable Company are now maintained and defended." Other articles bound the Peshwá even more closely to his foreign defenders.

The news of the Treaty of Bassein and the information he received as to its nature, roused Daólat Ráo Sindia to a sense of his errors. In that treaty he saw plainly not only a bar to a complete Maráthá Confederacy, but a threat against himself. Then, probably for the first time, he fully grasped the statesmanlike plans of Madhájí, at the very moment when the realisation of those plans had been rendered impossible for ever. Then he bestirred himself. He refused, after some hesitation, the invitation he received to become a party to the defensive portion of the treaty; and then, as earnest and active as he had been vacillating and dilatory, he strove to unite the Maráthás against their one dangerous foe. But he was too late. The Peshwá had been bought off by the British, and Jeswant Ráo Holkar, though he recognised as clearly as did Dáolat Ráo the gravity of the situation, allowed his policy to be overruled by his personal jealousy. It is more than possible that that jealousy was whetted by the conviction that the contest between the British and Dáolat Ráo would be prolonged, that it would leave the rival combatants exhausted; and that he, Jeswant Ráo, would then step in—the master of the situation. At all events, he refused his aid.

With Raghují Bhonslé, rájah of Barár, Dáolat Ráo was more successful. That Maráthá prince, equally penetrated with the danger of the situation, agreed to bring all the influence and power of the Bhonslé to support the national cause.

The two allies proceeded at once to make preparations for war. But though they masked their designs with secrecy, those designs did not escape the penetrating glance of the Governor-General; and he, on his side, prepared for the inevitable struggle. Not content with that, as soon as his own arrangements had been well advanced, he demanded of Sindia an explicit declaration of his intentions. Sindia, not yet prepared, replied that it was necessary, before he could answer, to consult with his ally, the rájah of Barár. He marched at once with his own troops to take up a position in proximity to the position occupied by that ally, close to the western frontier of the territories of the Nizám.

Long negotiations followed the meeting of the two chieftains, negotiations protracted on their side by the hope that Holkar might yet be tempted to unite his cause with theirs. Wearied at last of continued evasions General Wellesley, who commanded the main English force in that quarter, proposed as a test ultimatum that the armies of the several Powers should retire within the boundaries of their own territories; engaging, for his part, that if Sindia would retire to the North-west Provinces and the Bhonslé to Barár, he would withdraw every British soldier within the limits of British territories. Finding it impossible to evade a reply to this practical proposal, the two chieftains rejected it. As a consequence, the British Resident withdrew from their camp, and war ensued.

Marquess Wellesley, with that thoroughness which was a marked characteristic of his Indian administration, had made preparations to attack his enemies simultaneously on more points than one. Whilst, then, the commander-in-chief of the army in India, General Lake, marched from Kánhpúr, on the 5th August, at the head of about 8,000 men, to drive Sindia's troops from the North-West Provinces; whilst a smaller force of 3,500 assembled at Alláhábád to act on the side of Bundelkhund, and another of 5,216 marched to the eastward to conquer the districts of which Katak (Cuttack) was the capital; other, and, taken altogether, larger armies had been made ready to move in western and southern India. It is with these armies alone that we have to do just now.

In the Dakhan and Gujarát the forces assembled by Lord Wellesley's orders amounted to 35,596 men. Of these, 3,595 were assigned for the defence of the cities of Púnah and Haidarabád. To cover these places General Stuart, who commanded in chief in this part of India, at the head of 7,826 men, occupied a central position between the rivers Krishná and Tungabhádra. In advance of this covering army were three field forces; one, of 8,930 men, commanded by General Wellesley, was at Wálkí, eight miles south of Ahmadnagar; another, of 7,920 men, led by General Stevenson, but subordinate to Wellesley, was some miles to the east of Jálnah. The third field force was in Gujarát. It was composed of 7,352 men; but as 3,071 of these were required to garrison the strong places in that province there remained available for field operations only 4,281; these were commanded by Colonel Murray, who was subject to the control of General Wellesley.

But if the number of the British troops was considerable—enormous, in fact, if we compare it with the handful of men whom we have seen struggling, under Clive and Adams and Munro, to lay the foundations of empire—the forces wielded by their enemies were greater still. The combined forces of Sindia and the Bhonslé have been estimated at 100,000 men; and of these 30,000 were troops trained and armed after the European fashion, disciplined, and, in many instances, officered and led by Europeans. About two-thirds of these trained sipáhís occupied, however, Sindia's possessions in the North-West Provinces and in the more north-eastern parts of Central India. Besides the 10,000 of these regular troops, the allies had in south-western India some 40,000 horsemen, a splendid park of artillery, extremely well manned, and a mass of matchlockmen, very irregular infantry, formed on the old native system, which had degenerated into being no system at all. This army, when hostilities broke out, occupied a position below the Ajunta pass, on the frontiers of the Nizám's dominions, about fifty-five miles from Jálnah.

Before I proceed to give a detailed account of the events of the war, I propose to glance for a moment at the characters of the rival leaders. Of Dáolat Ráo Sindia the reader will by this time have formed an opinion. A man possessed of a slow brain and a vacillating nature can never be a great general. Throughout his life Dáolat Ráo was in leading-strings; he was the puppet of the man who for the moment had acquired the greatest influence over him. At this particular moment that influence was possessed by his ally, Raghují Bhonslé. Raghují was but a poor counsellor in difficult circumstances. He understood war, however, in the sense in which war was understood by the great founder of the Maráthá empire. According to him, war meant the ravaging of the country over which his enemy must march; the hanging on his flanks and rear; the avoiding of a general action; the cutting off his supplies. Raghuji impressed these counsels upon Sindia, and so long as he was by his side Sindia was disposed to conform to them. But the two chiefs could not always be together, and, when Raghují was absent, Sindia was swayed by men who dilated on the excellence of his trained troops, of his cavalry, and of his artillery, of his superiority in numbers, of the great advantage of striking a decisive blow. The result was an attempt to combine two opposite systems, an attempt which could not but end in failure.

The commander of the advanced British forces in south-western India, General Arthur Wellesley, was the very last man in the world in whose presence operations of the nature I have described could be carried out with impunity. Born in the year 1769, Arthur Wesley—as he was then called—had entered the army at an early age and had, in the days when everything was possible to a young man of good birth, very soon attained the command of a regiment. We find him, even in 1794, commanding with spirit and intelligence a brigade in the rear-guard which covered the retreat of the Duke of York's beaten army from Holland. In 1795, his regiment, the 33rd, was ordered to the West Indies. A succession of tempestuous weather accompanied by contrary winds, tossed the fleet for six weeks in the waters of the Atlantic, and compelled it finally to return to England. It became necessary to land the 33rd, and before it could be re-embarked, its destination was changed to India. Wesley, prevented from accompanying it, followed a few months later, and landed in Calcutta in February 1797.

At that time the Governor-General was Sir John Shore, afterwards Lord Teignmouth, a man distinguished amongst his other high attainments for his keen perception of character. It is said that after Wellesley—for his family shortly afterwards adopted this form—had retired from their first interview,—which took place at a levée—Sir John Shore turned to the gentlemen who surrounded him, and exclaimed, "If Colonel Wesley should ever have the opportunity of distinguishing himself he will do it—and greatly." *

Shortly after Wellesley had rejoined his regiment he was called upon to take part in an expedition against the Manillas. He seized the occasion to submit a recommendation to the effect that prior to such an attack the Dutch settlements of Java should be destroyed. The expedition sailed, and had reached Penang, when it was recalled to India in consequence of the hostile dispositions of Típú Sáhib. For the moment, however, these dispositions did not lead to warfare.

Shortly afterwards, 17th May 1798, Colonel Wellesley had the gratification of welcoming the arrival in Calcutta of the greatest of the many great men sent from England to govern India,—his brother—the Earl of Mornington—better known as Marquess Wellesley. Lord Mornington's arrival was coincident with the last effort made by the ruler of Maisúr to recover, in alliance with the French Republic, the position which his great father had gained prior to the battle of Porto Novo. The occasion was critical; for the French, led by the most brilliant general of the age, occupied Egypt, and that general was already in communication with Típú. The great Marquess—it may be convenient to style him by the title which he soon afterwards assumed—displayed on this occasion the acumen, the force of character, the resolution which mark every act of his career. He gave Típú every opportunity to prove the honesty of his intentions, and it was only when the last of these had been treated with contempt that he sent an army into his dominions.

That army conquered Maisúr and slew Típú defending his last fortress. With it served Colonel Wellesley. On the morrow of the successful assault of that fortress, Wellesley was appointed to command it, and he was shortly afterwards joined with other distinguished officers in a commission to regulate the affairs of

* *Life of Lord Teignmouth*

the whole country; and, when this work had been concluded by the re-formation of a Hindú kingdom under a sovereign of the ancient royal race, Wellesley was appointed to organise and command the army necessary to defend it.

Wellesley fulfilled the duties of this post—amongst which may be enumerated the successful extirpation of a very formidable band of freebooters—for upwards of a year. He was recalled from them towards the close of 1800 to command an expedition ordered to assemble at Tinomalli, and to proceed to the conquest of Java. The destination of the force assembled for this expedition was shortly afterwards changed to Egypt, and the command was given to a senior officer, Sir David Baird, under whom Wellesley was to serve as second. This change, which he bitterly regretted at the time, was one of the most fortunate occurrences of a very fortunate life. In two ways did Fortune display her favours. Fever prevented Wellesley at the last moment from accompanying the expedition. Firstly, the vessel in which he was to have sailed, and on board of which he had sent his baggage, the *Susannah*, was lost with all hands in the Red Sea; secondly, his enforced stay in India rendered him available for command in the war against Sindia and the Bhonslé.

Recovered from his fever, Wellesley was (April 1801) re-appointed to the command of the forces in Maisúr. He held this command nearly two years, was promoted to the rank of Major-General, and in March 1803 was appointed to the command of the advanced corps of General Stuart's army, and directed to move through the southern Maráthá country, to confirm the dispositions of the well disposed, and to march leisurely to Púnah, to establish there an order of things favourable to the return of the Péshwá. This mission Wellesley successfully accomplished, re-established the Péshwá (13th May 1803) and set out from that place on the 4th June to occupy the position facing the armies of Sindia and the Bhonslé, in which I left him when I turned aside to digress upon his earlier career.

On the 7th August 1803, the Governor-General issued a proclamation declaring that he had, on the day previous, directed the levying of war against the two Maráthá chieftains. On that day General Wellesley was at Wálkí, eight miles south of Ahmadnagar. Heavy rains prevented him from at once moving against that fortress, but on the 8th he set out to attempt it. Ahmadnagar is distant from Púnah but seventy-three miles. The fortress, formidable in appearance, bore the reputation of being impregnable. Wellesley has left upon record that it seemed to him, next to Vélúr, the strongest place in India. It was surrounded by a mud wall, and this again was defended by a ditch twenty feet in depth and forty in breadth. Arab soldiers, considered the best soldiers in western India, formed its garrison. Against it Wellesley at once raised his batteries, opened fire on the 10th, and forced its surrender on the 12th. His loss had amounted to twenty-eight killed and twenty-two wounded—of these, six were officers.

The capture of Ahmadnagar was a most important event, inasmuch as it secured the British communications with Púnah, afforded a secure depôt for stores, and severed the connection of the allied chieftains with the Dakhan. Leaving there a garrison, Wellesley (18th August) marched northwards, through a country wasted, in accordance with the suggestions of the Bhonslé, by the Maráthás, crossed the Godávarí on the 24th, and reached Aurangábád on the 29th. On the same day on which Wellesley crossed the Godávari, the Maráthá cavalry, covered by crowds of predatory skirmishers, ascended the Ajunta pass, and making a detour to avoid the camp of General Stevenson, reached Jálnah the day after Wellesley had arrived at Aurangábád. The distance between the two places is only forty miles, and by a proportion of that distance the Maráthás were nearer to Haidarábád. Hoping, then, to steal a march on their enemy, they stayed only a day at Jálnah, and then set off in a south-easterly direction.

The first care of Wellesley, on learning the course taken by the enemy, was to move so as to protect the country on which he greatly depended for supplies, and to ensure the safe arrival of the convoys of grain which had been despatched to him by General Stuart from the Krishna. Directing Stevenson, then, to secure Jálnah without delay, he moved down the Godávari. The action of the enemy on discovering this move proved that they had no guiding mind to direct them. It was still in their power, regard being had to their vast majority in cavalry, to push on to the heart of the Nizám's country. But the movement of Wellesley down the Godávari, whilst Stevenson, pressing after them, was endeavouring to bring them to action, greatly disturbed them. They at once renounced the projected movement on Haidarábád, abandoned their chance of predatory warfare, and manœuvred to avoid an action until the whole of their infantry should come up. In this they succeeded. Though surprised by Stevenson, who in the meanwhile had taken Jálnah, on the 9th September they managed to avoid a general action, and finally, on the 20th September, effected a junction with their infantry and artillery. The united army took up a position the day following at Bokardan, not far from the town of Jafarábád.

The very same day, the 21st, Wellesley and Stevenson, who had been following the enemy on different lines, met at Badnapúr, a little more than eleven miles from Jálnah, and on the road between that place and Aurungábád. At a conference which ensued between the two generals, it was agreed that their two corps should continue to move on separate lines, and should simultaneously attack the enemy from opposite points, on the morning of the 24th. The separation was necessary, not only because both divisions could not traverse the same defiles in one day, but because the roads through the hills required to be occupied to prevent any attempt on the part of the enemy to avoid the action by retiring. With this understanding they separated, and on the following morning each set out to perform the task allotted to him. It is necessary that I should first record the movements of Wellesley.

That general, leaving Badnapúr on the 22nd, reached the village of Kalní on the morning of the 23rd, and was about to pitch his camp when the scouts brought him the information that the combined army of the enemy was encamped on the banks of the river Kaitná, within six miles of him; that they had notice of his approach and were preparing to move off. Apprehensive lest an adherence to the agreement made with Stevenson would allow them to escape, Wellesley resolved to attack them at once. Sending word of his intention to Stevenson, who was within eight miles of him, and leaving a strong guard in his camp to protect the baggage, he set forth at the head of his army, numbering now only four thousand five hundred British and native troops—of whom one regiment of cavalry and two of infantry were Europeans—and five thousand Maisúr and Maráthá (the Peshwá's) horsemen. After marching about five miles, Wellesley, who was with the advance in front of the army, beheld from the summit of a rising ground the enemy's army drawn up in a vast line extending along the northern bank of the river Kaitná, near its junction with the Jewah. Their infantry and artillery, formed in dense masses on their left, rested on the village of Assaye, whilst their numerous cavalry, thirty thousand strong—the famous horsemen who had dealt the death-blow to the empire of the Mughul, and had bidden defiance to Aurangzíb in all his glory—completely filled the spaces on the right. Of the infantry, 10,000 had been trained on the European system, and the artillery was for the most part magnificent.

It was a sight to arouse all the warrior instincts in the breast of the young general—then in his thirty-fourth year—about to fight his first battle. He gazed long and eagerly, slowly advancing as he did so, on the array before him, examining with piercing glance every disposition. The instincts of a soldier soon told him that the true point of attack was on the flank which rested upon the enemy's line of retreat. To reach that he would have to increase the distance which separated him from Stevenson. Not for a moment did the fear of responsibility check his audacious genius. Exclaiming "They cannot now escape us!" he moved rapidly round to their left flank, crossed the Kaitná by a ford which the enemy had neglected to guard, close to its junction with the Jewah, and formed his infantry in two lines, in an open space between the two rivers, his cavalry forming a third line in the rear. Just as he was forming up his troops, information reached him that the cavalry of the Peshwá intended to betray him and join Sindia. Confident that they would join the victor, whoever he might be, Wellesley did not allow this information to affect his dispositions.

Meanwhile the enemy, noting the action of the British, had changed their front in consequence. They had moved up their three arms from the position they had occupied along the Kaitná, and had extended them in a line facing the English between the two rivers; but as the space was not sufficient to accommodate their entire masses, they had formed of those who were superfluous a shorter line running at a right angle to the first. The left of both these lines rested on Assaye, in which their artillery had been posted.

The preparations of the two Maráthá leaders had been completed whilst Wellesley was crossing the ford, and his order of battle had therefore to be made under a continuous fire from the artillery posted in the village of Assaye. No sooner, however, had it been arranged than he gave the order to advance. His plan was of the simplest. The enemy's right wing, resting on the Kaitná, was their weakest point: he would attack that, force it back upon the Jewah, and then use the advantage which a small body of disciplined troops employed against masses huddled together in a space too small for their operations always bestows.

The 74th Regiment occupied the right of the line. The order given was that whilst the skirmishers in front of this regiment should cover a very slow advance, sufficient only to draw the entire attention of the troops massed in Assaye, the 78th and the native regiments on the left should press forward rapidly and perform the work assigned to them. But whether it was that the order was imperfectly comprehended, or that the fighting instincts of the British soldier would not be restrained, the right, notwithstanding the very severe cannonade to which they were subjected, dashed forward at the same pace as the rest of the line. But so great was the execution of the enemy's guns that, before the line had made one half of the distance, the bullocks attached to the English light batteries had been killed. The forward movement of the guns was therefore rendered impossible; and the men, staggered for the moment by this accident, and by the terrible fire to which they were exposed, halted, whilst the officer commanding despatched an orderly to report the mishap to his guns. "Tell him to get on without them," was the brief and emphatic reply. It was, indeed, too late to think of anything else; there was absolutely no alternative; anything but advance meant destruction.

The leaders of the Maráthá army had, however, noticed the hesitation, the halt, the apparent confusion in the ranks of the English. It was just the sort of hesitation to which, in their wars against each other, they had been accustomed, and to take advantage of which they were prepared to use their cavalry. Instantly, then, Daolat Ráo ordered his famed horsemen to the front, and directed them to change the check into a defeat. But Wellesley saw the impending movement, and, a born leader of soldiers, took on the spot the only possible means to anticipate a charge which, made under the actual circumstances, could scarcely fail of being successful. As quick as thought, and quicker, fortunately, than the enemy, he brought up from the rear the 19th Light Dragoons, and ordered them to meet at full gallop the advance of the Maráthá horsemen. The Dragoons, who drew only three hundred and sixty sabres, came up, followed by the 4th, 5th, and 7th Madras Native Cavalry, passed with a loud huzza through the broken ranks of the 74th, and dashed at full speed at their enemy. Under the terrible shock which followed the swarthy troopers of Western India reeled. They had been taken before the speed of their horses had roused their excitement to fever heat, and now their very numbers impeded them. They offered, then, but a slight resistance to the impetuosity of the British, and were glad to take refuge, baffled, behind their infantry. The charge of the dragoons had given the infantry the cover and the breathing-time they wanted. During its continuance the artillery fire had ceased, and the British left and centre, under the personal direction of Wellesley, had rapidly pushed forward. When the space cleared again Wellesley charged the enemy's right on the Kaitná, and pushed them before him back on to their second shorter line, which was formed up almost resting on the Jewah. Simultaneously the victorious cavalry charged the village of Assaye. The 74th came up to support them. The village, after a long resistance, was carried, and the rest of the line pressing simultaneously forward, drove the enemy before them step by step until they forced them, at the point of the bayonet, into the Jewah!

So far success had crowned the efforts of the British commander; he had driven the enemy from the battle-field. But success not followed up is, in war, but the shadow of success. And there, now, were the enemy, their numbers but little diminished, on the ground beyond the Jewah, infinitely more suited for their peculiar mode of warfare than that from which they had been driven. It was clear that they recognised this fact, for they began, as soon as they had reached the opposite bank to rally and to make new formations. Wellesley, with the keen instinct of a great commander, anticipated here, as in the earlier part of the battle, their intentions. At a word from him the British cavalry, dashing across the rivulet, charged the infantry and pursued them with so much vigour that all thought of rallying was dispelled. The only troops who made good their retreat were the trained battalions.

The enemy's cavalry, however, still looked dangerous. They had been but little engaged, their self-love had been sorely wounded, and they numbered thirty thousand. Just at this moment, too, masses of the enemy who had thrown themselves on the ground as if dead, jumped suddenly to life and turned their guns on the British rear, now advanced beyond them. So effective was their action, that to stop it Wellesley was forced to move against them with the 78th and some native cavalry. The British cavalry then dealt with the Maráthá squadrons and with some of the fugitive infantry which had taken shelter under its wing. Led by Colonel Maxwell they again charged the masses before them—so effectually, that though Maxwell fell, the enemy, their pride completely abated, quitted the field, and did not halt till they had covered a distance of twelve miles.

Such was the battle of Assaye—in very deed a general's battle! For its result was due even more to the brain of the commander than to the valour of the men. It may be taken as certain that under an inferior commander the issue would have been different. Whether it was wise to engage in the battle with so small a force, when another was within eight miles of him, is a point which may be fairly argued. It was simply a question whether the political circumstances of the time rendered it advisable to risk much in order to gain much, or to witness, quiescent, an action which would have entailed disastrous consequences. Doubtless the "prudent" school would not have fought. To avoid risking a British army they would consequently have witnessed the uprising of the Dakhan, the union of the Nizám with the Maráthás, possibly also the rising of the Peshwá, and of Holkar, and the great injury of British interests in southern and western India.

From such issues Wellesley saved India. The battle, I repeat, was a General's battle. He "gave," wrote Munro, "every part of the army its full share: left no part of it unemployed; but supported, sometimes with cavalry, sometimes with infantry, every point that was pressed, at the very time it was necessary." The flank march to cut off the enemy from his communications before the battle, and the advance of the British cavalry to repel the Maráthá horsemen in its very crisis, were sufficient to establish his title to be a great commander. His readiness, his coolness, his quick and sure glance, his firm and decided action, were conspicuous throughout the day!

The casualties were heavy. The English lost, in killed, twenty-three European officers, a hundred and seventy-five European and two hundred and thirty native soldiers; in wounded, thirty European officers, four hundred and twelve European and six hundred and ninety-six native soldiers. Of the enemy twelve hundred were left dead on the field of battle; their wounded were scattered all over the field. Ninety-eight pieces of cannon fell into the hands of the victors.

Of the leaders on both sides it deserves to be recorded that whilst Wellesley was foremost in the fight, himself led two charges and had two horses shot under him, Raghují Bhonslé gave an example to his men of unsurpassed cowardice; after having by that example paralysed their action, he quitted the field. He was followed by Daolat Ráo as soon as the defeat of his cavalry had been pronounced. Thenceforward the soldiers of the latter fought without a leader, and many of them by their gallantry proved that they deserved a better.

The evening of the day after the battle Stevenson came up and at once proceeded in pursuit of the enemy. He soon found that the beaten army, after reaching the village of Anwah, had turned suddenly westward, apparently in the hope of gaining the southern Maráthá country by Tal Ghát and Kasára. Wellesley, on receiving this information, directed him to continue his march northward to reduce the important city of Burhánpúr and the fortress of Asírgarh, whilst he himself, south of Ajunta, should watch the movements of the enemy. These measures were successfully accomplished. Stevenson captured Barhánpúr without opposition (19th October), reduced Asírgarh —considered the key of the Dakhan—after battering it for an hour (21st October) and received, as a consequence, the submission of the independent districts of Khandesh. Wellesley, who up to that time, had acted strictly on the defensive, no sooner heard that Asírgarh had fallen than he dashed after the Bhonslé, who had quitted Sindia to proceed on a predatory expedition to the south. So greatly did the presence of the conqueror of Assaye terrify Raghují, that to avoid him he changed his camp five times in less than forty-eight hours, and finally beat a hurried retreat to his own territories. He had been sickened of fighting.

Wellesley then turned northwards to cover Stevenson on the march to besiege the strong fortress of Gúalgarh. Gúalgarh, a hundred and seventy miles to the north-east of Aurangabad, was a place of considerable importance, inasmuch as it commanded the main road across the mountain range which divides northern from southern India. It consisted of two forts built on the southern declivity of that range, and these owed their strength as much to the formidable nature of their works as to the fact that it was only with extreme difficulty that guns could be transported into a position to open upon them with effect. The capture of this stronghold would place the dominions of the Bhonslé at the mercy of the conqueror. On his way thither Wellesley received information that the Bhonslé's army, led by his brother, Manú Bápú, was encamped at Pahtarlí, six miles from the village of Argaum, and that Sindia's army lay within four miles of it. Wellesley, despite of the entreaties of Sindia's envoys who were pressing upon him terms of accommodation, sent instant word to Stevenson to join him at Pahtarli, and there attack the enemy. The junction was effected on the 29th September. The enemy had but that day decamped, and Wellesley, with troops tired from a long and fatiguing march, did not think proper to pursue them. The enemy, emboldened by this unwonted quiescence, sent forward parties of horse to beat up the surroundings of the English camp, and as these met with but a slight opposition from the Maisúr horse they supported them with many squadrons. Uneasy at this demonstration Wellesley directed the pickets to advance to the support of the Maisúr horsemen, and following them himself he discovered the combined armies of Sindia and the Bhonslé—horse, foot, and artillery—drawn up in order of battle in the extensive plain which covers the village of Argaum. Their position was well chosen. Their line, which was five miles in length, rested on the village of Argaum and the extensive walled enclosures adjacent to it, whilst to attack them the English would have to traverse a plain intersected by watercourses. Sindia, whose troops consisted wholly of cavalry, commanded on the right; Manú Bapú, who had under him men belonging to the three arms, including a powerful artillery, on the left. It was past 4 o'clock in the afternoon. The British troops had had their food and some rest. It was impossible to decline the combat. Wellesley then ordered his men to turn out, moved them forward in column till they arrived within range, then deploying the infantry into line, and having the cavalry behind as a support, advanced to the attack. The guns of the enemy were however, well served, and their fire, directed by accident or design at the three native regiments, produced upon these so great an effect that the men composing them, men who had behaved well at Assaye, turned and ran. Fortunately Wellesley was on the spot, and succeeded by his influence and example in rallying the fugitives and inducing them to resume their place in the line. He then urged on his right, somewhat thrown forward, in order to press upon the enemy's infantry and guns. It was soon clear that the enemy meant fighting. As the English line advanced, a body of infantry, five hundred strong, called Persian, but really Arabs, the chosen corps of the army, dashed forward to meet them. The 74th and 78th received them with steadiness, and marching calmly forward, swept them, almost to a man, into eternity. This movement had evidently been designed to engage the European troops, whilst the cavalry should deal with the sipáhís, whose conduct had not been unobserved. Accordingly, whilst the Europeans and Arabs were struggling for dear life, the enemy's cavalry, in dense masses, directed a charge towards the left of the British line. Before, however, they could reach it, the three regiments of Madras native cavalry, led by Wellesley in person, galloped from the rear and met them in full shock. The contest was neither long nor doubtful. The famed Maráthá horsemen recoiled disheartened and in disorder before the British-led troopers of Madras! This charge, and the simultaneous destruction of the Arab cohort, decided the battle. The enemy's long line broke and fled!

The sun was setting as the Maráthá host fled in disorder from the field of Argaum. The pursuit was continued by moonlight. "If we had had daylight an hour more," wrote Wellesley, "not a man would have escaped." As it was, they lost everything—thirty-eight pieces of cannon, their camp equipage, their confidence, their hope. The army dispersed never again to re-unite. Argaum, won with the loss of fifteen Europeans and thirty-one sipáhís killed, and less than two hundred wounded, was the complement of Assaye. It finished the war in southern and western India. The strong fortress of Gúalgarh was stormed on the 15th December. Two days later Raghují Bhonslé signed a treaty with the British, by which he yielded the provinces of Katak (Cuttack) and Barár; renounced all his claims on the

Nizám, and agreed to refer all disputes between that potentate and himself to British arbitration.

The treaty with Sindia, the treaty known as Surji Anjangáon, was signed thirteen days later. I shall consider its terms after I shall have described the great battle which not less than Assaye and Argaum forced it upon Dáolat Ráo—the battle of Laswárí. What Wellesley effected for southern and western, Lake achieved for central and north-western, India. Complete as were the operations of each in themselves, each required the other to produce a perfect result. Assaye decided the war in south-western India; Laswárí and the actions which preceded Laswárí decided it in the more northern parts. But taking a comprehensive view, it may be affirmed that neither without the other would have produced the result actually obtained. It is necessary, then, before summarising the results of the war, that the reader should accompany me to the camp of General Lake at Kánhpúr.

CHAPTER X.

LASWARI.

When Marquess Wellesley issued instructions to his brother to commence hostilities against the two Maráthá powers in south-western and western India, he had not been unmindful of the fact that the great bulk of the trained soldiers of Sindia, armed and officered by Europeans, held the North-Western Provinces; that they occupied Alígarh, the imperial cities of Dihlí and Agrá, and that a considerable portion of them were scattered over central India. Simultaneously, then, with the instructions given to his brother, he had directed the Commander-in-Chief in India, General Lake, to mass his troops at Kánhpúr, and to cross the frontier as soon as war should be declared.

The objects which the great Marquess had in view, and to accomplish which he had put forth all the resources of the British power in India, were worthy of his comprehensive and enlightened mind. Face to face with the Maráthá confederacy, whose avowed object was the expulsion of the British from India, he had realised that but one course was open to him. He must strike, and strike at the heart with a force which should be irresistible; break for ever the power for aggressive purposes of the great Maráthá chieftains; prevent Sindia, on the one side, from extending his possessions southwards, and rescue from his grasp, on the other, the two imperial cities. It had devolved, in fact, on Marquess Wellesley to do that, for the security of the British tenure in India, which five and thirty years previously the great Lord Clive had denounced as a policy certain to entail ruin on British interests. Clive would have retained the frontiers of Allahábád and cultivated amicable relations with the Maráthás. As a permanent policy, such a course was impracticable. What the Núwáb-Vazír of Awadh had been to Clive and his contemporaries, the Maráthás had become to his successors. Again was it a duel upon the issue of which depended the maintenance of the British power in India.

Lake, in pursuance of his instructions, issued from Kánhpúr, at the head of an army numbering five thousand infantry, two thousand five hundred cavalry, and the usual proportion of artillery, on the 5th August 1803, and crossed the British frontier about four miles to the south of Koil, the town protected by the fort of Aligarh, and separated from it by a plain, on the 28th.

The Maráthá troops in Koil were not much more numerous than the British army. They counted but two thousand infantry, eight thousand cavalry, and the usual proportion of guns. They were commanded by a Frenchman named Perron. Perron, who had risen to this position from that of a common sailor, was not a very strong man. He had arrived at that phase in the life of the adventurer who serves a foreign master when the interests of the master are subordinated to the interests of the servant. Daolat Rao Sindia, the master, had detected the arrival of this phase in the career of Perron, and had already made arrangements to replace him by one of his own countrymen, Ambají Inglia. Perron, aware that his disgrace was probably but a question of weeks, that Dudrenec, who was marching from Ujjén to Aligárh, was devoted to Ambají, that Bourquin, who commanded two brigades under his orders, was not to be depended upon, thought far more of making terms with the British than of opposing to them a stout resistance. When, then, on the 29th August, General Lake marched upon Koil, and in that operation exposed his flank to the enemy, Perron, who might have taken him at disadvantage, gave no orders. His men, waiting for those orders, were paralysed by the reserve of their leader, and when, a few seconds later the British galloper guns opened upon them, they lost heart and fled in all directions. Perron himself escaped to Mathurá, and from that place made terms with the English.

There remained the fort of Alígarh, which, garrisoned by two thousand trained infantry, commanded by a good officer, a Frenchman named Pedrons, seemed capable of offering a long resistance. Summoned to surrender, Pedrons flatly refused. To undertake the siege of the place would have interfered very much with the English General's plans regarding Dihlí, as it would have given time to the enemy's forces, then rapidly hurrying up from Central India, to concentrate for the defence of the place. Lake then carefully examined Alígarh. He found it very strong, but with one weak point. This weak point was a narrow passage leading across the ditch into the fort. But, weak as it was, it was guarded by a strong gateway, covering three other gateways behind it. It presented a forlorn chance. Such as it was, however, Lake, who made it a rule of life never to do things by halves, and who ever declared that boldness was prudence, resolved to attempt it and to try a *coup de main*. It was a bold resolve, for failure would give the Maráthá troops the morale which they wanted.

Early on the morning of the 4th September the British troops stormed Alígarh. It was a deed of splendid daring—for the defences were strong, the enemy watchful and brave. It cost in killed and wounded two hundred and sixty men, but it electrified India. To use the words of an officer then in the service of Sindia: "it was a mortal blow to the Maráthá war; it struck a panic into the minds of the natives and astonished all the princes of Hindústán; it gave them dreadful ideas of European soldiers and European courage."

From Alígarh Lake marched towards Dihlí (7th September). On the 11th, after a very fatiguing march, he had, at 11 o'clock, just reached the banks of the Jehna Nálá, six miles from the imperial city, when the Maráthá force, consisting of twelve battalions of trained infantry, five thousand cavalry, and seventy guns, the whole commanded by a Frenchman, named Louis Bourquin, was upon him. Bourquin was an inferior specimen of a class generally inferior. He was little fitted to lead an army, and, if we may draw conclusions from his career, Nature had not even endowed him with the animal virtue of courage. A great opportunity was here offered him. At the head of a superior force he had surprised—for he had done nothing less—the enemy's troops, tired after a long march. His position, too, was a strong one, for his front was covered by a line of intrenchments previously prepared; each flank was covered by a swamp, and the position of his guns was concealed by the long grass which covered the ground between him and the British camp. Lake, reconnoitring, noticed all this, the strength of the position, the impossibility of turning it. His own men were tired; many had undressed; many more were scattered. But Lake was essentially a man of action. He resolved to draw the enemy from their position, with his cavalry, and then to sever them from their intrenchments and pounce upon them.

He carried out this plan to the letter. Sending the cavalry in front at a trot, he moved his infantry slowly forward under cover of the long grass. The cavalry made a feigned attack on the intrenchments and then fell back as if beaten. This brought out the enemy with loud shouts from the intrenchments, and, as the British cavalry continued to fall back further and further, the enemy's infantry hastened to follow them. At last they reached a point within reach of the British infantry. Then the order was given; the cavalry opened out from the centre, and the infantry marching through, led by the Commander-in-Chief in person, made a dash at the intrenchments. They halted but once, within eighty yards, to fire one volley; then, despite of the showers of grape and round shot from the enemy's guns, they dashed forward with so much impetuosity, that the enemy gave way and fled. No sooner had this end been achieved, than the infantry formed into column of companies to allow the cavalry and galloper guns to pass through and finish the work. This was successfully accomplished. Never was a victory more complete. The enemy, who fought well, suffered heavily, for many of those who did not perish on the field were drowned in the Jamná. The English lost four hundred and eighty-six killed and wounded. Bourquin was the first man to leave the field. He surrendered with five other foreign officers, three days later, to the conqueror.

One important consequence of this victory was the capture of the city of Dihli. On the 14th September General Lake entered the city and released from confinement the blinded King, Sháh A'lam—the same whom we have seen, as Sháhzádah and as Emperor, the opponent of Clive and the ally of the Núwáb Vazír of Awadh, and who had subsequently been deprived of his sight by the infamous Ghulám Kadir (1788).* It was a pleasure to the English general to restore the venerable monarch to his throne, and to make arrangements for the peaceful enjoyment of his freedom and his dignities.

On the 24th September Lake set out with his army for Agrá. He arrived there on the 4th October, and encamped within long cannon-shot of the fortress. Agrá was then garrisoned by four thousand five hundred men, under the nominal command of George Hessing, an adventurer of Dutch extraction. The garrison, however, had noted the facility with which Perron, Bourquin, and other foreign officers had surrendered to the English, had conceived, consequently, a distrust of Hessing, and had placed him and the six European officers with him under restraint.

* The reader is referred to Mr. H. G. Keane's graphic history of the fall of the Moghul Empire.

Besides this garrison, there lay, encamped under the walls of the fortress, three battalions of the army which had been defeated near Dihlí, and four battalions of Perron's 5th Brigade, just arrived from the Dakhan with twenty-six pieces of cannon, the whole under the command of Major Brownrigg. The garrison had refused to admit these troops within the walls, because they feared that their admission would give them a claim to a participation in the twenty-five lakhs of rupees which formed the contents of the treasure-chest. In addition to these, again, twelve battalions of trained sipáhís, led by Dudrenec, from Ujjén, the flower of Sindia's army, occupied a position on the right rear of the British force, with the view, it was supposed, should the siege last long enough, of recovering Dihlí.

General Lake, having taken complete cognisance of the state of affairs, resolved, with his usual dash and energy, to dispose of his three enemies separately. The first he went against was the enemy outside the fortress, the remnants of Perron's and Bourquin's armies. These he attacked on the 10th October with so much energy that, with a loss of two hundred and thirteen in killed and wounded on his part, he inflicted upon them a severe defeat, placed six hundred of them *hors de combat*, captured all their guns, and so dispirited the remainder that, two days later, two thousand five hundred of them passed into the British service. Proceeding with the same vigour, he opened his batteries against the fortress, and compelled its surrender on the 18th. By this capture he not only became possessor of the cherished twenty-five lakhs, but he secured a line of defence along the left bank of the Jamná.

There now remained for him to deal with only the twelve battalions, about nine thousand strong, the flower of Sindia's army, led, for the most part, from Ujjén by the Chevalier Dudrenec. Unfortunately for Sindia, the conditions offered by the British Government to foreign officers to quit the service of their Indian master had been so much appreciated that Dudrenec himself and all the officers of the force had entered British territory. The flower of the army, the men victorious on many a field, were, then, led by their own countrymen. Supreme in command was Abaji, a Maráthá of great pertinacity and not without military talent. On realising the fall of Agrá, Abají had moved leisurely into the Jaipúr country, with the intention of taking post in the hilly country of Mewát, the only pass into which could easily be made impregnable.

Thither, on the 27th October, Lake, at the head of three regiments of dragoons, five of native cavalry, one regiment of European infantry (the 76th), and four battalions of sipáhís, followed him. So eager was he to catch him, that when he found that the heavy state of the soil, saturated with rain, retarded his progress, he came to a decision to leave the greater part of his artillery behind him, and to press on with his cavalry and infantry. Making forced marches with these, he reached, the night of the 31st, the ground which Abají had quitted that very morning. As this ground was but thirty-three miles distant from the pass into the Mewát country of which I have spoken, Lake, viewing the enormous importance of anticipating the enemy, resolved to push on with his cavalry alone, and encounter, if necessary, the Maráthás with that arm.

At midnight, then, he set off with his three cavalry brigades, leaving the infantry to follow. Pushing on without a halt, he came up at sunrise with the enemy, strongly posted about the village of Laswárí. On that village itself their left rested, whilst their right was covered by a rivulet the banks of which were steep and difficult; between these two points lay their centre, concealed from view by long grass, and defended by a most formidable line of artillery. Partly in consequence of this long grass, partly to the clouds of dust blown towards the British, General Lake did not at once realise the extreme strength of the enemy's position, and full of the idea that they intended to seize the pass in the Mewáti hills, from which they were now but eight miles distant, he resolved not to wait for his infantry, but attack them at once. Accordingly, he formed up his cavalry, and placing himself, as was his custom, at their head, directed successive charges from the advanced guard and first and second brigades on the left of the enemy's position, whilst the third brigade should turn their right. The charges on the left, where, it will be remembered, the Maráthás were massed about Laswárí, were executed with great precision and success; the enemy were driven into the village, several guns were taken, and, in some instances, their line was penetrated. The want of infantry to complete that which the cavalry had begun was, however, severely felt, for it enabled the enemy to re-form and recover their guns. The charge on the right was as brilliant and as resultless. The 3rd Brigade, which made it, was formed of the 29th Dragoons and the 4th Native Light Cavalry. They had been directed to turn the enemy's right. To enable them to take up a position to carry out this manœuvre, they had to ride along the front of the enemy's line, exposed to the fire of seventy-four guns, hidden from them by the long grass. Heedless of this fire, they galloped to the position marked out for them, then formed up as steadily as if on parade, and charged the hostile batteries. Here, again, the want of infantry was felt. The cavalry rode over the guns only to find the enemy's infantry securely protected by an intrenchment, from which they poured a galling fire. After they had vainly made heroic efforts to surmount the difficulty, the General, perceiving the inutility of persevering further, recalled his cavalry. If the attack had served to show the great strength of the enemy's position, it had at least also had the effect of preventing them from reaching Mewát.

At noon the infantry came up, eager, notwithstanding their forced march of twenty-five miles, for the attack. The General, however, ordered them, in the first instance, to take their morning meal. An hour later he ranged them for the battle.

Meanwhile, the enemy had been busy in strengthening their right, already the objective point of the British attack. Aware of the additional strength obtained by the occupation of houses they now caused it to fall back slightly on and about the village of Mohalpúr, in which, also, they concentrated many of their guns. Their preparations had just been completed when they became sensible of a movement on the part of the British.

This time the English General had resolved to attack the enemy's right seriously with his infantry, and, whilst one brigade of cavalry should threaten his left, the other two brigades were to be handy to support the infantry attack. That attack was made in two lines, in column. No sooner, however, was the movement of the first line, composed of the 76th and two native regiments, and led by the General in person, noticed by the enemy, than their infantry fell back, and from their guns in Mohalpúr, on its right, and on its left, there opened a concentrated fire on the advancing troops. Terrible as were its effects, great as was the slaughter, Lake was only impelled to press on the more quickly, careless, under the circumstances, of the fact, that, from some cause or other, the advance of the second line had been delayed. The decisive point in his eyes was the guns, and those, at any rate, must be captured. The gallant warrior, conspicuous on his horse, then led his men forward in face of a fire which, for intensity, has rarely, if ever, been surpassed. But the enemy were worthy even of him and his soldiers. Led only by their own countrymen, they did credit to the careful training they had received at the hands of Dudrenec and de Boigne. So firm was their defence, so steadfast their bearing, that the British troops could make no impression upon them. Just at the critical moment, too, when the English column was struggling forward under all the difficulties I have recorded, Abájí, with the true eye of a general, dashed his cavalry against them. The charge was repulsed, and Lake, whose mental energies, like those of Masséna, always redoubled under the roar of cannon, then directed the British cavalry to make a counter-charge. As the men were forming up for this purpose, the horse of the General, who had ridden up to them to superintend it, was shot under him: the next moment his son,* who had dismounted to offer him his own, was shot by his side and severely wounded. This affecting incident, witnessed by all the troops preparing to charge, inspired them with enthusiasm. When, a few seconds later, the order was given, they dashed forward with an *élan* which was irresistible. In vain did seventy guns pour shot and shell into their ranks; in vain did the dense masses of the enemy spring forward to repel them. Nothing stopped them; they carried the guns. Then Lake, with his infantry handy, dashed forward and secured the greater number of them. Still, however, the enemy fought on, disputing with a valour and a pertinacity not to be exceeded every inch of the ground. Nor did they quit the field till they had been driven from every position and had lost every gun!

In the desperate valour with which it was contested on both sides, in the equality of the numbers engaged, and in the proportion of the numbers lost, the battle of Laswárí ranks above all others in which the British troops had been engaged in India. To rival it we must cast our eyes forward more than forty years till they rest on Fírúzshahar and the Satlaj. A contemporary writer, who took part in the action, and to whose spirited narrative I am indebted for many of its details,† records that from the commencement of the conflict early in the morning to the close of the general action in the evening the enemy discovered a firmness of resolution and a

* Afterwards, when Lieutenant-Colonel of the 29th Foot, killed at the battle of Rolica (17th August, 1808), just when, at the head of his regiment, he had forced the pass, the possession of which decided the day.

† Thorn's *War in India*.

contempt of death which could not fail to command the admiration of their opponents. It was well that it was so! They were fighting for empire. To their master defeat meant more even than the failure to obtain empire; it meant the loss of the independent position which the House of Sindia had gained by the sword!

Yes—the war provoked by Sindia and the Bhonslé was a war in which they had staked that independent position to fight for empire. They lost the stake. First, the blow delivered by Wellesley on the 23rd September at Assaye ruined their aspirations with respect to south-western and western India—the early cradle of their power. But the blow dealt at Assaye did not affect the vast countries north of the Vindhayan range. In those—from Ujjén to Gwáliár, from Gwáliár to Agrá, to Dihlí, to Aligarh, and, it may be said, generally in Rájpútáná—Sindia was still master. In those were concentrated his best troops, his best guns, his best generals, his strongest places. By a succession of rapid manœuvres, and a rare display of fighting power, Lake wrested these strong places from him one after another, and then finally dealt a most decisive blow—the most decisive blow of the whole war—at Laswárí. It was the fairest, the most equally matched, and the most hotly contested battle ever fought between the British and the natives of India. It had the most important consequences. The battle of Laswárí brought to the ground, crumbled and trampled in the dust all the dreams of Madhají Sindia. From its effects the great Maráthá family never recovered!

To gain it cost the victors eight hundred and thirty-eight in killed and wounded, or one man out of every five engaged. The enemy's loss in the actual battle was probably not so great, but in the pursuit which followed it they suffered terribly.

Though Laswárí was fought twenty days before Argaum, it was not Argaum but Laswárí which decided Sindia to accept the terms offered by Marquess Wellesley. Argaum was a rout, the Maráthá troops engaged in which had been beaten before they had fought. Laswárí had taken the fighting stuff out of every man in the Maráthá dominions.

Its result, coming immediately after Argaum, was the treaty of Surjí Arjengáon. By this treaty Dáolat Ráo ceded to the British and their allies his territories between the Jamná and the Ganges, as well as those situate to the northward of Jaipúr, of Jodhpúr, and of Gohad; the forts of Ahmadnagar and of Bharuch (Broach), and the districts adjoining; his possessions between Ajunta Ghát and the Godávari. He renounced, likewise, all claims on the Mughul emperor, on the Peshwá, on the Nizám, on the Gáikwar, and on all the rájahs who had assisted the British. There were other minor concessions, but these were the principal.

Though the final blow dealt at the Maráthá empire was not dealt till fourteen years later, when the Peshwá was extinguished and Sindia and Holkar were still further reduced, the conditions of their existence never resumed the importance that had attached to them prior to the campaign of 1803. It may be said, indeed, that that campaign virtually decided beforehand the war which immediately followed with Jeswant Ráo Holkar, and which forced that potentate, a fugitive hopeless of aught but of his life, to throw himself on the mercy of the conqueror with the touching admission that "his whole kingdom lay upon his saddle's bow." The two Maráthá chieftains allowed themselves to be dealt with in detail, and there can be no doubt that, in spite of some accidents of the second war, such as Monson's retreat and the failure at Bharatpúr, Holkar's soldiers suffered throughout the campaign from the effects of Laswárí!

One word regarding the general who fought it. General Lake was a man whose influence with his soldiers was unbounded, whose calmness in danger, whose self-reliance, and whose power of commanding confidence have never been surpassed. He had but one way of dealing with the native armies of India, that of moving straight forward; of attacking them wherever he found them. He never was so great as on the battle field. He could think more clearly under the roar of bullets than in the calmness and quiet of his tent. In this respect he resembled Clive. It was this quality which enabled him to dare the almost impossible. That which in others would have been rash, in Lake was prudent daring.

If success justifies a general, then was Lake fully absolved from the criticisms of men who took not into consideration his peculiar qualities. With a force at no time exceeding eight thousand men, he, between the 29th August and the 1st November, destroyed the thirty-one battalions which French adventurers had trained and disciplined for the service of Sindia; stormed a strong fortress, captured Agrá, and entered as a conqueror the imperial city of Dihlí; captured four hundred and twenty-six pieces of cannon, and defeated the enemy in four pitched battles—the last of them, for the results it produced, one of the most decisive battles ever fought. There must be some credit due to the man who accomplished such great results in a period exceeding two months by only three days. What he might have accomplished had he lived to be employed against the soldiers of Napoleon no man can say. He died a victim to the climate of India. He left that country in February 1807, reached England in the September following, and died in February 1808. He had been created a viscount for his brilliant services.

CHAPTER XI.

BHARATPÚR.

I MENTIONED towards the close of the last chapter that the victory over Sindia virtually decided the war which immediately followed with Jeswant Ráo Holkar. That war was, however, marked by two events which for a time shook the prestige of the British. These were the retreat, still known in history as "Monson's retreat," and the abortive siege of Bharatpúr, commonly called Bhurtpore. The first of these was completely avenged the very year of its occurrence. The renown of the second continued for twenty years to point the moral to the malcontents and intriguers who flocked about the courts of native princes. These never failed to impress upon their masters that there was a limit to British prowess; that behind stone walls and earthworks they could be defied with impunity. To repress this growing feeling, to convince the natives who traded upon it that the "incident" of 1804 was but an "accident," a second siege was needed. The second siege, undertaken by Lord Combermere in 1825, terminated successfully for the British. In its result it decided the question as to the capacity of British troops, and native soldiers led by British officers, to prevail against stone walls and earthen ramparts. The story of both sieges may fairly claim a place, then, in a work which relates those military events which decided the question of British supremacy in India. For it must never be forgotten that though we won India by the sword we hold it mainly by opinion—by the conviction in the minds of the natives that we are strong enough to maintain law and order within its borders, to protect them against all enemies from without.

When Sindia and the Bhonslé had entered into that war with the British, the most striking incidents of which are related in the last chapter, Jeswant Ráo Holkar had held aloof, and, as the war proceeded, had watched with complacency the defeats of the two Maráthá princes. There was a feeling, additional to the feeling of jealousy of Sindia, which nourished this complacency. Jeswant Ráo was, in his way, a man of very considerable natural capacity. High-spirited, courageous, a splendid horseman, he was the very man to lead the Maráthás in the charges for which they were so renowned. Against Daolat Ráo he had grave cause of complaint. The son of the last Holkar by a concubine, he was a prisoner at the capital of the Bhonslé when Daolat Ráo, in the hope of obtaining possession of all the territories of the Holkars, murdered the rightful heir, Mulhar Ráo, a prince of great promise, and imprisoned his only legitimate brother, Khásí Ráo, a man of weak intellect, whom he proposed to use as a tool. This treacherous action was resented by the followers of the Holkars, and they instinctively turned their hopes to Jeswant Ráo. Informed of what had happened, the young chief escaped from his place of confinement and assumed the reins of sovereignty at Indúr in 1798. To avenge himself upon Sindia he invaded his territories shortly after, and, in June 1801, completely defeated his army at U'jjén. In the July following he made a daring attack upon Sindia's great park of artillery on the Narbadá, and, though he was repulsed, so thoroughly alarmed Daolat Ráo that that Máhárájah advanced at once in great force on the capital, Indúr. In the hotly-contested battle which followed near that place Sindia was the victor. But, by his dilatoriness, he cast away all the fruits of victory; allowed Holkar time to gather together a new army, at the head of which he plundered Rájpútána, devastated Khándesh, and, defeating, the 25th of October, the army of Sindia near Púna, occupied that capital, and terrified the Peshwá into signing with the British that treaty of Bassein which was the virtual abdication of his power!

Roused to a conviction of the danger which might await each of themselves from the fate which had attended the prince who had been, nominally at least, the lord of their confederacy, the three Maráthá chiefs, Sindia, the Bhonslé, and Holkar, forgot for a moment their jealousies of each other, and agreed, in the manner related in the last chapter, to band together against the British. But when the time for action arrived Jeswant Ráo held aloof, hoping, it is believed, that when the combatants were exhausted, he would be able to step in and dictate his own terms!

How the contest between the British and the two other Maráthá princes, Sindia and the Bhonslé, terminated, I have told in the last chapter. Jeswant Ráo had watched, I have said, the course of the contest with complacency. The sudden collapse of his former associates, the fact that within a period of little more than two months the English in northern and central India had taken A'ligarh, Dihlí, and A'gra, and gained the battle of Laswárí; whilst in the south-west they had triumphed at Assaye and Argaum, gave him, however, considerable cause for reflection, and he hesitated long as to whether he should attempt to plunder Sindia, weakened by his losses, or, cementing an alliance with him, turn his arms against the British. For a short time he seemed inclined to the former course; and it was only when he learned that Sindia, apprehensive of such action on his part, had agreed* to become a party to the defensive alliance subsisting between the British Government, the

* Treaty dated 27th February 1804.

Peshwá, and the Nizám, on condition that the British should maintain a subsidiary force of six battalions for his defence, that he reconsidered his position. With the cunning habitual to a Maráthá he resolved at last to play a double game: to endeavour, on the one hand, to induce Sindia to join him against the British; on the other, to solicit permission from the latter to allow him to deal as he might choose with Sindia. In both these attempts he over-reached himself. Sindia, smarting under blows the severity of which he greatly attributed to the abstention of Holkar, communicated to the British the overtures made to him. The perusal of the documents containing these, combined with the haughty tone of the letters addressed by Jeswant Ráo to the British generals, satisfied the Governor-General that Holkar was bent on war. Instructions were at once despatched to Lord Lake, who was encamped with his army at Biána, fifty miles south-west from Agrá, opposite the pass leading into the dominions of the Rájah of Jaipúr, to resist any attempt which Jeswant Ráo Holkar might make on the territories of Sindia.

Before he had received this communication, Lord Lake, desirous to avoid unnecessary complications, had despatched a letter to Jeswant Ráo warning him of the consequences of making war upon an ally of the British and strongly urging him to remain quietly within his own territories. But already the mind of Jeswant Ráo was made up. On the receipt of Lord Lake's letter, he sent for an English adventurer in his service, named Vickers, one of his best officers, a man whose coolness and powers of leading had contributed largely to the victory gained over Sindia near Púna (the 25th October 1802); informed him of his determination to fight the English; and asked him if he was ready to join in battle against his own countrymen. The reply of Vickers was clear and decided. He would fight against any other people, but not against his own countrymen. Holkar then summoned two other Englishmen in his service, Tod and

Ryan, and put to each the same question. They gave the answer which Vickers had given. Then Holkar ordered that the three men should be slain. Their heads were at once severed from their bodies and placed on three poles in front of his camp, whilst a crier proclaimed that such would be the fate of every European who should fall into the hands of Holkar!

This barbarous murder, the discovery about the same time of correspondence on the part of Jeswant Ráo with the Rohílahs and the Sikhs, and the threatening attitude which the troops of Holkar were assuming with respect to Jaipúr, determined Lord Lake to advance into the territory of that Rájah. Accordingly, having previously sent back his heavy guns to Agrá, he broke up, the 9th February 1804, from Biána, and marched leisurely twenty-one miles to Hindáon, in Jaipúr territory. Hence, as the negotiations still proceeding with Holkar seemed every day to assume a more unsatisfactory tone, he proceeded, the 8th March, to Rámgarh, still in Jaipûr territory, forty-one miles, north-west by west, from the capital of that name. He was here when he received letters from Holkar, to the haughty tone of which I have referred in a previous page. Haughty as was that tone, it was as nothing in comparison with the bearing of the messengers who conveyed the letters. These openly avowed that their master had concluded a treaty with the Rohílahs and with the Rájah of Bharatpúr; declared that a war with Holkar could never bring any profit to his opponents, since he was a marauder by profession; could dispose of one hundred and fifty thousand cavalry, at whose head he would be able to inflict terrible punishment on his enemies, whilst defeat in one place would not prevent reappearance in another. They boasted, likewise, of a secret understanding with Sindia and of an alliance with France!

Lord Lake contented himself with advising the emissaries of Holkar and Holkar himself to be more moderate in their language. On the 23rd he moved to Bálàhára, still in Jaipúr territory. There he received a copy of an insolent letter which Holkar had addressed to General Wellesley. A few days later he heard that Holkar had invaded and plundered the dominions of the Rájah of Jaipúr. He at once applied to the Governor-General for instructions. Marquess Wellesley, in reply, directed Lord Lake to treat Holkar as an enemy.

Still Lake was unwilling to do more than protect the princes who naturally looked to the English for defence. Of these the Rájah of Jaipúr was one. The territories of that prince had been plundered, and his capital was in danger. To protect that capital, then, Lord Lake despatched from Déosar, which place he reached on the 17th, a small force under Colonel Monson. The distance to be traversed was fifty miles.

Colonel Monson had a very good reputation in the army. He had led the storming party at A'ligarh, but the severe wound he had received on that occasion had not allowed him to take any further part in the campaign. From that wound he had but recently recovered, and it was to compensate him for his enforced absence from the fields of Dihlí, Agrá, and Laswárí that Lord Lake now gave him an opportunity of distinguishing himself. The force entrusted to him consisted of the two battalions of the 12th Regiment N.I., the 2nd Battalion 2nd N.I., a few European gunners, some native cavalry levies, and a small contingent of Sindia's troops under Bápúji Sindia, a relative of Daolat Ráo.

With this force Colonel Monson set out from Déosar on the 18th April and reached the vicinity of Jaipúr on the 21st. Lord Lake had not despatched him a day too soon, for he found Holkar's army occupying a position which threatened the city on its southern side. Whether it was that Jeswant Ráo was unwilling to strike the first blow at the British, or whether he had already conceived the design of enticing Colonel Monson into a position from which he would find it difficult to withdraw, may not be exactly known. It is certain, however, that when, on the morning of the 23rd, Monson reconnoïtred his position, Jeswant Ráo had disappeared!

Holkar had marched in a southerly direction, apparently without purpose. Meanwhile, however, Lord Lake had despatched Colonel Don with seven companies of native battalions, a native cavalry regiment, and a native battery, to gain possession of Tonk Rámpúra, a strong fort in the district of Tonk. Don had duly stormed Tonk Rámpúra. The news of this had a marked influence on the proceedings of Jeswant Ráo. Before the fall of Tonk Rámpúra he had carefully kept on the right bank of the Chambal, but, on hearing of Don's success, he crossed that river and marched hastily southwards.

Relieved by this retreat Lord Lake resolved to rest his troops and to postpone serious operations until after the rainy season. He directed Don, then, to join Monson with two native regiments; ordered that officer, whose force was thus strengthened to four thousand men, to march on Kotá and cover the Jaipúr territory, whilst he himself should move on Agra and Kánhpúr. Similarly, General Wellesley directed Colonel Murray to march with a small force from Gujrát upon Indúr, with a view to prevent Jeswant Ráo from attempting to recover ground in the north.

Monson had, we have seen, been ordered to defend, from Kotá, the territory of Jaipúr. Scarcely, however, had Lord Lake moved towards Agra than it occurred to Monson that by making a movement from Kotá southwards he would be able to open communications with Murray. In spite of the fact that such a move was opposed to the general instructions he had received from his Commander-in-Chief, he made it; marched through the Mokandara pass twenty miles to Sonára, detached thence one native regiment, six 6-pounders, and some irregular horse, under Major Sinclair, to seize the small but strong fort of Hinglajgarh; whilst he pushed on himself, notwithstanding very rainy weather and bad roads, to the village of Píplah. Here he received information that Holkar had suddenly retraced his steps and was then encamped with a strong force on the Chambal, some twenty-five miles distant, covering the town of Rámpúra, within the Indúr territory—not to be confounded with the Tonk Rámpúra—and guarding the only ford across the river by which it could be approached.

Monson had with him but three days' supplies, and he had experienced the greatest difficulty in obtaining any more from the country through which he had marched. Píplah was only a village, quite unable to furnish him, and he had counted on re-victualling at Rámpúra. To reach Rámpúra was now impossible, if Holkar should bar the way. Equally so to remain, with only three days' supplies, at the village of Píplah. He could not make up his mind to retreat. But Monson was a very sanguine man. He had absolute faith in the moral efficacy of a forward movement. He could not divest himself of the belief that if Holkar, who had shrunk from attacking him at Jaipúr, were to learn that he was marching on Rámpúra he would retreat before him. He resolved, then, in spite of the still continuing rain, to march on that place. Setting out on the morning of the 7th July, he halted for the night at Gurí, seven miles from Rámpúra. There, conflicting information of the movements of Holkar at first reached him. Finally, however, at 9 o'clock at night he received certain intelligence that Jeswant Ráo had crossed the river and was distributing largesses to his troops. This was regarded as the certain prelude to action, and Monson accordingly ordered his troops to remain under arms all night.

During that night he consulted with the commanding officers under him, and especially with the leader of the native contingent, Bápújí Sindia. Unfortunately, this man, who was in secret correspondence with Holkar, prevailed upon Monson to give the order to retreat. In a word, the resolution which had prompted Monson to advance from Píplah vanished when he was persuaded that his progress so far had not induced Holkar to evacuate Rámpúra. In vain did the commandants of the native regiments urge him to advance. In vain did Lieutenant Lucan, who commanded the native cavalry levies, beg him, on his knees, to attack Holkar, offering to encounter that chief with his own men. Colonel Monson had made up his mind. Telling Lucan that he might, if he chose, stay to encounter the whole Maráthá army, he gave immediate orders for a retrograde movement. During the night, indeed, he held his ground, but at 4 o'clock the following morning he despatched his baggage and camp equipage towards Sonára, and followed at 9 A.M. with his infantry and guns, directing Lucan to cover the retreat with his cavalry. His hope was to reach the Mokandara pass before the enemy could reach him. Once there, he calculated on being able to obtain supplies from the country beyond it, whilst his troops would defend the pass against Holkar's entire army.

But Monson had not left his ground at Gurí three hours before he found he had reckoned too much on the inactivity of Jeswant Ráo. Scarcely had that time expired when twenty thousand Maráthá horsemen, flushed with the conviction of their own superiority, dashed upon Lucan's scanty horsemen and speedily overpowered them. Lucan and his comrade, the Baraitch Nuwáb, after doing wonders, were wounded and taken prisoners, whilst Bápújí Sindia, throwing off the mask, boldly went over to the enemy. Monson, meanwhile, pushed on with his infantry, reached Sonára, a march of twenty miles, the same evening, and the Mokandara pass, nearly twenty miles further, early the next morning. There Jeswant Ráo summoned him to surrender. On his refusal, Jeswant Ráo attacked him; but Monson's troops responded nobly to the appeal which he made them, and, after a contest which lasted from 11 o'clock in the morning till 6 o'clock in the evening, drove back the Maráthá troops in confusion.

It had been, we have seen, Monson's intention to hold the Mokandara pass, the entrance to which was strongly fortified, and to await there provisions and supplies. But fearing on the evening of the 9th that the Maráthás might be induced, in consequence of their repulse, to endeavour to cut him off from Kotá, he resolved to leave Colonel Don, with one battalion, to defend the pass till the morning, and to retreat himself to that place.

Don successfully performed his part of the programme, then, pushing on, rejoined Monson. Three days of hard marching brought the force to Kotá, but the Rájah of that place declined to admit it, and even refused it provisions. At 9 P.M. of the 12th it started, then, for Ganiás on the Chambal. It reached that place, after a harassing march, on the 13th, crossed the river, not without great difficulty, the 14th; and pushed on, the 16th, without order, through a heavy country, the black soil of which had been reduced by the rain almost to the condition of a bog. On the 16th, it was found impossible to drag the guns through the sticky black soil, made more sticky by the heavy rain. They were, therefore, spiked and abandoned. The force pushed on, but in eight hours it was able to accomplish only as many miles. On the 17th the Chambali Nálá, close to the entrance of the Lakri pass, was reached; and here the force halted till the 26th, in great distress from want of food, and constantly harassed by the enemy. On the evening of the 26th the worn-out soldiers attempted the passage of the Nálá, threatened all the time by the enemy's cavalry, who cut off numbers of their baggage cattle. On the 27th, however, the passage was completed, owing very much to the exertions of Colonel Don, who commanded the rear-guard, and who had to beat off the attacks of the population, eager for plunder, as well as of the enemy's cavalry. All the baggage, however, had to be sacrificed. On joining the main body that same evening Don received a letter from Monson announcing that he had preceded the force to Tonk Rámpúra. The command then devolved upon Don, who, in two marches, characterised by great suffering, led the starving force to Rámpúra, where Monson re-assumed command, and, after many hesitations, resolved to remain until the reinforcements for which he had applied should reach him.

The reinforcements, consisting of two native battalions, one regiment of irregular cavalry, and six guns, reached Tonk Rámpúrá on the 14th August. They brought with them, however, no supplies. For a week Monson remained at the place, threatened on the one side by Holkar, on the other by Bápúji Sindia. He might have remained there longer until the further reinforcements promised by Lord Lake should have reached him. But—to use his own expression—"his mind was so distracted" that he could think coolly upon no point. In a moment of utter discouragement he gave orders to retreat on Kúshalgarh, telling his officers at the same time that it would be for them to make their way to Agrá, some ninety-eight miles further, as best they could!

In the march to Kúshalgarh Monson was attacked when crossing the Banás, on the 24th August, by Jeswant Ráo Holkar, and was very severely handled. Monson himself behaved with conspicuous gallantry; but the 2nd Battalion 2nd N.I. was almost annihilated; several of his best officers were killed or wounded; one howitzer was lost, and the spirits of both officers and men were greatly affected. He succeeded, however, in reaching Kúshalgarh on the night of the 25th, having marched that day thirty-six miles, exposed all the time to constant attacks. At Kúshalgarh he obtained supplies; but a detachment of Sindia's troops stationed there, which he had expected to support him, displayed a decidedly hostile disposition.

Great as had been Monson's difficulties up to the time of his arrival at Kúshalgarh, they now became infinitely greater. The town was ill-fitted for defence; the enemy were swarming around its walls; his troops were dispirited; he himself had no plan. After considering the whole day of the 26th, Monson at

20

last resolved to evacuate the place, though he scarcely knew in what direction to retire. At 8 o'clock that evening, then, he formed the troops that remained to him in an oblong square and moved off in that formation. The enemy, however, soon discovered his retreat, and twenty thousand cavalry started on his track, and soon came up with and attacked the rear face of the square. The steadiness of the men forming that face, the 2nd Battalion 21st N.I., however, kept the enemy at bay, though the attacks were repeated until noon of the day following. But their last remaining gun, a howitzer, was spiked and abandoned.

The retreating force took advantage of the cessation of the enemy's attacks at noon to hurry on to Hindáon, a large city with extensive fortifications. They came within sight of it—having marched twenty-seven miles without a halt—at sunset, only to find, to their intense disappointment, that it was partly occupied by the enemy. Unwilling, with a tired and partly demoralised force, and with an enemy still following in his rear, to risk a fight for its possession, Monson moved to an old fort in its neighbourhood and there gave his troops a few hours' repose. At 1 o'clock the following morning, however, he was again on his way, still marching in the same formation. As long as the darkness continued there were no signs of an enemy; but at daylight the Maráthá horse came swarming on his track, accompanied by camels carrying rockets and swivel-guns, which were occasionally discharged. The situation was soon to become even more perilous. For, at 7 o'clock, as he and his troops emerged in very straggling order from some intricate ravines, they perceived the enemy formed up in front and on both sides of them, whilst just at the moment the Maráthá horse came thundering on their rear. In this terrible extremity the sipáhís proved themselves worthy alike of their officers and of their training. Forgetting the long marches, the harassing disquietudes, of the previous two months, of the fact that the men who attacked them were men of their own faith and country, they formed up steadily, reserved their fire till the enemy were within fifty yards, and then began a continuous file-firing which emptied many a saddle. On the rear, on the front, on both flanks, did the horsemen of Jeswant Ráo make charge after charge. All in vain, however. They made no more impression upon those brave sipáhís than did the French cavalry of Napoleon upon the solid squares of the British at Waterloo!

Finding all their efforts to break the square with their horsemen ineffectual, the Maráthás then attempted the surer method of pouring in a steady fire from their matchlockmen and the camel-swivels. From this the sipáhís suffered terribly. Monson, therefore, gave orders to move on, still in square. But the enemy continued their attacks, and took advantage of the inequalities of the ground, caused by the many ravines and nálás in the way, to inflict very severe loss upon the retreating force. Nor with the waning day did they remit their attacks. Sunset came and there was no respite. Darkness followed almost immediately; still the matchlock fire continued. Under such circumstances halting was not to be thought of. The sipáhís pushed on, then, till they reached the entrance of the Biána pass, one of the most difficult, from its narrowness and steep ravines, in the country. Here the semblance of order almost entirely disappeared. To get through the pass was the object of every individual. Officers, sipáhís, camp-followers rushed through it in wild disorder. One battalion alone, forming the rear face, the 1st Battalion 14th N.I., kept some kind of formation, and, by preventing the rush of the enemy's horsemen, enabled their comrades to escape.

After they had emerged from the Biána pass, the force made no further attempt to rally. The next day some stragglers reached Fathpúr Sikri. But even here there was no rest for them, for the very townspeople treated them as fugitive outcasts and fired upon them. With the poor remnant of strength yet remaining, they pushed on then to Agrá, still twenty-three miles distant, and that day and the following, the 30th and 31st August, the arrival of wretched, footsore, half-starved, and dispirited fugitives conveyed to the garrison of Agrá some idea of the humiliation ever in store for the general who retreats before a barbarian enemy!

Such was Monson's retreat. What it cost in men was never ascertained. Of the officers, fourteen were killed, one was drowned; three were taken prisoners, one of whom was murdered and one died; nine were wounded. The misfortune was due entirely to the want of steadfastness of Monson. Unduly bold, he had advanced, in opposition to the general directions of Lord Lake, from Kotá. When he heard that Jeswant Ráo was at Rámpúra on the Chambal, he had still time to fall back. His resolution to advance and attack was a heroic resolution. Had he carried it out he would probably have succeeded. Even if he had failed, had he been destroyed, the effect would not have been nearly so bad as that which actually followed. But, having only three days' supplies, to advance, over a barren country, to within seven miles of an enemy, and then, morally frightened, to retreat, was of all courses the most insane. The retribution which followed was a righteous retribution. It served, for a long series of years, as an example and as a warning, never requiring, until 1841, when its teaching had been forgotten, a painful and humiliating renewal!

During this retreat the conduct of Jeswant Ráo had not been marked by the energy and decision for which the Maráthá world had given him credit. With sixty thousand horse and fifteen thousand footmen under him he had failed to destroy a demoralised enemy retreating under circumstances of great disadvantage. He himself had sent on, he had not led on, his troops. Though he had forced back, then, the British sipáhís, he had failed to destroy them. With the natives, indeed, who contrasted his comparative success with the constant defeats of Sindia and the Bhonslé, the fact that he had driven before him the unconquered British greatly augmented his credit. But his own estimate of his prowess was not apparently very high. Notwithstanding his success against Monson he would not even attack the city of Mathurá, rich as it was, until after the English had evacuated it. When on the 15th September they fell back to concentrate at Agrá, he then, the day following, entered Mathurá, but he showed no disposition to move nearer to his enemy.

The news of Monson's disaster inspired every Englishman in India, from the Governor-General downwards, to exert himself to the very utmost to avenge it. Fortunately that Governor-General was Marquess Wellesley—a real king of men—who shrank neither from responsibility nor from danger. Orders were instantly issued to concentrate a force under Lord Lake's orders for offensive operations.

Lord Lake, who was at Kánhpúr when the disaster occurred, marched from that place, with the troops stationed there, the 3rd September, and reached Sikandrah—the portion of Agrá where stands the mausoleum of the illustrious Akbar—the 22nd of the same month. There, another portion of the avenging army had been collected. It consisted, when united, of three regiments of dragoons—the 8th, 27th, and 29th—five regiments of native cavalry, the 76th Regiment of Foot, and the flank companies of the 22nd Regiment, ten battalions of native infantry, and the usual proportion of artillery.

On the 1st October Lord Lake marched towards Mathurá. Holkar, however, had no wish to fight a general action. His plans were conceived in a far abler spirit. He wished to delay the advance of his enemy, to harass him by flying parties, whilst, with his main body, he should make a dash at Dihlí and gain possession of the person of the ruling Mughul, the blind Sháh A'lam. He had already despatched his infantry in the direction of the capital, whilst, with his cavalry, he took a position at Aurang, a village nine miles to the west of Mathurá.

Unsuspicious of Holkar's device, Lord Lake, who had caused Mathurá to be re-occupied, moved against that chief early on the morning of the 7th. But, as soon as the vanguard of the British army appeared, Holkar evacuated his position and retreated more quickly than he could be pursued. On the 10th a similar attempt was attended with the same result. The next day Lord Lake received a despatch from Colonel Ochterlony from Dihlí, informing him that Holkar's infantry had appeared before that city on the 7th and were about to attempt its capture.

The defences of Díhlí were in a very dilapidated condition. The walls had not been repaired since the city was taken by Ahmad Sháh Duráni; the ramparts had mostly fallen, and the bastions were in a state of decay. The garrison consisted of two and a half native battalions and some—as the event proved, untrustworthy—matchlockmen. But as a set-off to the disrepair of the defences and the paucity of the troops was the fact that the men who wielded the chief authority within its walls were men of the stamp of those who have made England. They were Colonel David Ochterlony and Lieutenant-Colonel William Burn.

It is not necessary to describe here the details of the story of the defence inaugurated by these gallant officers. It must suffice to state that for seven days the troops of Holkar, nineteen thousand strong, with one hundred and sixty guns, commanded by Bápújí Sindia—the man who had proved a traitor to Monson—used all the means in their power to master the place. But all the assaults which they made were repulsed. On the 14th, learning that Lord Lake was marching to relieve the city, they made a grand attempt to escalade the walls simultaneously at several points. In not one did they succeed. Then, completely baffled, they retreated the same night, leaving the scaling ladders standing!

On receiving Ochterlony's despatch Lord Lake had started at once for Dihlí, leaving on the road, with a noble disregard of rule, unattacked and unmasked, three or four strong places which had declared for Holkar. He reached Dihlí the 18th. The necessity of providing supplies for his troops forced him to halt there for some days. He despatched, however, on the 25th a small force under Colonel Burn to relieve Sahâranpúr. Learning on the 29th that Holkar had crossed the Jamná at Pánipat and had poured into the Duab, he started, the next day, in pursuit of him, at the head of three regiments of dragoons, three of native cavalry, and Colonel Don's reserve brigade of infantry. Holkar, meanwhile, had attempted to destroy Burn's party, and, coming upon him with his whole force, had forced him to take refuge on the 30th, with but a small stock of provisions, in a mud fort near Shámli. Here Burn resisted for three days the repeated attacks of Holkar's army. On the fourth day the news of the approach of Lord Lake induced that wily chief to raise the siege.

Lord Lake, indeed, arrived the day following, the 3rd November, having marched eleven and a half hours the previous day. He halted, then, on the 4th, but resumed the pursuit by forced marches on the 5th. When, on the 15th, he reached A'liganj and found the village, which had been set fire to by the enemy, still burning, he resolved to push on the same night, with the cavalry and galloper guns, in pursuit. Just as he was starting, however, a courier reached him with the information that General Fraser, whom he had left in command of the army during his absence, had achieved, on the 12th, a victory over the main body of the enemy at Díg. To that event I must recur for a moment.

Fraser had been left at Dihlí with a force consisting of the 76th Regiment, the Company's European Regiment,* and six native battalions. Having ascertained that Holkar had left his infantry and artillery behind him when he made his raid into the Duab, Fraser, acting on instructions from Lord Lake, went

* Now the Royal Munster Fusiliers.

in search of them on the 6th November. He found them on the 12th occupying a very strong position close to the fortress of Díg. Their left rested on that fortress, which was very strongly armed, and was covered by a morass which extended likewise in front of the centre; their right was protected by a village on a height, bristling with guns. Fraser carefully reconnoitred the position and then formed his plan. He resolved to make a flank attack on the village, and, when he had carried it, to roll up the enemy from the right, and either to destroy them or force them within the fort. To do this he made a flank movement to his left beyond the morass and the village; then, having well cleared the latter, took ground to his right at a right angle to his first movement, then formed up on the right flank of the village, facing it, and dashed the 76th against it. That gallant regiment drove the enemy from the village, and then rushed down the declivity, supported by the European and four native regiments, to attack the first line of guns, which, in the meanwhile, the enemy had formed to protect their centre and left.

This line they carried; but they had no sooner done so when they found themselves exposed to a heavier fire from a second line. Under this fire they fell rapidly. One shot carried off their General's leg, as he was forming up his men to charge. The command then devolved upon Colonel Monson. Monson at once carried out Fraser's plan, charged, drove the enemy from the second line, and forced them to take refuge within the fortress. Whilst he had been thus engaged, the enemy's horse—who, on the first sign of Fraser's flank movement, had been despatched from the left to make, by a wider circuit, a movement conforming to his—came up on the rear of the British force, and, galloping forward, retook the first line of guns it had captured, and turned them upon the still advancing Europeans. They were thus occupied when Captain Norford of the 76th, who had noticed their action, charged them with twenty-eight men of his regiment and compelled them to relinquish their hold.

It was a very gallant action and it cost Captain Norford his life. There still remained a body of the enemy who had moved beyond the morass in the direction of the British baggage, which had been left there under the guard of two native regiments. Against that body Monson now turned, opened fire upon their flank and forced them back through the morass.

The victory was in many respects important. It was the first decisive reply to the disaster of the Monson's retreat. It proved that on the field of battle Holkar's infantry and artillery, even when resting on a fortress, were no match for the British. The circumstances connected with it made one thing clear. The fortress of Díg belonged to Ranjít Singh, Rájah of Bharatpúr; that Rájah was nominally the ally of the British; yet he had allowed Holkar, who was at war with the British, free use of his fortress: it was evident, then, that Ranjít Singh was prepared to cast in his lot with Holkar.

The battle of Díg cost the British six hundred and forty-three men killed and wounded. General Fraser died a few days after the action. The victors captured eighty-seven pieces of cannon, of which fourteen were pieces which had been lost by Monson in his retreat. The loss of the enemy was computed, probably with truth, at something under two thousand.

Lord Lake, I have said, received information of this victory just as he was setting out from A'liganj at the head of his cavalry in pursuit of Holkar. Its communication to the men he was leading encouraged them greatly. They set off at once, marched all night by the light of the moon, and at daybreak came in sight of Holkar's encampment at Farakhábád. Lake at once ordered the galloper guns to open fire.

Holkar was entirely unsuspicious of his vicinity. In the early part of the night which had just then terminated he had been enjoying a nautch, when, in the midst of it, a messenger communicated to him the information of the defeat which his troops had sustained at Díg. Troubled more than he cared to avow, he quitted the entertainment without communicating the news to his chiefs. He was still sleeping heavily when the fire of the galloper guns convinced him that the enemy he most dreaded was upon him. He was thoroughly panic-stricken. Forgetting the fame he had acquired, the boasts he had indulged in, his visions of empire and dominion, he hurriedly mounted his horse, and, followed only by those who had been as expeditious as himself, galloped at full speed to Mainpúrí, not even drawing rein till he had placed eighteen miles of road and a river between himself and his encampment. It was as well for him that he had made the haste he did make. For Lord Lake, after the first discharge of the galloper guns, had dashed with his cavalry into the encampment, and his men had had little to do but to sabre the beings who rose in hurry and confusion from their slumber. In the attack and the pursuit which followed, the enemy lost about three thousand men, whilst the desertions were even more numerous. The English lost but two men killed and twenty wounded.

It is as well, in the present day, to note and remember the particulars which made this surprise very remarkable. Lord Lake had quitted Dihlí the 31st October. Between that date and the date on which he surprised Holkar at Farakhábád—the 17th November—he had marched three hundred and fifty miles, rescuing in his way a beleaguered garrison. In the twenty-four hours immediately preceding the surprise he had marched seventy miles. Nor did this long march prevent him from attacking the enemy at once, and pursuing him for ten miles further!

Nor even then did he relax! Finding that the remnant of Holkar's army was making for Díg, he followed it, and, on the 28th, joined the force commanded by Monson between Mathurá and that fortress. He had to wait there a few days until the siege-train should join him from Agrá, but on the arrival of that he took up, the 13th December, a position before

Díg. He opened fire the following morning, effected a practicable breach in an outwork at an angle of the city on the 22nd; stormed and occupied that outwork the same night. This gallant deed so intimidated the garrison that they evacuated the fortress and retired to Bharatpúr. The British troops entered the citadel of Díg on Christmas Day.

There still remained Bharatpúr, the Rájah of which had openly declared for Holkar. It was necessary that he should be made to submit or should receive a lesson. As soon, then, as he had repaired the fortifications of Díg and had met the stores for the army which he was expecting, Lord Lake marched for that place. He took up his ground in front of it on the 2nd January.

The fortress of Bharatpúr was founded in the early part of the eighteenth century by the Jâts—a people recognised by Colonel Tod as the Getæ and Massagetæ of the ancient writers, belonging to the same family as the Jutes of Jutland—who emigrated from Múltán in the century immediately preceding, and settled in the Duáb. The fortress took its name from "Bharat," the younger brother of the Hindú divinity, Rámá, and "púr," the Hindú word for "city." It lies, thirty-four miles to the west of Agrá, in the midst of an almost level plain covered with jungle and abounding in several pieces of water or ponds. The town, eight miles in circumference, is bounded on the western side by a ridge of low, bare, flat rocks; whilst on the three other sides its limits are dotted by a few isolated eminences of no great height or size. The fortifications at the time of which I am writing consisted of a citadel and a continuous enceinte of thirty-four lofty mud bastions, connected by curtains, and in shape generally either semi-circular or like the frustra of cones. On some of these bastions there were cavaliers, and most of them were joined to the curtain by long narrow necks. In many cases the ramparts were strengthened by several rows of trunks of trees, which were buried upright in the mass of earth, and all of them were constructed of clay mixed with straw and cow-dung—a composition which, put on in layers, each hardened by the sun before another is applied, was, of all others, the best adapted to baffle the artillery-fire of that day. The enceinte was surrounded by a nálá or dry water-course, with steep, almost perpendicular, banks One source of weakness in it, however, arose from the fact that numerous small watercourses led into it from the ponds in the plain, thus affording in many places an easy descent. It possessed nine gates, and outside of each an equal number of semi-circular earthworks. The citadel, which completely commanded the body of the place, rose to a height of a hundred and fourteen feet above the level of the ground, and was very strong. The ditch, a hundred and fifty feet broad and fifty-nine deep, had its counterscarp faced by a perpendicular revetment of stone. From the bottom of the escarp rose a perpendicular stone wall of eighty feet, forming a *fausse-braye,* well flanked by forty semi-circular towers. Above this arose another stone wall, seventy-four feet in height, and flanked by eleven conical bastions, whose total relief reached a hundred and seventy-three feet. The strength of the fortress was further increased by the vicinity to it, on a higher level, of a lake called the Moti Jhíl. This lake was bounded on the side of the town by a bund or embankment, by the cutting of which not only could the ditch be filled, but a great portion of the surrounding country could likewise be laid under water. It was garrisoned by eight thousand men, composed partly of the hitherto unconquered Jâts, and partly, though to a lesser extent, of the refugees from Farakhábád. But, outside the walls had collected the still numerous cavalry of Jeswant Ráo Holkar and the considerable following of Amír Khán, a partisan leader, who had recognised the supremacy of Jeswant Ráo, and who became subsequently famous as the founder of the still existing principality of Tonk. It may be added that the confidence of the defenders was further increased by a prophetic legend to the effect that Bharatpúr would only be taken when a long-nosed alligator—a *kumbhir*—should drink up the water of the ditch surrounding the fortress.

Lord Lake, on the other hand, though at the head of a force flushed with recent victory, was ill-supplied with the guns necessary for the attack of a place so strong as Bharatpúr. When he came before it, on the 2nd January, he had but six 18-pounder battering guns, four 8-inch and four 5½-inch mortars. When these became inefficient from excessive firing, as proved the case with some of them, he had to use guns captured from Holkar, hurriedly furnished with *bouches* from Mathurá. Knowing his weakness in this respect, Lord Lake had been strongly in favour of attempting the place by a *coup de main*, but had been dissuaded. On the 7th January the 18-pounder batteries opened fire on the south-west front of the fortress, whilst the two mortar batteries shelled the town. On the 9th, a breach was reported practicable. That same night, three columns—one, commanded by Lieutenant-Colonel Maitland, and composed of the flank companies of the 22nd, 75th, and 76th, and the Company's European regiment and a battalion of sipáhis; the second, commanded by Lieutenant-Colonel Ryan, and consisting of an hundred and fifty men of the European regiment and a battalion of sipáhís; the third, led by Colonel Hawkes, and comprising two companies of the 75th and a third battalion of sipáhís—were told off for the assault. Ryan was to attempt the Nímdah gateway; Hawkes to storm the position to its right; Maitland, to penetrate by a breach between the two. At 8 o'clock the three columns started. Maitland, however, lost his way amid the swamps and pools which intervened between his point of departure and the point of attack, encroached upon Ryan's line of advance, and missed the breach altogether. A scene of incredible confusion followed. The enemy, roused by the clumsy advance of the assailants, received them with a continuous fire of musketry and grape, as well from the front as from the circular bastion nearest to the breach.

This completed their disorder. Twenty-three men of the 22nd did indeed wade through the ditch, breast-high, and even ascended the breach, but their number was too small to admit of their storming the enemy's batteries, and, unsupported, they fell back before reaching the crest. When, after a long interval, Maitland had concentrated his force in front of the breach, the enemy had brought to bear upon the approaches a fire which it was impossible to face. Hawkes, meanwhile, had driven the enemy from their advanced guns; and Ryan, after shaking off Maitland, had compelled the enemy to fall back, though he was prevented by a deep drain from following them. Everything depended upon Maitland's success. Feeling this very keenly, that officer advanced and gallantly led his men up the breach. He had approached the crest when he was shot dead. Other officers took his place, but to no purpose. The slaughter amongst them was terrible. At length, baffled but not humiliated, the survivors fell back to the trenches, exposed, in their retreat, to a galling fire from the enemy. They had lost five officers and eighty-five men killed, twenty-four officers and three hundred and seventy-one men wounded: about one-seventh of the total number of the three columns; more than a third of the number of the column, Maitland's, which was chiefly engaged!

Undaunted by this failure, which he rightly attributed to the fact that the centre column had lost its way, Lord Lake recommenced on the 16th the fire from his batteries, and on the 21st succeeded in effecting another breach a little to the right of the first one. This time he determined to attempt the assault in the daytime. He believed himself to be in every respect better prepared for success than on the first occasion, for, on the 18th, he had been reinforced by three sipáhí battalions, some convalescent Europeans, and a few field-pieces, and he had obtained, he imagined, correct measurements of the ditch at the point where he intended to cross it. In this latter matter he was deceived. The officer to whom he had entrusted the duty of ascertaining the measurements had confided its execution to a Havildar and two privates of native cavalry, and, on their vague assurance that the ditch at the point indicated was neither broad nor very deep, and that the breach was easy of ascent, had made a report which his superiors had accepted as correct.

At three o'clock in the afternoon of the 21st the storming party, composed of a hundred and fifty men of the 76th, a hundred and twenty of the 75th, fifty of the 22nd, supplied with three portable bridges, in the form of broad ladders covered with laths; and supported by the remaining portions of those regiments, and by three battalions of native infantry, the whole commanded by Colonel Macrae, advanced to the assault. On reaching the ditch, they found that not only was it much broader than had been represented, but that the enemy, by improvising dams across it above and below the selected point, had enormously increased the volume of water there. The portable bridges were thus useless, and an attempt made to lengthen one of them by fastening to it a scaling-ladder completely failed. At this conjuncture, and when the men stood powerless, exposed to a heavy fire from the defences, Lieutenant Morris of the Company's European Regiment jumped into the water, swam across the ditch, and began to clamber up the breach, followed by several men who had been inspired by his example. But the enemy had taken the precaution to range a battery behind, so as to command the breach, and the guns from these opened a fire, in addition to the musketry fire which had already begun to play, upon the comparatively few men who had passed the obstacle of the ditch. Seeing these exposed to certain death, and unable to send to them any assistance, Colonel Macrae sounded the recall. The survivors only came back, however, when their leader, Morris, had been severely wounded and many of their comrades killed. When these were once again safe on the British side the stormers retired in great confusion, leaving a large number of wounded, the scaling-ladders and bridges, in the hands of the enemy. The abortive and ill-arranged attempt had cost them, in killed and wounded, eighteen officers and five hundred and seventy-three men! It deserves to be added that whilst the storming party was thus fruitlessly employed, Holkar and Amír Khán had made a vigorous attempt upon the British camp, which was repelled only by the skilful use of the galloper guns.

The failure of this attack only rendered Lord Lake more determined to persevere. In a "general order" which he issued at this time to his troops he acknowledged the gallantry and steadiness they had displayed, and expressed a confident hope that in a very few days the obstacles which had baffled them would be overcome. This order produced the very best effect; and this effect was heightened by the defeat, a few days later, of Amír Khán, by Colonel Need and the 27th Dragoons, in an attempt made by that chieftain to intercept a convoy of provisions escorted by Captain Welsh from Mathurá. On this occasion Amír Khán only saved his life by stripping himself of the gaudy apparel which he habitually wore and by mixing then, half naked, with his fleeing troopers. An attempt made by Holkar upon a second and larger convoy escorted by Colonel Don from Agra was equally defeated by Lord Lake in person. These two repulses so discouraged Amír Khán that he renounced his alliance with Holkar, and made for Rohilkhand, followed in that direction, and until he had crossed the Ganges, by a British force under General Smith.

Meanwhile there had been a lull in the siege operations, during which the position of the besiegers' camp was shifted to the south, and considerable industry was employed in the preparation of fascines, pontoons, and rafts. On the 10th February the force was augmented by the arrival from Bombay of a division under General Jones, consisting of the 86th Regiment, eight companies 65th Regiment, four battalions of native infantry, and five hundred irregular horse. Measures were at once taken more in unison with the scientific character of siege operations; regular approaches were made; and the batteries were brought much closer to the defences. On the 19th February the breach effected by these was reported practicable, and it having been ascertained, likewise, that a mine, which had been laid for the purpose of blowing up the counterscarp, was ready for explosion, Lord Lake ordered the third assault. To command it he had selected Lieutenant-Colonel Don, an officer who had greatly distinguished himself during Monson's retreat, as well as before and after it. The storming party was composed of three columns; one, of two hundred men of the 86th Regiment, and a sipáhí battalion; the second, of three hundred men of the 65th Regiment, and two sipáhí battalions; the third and central, of details from the 75th, the 76th, and the Company's Europeans, and three battalions of sipáhís.

The arrangements for the storming party had been completed, and the orders that the storm should take effect at 3 o'clock the following afternoon issued, when, on the night of the 19th, the enemy made a sally, which was repulsed only with considerable loss and after very severe fighting. At daybreak they returned to the assault, and for some time gained a decided advantage; but after a conflict which lasted several hours and cost the besiegers several lives, they were again forced back.

These two sorties had not contributed to encourage the men of the storming party. Still no change was made in the disposition or in the hour of attack. It was arranged that Captain Grant, with the first column I have named, should attack the enemy's intrenchments outside the town; that Colonel Taylor, with the second, should carry the Birnarain gate, reported to be easily accessible; whilst the central column, led by Don in person, should simultaneously advance and enter by the breach.

The unhappy result is soon told. Grant, indeed, not only drove the enemy from their intrenchments, but nearly succeeded in entering the place upon their heels. He captured eleven guns, all of which he brought into camp. But Taylor was repulsed at the Birnarain gate. The task of Don, and its result, were still more disheartening. He gallantly led his men to the breach, but, in spite of all his entreaties, they refused to follow him into it. The head of the column halted under an enfilading fire, every shot of which told, and, discouraged either by the sight of the dead bodies of their comrades, killed in the sally of the morning, or apprehending that the approaches had been mined, the men composing it remained deaf alike to entreaty and exhortation. Don turned from them to the men behind them, those of the remnant of the 22nd Foot and 12th N.I. These responded to his call, and dashed gallantly to the front. Finding the ditch full of water and unfordable, they rushed to the right, to a point above the dam which had been made, crossed the ditch, and began the ascent of a rugged bastion which seemed to command an entrance into the place. Many men, amongst them the colour-bearers of the 12th N.I., reached the summit; but they remained there unsupported, and though just at the moment the enemy's mine exploded to the disadvantage of the enemy and threw them into considerable confusion, the head of the column still refused to budge. No exertions of their officers could rouse them; and when even fourteen of the former rushed to the front, not a man followed them! It was a day rare in the annals of the British army, a day of panic! Colonel Don, then, was forced to relinquish the attack. He had lost three officers and a hundred and sixty-two men killed; twenty-five officers and seven hundred and thirty-two men wounded!

Attributing the conduct of the men to exceptional causes, Lord Lake resolved to renew the attack the next day. He continued, therefore, all that night and the next day on the defences. Then, parading the troops who had displayed so much unwillingness to advance the previous afternoon, he addressed them in terms which went to their very hearts. For, when he concluded by offering them, then, an opportunity of retrieving their conduct, they came forward to a man. Lieutenant Templeton of the 76th offered to lead the forlorn hope.

This time Colonel Monson was selected to lead the storming party. It consisted of the Company's Europeans, the greater part of the 65th and 86th regiments, three sipáhí battalions, and the flank companies of a fourth. The attack was to be directed on the rugged bastion on the summit of which the 12th N.I. had succeeded in planting their colours the previous day. So steep, however, was the ascent, and so continuous and well directed the fire upon it by the enemy from the bastion nearest to it, that but few men succeeded in reaching the summit. The first of these was young Templeton, the leader of the forlorn hope, but he was at once shot dead. His place was soon taken by Major Menzies, Aide-de-camp to Lord Lake, who gave an example never to be surpassed, of cool and inspiring courage; but he, too, shared the fate of Templeton. After making many efforts to surmount the difficulties before him, Monson gave orders to retreat, not, however, till his losses in killed had amounted to six officers and a hundred and twenty-five men, and in wounded to twenty-eight officers and eight hundred and sixty-two men!

The four assaults had cost the besiegers a loss, in killed and wounded, of three thousand one hundred men, and had left Lord Lake in a position far worse than that he occupied when he commenced the siege. His battering train had become unfit for service: not one 18-pounder shot remained for use; the supply of gunpowder was almost exhausted; provisions were scarce; and there were but few stores of any kind. Whilst, too, the confidence of the enemy had increased, that of the besiegers had greatly diminished. On the 23rd February, the enemy succeeded in burning the British batteries. The following day, Lord Lake formally raised the siege, and took up a position, greatly harassed in his movement by Holkar's cavalry, six miles to the north-east of Bharatpúr, covering the road leading to the depôts at Agra, Mathurá, and Díg. Very soon after he went in pursuit of Holkar, followed him across the Satlaj, and, in December of the same year, forced him to implore his mercy. The Government of India reinstated the fugitive prince in his dominions.

I have now related the first siege of Bharatpúr. It failed for two reasons: the first, that it was begun and conducted throughout with inadequate artillery means; the second, that there was not an engineer in the force who was acquainted with the defences of Bharatpúr, or with the peculiarities of the ground immediately under its walls. The failure, however, was unfortunate; and though the Máhárájah, Ranjít Singh, shortly afterwards sued for peace, and made his submission, he had gained with his countrymen as much in prestige and credit as the English had lost. His capital was the only fortress in India from which British troops had fallen back repulsed. During the twenty years that followed, "Bharatpúr" was a word to conjure with in the habitations of disaffected princes and nobles throughout the country; and it required the reversal of the result of the first siege to deprive that word of its efficacy and its sting.

The opportunity came in the year 1825. Ranjít Singh died at the close of 1805. His eldest son, Randbir Singh, was loyal to the British during his reign of eighteen years. His brother, who succeeded him in 1823, died on the 26th February 1825. He left a son, six years old, named Balwant Singh, whose succession was recognised by the British Government. But his cousin, Durján Sál, supported by the Rájah of Karauli and others, attacked, dethroned, and imprisoned him. Upon this the British Resident at Dihlí, Sir David Ochterlony, who was also the Governor-General's Agent for Bharatpúr, assembled a force to re-instate the rightful heir; and there can be little doubt but that, had he been allowed to proceed, no serious hostilities would have followed. But the Governor-General, Lord Amherst, trusting to a peaceful adjustment of the family differences, and not considering that the recognition by the Government of India of an heir-apparent during the life-time of the father imposed upon it the obligation to maintain him in his position under the circumstances which had occurred, disapproved of Ochterlony's policy, and summarily removed him from his post. Ultimately, however, the Government was forced to take up and carry out the policy it had thus rejected, and under circumstances far less favourable. For Dúrjan Sál, in the interval, whilst negotiating with, and professing to leave the decision on his claims to, the British Government, had been engaged in preparing to assert them, by strengthening the fortifications of Bharatpúr, by levying troops, and by soliciting aid—which had been secretly promised—from the Rájpút and Maráthá princes. The attitude of Dúrjan Sál, combined with the prestige attaching to his capital, produced at last so great an excitement and commotion throughout the country, that, to prevent a general conflagration, Lord Amherst was forced to adopt the policy of Sir David Ochterlony and to expel the usurper. The carrying out of this resolve was at once entrusted to the Commander-in-Chief.

The army which assembled at Agrá in November to undertake the second siege of Bharatpúr numbered twenty-seven thousand men. It had a battering train of a hundred and two guns and fifty-two pieces of artillery. The English regiments employed were the 11th Dragoons, the 16th Lancers, the 14th and 59th regiments, and—a short time after the siege had commenced—the Company's European regiment. Lord Combermere, a friend and comrade in arms of the Duke of Wellington, had that year arrived in India as Commander-in-Chief. He assumed command of the force on the 1st December; moved with the right wing on the 5th to Mathurá, and marched thence, at its head, on the 9th, to Bharatpúr. General Nicholls, commanding the left wing, similarly received orders to quit Agra on the 8th and to take a position to the west of the place on the 10th.

These arrangements were carried out with but slight deviations, and Bharatpúr was invested on the 11th December.

Since the abortive siege of Lord Lake in 1805 the fortifications had been somewhat strengthened. Additions had been made to the enceinte, and one bastion, called Fath Burj, or Bastion of Victory—so named because the natives declared it had been built with the bones and cemented with the blood of those who had fallen in the last siege—had been added to the thirty-four previously existing. The garrison had been considerably augmented. The fortress was defended now by twenty-five thousand men, mostly Játs and Patáns, the two most warlike races in India. It was well stored with supplies, and the ramparts were plentifully furnished with guns.

Recognising the mistakes which originated in the first siege from want of accurate knowledge of the ground, Lord Combermere and his engineers spent the nine days after his investment of the place on the 11th in reconnoitring every part of the fortress. On the 20th he and they had arrived at definite conclusions. These Lord Combermere at once endeavoured to carry out.

Lord Lake had made his approaches to the south-west face of the town. Lord Combermere decided to attack the fronts about the north-east angle, which the defenders considered their strongest point. The reasons which led him to this conclusion were clear and simple. The north-east angle was, with the exception of one short face in another direction, the only part of the place totally unflanked; the ditch there was comparatively shallow and almost dry: a ravine which fell into the ditch gave great facility and cover to those desirous of descending into it. Moreover, whereas from that angle the heaviest artillery fire could be concentrated on the assailants at a distance, it could not touch those who should approach close to the ditch.

On the 23rd the investment was drawn closer, and Lord Combermere sent two columns to seize the village of Kadam

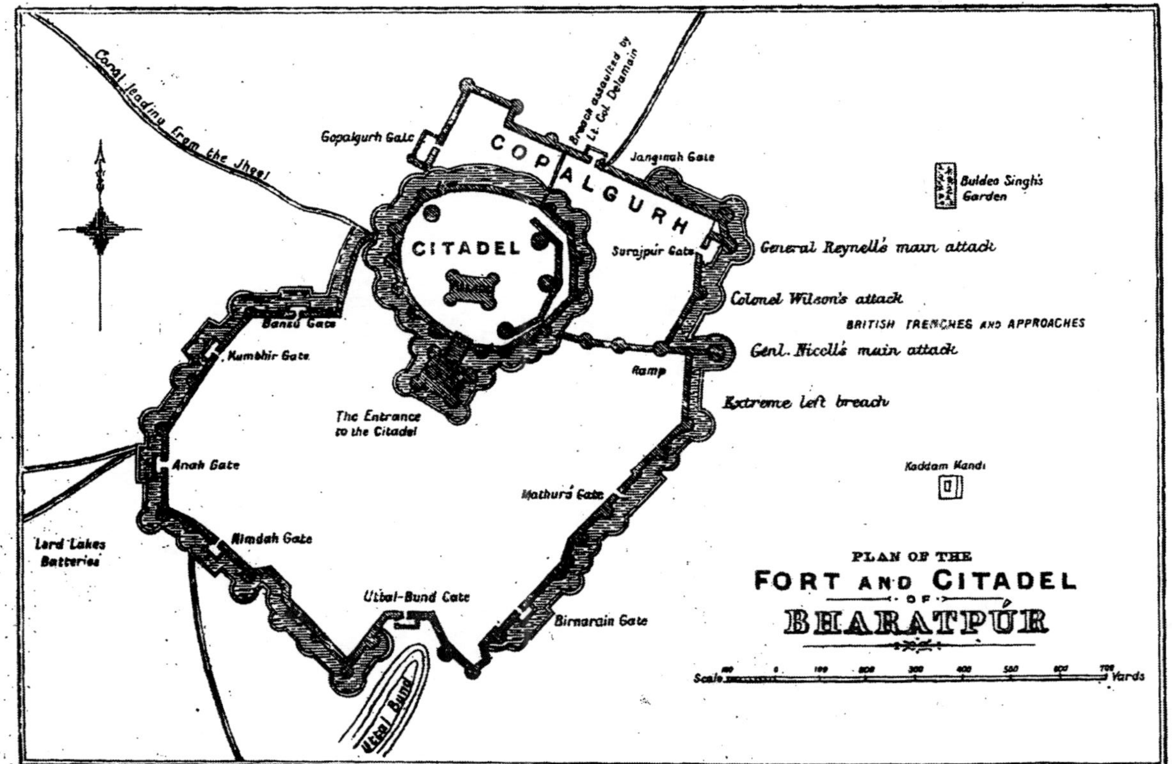
PLAN OF THE
FORT AND CITADEL
OF
BHARATPŪR
Canal leading from the Jheel
Gopalgurh Gate
GOPALGURH
Breach assaulted by Lt. Col. Delamain
Janginah Gate
Buldeo Singh's Garden
CITADEL
Surajpur Gate
General Reynell's main attack
Colonel Wilson's attack
BRITISH TRENCHES AND APPROACHES
Genl. Nicoll's main attack
Ramp
Extreme left breach
Banzu Gate
Kumbhir Gate
The Entrance to the Citadel
Anah Gate
Mathura Gate
Kaddam Kandi
Nimdah Gate
Lord Lakes Batteries
Utbal-Bund Gate
Birnarain Gate
Utbal Bund
Scale
Yards

Kandi on the right front, and Baldéo Singh's garden on the left front, of the attack, situated about seven hundred and fifty yards from the place, and about eight hundred yards from each other. Their possession was important, for they afforded good cover to the men supporting the parties about to work in the construction of the first parallel. The defenders made some attempts to disturb the operation, but without any practical result. That same night the first parallel was commenced, and so well did the men, Europeans and natives, work at it, that before daybreak a gun battery of eight 18-pounders and a mortar battery for six 8-inch mortars were finished and armed. As soon as it was light a fire from these batteries opened on the place. The enemy attempted to reply, but, finding that they could not sufficiently depress their guns, they ceased firing and withdrew them.

Before these approaches had been made, the fire from the mortars had caused great damage to life and property within the city. Lord Combermere, as a chivalrous soldier, was very unwilling that the injury intended for armed enemies should be inflicted upon women and children. He accordingly had written, the 21st, to Dúrjan Sál, offering safe conduct and escort to any women and children who might wish to leave the fortress. After some correspondence, Dúrjan Sál agreed to avail himself of the permission, and, on the 24th, all the women not belonging to the royal family emerged from the city and passed through the besiegers' lines, unmolested and unsearched. It transpired a little later that these fugitives had carried off precious stones to an enormous value secreted about their persons!

On the 24th the besiegers widened the parallel to a breadth of ten feet, and the same night carried out an approach in advance of it by means of the flying sap. They commenced, likewise, a breaching battery for ten—eventually for eleven—24-pounders and a small barbette battery. The party engaged in this work was, however, attacked, and, after a heavy loss, was forced to discontinue its labour. But, the enemy's fire slackening, it resumed it and had made considerable progress before daybreak. That day and the following the 18- and 24-pounders kept up a heavy fire on the place and silenced the enemy's guns. In the course of the second day, the 26th, the approaches had advanced to within two hundred and fifty yards of the place. It was evident that the feeling of the defenders was far less confident than had been that of their forerunners in 1805, for that same afternoon a body of their cavalry, laden, it was believed, with treasure, dashed out and succeeded in escaping.

On the 27th, the second parallel was completed at a distance of two hundred and fifty yards from the ditch. It was armed with two batteries, one for two 12-pounders, the other for twelve 24-pounders. The following day the approaches were brought to within forty yards of the ditch. On the 29th, the second parallel was extended; and a new battery for four guns was added to the left of the northern breaching battery, with a view to destroy the defences which were reported to exist in rear of the bastion intended to be assailed. Another battery for two guns was also thrown up in advance of the second parallel to enfilade the ditch of the north front. The fire now brought to bear on the fortress had a very discouraging effect on the garrison, and six hundred of them sent an envoy to the Commander-in-Chief to treat for terms. The negotiation came to nothing, because the six hundred declined the only terms that would be accepted—surrender at discretion.

On the 30th and 31st, and on the 1st January, the newly-erected batteries were armed, the approaches were extended, and the trenches were improved: one mine, which had been begun before, was pushed on, and a second was commenced. Two more were begun on the 2nd. On the 3rd, the third parallel was extended, and on the 4th a fifth mine was begun. The work in these mines was continued night and day till the 7th, when one was exploded, without, however, producing much effect. But, on the following day, the explosion of four mines blew in the counterscarp and procured for the assailants an excellent descent into the ditch. It was generally thought in the army that Lord Combermere would order the assault for that day. But he rightly considered that the defences had not yet been sufficiently broken down, and resolved to develop still further the system of mining and countermining.

In this work the engineers displayed great skill and daring. On the 9th, they exploded a scarp-gallery occupied in some force by the enemy. On the 12th, however, Captain Taylor and Captain Irvine of the Engineers, with a small following of Europeans and Gúrkhas, and a few sappers, failed in a very daring attempt to destroy a gallery which allowed the enemy to communicate, through the ramparts, with a newly-erected parapet of cotton bags. But, on the 14th, Irvine rendered signal service by destroying the same gallery and effecting a small but very practicable breach. On the 16th, the last supply of shot, shell, and gunpowder remaining in the Agrá arsenal reached the besiegers. The same day Captain Carmichael, of the 59th Regiment, responding to the expressed desire of his general, General Nicholls, to ascertain the nature of the obstacles which would have to be encountered behind the defences, performed an act of very great daring. Taking with him five or six Gúrkhas, who volunteered for the service, and accompanied by Captain Davidson of the Engineers, Carmichael walked, at midday, from the advanced trench to the foot of the breach—a distance of fifty yards. Although the space traversed was enfiladed by a well-manned bastion on its left and the top of the breach was strongly occupied, the volunteers reached the point I have indicated, and even made half the ascent of the breach, before the enemy perceived them. A few seconds later brought the whole party to the summit. The startled defenders, believing at first that they were the head of a storming party, seized their muskets and hurriedly delivered their fire. Fortunately it took no effect; and when the smoke had cleared away, the visitors, cool and collected, took a deliberate survey of the interior of the fort, storing every position in their minds. They continued the survey till the defenders, recovering from their astonishment, rushed forward to seize and punish them. But these, not awaiting the assault, turned, dashed down the breach, and, in spite of a fire from behind them and on their flank, which literally swept the earth, reached the trenches with the loss of but one man. Even he was hit so close to the goal that he actually dropped into the trench!

This gallant deed was productive of most important results. Captain Carmichael and his comrades imparted to the General information which determined him to risk an assault without further delay. For Lord Combermere had now certain evidence that the defences, though formidable, were by no means impregnable.

On the 17th, then, the Commander-in-Chief directed that the three principal mines to be exploded at the moment of attack should be charged with powder. One of these mines was under the angle of the north-east bastion or cavalier; the second was destined to widen the right gun breach; the third, about midway between the two, was to blow in the counterscarp. The explosion was to be the signal for the assaulting columns to advance.

These columns were composed and formed as follows:—The right column, commanded by Major-General Reynell, was subdivided in the manner now to be described: (1) Colonel Delamain, commanding a party composed of two companies of the Company's European regiment, a regiment of sipáhís, and a hundred Gúrkhas, was, on the extreme right, to storm the breach to the right of the Jangínah gate; Colonel Reynell, leading two brigades in person—Brigadier McCombe's, consisting of a company of the 14th Foot, leading and followed by a spiking party of gunners, supported by four more companies of the 14th, a regiment of sipáhís, and a hundred

Gúrkhas; and Brigadier Patton's, ranged behind McCombe's, and consisting of four companies of the 14th, five of one sipáhí battalion and another entire battalion, was to attack the centre or main breach—that at the north-east angle of the fortress.

To act in conjunction with the right was the left attack, subdivided into four columns, the whole directed by General Nicholls. Of these columns, that on the right, composed of two companies of the Company's Europeans, two of native infantry, and an hundred Gúrkhas, led by Colonel Wilson, and preceded by pioneers carrying six ladders, was to escalade the place at a re-entering angle to the left of the main breach. Immediately on its left, the second column, commanded by Brigadier Edwards, and composed of seven companies of the 59th Foot, one sipáhí battalion, and an hundred Gúrkhas, was to make what was termed the main attack. The order of this attack was to be as follows. Two companies of the 59th were to lead it, followed closely by pioneers carrying six short ladders; then the Brigadier and five more companies of the 59th; then the native battalion. On reaching the summit the seven companies of the 59th were to turn to the left; the sipáhís were to advance into the town, and then, moving in a parallel line, were to cover their right flank. The Gúrkhas, meanwhile, were to enter along the counterscarp and keep down the enemy's fire.

The third column of General Nicholls' attack was composed of the three remaining companies of the 59th Foot, accompanied by pioneers bearing ladders, followed by a hundred Gúrkhas, and having attached to it a body of sappers and twelve men carrying nooses to slip over the upright beams in the parapet, so that they might act as hand ropes. This column was to assail the gun breach in the curtain immediately on the left of the attack of the second column.

The fourth column, commanded by Brigadier Fagan, and composed of three sipáhí battalions, was held in reserve.

During the siege Lord Combermere had trained his men in the

use of ladders and of hand-grenades.* He had been very careful in seeing that the ladders were made of the material which, after trial, proved most suitable, viz. of bamboo; and to enable the attacking columns to advance promptly, he had caused steps to be cut in the parapet of the trenches. No precaution to ensure success had been omitted.

At half-past four o'clock on the morning of the 18th the columns told off for the assault quietly entered the trenches. A very brisk fire was kept thence on the defences. It was replied to rather fitfully, the enemy appearing every now and again to be apprehensive that mischief was brewing. A little after 8 o'clock the two smaller mines, that under the right breach, and that under the counterscarp, exploded. Startled at the sudden shock, the defenders crowded into the angle of the north-east bastion, some waving their swords in defiance, others beckoning eagerly for support. A few minutes later the ground shook beneath them; a violent concussion seemed to split the firmament; a dense cloud of dust and smoke arose, and their disjointed limbs were hurled, with stones, timber, and masses of earth, into the air. Some of the *débris* fell even into the British trenches, killed two sipáhís standing close behind Lord Combermere, struck down Brigadier McCombe at his side, and killed or wounded Brigadier Patton, Captain Irvine, Lieutenant Daly, and some twenty men of the 14th Foot. As soon as the eye could penetrate through the clouds of dust and smoke, the grenadiers of the 14th and 59th were seen rushing impetuously up the steep faces of their respective breaches. A moment later, as it seemed, and a loud cheer from the men in the trenches below announced that they had gained the summit. Lord Combermere had with difficulty been restrained from accompanying General Nicholls' main attack. Now he could hold back no longer. He ascended the breach, and hoisted the British flag on the summit.

* This was the last occasion on which Grenadiers carried the missile which gave them originally their distinctive appellation.

Nor had the main attack of General Reynell's two brigades been less successful. The cheers from the trenches below had announced, simultaneously with the success of the 59th, the success of the 14th, gallantly led by Major Everard. Arrived on the summit, Everard had at once given the colours to the wind. But there the defenders were congregated in the greatest force, and for a few minutes a hand-to-hand encounter took place not exceeded in fierceness by any encounter in our Indian wars. For there, the unconquered Jât and the death-scorning Patán, armed with *tulwar* and shield, met the British soldier, provided only with his bayonet. It was soon seen that the islanders had prevailed, for their main column was noticed to turn to the right and drive the enemy with fierce energy along the ramparts. Every now and again, as some vantage point was approached, the defenders were seen to rally and stand—then to give way and flee, only to rally and stand again. The sipáhís, meanwhile, were showing themselves worthy of this glorious comradeship; and though, in one or two instances, their firing was somewhat wild, they displayed a fearlessness deserving of all praise.

At length Everard reached the Jangínah gate. A moment later and he sighted Delamain's column, which, after storming the breach to the right of it, had turned to the left. The situation was peculiar. Between the two British columns was a steep and very narrow gorge, fully sixty feet deep, the only descent to which was by narrow flights of steps. To the right edge—from the town—of this gorge, Everard was driving the enemy he had beaten; whilst, to its left edge, Delamain was pursuing the enemy who had tried to bar the way to him. The fury of the battle here, then, exceeded anything that had gone before. A certain death stared the defenders in the face. The consciousness of this inflamed their resolution to sell their lives as dearly as possible. But the British were not to be withstood. Those that escaped the bayonet were pushed into the gorge below; and there, their cotton dresses igniting from the musketry fire at close quarters, they suffered a death compared to which death from the bayonet is merciful!

The two columns then united and pushed their way along the right to the Kumbhir bastion. Here Major Everard hoisted a red coat to signify his success to those below.

I have recorded already the first success of General Nicholls' main attack. The bastion they had gained was connected with the other part of the fortifications by a long neck. Along this the stormers had rushed without a check. At its mouth, however, the enemy made a stand, but were soon forced back. Exposed all this time to a severe fire from an outwork near the left main breach, they were not insensibly relieved when Brigadier Patton's brigade attacked that outwork and diverted the fire. It then proceeded to follow the enemy along the ramparts to the left, in face of a heavy fire, which killed the brigadier, Edwards. Nicholls, however, who had been only wounded by the consequence of the explosion to which I have referred, persevered, and, in spite of every obstacle, succeeded in gaining touch with Reynell and Delamain.

The right column of Nicholls' attack, commanded by Colonel Wilson, had meanwhile attempted to escalade the gun-breach. Wilson succeeded, though he was followed by only twenty or thirty men. The remainder went up by the left mine-breach and joined him on the summit. Thence he fought his way through the town, and, driving all opponents before him, finally remounted the ramparts.

Bharatpúr was now virtually gained. The citadel alone held out. In front of this a fight had already somewhat accidentally taken place. For an officer of the 41st N.I., Major Hunter, just after Everard's column had joined Delamain's, had, by mistake, entered the city and reached a bridge leading to the citadel. His presence had caused so much alarm to the enemy that, in their haste to shut the gates, they had excluded about an hundred of their own men, amongst whom was the brother-in-law of Dúrjan Sál, Khúshial Singh. Major Hunter had advanced to offer quarter to this nobleman, when the latter, with a terrific sword-blow, nearly severed his left arm from his body. A conflict had then ensued which had resulted in the extermination of the excluded warriors. Major Hunter and his men had then quietly made their way back to the ramparts.

This citadel was now summoned by order of Lord Combermere. As no answer was returned, guns were brought up against it. But after a short cannonade the garrison surrendered unconditionally. The prophecy had been fulfilled. The "*Kumbhir*"—for so they called "Combermere"—had, in very deed, drunk up the waters of their ditch.

But there was one man all this time who, in spite of the storming of the town and the fall of the citadel, had not despaired of escape. This was Dúrjan Sál, the pretender, whose conduct had caused all the bloodshed I have recorded. As soon as this prince had realised that the fortunes of the day were going against him he had hastened to the citadel. Collecting there a vast amount of jewels, he secured them on the persons of his wife, his two sons, himself, and forty chosen followers, and then started to cut his way out. Dashing upon a small party of the 14th at the Kumbhir gate, he cut his way through and entered a small jungle, where he was joined by some more horsemen. Thence he tried to find an outlet to emerge into the open. Long was it in vain, for every outlet was guarded by the British cavalry. At length a chance offered. At half-past two the Brigadier commanding the cavalry, believing that he had captured every fugitive, dismissed his brigade. Then Dúrjan Sál and his followers emerged. Had he waited a quarter of an hour longer he might have got off. But he was noticed by the Riding-master of the 8th Light Cavalry at the moment when the men of that regiment had but just dismounted.

Instantly pursuit was inaugurated. The fugitives were caught, and Dúrjan Sál surrendered!

Such was the second siege of Bharatpúr. The cost to the besiegers of its capture was a thousand and fifty in killed, wounded, and missing, including seven officers killed and forty-one wounded—a small proportion in comparison with the losses sustained by Lord Lake when commanding a force less than one-half as strong. The treasure captured realised nearly half a million.

But it was neither the treasure nor the comparative smallness of the casualties that invested the capture of Bharatpúr with immense significance. It completely restored the prestige of the British. It dissolved the formidable confederacy which had been secretly arranged. It proved to the discontented that not a fortress in India was impregnable; that the British were able to overcome all opposition within the empire of Hindustan. One more war, indeed, the Maráthá war of 1817–19, rendered necessary by the reversal by the immediate successors of the great Marquess Wellesley of the policy of that illustrious statesman, was required to enforce the absolute supremacy of Great Britain. But, thenceforth, that supremacy was universally recognized. But it must ever be remembered, never more vividly than at the present moment, that there is one condition which the princes of India demand as the price of their subordination to British authority. They are content to acknowledge the suzerainty of the Empress of India on condition that the servants of the Empress will protect them against every enemy from outside. The chapter which immediately follows shows how well those servants understood and performed that obligation, when the necessity arose in 1845–6. Let us hope that they will understand and perform it now (1885) when the horizon is far more threatening and the danger is infinitely greater!

CHAPTER XII.

FÍRÚZSHAHAR AND SOBRÁON.

THE founder of the Sikh religion was Nának, son of a petty Hindú trader named Kálú. Nának was born in the vicinity of Láhor in the year 1469. A youth much given to reflection, he devoted himself at an early period of his life to a study of the rival creeds then prevailing in India, the Hindú and the Muhammadan. Neither satisfied him. Though his first teacher had been a learned professor of the latter faith, the simple mind of Nának could find no resting-place in a religion in which the worldly element so largely predominated; nor was he more content with the specious abstractions of Hindúism.

After wandering through many lands in search of a satisfying truth, Nának returned to his native country with the conviction that he had failed. He had found, he said, many scriptures and many creeds; but he had not found God. Casting off his habit of an ascetic, he resumed his father's trade, married, became the father of a family, and passed the remainder of his life in preaching the doctrine of the unity of one invisible God, of the necessity of living virtuously, and of practising toleration towards others. He died in 1539, leaving behind him a reputation without spot, and many zealous and admiring disciples eager to perpetuate his creed.

The founder of a new religion, Nának, before his death, had nominated his successor—a man of his own tribe named

Angad. Angad held the supremacy for twelve years, years which he employed mainly in committing to writing the doctrines of his great master and in enforcing them upon his disciples.

Angad was succeeded by Ummar Dás, a great preacher. He, and his son-in-law and successor, Rám Dás, were held in high esteem by the emperor Akbar.

But it was the son of Rám Das, Arjún, who established on a permanent basis the new religion. Comprehending the applicability of the teaching of Nának and his successors to every state of life and to every condition of society, Arjún arranged their several writings, added to them the most suitable compositions of preceding religious reformers, and, completing the whole with a prayer and some pious exhortations of his own, he produced the sacred book, the Grunth, of the new faith, and imposed it upon his followers as containing the guide to their religious and moral conduct. Simultaneously he fixed the seat of the chief Gúrú, or high priest of the religion, and of his principal followers, at Amritsar, then an obscure hamlet, but which, in consequence of the selection, speedily rose into importance. Arjún then regulated and reduced to a systematic tax the offerings of his adherents, to be found even then in every city and village in the Panjáb and the cis-Satlaj territories. Nor did he disdain to increase the wealth of the holy city he had founded by traffic of a very extensive character. Meddling, however, in the political contests which almost invariably supervened on the death of a Mughul sovereign Arjún unfortunately espoused the losing side, was imprisoned, and died.

The real successor of Arjún was his son, Hur Govind. Hur Govind founded the Sikh nation. Before his time the followers of the Gúrú had been united by no tie but that of obedience to the book. Govind formed them into a community of warriors. He did away with many of the restrictions regarding food, authorised his followers to eat flesh, summoned them to his standard, and marched with them to consolidate his power.

A military organisation based upon a religious principle, and directed by a strong central authority, will always become powerful in a country the government of which is tainted with decay. The ties which bound the Mughul empire together were already loosening under the paralysing influence of the bigotry of Aurangzíb, when, in 1675, Govind, fourth in succession to the Hur Govind to whom I have adverted, assumed the mantle of Gúrú of the Sikhs. Intolerance reigned supreme throughout India. Tégh Buhádur, the father and immediate predecessor of Govind, had been put to death by Aurangzíb, a martyr to his faith, and his body had been exposed with ignominy in the streets of Dihlí. This murder made of Govind, then only fifteen years old, the irreconcilable enemy of the Muhammadan name. Acting under the advice, almost under the authority, of his father's friends, he for the time concealed alike his enmity and his ambition, spent twenty years in comparative obscurity, hunting the tiger and the wild boar, learning the Persian language, studying the best means of swaying the races whom he would have to influence, and perfecting in his own mind the means of shaking the empire held together by the iron hand of the man who had slain his father.

The better to work out his end Govind still further simplified the dogmas of the faith. Assembling his followers, he announced to them that thenceforward the doctrines of the "Khálsa," the sáved or liberated, alone should prevail. There must be no human image or resemblance of the One Almighty Father; caste must cease to exist; before Him all men were equal; Muhammadanism was to be rooted out; social distinctions, all the solaces of superstition, were to exist no more; they should call themselves "Singh" and become a nation of soldiers.

The multitude received Govind's propositions with rapture By a wave of the wand he found himself the trusted leader of a confederacy of warriors in a nation whose institutions were decaying.

About 1695, twelve years before the death of Aurangzíb, Govind put his schemes into practice. He secured many forts in the hill-country of the Panjáb, defeated the Mughul troops in several encounters, and established himself as a thorn in the side of the empire. At last Aurangzíb took the alarm. He directed the governors of Láhor and Sirhind to move against the Gúrú, and even threatened to send his son, Buhádur Sháh, to command the army against him. Against such forces Govind could do but little. After a series of manœuvres he found himself surrounded at Anandpúr. His adherents, who had till then followed him with implicit trust, murmured in this hour of his supreme necessity; many of them even deserted him; but Govind himself never quailed. Sending his mother, his wives, and his children* to Sirhind, he threw himself into the fort of Chamkáur. Besieged there, he still bade a haughty defiance to the enemy, and, after a desperate defence, in which he saw his two remaining sons and nearly the whole of his band perish, he escaped by night to Behlolpúr, and thence to Damdamma, midway between Fírúzpúr and Hánsi. There he remained, unmolested, for several years, engaged in adding another book to the Grunth, and in devising measures for rousing the energies of his followers.

Aurangzíb died in 1707. Buhádur Sháh, who succeeded him, summoned the Gúrú to his camp in the valley of the Godávari. Govind complied, was received with respect and even trusted with a military command. But in the midst of his new prosperity he was assassinated by the sons of an Afghán whom in a sudden fit of anger he had killed.

Before leaving the cis-Satlaj territory Govind had bequeathed his temporal power to Banda, a native of southern India. Banda justified the selection. Recognising the fact that the death of Aurangzíb had dissolved the bond which kept

* The boys were, on their arrival there, betrayed to the Muhammadans and put to death.

the Mughul empire together, Banda raised an army of devoted followers, defeated the Mughul governor of Sirhind, avenged the death of Govind's children, and occupied the country between the Satlaj and the Jamná. This success brought upon him the army of Buhádur Sháh, and, surrounded, as his predecessor had been, by the emperor's army, Banda owed his escape only to a stratagem. Escape he did, however, with all his followers; and, making his way to Jammá, laid the fairest part of the Panjáb under contribution.

Every day, however, loosened the bonds of union throughout the Mughul empire. The death of Buhádur Sháh in 1712, and the contests amongst the rival candidates for the succession, gave strength to the nobles and the confederacies who were playing for their own hands. Banda took advantage of the surrounding turmoil to build a strong fort, Gúrdáspúr, between the Bíás and the Ráví, and, when the turmoil had subsided, he issued from the vicinity of that fort, defeated the army of the Viceroy of Láhor, and once more occupied Sirhind. Again were the chosen troops of the Mughul empire, led by their best general, Abdul Samad Khán, despatched against him. Again were the Sikhs, beaten in the open, compelled to flee before the foe. At last they took refuge in the new fort of Gúrdáspúr. Besieged here, they defended themselves to the last extremity. It was only when every means of defence was exhausted that they submitted. They had better have died of starvation; for the tortures inflicted by the victors on Banda and on many of his followers were so cruel that the pen refuses to record them. The blow was a serious one, and it was followed up by a rigid persecution. Recantation or death was the Muhammadan cry. Carried out unsparingly, it almost seemed as though it had produced the desired effect, for, for the period of a generation, the Sikhs were hardly heard of again in history.

But the principle which bound them together was a pure and a strong principle. Decay, too, was doing her work on all the surrounding institutions. Gradually, one after another, whole provinces became dissevered from the Mughul empire. Bengal, Awadh, Haidarábád, disclaimed dependence on Dihlí. The Maráthás ruled in western and central, and were steadily pressing up towards north-western, India. The invasion of Nádir Sháh came to deal a fatal blow to an empire already a shadow of its former self. In the turmoil which followed, the Sikh confederacy gradually reconstituted itself. Then followed the several invasions of Ahmad Sháh Duráni. The Panjáb fell for a time under the sway of the Afghán. The Sikhs, often rising in arms, and as often dispersed, succeeded at length, under the leadership of Jassa Singh, a carpenter by trade (1758), in temporarily occupying Láhor. Three years later was fought the decisive battle of Pánipat. But though, the year following, the victor of Pánipat inflicted a crushing defeat upon the Sikhs near Lodiáná, destroyed their temples, and slew his prisoners by hundreds, the time had gone by when such a community could be rooted out. The Duráni had to leave India—an India about to be re-parcelled. Amongst the new claimants for dominion were the English, the Núwáb-Vazír of Awadh, the Maráthás, and last, but not least, the Sikhs.

Of these several claimants the last-named were not the least resolute. The year following their defeat by Ahmad Sháh they avenged that misfortune by inflicting upon the Afgháns an overthrow even more decisive in the plains of Sirhind. Uniting then with the Játs, and in alliance with Holkar, they laid siege to Dihlí, and though forced by another irruption—speedily abandoned—of Ahmád Sháh, and by the defection of Holkar, to raise that siege, they hurried back across the Satlaj, attacked and seriously maltreated the great Duráni, near Amritsar, took possession of Láhor, and parcelled out amongst themselves the whole country between the Satlaj and the Jhelam. The chiefs then convened a solemn assembly at Amritsar, at which they formally proclaimed the sway of the Sikh nation and the prevalence of their faith. To commemorate this event, to bind it on the tablets of the hearts of their followers, they struck from their mint a coin bearing an inscription to the effect that Gúrú Govind had received from Nának the three virtues—grace, power, and rapid victory.

For two years the Sikhs remained unmolested in their new dominions. In 1767, however, Ahmad Sháh, bent on recovering the Panjáb, made his last attempt to enslave India. The attempt failed, mainly in consequence of the defection of his own troops. Left then to themselves, the Sikhs, divided into twelve confederacies or misls, each of which had its chief equal in authority to his brother chiefs, felt the want of the organization which a central authority alone could bestow. Each misl or confederacy fought for itself, and it was not until 1784 that a young chieftain named Mahá Singh, gained, mainly by force of arms, a position which placed him above his fellows. The only other chief who could at all pretend to rivalry with Mahá Singh was the leader whom he had defeated, Jai Singh Kunaia. But Mahá Singh, as great in diplomacy as in war, found means to conciliate even him. A marriage between his son and the grand-daughter of Jai Singh cemented a union which was never afterwards broken. The name of the son of Mahá Singh was Ranjít Singh.

Ranjít Sing was born in 1780. At the early age of eleven he lost his father. Before he had attained maturity evil days befell the territories of which he was the nominal chieftain. In 1797, six years after his father's death, the Panjáb suffered again from the horrors of an Afghán invasion, conducted by Sháh Zamán. Láhor was taken by the invader, only, however, to be almost immediately evacuated. The invasion was renewed the following year, and Láhor was again occupied. But eighteen summers had formed the character of Ranjít Singh. A true follower of Gúrú Govind, he hated the Afghán invaders with an intensity inspired by the conviction that they were the determined enemies of the freedom and the toleration which were the watchword of his tribe. For the time, however, his weakness forced him to dissemble. By a show of service well appreciated he obtained from the Afghán ruler the investiture of the capital of the Panjáb (1799). Immediately afterwards serious occurrences in his own country forced Zamán Sháh to return to Kábul.

Ranjít Singh became then the recognised ruler of the Sikhs, just after the English had destroyed the power of Típú Sáhib, and just before the contest for supremacy with the Maráthás, which was really decided at Assaye and Laswári. The campaign against Holkar which followed the crushing overthrow of Sindia, had been virtually decided before the war broke out. Holkar, after a show of success, crossed the Satlaj in the autumn of 1805, a fugitive, with, as he said himself, " his kingdom on his saddle's bow," and implored the assistance of Ranjít Singh. But " the Lion of the Panjáb," as he was called about this time, had no wish to embroil his young nation with the veterans who had destroyed the powerful hosts of the Maráthás. Lake, with his victorious army, was on the track of Holkar, and Lake was not the man to fail to push his advantage to the utmost. Ranjít Singh, then, received Jeswant Ráo Holkar at Amritsar, and made it clear to him that the aid he wished for would not be given. By this time Lake was on the Bíás, and Holkar, after hesitating for a moment whether he should not traverse the Panjáb and invoke the aid of the Afgháns, finally accepted (24th December 1805) the terms offered by the English general.

Ranjít Singh himself exchanged at this time friendly communications with General Lake. It is even said that he entered in disguise the English camp in order to inspect the troops who had overthrown such famed warriors as Sindia, the Bhonslé, and Holkar. The communications led, however, to no practical result.

But the visit made by the English commander to the country of the Sikhs was not altogether void of consequences. In the cis-Satlaj territory Lake had been joined by two Sikh chieftains of repute, Lál Singh of Khaital, and Bhág Singh of Jhind, uncle to Ranjít Singh. These chieftains had already rendered good service to a British detachment at Shámli when it had been hard pressed by the enemy. On his passage through Patiála, too, Lake had received promises of devotion from its ruler, Sáhib Singh. Before the war had terminated the two first of these chieftains received handsome acknowledgments from the Indian Government, and there can be no doubt but that, had the policy of Marquess Wellesley not been suspended, the cis-Satlaj chieftains as a body would have acknowledged the over-lordship of the British. The temporary reversal of Marquess Wellesley's system delayed this acknowledgment, but the kindly memory of the British remained, and in due season bore abundant fruit.

Meanwhile Ranjít Singh had applied himself zealously to the task of consolidating his dominions, of giving unity to diverse and scattered elements, of welding the increasing Sikh nation into a well-ordered commonwealth. Beyond the Satlaj he succeeded almost to his fondest hopes. But in the cis-Satlaj territories a spirit of independence had been awakened strong enough to dispose the chiefs to resist the claim made by the Panjáb ruler even to nominal overlordship. In 1808 these chieftains combined to resist the aggressive system which Ranjít Singh threatened to introduce amongst them—a system which would bring them into direct subordination to Láhor. Recollecting their friendly intercourse with General Lake, they despatched messengers to the British Resident at Dihlí, praying for support in case of need. But the Cornwallis policy—the policy of under no pretence interfering in the affairs of native states—was in the ascendant, and from Dihlí no assuring replies reached them.

But the dread of the ambition of Napoleon changed the course of events. That dread inspired the British Government with the idea of seeking alliances for British India not only beyond the Jamuná but beyond the Indus. To secure these alliances Mr. Elphinstone was despatched to the court of Sháh Shúja, then ruler of Kábul, and Mr. Metcalfe to that of Ranjít Singh. In view, too, of an impending crisis, the Cornwallis policy was still further suspended; and the chiefs of Patiálá, of Jhínd, and of Khaital, were verbally assured that they had been brought under the protection of the British Government.

Ranjít Singh heard of this act while Mr. Metcalfe was still with him. He resented it so much that but for the earnest entreaties of two of his most trusted councillors he would have declared war against the English. As it was, he broke off the negotiations, crossed the Satlaj at the head of his army, seized Farídkót and Ambálá, levied exactions in Malarkóta and Thanesar, and entered into an agreement or alliance with the ruler of Patiálá.

The proceedings of Ranjít Singh seemed to the Governor-General, Lord Minto, to be of a character to demand a vigorous counter-demonstration. He accordingly ordered Sir David Ochterlony to march northwards with a force to support Mr. Metcalfe and to confine Ranjít Singh to the north bank of the Satlaj. Ochterlony on entering Sirhind, was received with open arms by all the chiefs, one only excepted, and then halted at Lodiáná, near his supplies, to wait for the next move of Ranjít Singh.

Ranjít Singh was in this position. His hold on the Panjáb was not absolutely secure. Multán, Pesháwar, and many other strong places were held by the Afgháns. He could not, until he had secured his kingdom beyond the Satlaj, engage in a war with the English. Reluctantly, then, he gave way, and recognised the protectorate of the British Government over the cis-Satlaj states, those only excepted which he had originally acquired south of that river.

During the five years which followed Ranjít Singh was occupied in carrying out, not always successfully, his ambitious schemes beyond the Satlaj. Some acquisitions he did make, but he failed, for the second time, before Múltán, in 1810; and he was foiled in an attempt upon Káshmír in 1814. But he never lost heart. He had placed one aim before him, the unification of the Panjáb under his sceptre, and he kept that ever in view. In 1818 he captured Múltán, and gained a post on the north bank of the Indus which secured to him the passage of that river. In 1819–20 he conquered Káshmír and annexed the Déraját. Four years later, 14th March 1823, he defeated the Afgháns at Naoshéra, and sacked Pesháwar, which, from this time forward, may be regarded as an integral portion of his dominions. From this year, indeed, his aim may be said to have been attained, his dominions to have been welded into one whole. He had become the feudal chief of a large population, devoted to war and to the preparation of military means and equipment. To this end were directed the wealth, the energies, the longings of the people.

A circumstance had occurred, the year previous to the consolidation of his dominions, which had greatly stimulated the ambition of Ranjít Singh to possess an army equal to any emergency. This was the arrival at Láhor of two officers who had made their proofs under Napoleon, Generals Allard and Ventura. Ránjít Singh persuaded these officers to accept positions in his army not dissimilar to those which de Boigne and his coadjutors had held in the armies of Sindia. At a later period two other officers, who had undergone the same training, Generals Court and Avitabile, were added to the list. Possessing great capacity and experience, these officers succeeded very speedily in engrafting on the most promising raw material in Asia the discipline and the dexterity of the European soldier. Strong of body, active, intelligent, unfettered by the bonds of caste prejudice, full of courage and gifted with a wonderful stamina, accustomed to live on flesh or to dispense with it, the Sikh has the making of the finest soldier in the world. And it is not too much to affirm that the rank and file of the Sikh army became, under the training of the skilled officers I have named, the finest rank and file in the world. They wanted but officers, from general to subaltern, to be invincible. These, happily for England, they had not.

An interview betweeen Ranjít Singh and the Governor-General of India, Lord William Bentinck, at Rúpar, on the Satlaj, in October 1831, seemed only to confirm the conditions of friendship between the two nations. There can be no doubt, however, but that Ranjít always regarded the advances of the aggressive foreigners with suspicion. Already had they thwarted his projects on Sirhind and Málwá, and he feared lest, fixed now on the banks of the Satlaj, at Firúzpúr and Lodiáná, they might interfere with the designs which he had already nurtured regarding Sindh. To bring his suspicions to a test he laid a claim, the year following the interview, to a paramount right over Shikarpúr. But eventually he had to yield—and not only to yield, but to grant, unwillingly, the opening of the Satlaj to British traders. It was about this period that, glancing at a new English map of India with the political agent, Captain Wade, and noticing how many portions of it were encircled by the red line betokening the supremacy of England, he exclaimed with a sigh: "All will become red."

It would be interesting to study the history of Ranjít Singh's dealing with his powerful neighbours from this period to the hour of his death. He never trusted them. He saw the beginning of those trading aspirations which, by bestowing a power to interfere, had led to the absorption of Bengal and of the North-west Provinces. Had he been younger, or had he felt within him the power to command, he would have resisted and fought. But, at his age—and he was old for his age—he feared to risk the empire he had made on a single battle. He preferred the impossible task of conciliating an aggressive race. He had not sufficiently realised the fact that a race which, from small beginnings, had succeeded in appropriating one-third of the globe, can never be diverted by conciliation from its natural bent. He tried it, however, first when Sir Henry Fane, the Commander-in-Chief of the army in India, visited Láhor in 1837, and, again, when the Governor-General of India, Lord Auckland, demanded, in 1838, permission to allow the English troops to traverse the Panjáb in order to seat Sháh Shújá on the throne of Afghánistán. Unwillingly, most unwillingly, did Ranjít Singh yield to this demand. The idea that he was to be girt about by the armies of England chafed him. He entertained no doubt that the men who had overcome the Maráthás in all their glory could easily conquer and retain the northern province which had always been the outer rampart of the Mughul empire. And then where would he be? With the English south of the Satlaj, the English north of the Indus, the English protecting Sindh, what chance of independence would remain for the Panjáb? Still—he yielded. Again he tried conciliation: he became a party to the alliance against Dost Muhammad.

What he hoped cannot be doubted. He hoped, though he believed it not, that the resistance of the mountaineers might so weaken his aggressive allies that he would be left master of the situation—master to conquer Sindh, master to recover the cis-Satlaj districts—possibly to acquire more. Nor can it be questioned that had a few years of vigorous life yet been spared to him he would have used to the advantage of the Sikh nation the mishaps which overwhelmed the English army a little later.

It was not to be. Ranjít Singh lived only long enough to hear that the English had taken Kandahár. He died on the 27th June 1839, aged in years only fifty-nine, but older in physique by at least twelve or fifteen years.*

* When Lord Auckland paid his return visit to Ranjít Singh in 1839, the Sikh ruler, says Sir Henry Lawrence, had completely lost the power of speech. Before he died, the same year, the faculties of his mind gave way, and the powers of the State had been usurped by the rájahs of Jamú.

His eldest son, Kharak Singh, succeeded him. He was almost an imbecile. But his son, Nao Niál Singh, had inherited much of the ability of his grandfather. He was a man who could rule as well as govern; who distrusted the rájahs of Jamú, and who was resolved to be master. Everything seemed to favour him. Karak Singh, always ailing, showed every disposition still further to abridge his life by his excesses.* In October 1840 it was clear that his days were numbered. On the 5th of the following month he died.

Nao Nihál Singh became ruler of the Panjáb. But the accession of a prince so able, so resolute, so self-reliant, did not suit the views of the ambitious rájahs of Jamú. Returning from performing the last rites at the funeral pyre of his father, Nao Nihál was passing under a covered archway with the eldest son of Guláb Singh by his side, when a portion of the structure fell, killed the son of Guláb Singh, and so severely injured the Rájah that he died that night. The day of his accession was the day of his death.†

Shér Singh, a reputed son of Ranjít's, succeeded to the thus vacated throne. A voluptuary without talents, Shér Singh conciliated neither respect nor affection. Suddenly an unexpected rival appeared in the person of Chand Kaur, widow of Kharak Singh, and mother of the deceased Nao Nihál. Matters were further complicated by the opportune recollection that Ráni Janda Kaur, a favourite wife of Ranjít Singh, had borne to him a son, named Dhulíp, a few months before the conferences regarding the re-seating of Sháh Shúja on the throne of Kábul had taken place!

For the moment, the sword decided the question. Shér

* Sir Henry Lawrence says he was the victim of a slow and subtle poison.

† Captain Cunningham states: "It is not positively known that the rájahs of Jamú thus designed to remove Nao Nihál Singh; but it is difficult to acquit them of the crime, and it is certain they were capable of committing it." Sir Henry Lawrence would appear to have been of the same opinion (*vide Calcutta Review*, vol. i. p. 479). Captain Gardner, who witnessed the accident, recorded his belief that it was premeditated.

Singh, having gained over the Jamú rájahs, marched on Láhor, captured it, and caused himself to be procalimed Mahárájá. Mái Chand Kaur was treated at first with outward respect; but, after a time, she was placed under surveillance, then in confinement. In the course of time, her paramour, who had been allowed to share her fate, was seized, tortured, and put to death; and a little later, about a year after her overthrow, Mai Chand Kaur herself was, at the instigation of higher authority, beaten to death with slippers by her own slave girls!

Shér Singh had gained his throne by the army, and the army had become his master. From that moment, until it invaded British territory, the Sikh army never ceased to be master in the Panjáb. No longer was it the willing instrument of a despotic but genial government. It had come to look upon itself as the representative body of the people, as the Khálsa itself, commissioned by the various tribes to take a leading part in public affairs. Distrustful of the English, the Sikh chiefs and soldiers yet behaved with singular loyalty to that people in the hour of their calamity in Afghánistán, and even aided them to force their way through the Khaibar. After the disaster had been retrieved, and the English army had returned to the south of the Satlaj, Lord Ellenborough, then Governor-General, expressed a desire that Shér Singh should visit the British camp at Firúzpúr. But neither Shér Singh nor his Jamú advisers desired an interview which, they imagined, would be used to force from them new concessions. Advantage, then, was taken of a misunderstanding to postpone it indefinitely.

But events were marching too fast for the repose of the voluptuary who ruled the Panjáb. The year following the return of the English from Kábul, he was deliberately murdered by his boon companion, Ajít Singh Sindhawála, a man whom he had recalled from exile. The assassin then murdered the son, Partáb Singh; then the minister, chief of the Jamú rájahs, Dhián Singh; and then proceeded to the citadel to proclaim a new king. But, meanwhile, Hírá Singh, son of the murdered Dhíán Singh, had thrown himself on the army, and promised them rewards if they would avenge the death of their friend and his father. The issue was doubtful, because the Jamú rájahs were hated by the troops, and it is probable that if Ajít Singh and his confederates had been able to maintain their position in the citadel for three days, the army would have come round to them, and the days of the Jamú rájahs would have been numbered. But, on the spur of the moment, the army responded to the call of Hírá Singh; the citadel made a poor defence; Ajít Singh and his brother were killed; and the next day, Dhulíp Singh, the only surviving son of the great Ranjít, was proclaimed Mahárájá. Hírá Singh was nominated his Vazír!

Be it remembered that the new rájah was then in his fifth year, an irresponsible minor. His mother, Rání Janda Kaur, became, in virtue of his age and of her relationship to him, regent of the kingdom. Of this lady it is not necessary to say more than that, gifted with considerable talents, she had not been endowed with the faculty of rightly directing those talents. Nor had education supplied that which nature had denied. With all her abilities, she was, and remained to the end, a spirited, hot-tempered, intriguing woman, swayed always by her passions, and possessing a large capacity alike for love and for hate!

The Rání had, on her accession, an intuitive conviction of the necessity of crushing the ambition of the Jamú rájahs. But she chose her instrument badly. Perhaps because there was no one else upon whom she could thoroughly depend, she selected her brother, Jowáhir Singh. Jowáhir Singh was a weak debauchee, without character and without influence. He made the attempt and failed. Scarcely had the failure been recognised than a new peril arose. Káshmira Singh and Peshora Singh, two princes who claimed relationship to Ranjít Singh by adoption, if not by blood, rose in revolt. Though the revolt collapsed, mainly through the imbecility of its two leaders, it proved the beginning of many others. Noble after noble rose in rebellion, nor was the spirit of sedition satisfied until the rule of the Jamú rájahs had been overthrown, and their leader, Hírá Singh, been slain (21st December 1844).

To the government of the Jamú rájahs succeeded an administration—if, by courtesy, it can be called such—of which Jowáhir Singh, the brother, and Lál Singh, the lover, of the Ráni, were the responsible heads. Of the first I have already spoken. Lál Singh was a man of greater ability and cunning. Of the Sikh nobles, he and another, Téj Singh, had been foremost in recognising the necessity of curbing the insolence of the army. There is reason to believe, indeed, that at this early period they had begun to nurture the idea that if they should fail to master those all-powerful soldiers, it would be wise policy to throw them on the bayonets of the British!

The first measure of the new confederates was to humble Guláb Singh, now become chief of the Jámú family. The army, which Hírá Singh had attempted to conciliate by a monthly increase of two and a half rupees to the pay of each common soldier, was further propitiated by a new increase of one-fifth of that sum. It was then ordered to march against Guláb Singh. That rájah, one of the most astute men of his day, submitted without a struggle, scattered his rupees broadcast among the soldiers, and returned with them to Láhor, where, to save his life, he surrendered without a murmur a considerable portion of his ancestral domains. He was then permitted to return to Jamú.

Meanwhile, Jowáhir Singh had been appointed to the fatal post of Vazír (14th May 1845). Shortly there followed a second rebellion of Peshora Singh, terminated very quickly by the surrender of that insignificant political personage. His very insignificance should have saved him. But Jowáhir Singh no sooner had him in his power than he caused him to be put to death. The news of this outrage roused into action feelings

2

which had for some time been fomenting in the army. Long had the soldiers despised Jowáhir Singh; the crime perpetrated on Peshora changed that feeling to hatred. At a solemn meeting of the Panchayats, or regimental councils, of the army, Jowáhir Singh was sentenced to death. He was required, in consequence, to appear before the assembled Khálsa to answer for his misdeeds. Tremblingly he obeyed; but, to ensure, if possible, his safety, he placed beside him, in the howdah of his elephant, the boy Mahárájá, Dhulíp Singh. The troops, however, thoroughly in earnest, were not thus to be baulked of their prey. The Mahárájá was made to descend and enter a tent. A party of soldiers then disposed of Jowáhir Singh by a volley of musketry!

The army, thus become the arbiter of the fate of the rulers of the country, was now more than ever master. To men like Lál Singh, Téj Singh, and others who had a stake in the country, the situation had become intolerable. Earnest secret efforts were then made by these men to arouse in the ranks of the army a spirit of hostility to the English. They bore no grudge against that people; they wished them no ill-will; they rather hoped that the power which ruled India south of the Satlaj would rid them of those all-powerful Janissaries who, at a word, might sentence them and their families to death. By degrees they succeeded. The soldiers, roused to a determination to conquer India, selected as prime minister and as commander-in-chief Lál Singh and Téj Singh, the two nobles who had most openly declared in favour of the new aggression; and, on the 11th December 1845, tumultuously crossed the Satlaj some twelve miles below Firúzpúr.

What sort of reception were the English prepared to give them? The Government of India had been neither blind nor indifferent to the anarchy which had prevailed in the Panjáb since the day when Shér Singh refused the invitation of Lord Ellenborough. That nobleman, strong in his conviction that a crisis was imminent, and might occur at any moment, had made every preparation in his power to meet it. He had established a new cantonment, the head-quarters of a division, at Ambála, in Sirhind, and had located there the troops who had previously occupied the far less commodious station of Karnál. He had directed the throwing-up of an intrenchment round the magazines and stores at Firúzpúr. He had even contemplated more. It had been his intention to establish a fortified camp between Múdkí and Jagráon, and he was only prevented from carrying out this project by his untimely recall.* He did not the less commend the plan to his successor, Sir Henry Hardinge. But like every Governor-General who has landed in India, from the time of Clive downwards, Sir Henry Hardinge had quitted England with the most sincere and loudly-proclaimed resolution to maintain a policy of peace. It can easily be understood, then, that he was unwilling to inaugurate his assumption of power by sanctioning a line of policy which would most certainly have been denounced as menacing the independence of a free people. But Sir Henry had not been long in India before he recognised, as clearly as had Lord Ellenborough, the danger of the situation. Quietly and unostentatiously, then, he strengthened the force in the north-west; increased the number of native regiments at Firúzpúr to seven; placed at the head of the brigade there the best officer in the Bengal army, General Littler; and brought up to support the frontier force every man who could be spared from the eastern, and even from the southern, portions of the empire. He did not mass the troops in the north-west on any particular spot, for such action on his part would have been liable to afford to the Sikhs the excuse they wanted; but he kept them handy, in readiness to move at the first signal.

On the 11th December, we have seen, the Sikhs gave that signal. They crossed the Satlaj twelve miles from Firúzpúr,

* I received this information from the late Earl of Ellenborough himself.

and at once intrenched themselves on the south bank of the river. Their counsels were divided. Whilst many amongst the rank and file were eager to push on at once, and overwhelm the weak British force at Firúzpúr, others, stimulated by Lál Singh and Téj Singh, who dreaded a victory of the Khálsa over the British, and whose main object was the destruction of the army which threatened them, were eager to push on, and have the glory of capturing or slaying a British Governor-General. Still, Firúzpúr was so temptingly near, and was so weakly defended, its arsenal being three miles from the station, that it is probable the advocates for an attack on that place would have carried the day, but for the conduct of the British general commanding there, General Littler.

Littler was a very capable soldier, daring, resolute, and self-reliant. He had seven thousand men under his command; but of these, rather less than one thousand were Europeans. As soon as he heard that the Sikhs, in large force, were attempting the passage of the Satlaj, Littler at once summoned the commanding officers of regiments to his quarters, and asked their advice. Without one exception, they recommended throwing up intrenchments to fortify the station. Littler listened to them all, dismissed them without a word from himself, and learning the next morning that the Sikhs had crossed the river, and were intrenching themselves on its south bank, marched out and offered them battle!

This bold and judicious action had an excellent effect. If the Sikhs ever had any intention of attacking Firúzpúr, the movement of Littler effectually dissipated it. They left, then, uninjured a position they might easily have carried, and the occupation of which by them would have effected incalculable damage to the British army, and prepared to carry out the design craftily instilled into them by their leaders.

Meanwhile the news of the passage of the Satlaj had reached the Governor-General, and the Commander-in-Chief in India,

Sir Hugh Gough. Instantly, from every station in the north-west, horse, foot, artillery were in motion. From the hill stations of the Himaláyas there hurried down two European regiments. The divisions stationed at Ambála and at Mírath marched on one common point. The Lodiáná force was concentrated at Bassián. On the 13th, Sir Hugh Gough, who had started from Simlah, was with the Ambála troops at the town of Sirhind; on the same day, he opened out communications with Sir Henry Hardinge. On the 14th the army was formed into brigades and divisions. On the 15th, Gough's division marched twenty-six miles to Lattála, and the day following thirty miles to Wadní, effecting on the way, at Bassian, a junction with the Governor-General and the Lodiáná force.

Wadní belonged to the Sikhs, and the officer who held the place refused the British army supplies. He yielded, however, to force. The next day the army marched ten miles to Charak; and the following day, the 18th, twenty-one miles further, to Múdkí. They had scarcely taken up their ground here, however, when they found themselves threatened by a detachment of the Sikh army.

It happened in this wise. The Sikh army, having crossed the Satlaj on the 11th, had remained for some days motionless. The influence of its leaders, Lál Singh and Téj Singh, caused them to waste those precious days. Intimidated by Littler's bold challenge, they had spared Firúzpúr. Their intelligence department being extremely defective, they had but imperfect news of the movements of the British army. A bold and sagacious enemy would have found it comparatively easy to destroy that army in detail. But boldness and sagacity were alike wanting in the councils of the Sikh leaders. At last, after they had rested six days idle on the south bank of the Satlaj, information upon which they could rely reached their camp (17th December) that the British army would certainly arrive at Múdkí the following day. Here was an opportunity.

The Sikhs had thirty thousand men on the south bank: the English, of all arms—not including Littler's force, which had not yet effected a junction with Gough—numbered eleven thousand: they would reach Múdkí tired and unprepared: how easy then to surprise and overwhelm them! Such were the counsels of common sense. But the Sikh army, under the baneful influence of the leaders who were bent on its destruction, had no regard for such counsels. Instead of marching *en masse* to overwhelm the enemy, they were persuaded to detach only a brigade consisting of less than two thousand infantry, supported by twenty-two guns and eight or ten thousand cavalry.*

The British force had, I have said, just arrived at Múdkí when the proximity of the enemy was reported to Sir Hugh Gough. Few men braver than the soldier who commanded the British army have ever lived; not one who was less of a strategist or a tactician. Of Clive, of John Adams, and of Wellesley it has been recorded that under the roar of cannon their mental energies redoubled, and that never was their vision so clear or their action so cool as when the battle raged furiously and doubtfully around them. Sir Hugh Gough possessed the opposite characteristic. Under the excitement of battle he forgot all his plans; he could only push forward. He chafed under the delay caused by the preliminary fire of his artillery; he burned with impatience to let his infantry get at the enemy. Such a disposition, less harmful against an Asiatic foe than any other, was dangerous when allowed to have its way against an enemy so formidable as the Sikhs. It would have been fatal had the opposing army been European.

* *Vide* Cunningham, p. 306. Captain Nicholson, who was at that time British agent at Firúzpúr, estimated the detached force as considerably smaller. The numbers given in the official despatches (fourteen thousand to twenty thousand infantry and the same number of cavalry) are absurdly unreliable. Personal inquiries on the spot enable me to state that the numbers given in the text are correct.

Such was the leader to whom it was reported, about 3 o'clock in the afternoon (18th December), that the Sikhs were advancing. The men, tired after their march of twenty-one miles, were cooking their dinners. Instantly the bugle sounded; the half-cooked dinners were abandoned, the men turned out, the line of battle was formed, and the order to advance was given. The front line was formed of the three arms, the artillery being in the centre, flanked on both sides by infantry, and the infantry again by cavalry. Behind this line came the main body of the infantry in contiguous columns; and in rear of all a small reserve. After marching a mile and a half the advance came under the fire of Sikh guns in position. Still the British troops pressed on. A few minutes later and the enemy's cavalry threaten both flanks of the British. To repel these Gough launches his own cavalry against them, and, under cover of their brilliant charge, deploys into line his infantry columns and sends them against the enemy. The enemy's hope, at this crisis of the battle, was in their guns. What could their handful of infantry effect against the superior numbers of the British? Still they remained firm, opposing, with steady discipline, a continuous musketry fire to that of the enemy. All at once, however, their flanks were uncovered; their cavalry gave way! Even in that hour the troops of the Khalsá were true to their renown. They retired, steadily, their faces to the foe, disputing every inch of ground. For five miles they fell back, still doggedly resisting, seizing every opportunity, every vantage ground* to turn upon their pursuers. With nightfall only did the contest cease. Of their twenty-two guns the Sikhs

* In his article on this campaign in the *Calcutta Review*, vol. vi. pp. 263–4, Sir Herbert Edwardes involuntarily renders justice to the Sikh army at Múdki. Sir Herbert was then under the impression (1846) that the number of the Sikhs greatly exceeded the actual amount. He calculated the infantry at about four thousand five hundred, and the cavalry from twenty thousand to thirty thousand. Whilst, then, exalting the prowess of the British soldier, he renders perfect justice to the gallant stand made by less than two thousand men against four times as many.

had lost seventeen; they had lost also the field of battle; but they at least had not lost their honour!

In this combat the English lost eight hundred and seventy-two men killed and wounded, amongst the former the famous Sir Robert Sale and General M'Caskill. How many of the Sikhs were slain can never be known. In all probability their casualties did not exceed those of their enemy.

That the victory of Múdkí was not considered in the British camp to be very decisive was shown by the determination arrived at that evening to effect a junction with Littler before attempting anything further. Orders to that effect were accordingly transmitted to that officer. It was ascertained the next day that the main body of the Sikhs, consisting of twelve battalions of infantry, eighty guns, many of large calibre, and from ten to twelve thousand horsemen, or in all under thirty thousand men,* were encamped in a deep horse-shoe form round the village of Fírúzshahar. Before venturing to attack such a position it was necessary that the army should be reinforced.

That same day some reinforcements, the 29th Foot and the 1st Europeans, the 11th and 41st Native Infantry, and a small detachment of heavy guns, arrived in camp. The day following, the Governor-General, Sir Henry Hardinge, notified to the Commander-in-Chief his willingness to serve under his orders as second in command. The offer was accepted. Sir Henry brought to the army a great accession of strength; for, in calm, cool, clear judgment on the field of battle he was surpassed by no one then in India.

The village of Fírúzshahar is ten miles from Múdkí, nearly midway between that place and Fírúzpúr. Early on the morning of the 21st December the army, led by Sir Hugh Gough, left its encamping-ground to effect a junction with Littler, who, on his part, quitted Fírúzpúr to march across country to meet it.

* Edwardes estimates them at thirty-five thousand with between eighty and ninety guns. —*Calcutta Review*, vol. vi. p. 271.

The junction was effected four miles from the Sikh position, about half-past one o'clock in the day. The skilful manner in which this manœuvre was effected by Littler completely deceived the Sikh reserve which, under Téj Singh, had been set to watch Fírúzpúr, and severed it from the main army.

The junction having been effected, Gough marched on the enemy's position. He found it, to use his own language, "a parallelogram of about a mile in length and half a mile in breadth, including within its area the strong village of Fírúzshahar; the shorter sides looking towards the Satláj and Múdkí, and the longer towards Fírúzpúr and the open country."

The dispositions for the attack were not completed till an hour before sunset. The left division was Littler's, next to him was Wallace, then the whole force of artillery, with the exception of three troops of horse artillery, one on each flank and one in support, to be used as it might be wanted; on the right was Gilbert's division. The division of Sir Harry Smith and the cavalry formed the reserve, a brigade of the cavalry being thrown forward in support of each wing. Sir H. Hardinge commanded the left wing, Sir H. Gough the right.

The order of the battle was as follows: Littler was to attack nearly the whole of the west face, that looking towards Fírúzpúr and the open country, Wallace the corner of the west and south face; Gilbert the rest of the south and as much of the east as he could manage. Littler came first under fire, just about, as I have said, an hour before sunset. To him the hardest work had been allotted, for on the west face the Sikhs had massed their best troops and their heaviest artillery. Boldly, however, did he advance, his troops in the highest spirits: so boldly, indeed, that the issue appeared certain to Littler. When he was within a hundred and fifty yards of the intrenchment, he gave the order to charge. Gallantly did the troops respond to this call, until, within a few yards of the enemy, the European regiment on the right of the line, crushed, apparently, by the overwhelming fire from the intrenchment, halted, turned about, and fell back, accompanied by the native soldiers, who took their cue from them.* Then, amongst many, undoubted panic set in. The cry of "India's lost" was heard from one commanding officer as he tried in vain to rally his men. The left attack on the Khálsa had failed so signally that it could not be renewed.

It was not until Littler had been beaten back that General Wallace was able to bring the next division into fire. Sufficient time elapsed between the two attacks to allow a part of one of the native regiments belonging to Littler's divison, the 14th, to rally and join in the new attempt. Wallace was more successful than Littler. The European regiment in his division, the 9th, and one of the native regiments, the 26th Native Light Infantry, had been comrades in the Afghán campaign, and they now vied with each other in generous rivalry in the field. The two sides of the angle on which they directed their efforts were well manned and well defended. But nothing could withstand their ardour. They carried the position at the point of the bayonet, in the face of a fire which cost the 9th Regiment alone two hundred and seventy-three men in killed and wounded.

To Gilbert had been assigned the storming of the south and south-east faces of the intrenchment. He had two splendid European regiments, the 29th and the 1st Europeans—now the 101st Fusiliers—under his command, and native regiments worthy of being their comrades. With great gallantry, and suffering much loss, the division carried the two faces. They carried them, however, only to find that their work was but just beginning. Behind the guns they had captured were posted the unsubdued infantry of the enemy, and these poured forth a continuous galling fire of musketry upon the English now face to face

* Sir John Littler's despatch; Sir Herbert Edwardes in the *Calcutta Review*, vol. vi. p. 273-5. It was well known that the commanding officer of the regiment in question had given the order to retire

with them. To add to the horrors of the situation, one of the enemy's magazines exploded under the feet of the 1st Europeans, blowing up many men and officers and rending the regiment in two. Undismayed, however, the gallant division pressed on, and drove back the foe. It was only on the approach of darkness that they retired, and took up a position about three hundred yards from the intrenchment, ready to advance again with the morning's light.

The battle, then, was not yet won. On the right the Sikhs held their own, and the fire from their guns continued to pour death and havoc into the British ranks. To deal finally with them the reserve under Sir Harry Smith was ordered up; the 3rd Dragoons were at the same time launched upon a battery which kept up its deadly shower. The manner in which they carried out this order is thus described by an eye-witness:* —"They charged, and carried the battery they were opposed to,—the leaders filling up the yawning trench with their own numbers, and those who followed crossing on a living bridge of their comrades. . . . But this was not all. Having put the artillerymen to death and silenced the battery, this gallant band faced the whole Khálsa army within the intrenchment, swept through their camp with loud huzzas over tents, ropes, pegs, guns, fires, and magazines, cutting down all who opposed their passage; and having traversed the enemy's position from side to side, emerged among their friends with numbers thinned, indeed, but covered with imperishable glory."

But the effect of this brilliant feat of arms was but temporary. Night fell before victory had been achieved. The Sikh infantry still offered a steady, and so far a successful, resistance to the British army. The position when darkness covered the field may thus be briefly summarised. On the extreme left Littler, repulsed, had fallen back on a small village directly west of the Sikh intrenchments. Two regiments of Wallace's division, the

* Sir Herbert Edwardes, *Calcutta Review*, vol. vi. pp. 276-7.

9th Foot and 26th Light Infantry, had, in the confusion of the battle, taken ground to the right, and were intermingled with those led by General Gilbert. Sir Harry Smith, whom we have seen brought up to finish the action, had penetrated to the very heart of the great parallelogram and had halted there ready to resist any attack. Gilbert's division on the right, reinforced, as just stated, by the 9th Foot and 26th Light Infantry, and increased by stragglers from broken regiments, and Smith's, were the only two left on the field of battle. But Gilbert was soon to find himself alone. Between two and three in the morning the enemy forced Smith to fall back, to evacuate the intrenchment, and to retreat on a village two miles to the south-east of Fírúzshahar. Gilbert was thus left alone to face the enemy. But with Gilbert were Hardinge and Gough, and these three gallant soldiers had laboured indefatigably since nightfall to restore order among the stragglers and to encourage the troops. This at last accomplished, the men lay down to take some fitful repose.

Soon they were roused again to action. As the night was wearing away the Sikhs brought up their heavy guns and played them with deadly effect upon the British troops only three hundred yards distant. Sir Henry Hardinge, cool and ready, at once called upon the two regiments nearest him, the 80th and the 1st Europeans, to "see if they could not stop that gun." The two regiments appealed to sprang at once with alacrity from the ground, dashed forward into the intrenchment, spiked the gun, and "returned again to their cold bivouac on the frosty ground."* They were not again disturbed.

Let us take a glance now at the Sikh camp. The brave, untutored warriors who defended it, led by generals who were betraying them, had, if they had only known it, won a victory. They had repulsed the British attack. They had driven back Littler, forced Smith to retire, compelled even

* Edwardes.

Gilbert to evacuate the position he had gained, and thrown the whole British army into disorder. What was more; they had still ten thousand men under Téj Singh, watching Firúzpúr, who had not been engaged, and these could not fail to join them with the morning's light. Had a guiding mind directed the movements of the Sikh army nothing could have saved the exhausted British. But the Sikhs, as we know, possessed no guiding mind. The honest men amongst them either did not recognise the advantage they had gained or were powerless in the presence of those who saw, in the attitude of Gilbert's division, the certainty of a renewal of the attack on the morrow. To these divided counsels were added the fatal suggestions of the traitors who desired nothing less than the victory of the Khálsa. The result was stormy counsels, bitter words, plunder, desertion. All cohesion vanished; the *morale*, which alone could have insured victory, disappeared.

When the day broke, then, and the English line again advanced, it encountered no opposition. The Sikhs were driven out of the village of Fírúzshahar.* The British line, then changing front to its left on its centre, swept the camp, marched round two sides of the parallelogram, and emerged on the north-east of the plain.

The line then halted, and its two leaders, riding along its front, were received with cheers. Every man thought that the work was done, that the victory had been gained. But, suddenly, the scene changed. A dense cloud of dust appeared on the horizon. It approached nearer and nearer. From it there emerged the advance guard of a fresh army of Sikhs. It was the army of Téj Singh, marching from the leaguer of Firúzpúr to recover the advantage which Lál Singh had thrown away!

Téj Singh had it in his power to recover that advantage.

* There was no real opposition. It was "little more than the passive resistance of the wreck of a great army."—Sir Herbert Edwardes, *Calcutta Review*, vol. vi. p. 279.

The true and loyal men who had served under him had urged him to fall upon the English army at daybreak when they were entangled in the intrenchments. He might have done this. He would have done it had he been as loyal as the least of his followers. But Téj Singh had but one object—to see the Khálsa troops overcome and dispersed. He waited, then, till the army of Lál Singh had been put to flight, till the British had had time to re-form. He then skirmished with their line, and opened an artillery fire upon the British left. This fire evoked no response. The English had exhausted their ammunition; they "were unable to answer him with a single shot."* This fact, which would have inspired a true man with a determination to continue the contest, produced an opposite effect upon the traitor who commanded the Sikh forces. He suddenly ordered the firing to cease, and, turning his horse's head, galloped as fast as he could towards the Satlaj. He did this at the moment when victory was in his grasp, for a portion of the British army was, at the moment, retiring upon Fírúzpúr!†

Such was the battle of Fírúzshahar—a battle gained after it had been lost, and then re-gained after its success had once more been imperilled—a battle which shook the edifice of British dominion in India to its very basis, which impressed our native soldiers with the conviction that the English were not invincible.

* Sir Hugh Gough's despatch.

† Cunningham's *History of the Sikhs*, pp. 308, 309, and notes. Sir Herbert Edwarde's narrative bears out the view taken in the text so far as relates to the practical result of Téj Singh's conduct. He says, after recording the facts: "To what the army of the Satlaj are indebted for this *deliverance*; whether to cowardice or treachery, or ignorance on the enemy's part of the British numbers, or whether, after all, Téj Singh's whole object was a chivalrous wish to cover his friend's retreat—remains to be guessed and wondered at, but we fear not to be satisfactorily decided." We may dismiss at once the last supposition, that regarding the "chivalrous wish," for the British were not pursuing. Cowardice can scarcely have been seriously suggested; nor can ignorance of the English numbers be pleaded with better grace. There is only one possible solution, and that is the solution adopted in the text. The object of Téj Singh was to destroy the Khálsa army, and then to claim credit with the British for having destroyed it. He succeeded in both objects.

More, far more, than the Kábul disaster of 1841, did the battle of Fírúzshahar give birth in the minds of the sipáhís to the conviction that great numbers might prevail even over their foreign masters.

For, be it remembered, the numbers on both sides were not very disproportionate. The English army mustered over 16,000; the Sikhs, excluding Téj Singh, who was not near the battle-field, did not certainly exceed 30,000; and if the latter possessed a slight superiority in artillery and a strong position, these advantages were more than counterbalanced by the treason of their leaders, the want of unity in their counsels. It was these two circumstances alone that lost them the day.

The results of the battle have been so well described by the faithful and accurate author to whom I am so largely indebted* that I cannot do better than record them in his own impressive language: "A battle had thus been won, and more than seventy pieces of artillery, and some conquered or confiscated territories, graced the success; but the victors had lost a seventh of their numbers,† they were paralysed after their prodigious exertions and intense excitement, and the Sikhs were allowed to cross the Satlaj to prepare for fresh contests. The Sípáhí mercenaries had for the first time met an equal antagonist with their own weapons—even ranks and the fire of artillery. They loudly complained of the inferiority of their cannon; they magnified banks two or three feet high into formidable ramparts, and exploding tumbrils and stores of powder became, in their imagination, designed and deadly mines. Nor was this feeling of respect and admiration confined to the Indians alone; the European soldiers partook of it."

The moral effect of this hard-gained victory was seen in the demeanour of the cis-Satlaj feudatories. Whilst the beaten

* Cunningham's *History of the Sikhs*.

† They lost six hundred and ninety-four killed, seventeen hundred and twenty-one wounded, or a total of two thousand four hundred and fifteen.

army was allowed to cross the Satlaj leisurely, and then to re-cross again and construct a bridge-head to ensure freedom of passage, the cis-Satlaj feudatories kept as much as possible aloof from their new masters. The Rájah of Ladwá even joined the enemy, and subsequently burned a portion of the cantonment of Lodiáná; and, generally, the demeanour of the petty princes was such as to indicate their conviction that the hour of independence was approaching.

The English army, meanwhile, gradually reinforced, had advanced to the Satlaj, and taken up a strong position on the left bank stretching from Firúzpúr towards Haríkí. Thence, whilst waiting for his heavy guns, Gough, on the 17th January 1846, despatched Sir H. Smith to capture Dharmkót, and to cover the march of the expected convoy of guns, ammunition, and treasure. Dharmkót having surrendered without bloodshed, and the progress of the convoy having been thus made more secure, Smith was ordered to proceed to the relief of Lodiáná, threatened by a Sikh army under Ranjúr Singh. On his march thither, Smith received information (21st January) that Ranjúr Singh, with an army estimated at eight thousand irregular cavalry and nearly seventy guns,* had the previous day occupied Badiwál, eight miles distant. Smith then concluded that by making a detour to the right, so as to leave his left flank three miles distant from the Sikh position, he would be able to effect a junction with the Lodiáná brigade without molestation, and he attempted to give effect to this idea. As he approached Badiwál, however, it became clear to him that he would not be allowed to carry it out with impunity. Ranjúr Singh moved from that place with the apparent intention of heading the English force. But as Smith, who wished to avoid a combat, inclined more and more to the right, the Sikhs pounced upon the English rear-guard, and captured nearly the whole of their baggage!

* Sir Herbert Edwardes.

This misfortune, which gave heart to the malcontents all over India, which made Téj Singh and Lál Singh tremble with fear, and which drew the head of the Jamú family, Guláb Singh, to Láhor, to gain supremacy should the Sikhs be victorious, or to share in the spoil should they be beaten, was very soon avenged. On the 28th January, Smith—his army reinforced to a strength of eleven thousand men—marched to give the enemy battle. He found them, strengthened by the addition of four thousand infantry, their left resting on the little hamlet of Alíwál, their right on the village of Búndrí. So little did they expect the English, that they had but just time to throw up banks of earth to protect their guns, when the battle commenced. Smith, seeing that Alíwál was the key of the position, sent his infantry against that hamlet. The Sikhs who defended it were hill-men, with no heart in the cause of the Khálsa. After firing a straggling volley, they gave way, and fled from the field, headed by the commander of the army, Ranjúr Singh. Whilst this was going on on the left, the English cavalry, led by the 16th Lancers, made a magnificent charge on the Sikh right. There the Khálsa regiments behaved in a manner worthy of their renown. They knelt to receive the dashing charge of the Lancers and their Indian comrades; but, as these approached, they instinctively rose and delivered their fire. Beneath the charge that followed they did not yield, nor was it till they had been three times ridden over that they gave way. After the battle it was found that the ground was more thickly strewn with the bodies of the victorious horsemen than of the beaten infantry. An attempt made to rally behind Búndrí was ineffective. The English pushed their advantage to the utmost, nor did they cease till they had forced the Sikhs to recross the Satlaj, and had captured more than fifty of their guns.

This victory changed the aspect of affairs. Whilst it raised the hopes of Lál Singh and of Téj Singh, it encouraged the astute rájah of Jamú to open negotiations with the British.

Guláb Singh possessed at this time the reputation of being the most able and the most formidable of the Sikh aristocracy, and it was by no means displeasing to Sir Henry Hardinge to receive proposals of accommodation from one in so high a position. In reply, then, to Guláb Singh's overtures, the Governor-General intimated that he would be prepared to acknowledge a Sikh sovereign in Láhor after the Sikh army should be disbanded.

Neither, however, had the Sikh army any intention of disbanding itself, nor did Guláb Singh, Lál Singh, or Téj Singh possess the power to force it to such a step. Its destruction then became a necessary preliminary to the carrying out of the plans of the Sikh rulers.

By degrees, by means of the bridge-head they had constructed, the Sikhs crossed over into the intrenchment they had formed on the left bank of the Satlaj. But alike in the construction of the intrenchment and in the means taken to fortify it there was evidence of the want of a guiding mind. Each regiment seemed to work for its own hand, and for that alone. Instead of being a position possessing defensive works regular in design, the intrenchment at Sobráon presented the most glaring anomalies. Whilst on the left and centre, where the regular battalions were mainly posted, batteries and salient points had been constructed as high as the stature of a man, defended by ditches which an armed soldier could not leap without exertion, on the right flank the parapets were thrown up at intervals, and constructed in a very slipshod fashion. As some compensation, however, this flank derived support from a salient battery, and from heavy guns on the right bank of the river. Whilst the left and centre faces had fifty-seven pieces in battery, the right was protected only by two hundred *zumburaks* (falconets). A bridge of boats connected the intrenchment with a smaller camp on the right bank. It should be added that, owing to the carelessness of the English, the Sikhs had captured and continued to hold a post of observation almost within hail of the British pickets.

The strength of the Sikh army within the intrenchment on the left bank did not exceed twenty thousand men.* They were commanded by Téj Singh. But, outside, higher up the river, Lál Singh disposed of a body of ten thousand horsemen.

The English had been forced to watch the gradual growth of these works, pending the arrival of the siege train and reserve ammunition for a hundred field guns. The first instalment of these reached the British head-quarters on the 7th and 8th of February. On the latter day joined also the brigades which had been detached for operations in the neighbourhood of Lodiáná. On the 9th the plan of operations was decided upon, and it was determined to attack the enemy's position the following morning.

The general plan of attack adopted by the British general was to force the right or weaker end of the intrenchment close to the point where it rested on the river, and thus take the guns on the outer face in reverse. To carry out this plan, he had resolved to prelude the attack by a fire from his heavy guns, then to launch his left, commanded by Sir Robert Dick, against the right; whilst his centre, Gilbert, and his right, Smith, should divert the attention of the enemy by a false attack; and his cavalry, Cureton, should occupy the attention of Lál Singh.

Before dawn the British columns were in motion. The morning was dark and foggy, favourable to a surprise. The advance guard, composed of the 62nd Foot, dashed upon the post near the British camp, and another in the village of Little Sobráon, only to find it unoccupied.† Thus favoured alike by the fog and the carelessness of the enemy, the British pushed forward until, at a little before seven o'clock, they had been able unobserved to place their heavy guns in position. Exactly at seven o'clock these opened their fire, and, by a curious

* Cunningham, p. 321. My own investigations confirm this calculation.

† It was the bad practice of the Sikhs to occupy the place strongly during the day, and to abandon it at night.

coincidence, precisely at the same moment the fog lifted, and "the surprised Khálsa at once heard and saw that the avenger had come upon them."*

Clamorously did the Sikh drums beat to arms; eagerly did the gallant defenders rush to their posts. Not for long had the British guns opened before an answering fire from the intrenchment proved to their army that they had all their work before them.

The cannonade had lasted two hours, and but little impression had been made on the intrenchment, when it was reported to Sir Hugh Gough that the ammunition of the heavy guns was "well nigh expended." The gallant soldier, who had been fretting for the time to arrive when he could launch his infantry at the enemy, felt his heart bound with a secret joy as he gave the order to his left to advance and carry out the preconcerted programme.

Under a slackening fire from their own guns, formed in line, the first brigade of the British left, "in even order and with a light step," advanced to the attack. It was composed of the 10th and 53rd Foot, the 43rd and 59th Native Infantry, was led by Brigadier Stacy, and was supported on the flanks by Horsford's and Fordyce's batteries and Lane's troop of Horse Artillery. No mean authority, the late Sir Herbert Edwardes, himself an eye-witness, has pronounced this to have been "beyond all comparison, the finest attack of the campaign." I cannot do better, then, than describe it in his own words. "The artillery," he writes,† "galloped up and delivered their fire within three hundred yards of the enemy's batteries, and the infantry charged home with the bayonet, and carried the outworks without firing a single shot. As it was the finest attack, so also did it meet with the most determined hand-to-hand resistance which the Khálsa soldiers had yet opposed to

* Edwardes, *Calcutta Review*, vol. vi. p. 294. *Vide* also Cunningham, p. 325.
† *Calcutta Review*, vol. vi. p. 294.

the British. Like lightning, the real plan of the attack seemed to flash on the minds of all the desperate men in that intrenchment; and, disregarding the distant feints of Gilbert's and Smith's divisions on their left and centre, they rushed to the right to repel the real danger that was upon them. In vain Stacy's brigade tries to withstand the mass which every moment is growing denser; in vain Wilkinson's brigade"—second brigade, left division—"comes up to the support; in vain Ashburnham's reserve swells the furious tide of the assault."

In one word, the attack so gallantly made was, for the moment, repulsed. The Sikhs, fighting with the same steadiness and resolution which they have since invariably displayed when fighting for the British, had, in an incredibly short space of time, turned their guns on the advancing enemy. When the combatants paused for breath the British found that the line of trench alone was all that they had gained.

Sir Hugh Gough had observed, with passionate excitement, the splendid advance of his left, then their sudden check. Divining that to gain such a result, the enemy had concentrated all their efforts on their right, he despatched orders to his right and centre to make of their feigned a real attack. Smith and Gilbert responded to the call and at once pushed forward. But before them were the strongest parts of the intrenchment, high and continuous ramparts, guarded by deep and broad ditches. The Sikhs, too, noticing their movement, rushed back tumultuously to the defence. Grape, round shot, and musketry, poured forth at a distance at which almost every shot was bound to tell, forced the assailants for a moment to recoil; only, however, for a moment. In spite of their enormous losses* they re-formed and returned to the charge—this time under happier auspices; for the British left, taking advantage of the slackening of opposition to them caused by the rush of the

* Gilbert's division lost six hundred and eighty-five men, and Smith's four hundred and eighty-nine, in about half-an-hour.

defenders to oppose the centre and right divisions, had again pushed forward, and had penetrated within the intrenchment sufficiently far to give a hand to the extreme left of the British centre. The tide of the fight was now turning against the defenders, and to make its turn irrevocable, the traitor commander-in-chief, Téj Singh, instead of leading fresh men to sustain the failing strength of his right, fled across the bridge, and, either by accident or design, sank its centre boat.* Thenceforward, steadily advancing, the assailants, though still gallantly opposed, carried one position after another, and, pushing on, pressed the defenders towards the banks of the, now to them, formidable river. But, fiercely assailed, the Khálsa warriors viewed with calmness the inevitable fate before them. "No Sikh offered to submit, no disciple of Govind asked for quarter. They everywhere showed a front to the victors, and stalked slowly and sullenly away, whilst many rushed singly forth to meet assured death by contending with a multitude. The victors looked with stolid wonderment upon the indomitable courage of the vanquished and forbore to strike when the helpless and dying frowned unavailing hatred. But the warlike rage or the calculating policy of the leaders had yet to be satisfied, and, standing with the slain heaped all around them, they urged troops of artillery almost in the waters of the Satlaj, to more thoroughly destroy the army which had so long scorned their power." † At half-past ten o'clock not a single Sikh soldier remained on the left bank of the Satlaj!

Such was the battle of Sobráon. Though in point of actual fact it terminated the Sikh invasion, and threw the fate of the Sikh nation into the hands of the British, Sobráon, as

* Cunningham, p. 327.

† Cunningham, p. 328. This is confirmed by Edwardes, *Calcutta Review* vol. vi., pp. 295, 296. Gough writes in his despatch: "In their efforts to reach the right bank through the deepened water, they suffered from our horse artillery a terrible carnage."

a decisive battle, must be considered not by itself, but as the complement to and natural consequence of Fírúzshahar. Of the two, the latter was really the decisive battle. There victory long hovered in the balance. There, victory for the Sikhs—a victory twice within their grasp—would have meant to the English the loss of India. When the Sikhs were beaten at Fírúzshahar they had really lost the game. Thenceforth they had to get out of the difficulty the best way they could. They were persuaded by their treacherous leaders to make one more attempt at Sobráon. But there they never had a chance of victory. The overthrow at Fírúzshahar still hampered them. Nor, even if the English had been repulsed, would the consequences have been so tremendous as would have been entailed by a defeat at Fírúzshahar. That would have meant the destruction of the British army. A repulse from Sobráon, had it been possible, would still have left the British army in a position to renew the attack.

Rightly, then, must we regard Sobráon as the complement to Fírúzshahar. The result of the latter really decided the question of empire!

There was no great disproportion between the numbers engaged at Sobráon. The fighting strength of the English engaged was about fifteen thousand; that of the Sikhs fell somewhat short of twenty thousand. But, whilst the English were led by a gallant soldier, with his whole heart in the cause, the worst enemy of the Sikh soldier was their general. It is beyond a doubt that he betrayed them. The English lost 320 killed and 2,083 wounded. The casualties of their beaten foe have been calculated from five to eight thousand; most of these happened after they had lost the battle.

The battle gained, the English army crossed the Satlaj, and on the 12th occupied the fort of Kasúr within thirty miles of Láhor. The Sikh army had meanwhile retired, its spirit broken, to Amritsar. From this place they gave their assent, on a requisition made by the Court, to the proposition that Guláb Singh, the Jamú chief, whose treachery had not been apparent to them, should have full powers to treat with the English on the admitted basis of recognising a Sikh Government in Láhor. Finally, after some negotiation, a treaty was concluded at Kasúr on the following conditions:—(1) That the country between the Biás and the Satlaj, known as the Jálandhar Doáb, comprising the districts Jálandhar, Hoshiápúr, and Kángrah, with an area of eleven thousand four hundred and eight square miles, and a population of two million four hundred and seventy thousand souls,* should be transferred to the conquerors; (2) that the Sikh Treasury should pay a million and a half sterling for the expenses of the war. It was soon found, however, that it would be impossible for the Sikh Treasury to find two-thirds of the sum agreed upon. A way, creditable to none of the parties concerned, was then found to meet the difficulty. In lieu of one million of the sum they had agreed to pay, the Sikh Darbár yielded the magnificent province of Káshmír, a country famed for the beauty of its scenery, the mildness of its climate, the industry of its inhabitants, to the British. The British, retaining only the suzerainty, sold the province to the chief of Jamú, Rájah Guláb Singh.

The reasons for this transaction have never been sufficiently explained. Sir Henry Hardinge declared that he required the money, and that he had not sufficient troops to occupy Káshmír. But a mountainous country like Káshmír, possessing a few strong passes, would have been easily garrisoned by a brigade. The fallacy of the reasoning is further proved by the fact that very shortly afterwards Sir H. Hardinge effected a considerable reduction in the native army, thus giving evidence that he had actually more troops than he required. To a rich country like England the million of money was but a small compensation for the possession of the finest mountainous tract in the whole

* Blochmann.

world. Subsequent events have proved that the transaction was a blunder, politically and morally. Politically, because England thus gave away the opportunity of strengthening her frontier and of gaining a position which, in the event of an invasion, would be of incalculable value; morally, because the Governor-General had no right to sell a hard-working and industrious people to a chief alien in race and religion, and harsh and oppressive in nature.*

The treaty concluded, Lál Singh was rewarded for his treachery by being made Vazîr, and a high position as the nominal head of the army was secured to Téj Sing. But these chiefs and those associated with them were still afraid of their broken and diminished army. Thinking only of themselves, not at all of their country or of the child Mahárájah, in whose name they exercised authority, they pressed upon the British Government a policy of the kind which has ever proved, sooner or later, fatal to the native Government which has adopted it. They requested, and the request was granted, that a British force should remain at Láhor till the last day of December 1846. Before that day had arrived they had again requested, and the request was agreed to, that the British force should remain at Láhor till the Mahárájah should attain the age of sixteen.

Further, and what was of far greater importance still, it was, on the motion of the Láhor Darbár, agreed at this period (16th December 1846) between the two Governments, that "a British officer, with an efficient establishment, shall be appointed by the Governor-General to remain at Láhor, which officer shall have full authority to direct and control all matters in every department of the State."† 2nd. That a regency should be appointed of six selected Sikh nobles, chiefest of whom was

* "The transaction," writes the fearless and conscientious Cunningham (p. 332), "scarcely seems worthy of the British name and greatness." His remarks in continuation are well worthy of perusal.

† Agreement between the British Government and the Láhor Darbár, 16th December 1846, Art. II.

Téj Singh, and that "no change shall be made in the persons thus nominated, without the consent of the British Resident, acting under orders of the Governor-General."*

This, then, was the result of Fírúzshahar and Sobráon! The English Government assumed virtually the protectorate of the Panjáb during the minority of the Mahárájah Dhulíp Singh; constituted that sovereign prince its ward; and, the better to ensure the proper government of his country and the due transmission to him of his power intact at the proper time, nominated as Controller of the native regency, "with full authority to direct and control all matters in every department of the State," a British officer, having under him British assistants. In a word, by the agreement of the 16th December 1846, the English assumed the responsibility of the Government of the Panjáb.

In the light of the events which followed, this is a very important consideration. It is necessary that the reader should bear it in mind when he comes to consider the causes and consequences of the second Sikh war.

It remains only to add that the officer to whom the Governor-General delegated the important trust set forth in the last paragraph but one, was Colonel, afterwards Sir Henry, Lawrence.

* Agreement between the British Government and the Láhor Darbár, 16th December 1846, Art. V.

CHAPTER XIII.

CHILIÁNWÁLÁ AND GUJRÁT.

For fifteen months after the agreement made, the 16th December 1846, between the British Government and the Láhor Darbár, the Panjáb remained apparently quiescent under the control and guidance of a British officer. That officer was not always Sir Henry Lawrence. After administering the affairs of the Sikh State for less than a year, that distinguished officer had, to recover his shattered health, accompanied the retiring Governor-General, Lord Hardinge, to England.

But during the few months of his tenure of office Sir Henry Lawrence had laid down the principles upon which he proposed to guide and reform the administration of the Panjáb, The chief of these was English supervision. With this object he had deputed two of the ablest of the officers placed at his disposal—men already famous, and both of whom have an imperishable record in the Temple of Fame, Herbert Edwardes and John Nicholson—to Bannú, a district in the Deráját, north of Derá Ismáil Khán, a portion of the Panjáb territory, which, though nominally ceded to it by the Afgháns, had neither been completely conquered nor thoroughly occupied. Ultimately it was arranged, Nicholson's services being at the time required elsewhere, that Edwardes should proceed to Bannú alone, and this arrangement was carried out. It was a bold step indeed to send to a country which had never been properly subdued, one month's march from Láhor, to control its inhabitants, a solitary Englishman. But the result proved the correctness of the view taken by Sir Henry Lawrence, alike of the selected Englishman and of the feasibility of the task to him entrusted.

To other parts of the Panjáb, likewise, Sir Henry deputed officers of his selection. His brother, George Lawrence,* not the least able and the least distinguished of a very remarkable family, was sent to the still more distant post of Peshâwar. Accompanying him was a promising young officer, Lieutenant Bowie, already noted for the sureness of his judgment. To Attock had been sent Herbert; to Hazárah, Abbott of the Artillery, the noblest and gentlest of men, endowed with a heart which comprehended all mankind, and who had previously, alone and unattended, made the romantic and dangerous journey from Herát to Khiva and Bokhara, and thence to the frontier of Russia, for the purpose of negotiating the freedom from slavery of Russian subjects detained in those countries; to other difficult districts, John Nicholson, already referred to, Lake, an officer of the Engineers, of cool and calm judgment, Reynell Taylor, Lewin Bowring, afterwards Chief Commissioner of Maisúr, Cocks, and some others. The main instructions given to these officers were to report freely to Sir Henry regarding the state of the several districts, to resettle the country, to make recommendations as to reforms, and to do their best to maintain peace and order, and to instil confidence as to the intentions of the British into the people.†

* Now Sir George Lawrence, K.C.B.

† "I offer you liberty," said Edwardes to the people of Bannú, "and not only offer it, but guarantee it so long as the Sikh treaty with the English lasts. Only pay of your own free-will, into any treasury you like, an annual tribute of forty thousand rupees, and no army shall again enter your valley, no Sikh show his face within your boundaries, you shall be left in the undisputed enjoyment of your own country and your own laws."—Edwardes's *A Year on the Punjab Frontier*, p. 23. This offer supplies the keynote of the British policy of 1847.

It may well be doubted, judging from the knowledge we now possess, whether, even if Sir Henry Lawrence had remained at his post, the system of controlling the Sikh Darbár by means of reports received from British officers at the extremities of the Panjáb could have long resisted the strong national feeling which was silently growing up throughout the country. The fact is that neither Lord Hardinge, Sir Henry Lawrence, nor any of the able coadjutors of the latter, recognised the fact that though the Sikh army had been decisively beaten at Sobráon, the Sikh people had never felt themselves subdued. On the very morrow of their great defeat, the soldiers, and the classes from whom the soldiers were enlisted, had recognised that they had been betrayed; that they and their country had been sacrificed to the chiefs who were now reaping the reward, thanks to the protection afforded them by the foreigner, of their combined cowardice and treason. At the very time, then, when the English officers I have enumerated were performing the dangerous duties allotted to them with marked success among the rude tribes on the extremities of the kingdom, within the Khálsa itself there was being nurtured a feeling which tended every day to render certain, at no distant day, a national rising.

It was not to be expected that the English officers deputed to outlying districts on the frontier, inhabited, be it remembered, not by Sikhs, but by tribes who had been subdued by the Sikhs, should realise the thoughts which coursed through the heart of the Sikh nation. They were, after time had allowed their true position to become understood, regarded for the most part as the friends of the tribes, as their protectors against the oppression of the nearest Sikh authorities. The officers in question, recognising this feeling on the part of the populations amongst whom their lot was cast, reported, with just pride, to Sir Henry the success of their mission. Nor is it to be wondered at that Sir Henry, coming in contact at Láhor with the chiefs who had betrayed their own people in the late campaign, should consider that the reports of his officers justified him in looking forward to a long period of tranquillity in the province of which he had the control.

It is certain that unless Sir Henry Lawrence had been satisfied that affairs in the Panjáb were progressing in a satisfactory manner, he would not have yielded to the wish expressed by Lord Hardinge that he should accompany him to England at the end of 1847; nor, unless Lord Hardinge had been impressed by the same view, would he have signalised the last few months of his administration by a reduction of the army; nor would his friends have declared, as they loudly declared on his departure, that there would not be another shot fired in India for another ten years.*

The successor of Sir Henry Lawrence was the Foreign Secretary of the Indian Government, Sir F. Currie. An able Foreign Secretary, Sir F. Currie had had little experience of administration, still less of the administration of a country peopled by a race of warriors only half subdued, and chafing every day under the recollection of the means by which they had been subdued; warriors, whose chiefs, the men whom he had to control, were as smooth-tongued, as slippery, and as oily as the subordinates with whom he had had to deal in the early days of his official life. Moreover, it must be recollected that, as Foreign Secretary, Currie had been the recipient of the secret reports of Lawrence, and that when he relieved him of his office he was prepared thoroughly to endorse the opinions regarding the tranquillity of the country to which Sir Henry had given utterance.

And yet the period in question was really most critical Smooth as was the outer surface, the currents below were in violent commotion. The true Sikh leaders, the leaders who preferred independence to servitude, however gilded, had taken

* *Calcutta Review*, vol. xv. p. 257. Personal observation.

their measures with the Sikh soldiery, and were waiting only for their opportunity.

It is just possible, seeing what sort of a man Sir Henry Lawrence was, that, had he remained at Láhor, the opportunity would not have been given, and that, under any circumstances, he would have dominated the situation. His noble bearing, his gentle manner, his lofty character, had already gained for him respect, and, it is not too much to say, in some cases, even affection, even from those who were plotting against the English. It is certain, moreover, that Sir Henry Lawrence would not have given to the confederates the opportunity of which they took advantage; as certain, that, had an outbreak occurred in his time, he would have met it in a different manner.

The crisis which occurred soon after Sir F. Currie had assumed the control at Láhor occurred in this wise :—

Mulráj, eldest son of Sáwan Mall, had succeeded his father in 1844 as Díwán or Governor of Multán. The conditions of the succession were, that while the Díwán should transmit a certain fixed amount yearly to the Láhor Darbár he might keep for himself the remainder. These terms had been enjoyed by his father with so much advantage, that, on his death, after an administration of twenty-three years, he had left £900,000 to be divided amongst his sons!

On his accession, Mulráj was expected to pay to the Láhor Darbár a fee of thirty lakhs of rupees. He was quite prepared to pay that amount, but the Government at Láhor was in a state of revolution, and the matter stood over, therefore, until after the abortive invasion of India.

In 1846, after the close of the war, the Láhor Government, during the premiership of Lál Singh, demanded payment, and sent a detachment of troops to enforce it. Either confident in his strength, or imbued with contempt for the Darbár, Mulráj refused compliance, and, meeting force by force, defeated the Darbár troops near Jhang. The British then intervened, and it was finally settled that Mulráj should give up the district of Jhang, north of Multán, and comprising nearly one-third of the province theretofore held by him; that he should pay twenty lakhs as the succession-fee; and that the revenues of the districts still left in his charge should be raised in amount by rather more than a third. Mulráj expressed himself well pleased with this arrangement.

Faithfully did Mulráj fulfil the engagements he then made. But he did not satisfy the Láhor Regency. Complaints reached that body and its controller, Sir Henry Lawrence, to the effect that the weight of Mulráj's little finger was heavier than his father's loins. Called upon to remedy the evils complained of, Mulráj fired up. The summons was, he contended, outside the agreement he had made with the Darbár, and which he had faithfully kept. He might have added that the revenue demanded from two-thirds of his father's territory exceeding by one-third the amount which his father had paid from the whole, rendered necessary an increase of taxation. After some fruitless interchange of communications, Mulráj, on learning that Sir Henry Lawrence was about to leave for England, came to Láhor and tendered resignation of his office (November 1847).*

Sir Henry Lawrence had left Láhor for England when Mulráj arrived. Mr. John Lawrence, therefore, received him. With him, after much but fruitless persuasion not to persist in his idea, Mulráj came to the following agreement:—First: That his resignation should be accepted, but should be kept a profound secret from the Láhor Darbár. Secondly: That it

* Evidence of Mr. John Lawrence at Mulráj's trial, *vide* Edwarde's *A Year in the Punjab*, pp. 36, 37. Mulráj gave as his reason for resolving to resign—Firstly: That the new Custom arrangements in the Panjáb had an injurious effect upon his revenues, for, though they had not been introduced into Multán, his people did not like to pay any longer those dues which had been abolished everywhere else. Secondly: Because an order had been passed by the Regency, giving his people a right of appeal against his judicial decisions. It was this last grievance, so completely outside the convention he had made, under the auspices of the Resident, which specially weighed upon him.

should take effect from the end of the following April, up to which time Mulráj was to account for the revenue. Thirdly: That two or three months before his actual resignation, two British officers should proceed to Multán to be initiated by Mulráj into the state of the country, and ultimately to be installed by him in charge of it.* This agreement settled, Mulráj returned to his government.

Sir F. Currie was unable to assume charge of the office held by Sir Henry Lawrence till the 6th March. Meanwhile, notwithstanding the engagement to secrecy, the story of Mulráj's intended resignation had been noised abroad. The consequence was that when Sir Frederick arrived, considering the pledge to secrecy to be at an end, he insisted, against Mr. Lawrence's remonstrance,† on consulting the Láhor Darbár. Before doing so, however, he wrote to Mulráj to request him to withdraw his resignation. Mulráj refused. Sir F. Currie, then, in consultation with the Darbár, resolved to carry out the third clause of the agreement made between Mr. John Lawrence and Mulráj, and to send to Multán two English officers to be initiated into the affairs of the province. He selected for this purpose Mr. P. A. Vans Agnew, of the Civil Service, and Lieutenant W. A. Anderson, of the Bombay Fusiliers.

I must ask the reader always to bear in mind that Multán was considered the strongest fortress in the Panjáb; that Shér Singh, who subsequently led the popular movement, was a prominent member of the Regency, and believed to be extremely well affected to British interests; and that the word had been passed to all the able-bodied men in purely Sikh villages that the time was approaching when their services would be urgently required.‡ With the knowledge of these incontestable facts it

* Edwardes's *A Year in the Punjab*, pp. 40, 41.

† *Ibid.*

‡ *Calcutta Review*, vol. xv. p. 257, Art. "The Second Sikh War." This article has since been republished with the name of the author attached—the late Sir Henry Durand. "Towards the close of 1848," wrote Sir Henry,

is difficult, looking back, to resist the conclusion that the resignation of Mulráj, proposed the moment Sir Henry Lawrence had quitted Láhor, was part of a deep scheme to inveigle the English into hostilities, at the hottest season of the year, against the strongest fortress in the Panjáb, to be detained there until the general rising, already determined upon, should be accomplished. The father of Mulráj, though of low origin, had been emphatically one of Ranjít Singh's men. Mulráj had been brought up in the same school. In common with the Sikh nation, they loathed the idea of being dragged at the chariot wheels of the conqueror, who, they one and all believed, had not vanquished them in fair fight.

Still, however clear this may appear to us, who, with the knowledge of subsequent events, can trace their cause, it can easily be understood how it was a sealed letter to every Englishman at that time in authority. The arrangements made with respect to the Panjáb were so perfect, the contentment of the people was so assured, the reforms introduced by the English were so popular, that it was heresy to dream of Sikh disaffection. And, in point of fact, no one on the spot did dream of it.*

With a light heart, then, Currie despatched Agnew and Anderson to Multán, there to be tutored by, and ultimately to relieve, Mulráj. To escort them there was detailed a body of about fourteen hundred soldiers of the Sikh army. Of these, the infantry, upwards of six hundred in number, were hill-men,

"many a village seemed to possess no other inhabitants than old decrepit men, women, and young children. Our two years' sway had not proved popular; and the able-bodied flocked to the rebel standard of the chiefs, even from districts under our immediate supervision and control, without the slightest check or hindrance."

* I have used deliberately the words "on the spot," because a soldier not on the spot, the greatest man I ever met in India, the late Sir Henry Durand, did see it. I have often heard him relate how, being in England at the time, he had endeavoured vainly to impress his forebodings alike on the India Office and the Board of Control. He has himself told how his warnings, after Multán had defied our troops, were received at both those high places.—Vide *Calcutta Review*, vol. xv. p. 258.

the troops least affected to the Khálsa, and therefore likely to be influenced by a display of manly qualities on the part of their officers; the cavalry, regular and irregular, Patáns and Sikhs, numbered about seven hundred, and there was an excellent troop of horse artillery. The whole were commanded by a Sikh officer, Sirdar Khán Singh, who was to succeed Mulráj as Názim, or Governor, of the Multán districts.

Regard being had to the fact that the infantry of the escort were hill-men, very lukewarm in their devotion to the Khálsa, wisdom would have dictated to the two British officers the advisability of accompanying them in the march to Multán. But the hot season had set in, and it was pleasanter to travel by water. By water, then, the two English officers and the new Názim, Sirdár Khán Singh, proceeded, whilst the troops, left to themselves, marched by land. The result was, that, on the 18th April, the two parties, the troops and their commanders, met each other for the first time in front of Multán. They encamped then at the 'I'dgah, a spacious Muhammadan building, within cannon-shot of the north face of the fort, and about a mile from Mulráj's own residence, a garden house outside the fort, called Am Khás.

Into the events which immediately followed, it is not necessary to enter into great detail. They are very simple. Mulráj and the British officers exchanged visits on the 18th, and it was arranged that on the following morning Mulráj should make over the fort to Sirdár Khán Singh.

Early on the morning of that day that official and the two British officers, accompanied by Mulráj, entered the fortress; were shown all over it, received the keys, planted sentries from the men of their own escort, mustered Mulráj's garrison, endeavoured to allay the sullen feeling of which they gave evidence at being thrown out of employment, and set out to return to their camp.

On their way, crossing the bridge over the ditch, one of the late garrison, standing upon it, struck Agnew from his horse with his spear. Agnew jumped up to return the blow with his riding-stick, when the man rushed in with his sword and inflicted two severe wounds on the Englishman. A crowd collected: soon the news was noised in the fort; the late garrison came pouring forth, set upon Anderson and cut him down, leaving him for dead. Mulráj, at the first signs of tumult, put spurs to his horse, and forced his way to his private house. Anderson was carried, seemingly dead, by the men of his escort to the 'I'dgah; Agnew was, about the same time, extricated from the mob by Sirdár Khán Singh, lifted on to his elephant, and conveyed to the same building.

Of the two Englishmen, Agnew was the less injured. In the trying situation in which he was placed he displayed the calmness, the courage, I might even add, the generosity, of his race. Unwilling to condemn Mulráj for an outbreak which might well have been caused by the fanaticism of a solitary soldier, he wrote to him (11 A.M.) to express his utter disbelief in his culpability, and to beg him to prove his good opinion by seizing the guilty parties and coming himself to the 'I'dgah. Three hours later, as Mulráj gave no sign, Agnew despatched letters to Herbert Edwardes at Bannú, and to General van Cortlandt, Governor for the Sikhs of the province of Déra Ismáil Khán, to ask for assistance. At 4 o'clock a message came from Múlráj to the effect that he could neither give up the guilty nor come himself, as he, after some efforts, had been forced to desist from attempting to control the storm; "that all the garrison, Hindú and Muhammadan, were in rebellion, and the British officers had better see to their own safety."

The die, in fact, had been cast. Whether Mulráj designed that the outbreak should occur at that particular time, or in that particular manner, may be doubted; but, the outbreak having occurred, he had but one thought—to place himself at the head of the movement. The messenger who had conveyed to Agnew the reply of Mulráj returned to find his master presiding at a council of his chiefs! That same night Mulráj, to prevent their flight, carried off the whole of the carriage cattle of the English officers and of their escort!

Agnew, undismayed, showed a bold front to the foe. He had still the escort and their six guns. If he and his comrade had only but marched with that escort and won their esteem! It was too late to think of that now! Still, he placed his guns and posted his troops in the manner best calculated to offer successful resistance. He made, too, one effort, unhappily fruitless, to induce the chiefs round Mulráj to obey the orders of the Láhor Regency. Presently guns opened upon his position, alike from the fort and the private house of Mulráj. Then emissaries came to tempt the escort. Despite of all the efforts of Agnew, they succeeded. Before the sun set all the troops—horse, foot, and artillery—had gone over, "except Sirdár Khán Singh, some eight or ten faithful horsemen, the domestic servants of the British officers, and the múnshís of their office." *

"Beneath the lofty centre dome of that empty hall (so strong and formidable that a very few stout hearts could have defended it)," continues the author from whom I have just quoted, "stood this miserable group around the beds of the two wounded Englishmen. All hope of resistance being at an end, Mr. Agnew had sent a party to Mulráj to sue for peace. A conference ensued, and, 'in the end,' say the Díwán's judges, 'it was agreed that the officers were to quit the country, and that the attack upon them was to cease.' Too late! The sun had gone down; twilight was closing in; and the rebel army had not tasted blood. An indistinct and distant murmur reached the ears of the few remaining inmates of the 'I'dgah, who were listening for their fate. Louder and louder it grew, until it became a cry—the cry of a multitude for blood! On they

* Edwardes.

came, from city, suburbs, fort; soldiers with their arms, citizens, young and old, and of all trades and callings, with any weapons they could snatch."

Then was consummated the murder of the two gallant Englishmen. The head of Agnew was severed from his body, whilst Anderson, who, since he had been brought in grievously wounded from the fort, had been incapable of stirring from his bed, was hacked to pieces with swords. Sirdár Khán Singh, faithful to the last, was conveyed a prisoner into the presence of Mulráj, laden with taunts and insults!

I have said that at 2 o'clock on the day on which he was assaulted, Van Agnew had despatched a letter, asking for aid, to Edwardes. The letter reached Edwardes at Derá Fath Khán, ninety miles from Multán, on the afternoon of the 22nd of April. With the prompt resolution which ever characterised him Edwardes at once transmitted a despatch to the British Resident at Láhor, informing him of the attack made upon the two Englishmen, and announcing his own intention of marching upon Multán with the raw native levies* of whom he could dispose. Leaving Edwardes, for the present, I must precede his letter to Láhor.

Sir Frederick Currie received the first news of the outbreak at Multán on the 21st of April. He rather made light of it, considered the affair unpremeditated, and that though Mulráj's conduct was very suspicious, yet that his share in the outrage was doubtful. Impressed with the idea that Mulráj was very unpopular both with the army and the people, and that it was quite possible he might have been urged to extreme measures by "unfriends"† desirous of effecting his ruin, he deemed, at the moment, that the crisis would be adequately met by the despatch against Multán of a force composed of

* There were twelve infantry companies, three hundred and fifty mounted men, two guns, and twenty zumbúralís (falconets).

† Sir F. Currie's own word; *vide* extract from Blue Book, Edwardes's *A Year in the Punjab*, vol, ii. pp. 122–23.

seven battalions of infantry, two of regular cavalry, twelve hundred irregular horsemen, and three troops or batteries of artillery—all belonging to the Khálsa army—to proceed or be stopped according to the accounts he might receive in the next twenty-four hours. Such a force he despatched accordingly.

When, two days later, Currie received an account of the attack upon, but not of the massacre at, the 'I'dgah, he was as far off as ever from arriving at a just conclusion. Still implicitly trusting the Sikh sirdárs, and wrongly attributing the movement to "Patán counsel and machination,"* he directed the Sikh sirdárs, "all the chiefs of the greatest note," with the few Sikh troops at Láhor, to take part in the operations already ordered, intending to support them with the British moveable column, stationed at Láhor. The idea of a general conspiracy on the part of the Sikh chiefs and population never having entered his head, Currie was sanguine enough to believe that a demonstration only would be sufficient.†

The receipt, the next day, of a more complete account of the events at the 'I'dgah, comprising the murder of the two British officers, caused another modification in the views of the Resident. The facility with which the Sikh escort had gone over to Mulráj, for the first time aroused within his mind that, possibly, the entire Sikh army might follow their example. He abandoned, then, at once, as impracticable, his dream of a demonstration, recalled the order given to the officer commanding the British moveable column, and informed the Sikh sirdárs that they must put down the rebellion themselves!

The Sikh sirdárs, all men, in the view of the British Resident, "implicitly to be relied upon," did not view matters quite in the light in which they presented themselves to the mind of that high official. They declared themselves unable to coerce

* This was absolutely the reverse of true. If we had any friends in the Panjáb they were the Patáns: our enemies were the pure Sikhs.

† Blue Book. Sir F. Currie to the Governor-General, 24th April.

Mulráj without the aid of British troops; and, admitting that their own men could not be depended upon, urged that they should not be employed at all in the operations against Multán. Sir F. Currie, then, recommended that the British army should itself undertake the operation, not in the interests of the Sikh Government, but—his mind curiously running on the Patán scare—to prevent the Afgháns establishing themselves upon the Indus! * On the same date he wrote to the Commander-in-Chief, Lord Gough, recommending that a British force should at once move upon Multán, capable of reducing the fort and occupying the city, independent of any assistance, or in spite of any opposition, from the Sikh troops.

Lord Gough, however, who was at Simla, conceived that at the advanced season of the year operations against Multán would be uncertain in their results, if not altogether impracticable. He therefore not only declined to commit himself to the plan urged by Currie, but even deprecated the weakening of Láhor in view to the very uncertain disposition of the Sikh army. In this view the Governor-General concurred.†

The siege, then, having been postponed till the autumn, it is time we should return to Edwardes.

We left that officer at Derá Fath Khán preparing to march with his raw levies, numbering only about sixteen hundred men, against Multán. Between him and that fortress flowed two broad and rapid rivers. Writing to his friend Reynell Taylor at Bannú to send him a regiment of infantry and four guns "sharp," he crossed the Indus, reached Leia on the 25th April, and was joined there by many of the Patán gentry of the neighbouring districts. Múlráj, hearing of this movement, sent a

* Blue Book. Sir F. Currie to Governor-General, April 27, 1848.

† Edwardes is of opinion that the delay, thus sanctioned, precipitated the war (vol. ii. pp. 144-7). I am inclined to believe that the war had already been pre-determined upon by the Sikh nation, and that the hostile action of Mulráj was prompted by a desire to drag the English into it at an unfavourable season.

force against him. On its approach Edwardes evacuated Leia, recrossed the Indus, and effected a junction, on the night of the 3rd May, with a Patán force under General Van Cortlandt. Four days later Mulráj recalled his army from Leia, and Edwardes at once occupied that place with a picket. Whilst Van Cortlandt, then, under orders from Láhor, proceeded to enter the trans-Indus territories of Mulraj, Edwardes waited at Derá Fath Khán till the situation between Leia and Multán should develop itself. Learning on the 15th May, from his picket, that a Sikh force had arrived within striking distance of that place, he crossed the Indus during the night with two hundred men, and, joining his picket, repulsed the enemy with the loss of all their zúmburaks (falconets) and twelve men killed. Four days later the loyal Bilúchís and Patáns defeated the Sikh party near Derá Ghází Khán, and took possession of that place for the English. This victory deprived Mulráj of all his Trans-Indus dependencies. Edwardes then occupied Derá Ghází Khán, and watched thence the movements of the enemy. Learning at length that Mulráj's best army had taken the field to secure the country between the Indus and the Chináb, Edwardes, now joined by the loyal Núwáb of Baháwalpur, marched against it, met it at the village of Kináiri on the Chináb, and, after a contest which lasted nine hours, completely defeated it. The effect of this victory was to deprive Mulráj of the country between the Indus and the Chináb, and of nearly all between the Chináb and the Satlaj. Following it up, Edwardes, reinforced by Van Cortlandt, and joined by Lake, pushed on towards Multán, met the last army of Mulráj, commanded by that chief in person, at Sadusám, close to the walls of the fortress, completely defeated it, and confined the enemy thenceforth to the city and its defences. They never again emerged from it except to resist the siege of the British army. This is not the place to do justice to the energy, the daring initiative, the greatness of character displayed by Herbert Edwardes. Alone, unsupported, he achieved a result of which a British army might have been proud. And it is not too much to affirm that had he been then and there supported by a few British troops and guns, placed under his own orders, he might have taken the fortress, and possibly have nipped the rising in the bud! *

Meanwhile, whilst Edwardes and his gallant comrades were thus combating, with means of their own manufacture, against the chief who had revolted against the Láhor Darbár, Sir F. Currie was preparing, in concert with that Darbár, and in correspondence with the Governor-General and the Commander-in-Chief, for the autumn siege of Multán. But before the autumn arrived, the horizon had become more clouded still. In the month of July a plot was discovered in which the Rání Janda, "who had more wit and daring than any of her nation,"† was seriously implicated. The chief conspirators were brought to trial and were hanged, and the Rání was exiled to the fort of Chunár, there to be kept as a state prisoner. Information reached Láhor about the same time that the Hazárah was shaky, and that a suspicious movement had been observed in that province. Notwithstanding the confidence justly felt by Currie in Abbott, the English representative in the Hazárah, and the assurances of Chattar Singh, father of Shér Singh, a prominent member of the Láhor Council of Regency, that there was nothing really to be apprehended, there was sufficient disturbance in the air to cause great anxiety to a man in the position of the British Resident. Just at this crisis Currie was cheered by the news of the battle of Sadusám, and incited to action by the recommendations from Edwardes which accompanied that news. At once, then, on his own responsibility, he directed the British brigade at Láhor to march upon Multán. Currie's conduct in this respect was confirmed very

* Edwardes, vol. ii. chap. viii. It is to be regretted that no detailed record of this noble life should have, as yet, been given to the world.

† Edwardes.

grudgingly by the Governor-General. As for the Commander-in-Chief, in the promise of facility and aid he despatched to the Resident he took care to remind him that the troops had been ordered to move upon his responsibility. Upon Lord Gough, however, it devolved to arrange for the strength and composition of the British force to be employed.

It was speedily decided that the Láhor brigade should be reinforced by that at Fírúzpúr. The force would then consist of about seven thousand five hundred men, including two European regiments, the 10th and the 32nd, with a proportion of artillery, including a siege train, and cavalry, and would be commanded by General Whish, the commander of the brigade at Láhor. Currie, meanwhile, in concert with the Regency, had decided to despatch a purely Sikh force to Tolomba, under the command of the ablest of its members, Shér Singh Atáriwálá. This force, consisting of about five thousand men, was not, however, content with marching to Tolomba, but pushed on, on the 6th July, to Multán.

Whish left Láhor with his brigade on the 24th July, and encamped at Sital-ki-mári, before Multán, on the 18th August. The following day he was joined by the Fírúzpúr brigade, commanded by Brigadier Salter. Whish found Edwardes's army, now composed of fourteen thousand infantry and over eight thousand irregular cavalry, encamped at Súrajkúnd, about six miles distant. His first care was to lessen that distance by bringing Edwardes two miles nearer to the fortress, a movement which was not accomplished without some hard fighting, in which Lake and Pollock—now Sir Frederic Pollock—distinguished themselves.

Pending the arrival of the siege train, Whish and his chief Engineer, Major Napier—now Lord Napier of Magdála—closely reconnoitred the fort. The two officers named, with a small party of the staff, crept forward into the 'I'dgah, and thence made a leisurely observation. They emerged with the conviction that "it was no contemptible place of arms." They could do nothing, however, till the arrival of the siege guns, and those guns reached the camp only on the 4th September.

But before their arrival an event occurred which greatly affected the course of action. The threatened outbreak in the Hazárah had taken place, and Chattar Singh, father of the Shér Singh who commanded the Darbár troops before Multán, had placed himself at the head of it. It is true that Shér Singh cleared himself, in the opinion of Lieutenant Edwardes, from any complicity in his father's conduct; but the fact that that father was at the moment at the head of a great national movement was not encouraging. Under these somewhat unfavourable auspices, the siege of Multán began (7th September 1848). I do not propose to do more than give a summary of it. On the 9th, a night attack made upon some gardens in front of the trenches, though conducted with great gallantry, and illustrated by the splendid valour of Lieutenant Richardson, of the Indian Army, and of Captain Christopher, of the Indian Navy, both of whom showed the way to their followers, was repulsed.* On the 12th, Whish, after a very hot encounter, productive of loss on both sides, especially on that of the Sikhs, cleared his front, gaining a distance in that direction of eight or nine hundred yards, and driving the enemy into the suburbs. The place seemed now at the mercy of the British general. He was within easy battering distance of the city walls. A few days more, and Multán would have been his. But, just at this critical moment, he was baffled by an action which, though foreseen by some acute minds,† had not been provided against. On the morning of the 14th September, Shér Singh and his whole force gave their adhesion to the national movement, and entered Multán!

* Richardson was brought from the combat covered with wounds; he still, I believe, lives. Christopher was mortally wounded.

† The mind of Edwardes, for instance. See his letters of the 4th and 10th September, vol. ii. pp. 487–498.

In consequence of this defection General Whish at once raised the siege, but remained encamped before the place, at first on the field of Sadusám, later on a more convenient spot close to the suburbs of the town, waiting for reinforcements or orders. He remained there inactive, but still in a way blockading the town, till the 27th December, when, reinforcements having arrived, he resumed the siege. Long before that period the decisive action of the national movement had passed to another part of the country. To that part I propose, now, to transport the reader.

The rising of Chattar Singh, the defection of Shér Singh, the consequent raising of the siege of Múltán, brought matters in the Panjáb to a crisis. There could no longer be any doubt. The Khálsa had resolved to strike a great blow for independence.

The Government of India was neither blind nor deaf to the signs of the time. The Governor-General, Lord Dalhousie, in a famous speech delivered at Barrakpúr, which resounded all over India, declared that as the Sikh people wished war "they should have it with a vengeance." The Commander-in-Chief, Lord Gough, issued, early in October, a general order announcing the formation, at Fírúzpúr, of an army, to be styled "the army of the Panjáb," under his own personal command.

Whilst this army was assembling, Cureton with a brigade of cavalry, and Colin Campbell* with a brigade of infantry, were directed to march from opposite directions on Gújránwálá, a small fort about three days' march from Láhor, which it was expected the Sikhs would occupy. Cureton, who arrived there first, found the place unoccupied. So much, at this time, did the British undervalue their enemy, that a very general impression prevailed that if Cureton and Campbell had pushed on from Gújránwálá they would have finished the war!

Similarly Brigadier Wheeler's brigade, which, since the month

* Afterwards Lord Clyde.

of August, had been engaged, under the direction of Mr. John Lawrence, in putting down the national movement in the Jálandhar Doáb, and Brigadier Godby's brigade, were pushed on, about the 3rd of November, towards the Rávi.

The entire army formed by Lord Gough, including the three brigades already mentioned and the division under General Whish still before Multán, was composed of seven brigades of infantry, four of cavalry, and a numerous artillery. It numbered about seventeen thousand infantry and four thousand cavalry. Of the former arm, however, between four and five thousand were with General Whish. The army, then, which Lord Gough found under his own immediate direction when, after crossing the Satlaj and the Rávi, he arrived at the small village of Noiwálá, thirteen miles from the Chináb, on the 20th of November, consisted of about twelve thousand five hundred infantry, of whom one-fourth were Europeans, and three thousand five hundred cavalry, comprising three British regiments.*

Ten miles from the British camp, and three only from the banks of the Chináb, near the walled town of Rámnagar, lay detachments of the Sikh army. They were encamped in an open plain covered with a low scrub jungle extending to the river. Midway between their position and the river was a small grove.

The position was admirably chosen. From it the Sikh commander, who was no other than Shér Singh Atáríwálá, whose desertion to Mulráj had caused the raising of the siege of Multán, could intercept the movements of the ruler of Káshmir, Gúláb Singh; could cover his communications with his father in the Deráját; and could draw his supplies from the productive districts in the upper part of the Chináb. Such a position was

* These were the 3rd Dragoons, the 9th Lancers, the 14th Light Dragoons (now 14th Hussars). The European infantry regiments were the 24th, the 29th, the 61st, and the 2nd Europeans (now the 104th Foot).

worth fighting for. Indeed, Shér Singh would have been justified in seeking an opportunity to bring the British to action to maintain it.

Apparently, however, Shér Singh regarded the ground about Rámnagar as not worth fighting for. For, when, on the morning of the 22nd of November, Lord Gough moved with a force composed of cavalry and artillery, supported by an infantry brigade* and two batteries of artillery, to reconnoitre the position of the enemy, Shér Singh directed the detachments on the left bank to recross the river by the ford and to rejoin him on the right bank.

Lord Gough belonged essentially to a "fighting caste." In the presence of an enemy he could think only of how to get at him. At that time of supreme excitement all ideas of strategy, of tactics, of the plan of the campaign, vanished from his mind. How a momentary triumph might be gained became his dominant and fixed thought. On the occasion of which I am writing a calm and cool leader would have rejoiced to see an enemy voluntarily abandoning, in the face of a military demonstration, a splendid military position, and retreating to a country where supplies were difficult and whence he could not control the ruler of Káshmír. He would even have aided him by making the demonstration more pronounced. But no thought of that kind ever entered the brain of Lord Gough. He had joined and placed himself at the head of the advanced party of cavalry that morning "unknown to the majority of his staff,"† and he now saw the enemy retiring without his striking a blow! Little recked he of the fact that his own advanced

* The advanced force was composed of the 3rd and 14th Light Dragoons, the 5th and 8th Native Light Cavalry, the 12th Irregulars, and the Horse Artillery of Lane and Warner, all led by General Cureton. The supporting infantry brigade was commanded by Brigadier Godby, and consisted of the 3rd Europeans and the 31st and 70th Native Infantry. The two batteries of artillery were Dawes's and Austen's.

† *Commentaries on the Punjab Campaign, 1848-9*, by Captain J. H. Lawrence-Archer, p. 9.

party was few in numbers, that he had left the main body of his troops behind him without orders and without a head; it never occurred to him to reflect that in all probability the Sikhs were but retiring to a selected position, covered with heavy guns, on the right bank of the river. He thought of nothing but that the enemy were escaping him when they were within measurable distance of his small force. Rendered wild at this thought he dashed his cavalry and horse artillery at them as they were crossing the ford.

The horse-artillery guns of Lane and Warner, opening upon the enemy engaged in a movement of retreat, caused them at first some slight loss; but as the British guns pressed on, they came, as might have been expected, under the fire of the enemy's guns on the right bank, a fire so superior to their own that their position became untenable. The English then endeavoured to retire. But this had become a matter of great difficulty. Their guns, one of them especially, had become deeply embedded in the heavy road of the river bank. It was difficult to extricate them, and, after superhuman efforts, the English, to save the remainder, were forced to abandon that one.

To cover the retreat of the British artillery Captain Ouvry, with a squadron of the 3rd Light Dragoons, made a gallant charge on a body of the enemy who had taken up a position on an islet surrounded by stagnant pools. This charge was followed by others; but the Sikh infantry, cool and resolute, maintained on the cavalry a galling fire, and then, as the charges ceased, advanced to capture the abandoned gun.

Burning with indignation at the very idea of the enemy carrying off a trophy in the very first action of the campaign, Colonel Havelock, commanding the 14th Light Dragoons, demanded and obtained permission to drive the enemy back. The 14th, accompanied by the 5th Native Light Cavalry, charged, then, upon the advancing Sikhs with so much fury that they rolled them back in disorder. Hoping then to recover the gun, the 14th pursued their advantage, and dashed forward to the ground on which it lay. But here, not only did the heavy sand tell on the horses, but they came within range of the batteries on the right bank. Under cover of this fire, too, the Sikh infantry rallied and returned to the charge. In the fight that followed Havelock was slain. Cureton, who had witnessed the charge, galloping down to withdraw the 14th from the unequal contest, was shot through the heart. The cavalry then fell back, leaving the gun still in the sand. During the day the enemy succeeded in carrying it off.

Such was the combat of Rámnagar, an affair entailing considerable—the more to be regretted because useless—loss on the British army. The object aimed at—the retirement of the Sikhs to the right bank—had been gained by the mere display of the British troops. The subsequent fighting was unnecessary butchery, which caused the loss to the British army of two splendid officers, Cureton and Havelock, and eighty-four men, killed, wounded, and missing. Besides this, it gave great encouragement to the Sikhs, who could boast that in their first encounter they had met the British not unequally.

The Sikhs, having crossed to the right bank of the Chináb were now in the strong but inhospitable territory between that river and the Jhelam. A really great commander would have been content that they should remain there, eating up their scanty supplies, until Multán should have fallen, when, with a largely increased army and greatly enhanced prestige, he could assail them with effect. The true course and position of the English commander, was, in fact, to use the language of the most competent critic of the time, "marked out by the manifest objects of the enemy. To remain in observation on the left bank of the Chináb; to regard himself as covering the siege of Multán and holding Shér Singh in check till that place fell; to cover Láhor and cut off all supplies from the districts on the left bank of

26

the Chináb reaching the enemy; jealously to watch the movements of the latter, whether to the northward or southward: these should have been Lord Gough's objects. So long as Shér Singh was disposed to have remained on the right bank of the Chináb, Gough should have left him undisturbed, and patiently have awaited the fall of Multán." *

But Gough cared for none of these things. He saw only the enemy. The enemy being on the right bank, he must cross to that bank and get at him. His mission, as he read it, was to seek the enemy wherever he could be found, attack him, and beat him. Larger aims than this lay outside the range of his mental vision.

The English general prepared, then, to dislodge the enemy from the right bank, and to cross the Chináb. To make a direct attack on his position would have been dangerous; for the right bank was considerably higher than the left, and the ford across it was covered by a very powerful artillery. But rivers rarely present a serious obstacle to a resolute commander. This was especially the case with the Chináb in the cold months of the year, for at that season the stream contracts itself to a comparatively narrow channel, fordable in many places. It was not difficult, therefore, for Lord Gough to turn the position of the army which faced him on the right bank.

Between Rámnagar, which had now become the head-quarters of the British army, and the town of Vazírábád, some twenty-five miles to the east of it, on the same side of the river, were three fords across the Chináb—the fords of Gharí, of Ranikan, and of Ali Shér; the first-named being eight, the others about thirteen, miles distant from the British camp. There was also a ford

* Sir H. Durand's article in the *Calcutta Review*, vol. xv. p. 261. The justice of this criticism is proved by the fact that, before he could strike an effective blow, Gough was compelled to wait for the fall of Multán, and for the reinforcements which that fall secured to him. The crossing of the Chináb would serve no good purpose unless it would enable him to strike at once a decisive blow at the enemy. This Gough failed to do.

opposite Vazírábád itself. Lord Gough had before him, then, a choice of passages across the river.

But, extraordinary fact! although, as I have shown, time did not press him, although sound policy would have induced him to remain altogether where he was, yet so eager was Gough to "get at" the enemy, that he would not spare a single day to have the fords I have named properly examined.* He would appear to have been satisfied with the report of his staff that the fords were practicable, but that they were strictly watched by a numerous and vigilant enemy. Such "strict watching" has not, under other leaders, prevented British officers from making the strictest examinations. There was plenty of time for such, for, anxious as was Gough to look the enemy in the face, he could not put in action the turning movement till the heavy guns should have arrived, and those reached him only on the 30th November.

The very next day Lord Gough directed his divisional general of cavalry, Sir Joseph Thackwell, to march, at 1 o'clock in the morning, with the force destined for the turning movement, upon the ford of Ranikan. His force consisted of three troops of horse artillery, two light field batteries, two 18-pounders; of the 3rd Light Dragoons, the 5th and 8th Native Light Cavalry, the 3rd and 12th Irregulars; of the 24th and 61st Regiments of the Line, and of the 25th, 31st, 36th, 46th, 56th, and four companies of the 22nd Native Infantry—in all about eight thousand men. It was accompanied by a pontoon train. The infantry was commanded by Brigadier-General Sir Colin Campbell.

Thackwell had resolved to cross by the ford of Ranikan on the ground that, being further from the position of the enemy than that of Gharí, it would not be so fiercely disputed; but,

* "That these fords were not subjected to a minute scrutiny, in which the highest authorities should have actively participated, was afterwards deeply lamented."—*Narrative of the Second Sikh War in 1848-9*, by Edward Thackwell, late A.D.C. to General Thackwell. 1851.

to make assurance doubly sure, he detailed a small force to secure if possible the ford in front of Vazírábád.

To assure the success of the movement Thackwell was undertaking, silence, secrecy, and despatch were absolutely requisite. All three, on this occasion, were conspicuous by their absence.* Not only did the camp-followers raise an astounding din, but the infantry, unprovided with a guide, became entangled in the intricacies of the vast camp, and finding it impossible, owing to the intensity of the darkness, to see, and difficult to feel, their way, did not reach the rendezvous till two hours after the appointed time. As a natural consequence, the turning force, instead of reaching Ranikan at eight o'clock, as had been laid down in the programme, arrived there only at eleven o'clock.

Thackwell rode to the front to reconnoitre. The view that met his gaze was not encouraging. He saw before him a broad river-bed—far broader here than in front of Rámnagar—the water flowing swiftly over which was divided into four separate channels, with sandbanks, and, as the natives reported, with dangerous quicksands. The opposite bank was out of range and was guarded by the enemy.†

Thackwell, Colin Campbell, and other high officers, spent three hours in debating the course to be pursued. Evidently the ford of Ranikan presented great and previously unthought-of difficulties. By degrees one and all recognised the impossibility of attempting it. Campbell then counselled a return to camp, but Thackwell, wishing to prove the matter to the utmost, resolved to attempt the ford at Vazírábád. He accordingly resumed the march, and reached his destination at six o'clock in the evening.

* Lawrence-Archer's *Commentaries on the Panjáb Campaign*, p. 16.

† The surprise of Thackwell is a sufficient proof that any previous examination of the ford must have been of a most cursory character. Neither he nor his staff had any idea of its actual features before he saw it. Yet, compare these facts with Lord Gough's bulletin of the 5th December!

Here, too, but for the fortunate unforeseen and unexpected, he might have been again disappointed. But this time a good genius, in the shape of a man who, already great, afterwards astonished the world by his brilliant feats of war, the illustrious John Nicholson, had made his task easy. John Nicholson was at this time a political officer attached to the head-quarters of the army, for the purpose of facilitating the communications of its chief with, and of bringing his own influence to bear upon, the nobles and people of the country. On this occasion, foreseeing the difficulties which might possibly baffle Thackwell at the fords, Nicholson had ridden forward with a few of the Patán horsemen whom he had raised and trained, and secured at Vazírábád seventeen large boats. These constituted the acceptable present which gladdened the heart of Thackwell as he rode into Vazírábád.

Darkness had already set in. It was one great fault of the Sikh army, as apparent in this campaign as in that which was concluded at Sobráon, that they trusted too much to the darkness of the night. Not accustomed to attempt night surprises themselves, they posted no guards. But for this, under the circumstances, Thackwell might have been again baffled. The darkness of the night and the neglect of the Sikhs, however, greatly befriended him.

Thackwell wisely resolved to take advantage of these two circumstances to cross at once, and gain a footing on the right bank.

The result showed how fatal would have been the attempt had the enemy been on the alert. On the assurance of Nicholson's Patáns that the enemy were not watching on the other side, the guns were first crossed over. Of the two brigades of infantry, one, Pennycuick's, then passed over in the boats. The other, Eckford's, attempted wading; but, after mastering the first and second branches of the stream, they were brought to a dead stop by the third, and were forced to bivouac for the night on a sandbank. Of the cavalry, Tait's Irregulars crossed the ford as indicated by stakes: not, however, without the loss of some men from drowning.

The troops who had crossed, as well, it can easily be imagined, as those who had stuck half-way, passed a miserable night. They were all more or less wet; the cold was the intense, cutting cold of a Panjáb December night; they had eaten nothing, or but little, all day; they had no food with them, and they were unable to light fires lest they should attract the enemy. The agony of such a situation is simply indescribable.

But the darkest hour comes to an end. With daylight, and the glorious sun which soon followed daylight, the men revived. They had at least an undisturbed footing on the right bank, and their comrades were crossing. Food would soon give them back their strength, and a brisk march restore their circulation. At length, by about noon, all the force had passed over except the 12th Irregulars and two companies of the 22nd Native Infantry. These were detailed to escort the useless pontoon train back to Rámnagar.

It was 2 o'clock before the men had finished their meal and were ready to march. Meanwhile Thackwell and Colin Campbell were discussing the line of advance to be adopted. They knew nothing of the country in which they were. They had only, then, to push on by the compass in the direction of the enemy. They marched that afternoon about twelve miles, to Dúriwál, without encountering the Sikhs. There Thackwell received a message from Gough congratulating him on his successful passage, and urging him to attack the enemy in flank the following day, whilst he should assail him in front.

The next day this order was countermanded. After marching six miles, Thackwell received a despatch from the Commander-in-Chief forbidding him to attack till he should be joined by Godby's brigade, which was to cross at the ford of Ghari. To facilitate this junction, Thackwell then directed his march towards the three villages of Tárwalur, Rattai, and Rámúkhail; but, too intent on the idea of holding his hand to Godby, he made the mistake of not occupying the line of those villages, and of throwing out his advanced guards and pickets well in front of them.* Instead of so doing, he encamped on the grassy plain in front of the larger village of Sadúlapúr, having the three villages I have named in front of him.

Whilst they are breakfasting, let us cross the river and see what Lord Gough was doing at Rámnagar.

Lord Gough, we have seen, had despatched Thackwell to effect the turning movement early on the morning of the 1st December. It was not till midday of the 2nd that he learned the complete success of the operation. To distract the enemy's attention from Thackwell, then, he immediately opened a heavy fire upon the enemy's position on the opposite bank. The Sikhs replied by directing a return fire from the few guns which effectually guarded the ford, and which were so placed, that, though the fire of the British artillery was admirable, it could not, from the width of the river, silence them.†

Whilst the artillery fight was thus raging, Shér Singh was made aware of Thackwell's successful passage and his subsequent movement. The idea which flashed across his mind was an idea worthy of a great commander. He resolved to march at once to crush Thackwell before Gough could possibly come to his support. He would then deal with Gough.

He broke up his camp, then, without delay, and drew back his whole force about two miles, preparatory to the contemplated movement. Meanwhile he gradually slackened his artillery fire against the British, until at length it ceased altogether.

But the movement to the rear was scarcely effected when other thoughts came over the mind of the Sikh leader. What if Lord Gough, encouraged by the cessation of fire, should cross

* Vide *Calcutta Review*, vol. xv. pp. 264, 265.

† Lawrence-Archer, p. 29,

at once? He would be between two fires. He somewhat modified his plan, then, and, leaving the larger moiety of his forces to amuse Gough, marched with ten thousand men against Thackwell. This change in resolution was a half measure, and in war half measures rarely succeed. The action of Lord Gough proved that audacity on this occasion would have been justifiable. For that general, completely deceived, renounced the idea he had communicated to Thackwell, of immediate crossing. He spent the night of the 2nd in pushing forward breastworks and batteries, just as if a formidable enemy had been in front of him. It was not till the night of the day following that he discovered the abandonment by the enemy of his position, nor was he able to bring his army to the opposite bank till after Shér Singh had met Thackwell and was taking up a new position on the left bank of the Jhelam! Audacity was, therefore, not wanting on one side only.*

Whilst Gough was thus throwing up his earthworks and his batteries, Shér Singh was marching against Thackwell. He caught him about 11 o'clock on the 3rd, just as the English leader had taken up the position I have already described, in front of Sadúlapúr and behind the three villages. Thackwell's men had but just piled arms and fallen out, when, suddenly, a peculiar sound was heard overhead, and, on looking up, a shell was discovered bursting in mid-air, between the British line and the villages in front—a distance of about half a mile of level turf. After this came round shot.† It was Shér Singh who had thus surprised the British, badly posted facing three villages which he now held. In that supreme hour he must have deeply

* Lawrence-Archer, p. 29 *note*; *Calcutta Review*, vol. xv. p. 266.

† Lawrence-Archer, p. 23. The extraordinarily careless manner in which the British generals conducted their operations in this campaign is proved by the admission of Captain Thackwell, who acted as A.D.C. to the General of that name throughout the campaign. "It was difficult to believe," he wrote, "that this shot was fired by the enemy, for the scouts and patrols had raised no alarm of their approach." The question naturally arises: had any scouts been sent out, or any patrols been posted?

regretted that he had not brought with him his whole army! The English troops at once fell in. The infantry deployed, and the advanced guard, which by this time was about equidistant between the enemy and the British main body, was ordered to fall back. When this had been accomplished, Thackwell, in order to have a clear space in front of him, retired about two hundred yards further.

Meanwhile, Shér Singh, still wanting in audacity, had contented himself with holding the three villages, and in pouring in a continuous fire from his guns. This fire could not have failed, under ordinary circumstances, to produce a murderous effect; but on this occasion its result was minimised in consequence of the precaution taken, on the advice of Colin Campbell, by the British general, to make his infantry throw themselves on the ground.

For nearly five hours the British force sustained this fire without replying. At last, at nearly 4 P.M., Thackwell's patience was exhausted, and he ordered his guns to reply. The artillery duel then continued till sunset, varied only by two feeble attempts made by the Sikhs to turn both flanks of the British force. That on the left was baffled by Biddulph's Irregular Cavalry and Warner's troop of Horse Artillery, supported by the 5th Light Cavalry; that on the left by Christie's Horse Artillery, the 3rd Light Dragoons, and the 8th Light Cavalry.

By sunset the firing on both sides ceased, and Shér Singh, still haunted by the fear lest Gough should take advantage of the night to cross, fell back on his position without loss and without pursuit. The loss of the British was only seventy-three.

Such was the artillery combat of Sadúlapúr, dignified, in the inflated language of the British commanders of the day, with the name of a battle. It must be a strange kind of battle in which, by the admission of the general, "the infantry had no chance of firing a shot, except a few companies on the left of the line," to repulse a turning movement, and the cavalry never charged, No, Sadúlapúr was nothing more than an artillery combat. The armies never came to close quarters; the English, because Shér Singh held a very strong position in the three villages, and the ground between them and their position was unfavourable to an advance; the Sikhs, because their leader feared to commit himself to a battle when he might, at any moment, hear the guns of Lord Gough thundering on his rear. There can be no doubt but that his want of audacity in not bringing up his whole army lost him a great opportunity; for no position could have been weaker than that of the English—and in war opportunities do not return.*

Meanwhile, Lord Gough, still encamped at Rámnagar pending the construction of a bridge of boats across the Chináb, had, on the 4th, despatched Sir Walter Gilbert with the 9th Lancers and the 14th Light Dragoons to the right bank of that river. Gilbert returned to report that the enemy had disappeared. Shér Singh had, in point of fact, fallen back during the night of the 3rd on his main body, and, in view of taking up a new position on the Jhelam, had marched a few miles in that direction.

* It is ludicrous to read Lord Gough's despatch on this battle. Alike in the statement of facts (?) and in the inferences drawn from those—facts, it is throughout a supreme effort of the imagination. Beginning by the statement "It has pleased Almighty God to vouchsafe to the British arms the most successful issue to the extensive combinations rendered necessary for the purpose of effecting the passage of the Chenab, the defeat and dispersion of the Sikh force under the insurgent rajah Sher Singh," it proceeds to give a description of the battle of Sadúlapúr—a battle not brought to a decisive issue solely in consequence "of the exhausted state of man and horse" on the British side. (The men had marched six miles and had lain down for five hours!) After stating, then, the fact of his own passage of the Chináb, and the retreat, in disorder (?), of the Sikhs, he draws the inference—soon, to his dismay, to be proved utterly baseless—that the movement to the Jhelam of the Sikhs has "become more a flight than a retreat," and that "a great portion of those not belonging to the Khálsa army have dispersed and returned to their homes." It may be said of all Lord Gough's despatches that they should be left unread by those who wish to possess a true knowledge of the actions which they profess to describe.

"The ill-advised passage of the Chináb," writes the most competent critic of this campaign,* "the failure to strike a blow, and the withdrawal of the enemy intact to positions of their own choosing, were doubtless sufficiently irritating" to the British commander-in-chief. If the passage of the Chináb was to be justified at all, it could only be justified by following it up by a rapid advance on the enemy. Under the circumstances it was simply a useless piece of bravado. In spite of it, Gough with his main army was still chained to the left bank; he had no reserves; the commissariat arrangements were still incomplete; a feeling of insecurity was beginning to arise in Láhor; Multán was still unsubdued; Wheeler's brigade was still busy in the Jálandhar Doáb. In spite of Lord Gough's bulletins, which imposed upon nobody, it was universally felt that up to that point the campaign had been a failure.† The public, in fact, had lost all the confidence they ever possessed, never very much, in the military capacity of Lord Gough.

Nor, with time, did matters improve. After his affair at Sadúlapúr Thackwell had pushed on, in a blind sort of manner, after the enemy. He had been joined by Godby's brigade at 9 A.M. of the 4th, and by the 9th Lancers and 14th Light Dragoons on the evening of the same day. On the 5th he moved to Hélah, a mud village which had arisen on the accumulated *débris* of other villages. From this place, if he had only known it, Shér Singh and his army were distant only ten miles. But, so vicious was the system of reconnoitring, and so hostile to the English was the feeling of the people, that although Thackwell sent out two large observation parties of cavalry and artillery, these returned to camp only to report that they had seen, indeed, small bodies of the Sikhs, but that the villagers persistently asserted that Shér Singh had already crossed the Jhelam.

* Sir Henry Durand, vide *Calcutta Review*, vol. xv. p. 266.

† *Calcutta Review*, vol. xv. p. 267.

On the 18th December, the bridge of boats being ready, Gough crossed to the right bank, and marched forthwith to within three miles of the position which Thackwell still held at Hélah. Shér Singh, well informed of the British movements, thought the moment opportune to march on Dinghi, a post from which he threatened the ford at Vazírábád and Vazírábád itself. He so imposed upon the English general that the latter resolved on the moment to fall back on Gujrát, and actually sent orders to Thackwell to support him in that movement. Under inspiration happier than his own, however, he cancelled the order, and despatched instead a brigade of cavalry and three guns to guard the ford. The army remained in Hélah and its immediate vicinity.

The Governor-General, Lord Dalhousie, had been very unwilling to give his sanction to a general attack upon the main Sikh army until Multán should have fallen. His position in this respect was not very logical. Holding the views he did, he should have kept the British army on the left bank of the Chináb. Once having allowed Gough to cross, he should have urged him to immediate action. By his steering a middle course, by his allowing Gough to move to the right bank and then holding his hand, there came about a state of affairs which might be regarded almost as alarming.

Gough was still halted at Hélah, when, in the beginning of January, the important fortress of Atak on the Indus, held till then by Lieutenant Herbert, surrendered to the Sikhs. The fall of Atak effected an immediate change in the views of Lord Dalhousie. Regarding it as an event which let loose the besieging army led by Chattar Singh, father of the Sikh commander-in-chief, and which opened the way for the advance of an Afghán contingent, for which it was known that chief had been negotiating, he at once, 10th January, sent pressing orders to Gough to strike, if he should deem himself strong enough, an effectual blow at the enemy in his front, and to strike it "with the least possible delay."

In consequence of these instructions Gough broke up his camp near Hélah, and advanced, at daylight on the 12th, to Dinghi, some twelve miles distant. Here he received information, subsequently proved to be true, that the Sikh army was in position some fourteen miles distant, that its left rested on the low hills of Rasúl, its centre on the village of Fathsháh-ki-chak, its right on Múng.

That afternoon Gough summoned some of the officers whom he most trusted to confer with him on the best mode of carrying out the Governor-General's instructions. Amongst the officers so summoned was one who had but recently joined the camp. The high character borne by this officer more than warranted the extension to him of the summons to attend the meeting, and it was upon the advice he gave that the commander-in-chief decided to act.

The officer in question—after alluding to the fact, a report of which had been made to head-quarters, that though the front of the enemy's position was covered by a thick belt of jungle, yet along the frequented road which led from Dinghí straight upon Rasúl the country was more open—pointed out that a line which extended from Rasúl to Múng must be thin and weak, and recommended, therefore, that the British army should march on Rasúl, and, taking the enemy in flank, should double up his line, thrust it back upon Fathsháh-ki-Chak and Múng, into a country void of supplies, where he would be hemmed in between rivers he could not cross, and thus cut him off from the fords of the Jhelam, sever his communication with Chattar Singh and with Atak, and render it impossible for him to receive further aid in men and provisions. This plan, constituting an *echelon* attack quite in the style of the Great Frederic,* was, I have said, adopted by Lord Gough.

In the chapter immediately preceding, when I introduced Lord Gough to the reader, I described him as a general the

* *Calcutta Review*, vol. xv. p. 268.

reverse in one respect of Clive, of Adams, of Wellesley, of Masséna, and of other great captains who were remarkable for their clearness of vision and coolness under the roar of cannon, inasmuch as he, under the same circumstances, forgot all his previous plans and sought only to get at the enemy. The events which followed the deliberations of the 12th January illustrate this remarkable feature of his character.

Gough had resolved, I have said, on an *echelon* attack on the enemy. It was intended that Gilbert's division, forming the extreme right, should force the left of the enemy, whilst "the heavy and field artillery, massed together, should sweep in enfilade the curvilinear position of their centre and right"; that then, as soon as Gilbert had shaken and broken up the left, Campbell, till then kept in reserve with the massed artillery, should, with Gilbert and the cavalry, "throw himself fairly perpendicularly across the left centre of the opposing force, and hurl it to the southward."*

Full of carrying out this plan, Gough marched from his ground early on the morning of the 13th January. "It was one of those pleasant mornings," writes Captain Lawrence-Archer, himself a combatant, "peculiar to the cold season of upper India. The air was still and bracing, and the increasing warmth of sunshine, in an almost unclouded atmosphere, produced the glow so welcome after the cold of the early dawn." After proceeding five or six miles, Gough halted and sent on the Engineers to reconnoitre. They returned about 10 o'clock to report the road clear and practicable for guns, and that the enemy were marching down from Rasúl apparently to take up a position in the plain. The view which had been urged upon him being thus confirmed, Gough pushed on along the road to Rasúl. He had not, however, progressed very far when deserters informed him, through the political agent, Major Mackeson, that the enemy were in some strength on the left of the British

* *Calcutta Review*, vol. xv. p. 268.

advancing column in the neighbourhood of the villages Mujiánwálá and Chiliánwálá. On receiving this information, Gough, renouncing the plan of the previous evening, quitted the Rasúl road and inclined to the left. Further information having made known to him that small detachments of the enemy's horse had been visible on the plain in advance of the mound and village of Chiliánwálá, and their infantry on the mound itself, he turned directly to the left and marched straight on that point, leaving the Rasúl road in the rear of, and parallel to, his line when it was deployed.*

The Sikh detachment at the mound of Chiliánwálá, for it was no more, did not await the threatened attack, but fell back precipitately upon its main line by the Múng road. Gough speedily gained the vacated mound, and from its summit obtained a good view of the enemy's position. To bring his army in front of and parallel to it he had to bring his left forward. Whilst this movement was being effected he had time to examine in detail the enemy's position. He saw them—to the number of about twenty-three thousand†—their right facing Chiliánwálá, about two miles from that village, but less from the British line, which was deploying about five hundred yards in front of it, their left resting on the high ground of Rasúl. There was a great interval between the left of their right wing and the right of the centre. "It was evident," writes Durand, "that the enemy occupied a position too extended for his numbers." His extreme right was refused, and inclined back towards Múng.

* "It would have been a very hazardous movement," writes Durand, whose account of this movement I have followed almost verbally, "in front of an intelligent general, with troops quick and ready at manœuvre; for Gough offered his right to an enemy in position within four thousand yards of him, with a thickish belt of jungle, which would have covered their approach until they debouched and formed across his exposed flank."—*Calcutta Review*, vol. xv. p. 269.

† The official report, as usual, greatly exaggerates the enemy's numbers. It says from thirty to forty thousand. It should rather have been from twenty to twenty-five thousand.

When the British army had deployed it was noticed that its line of infantry, solid and compact, did little more than oppose a front to Shér Singh's centre. It is true it somewhat overlapped it, with the result, however, that its left brigade (of Campbell's division) faced the gap of which I have spoken as existing between the Sikh right wing and centre.

Gough had no intention of engaging. It was 2 o'clock in the afternoon, and his troops had been under arms since daybreak. He gave orders, therefore, to his Quartermaster-General to take up ground for encampment. Meanwhile, pending the completion of that officer's labours, the troops piled arms.

But Shér Singh was determined to force on a battle that afternoon. Knowing the temperament of the British commander, that the fire of artillery was the music which would make him dance, he despatched to the front a few light guns and opened fire on the British position.

The fire was distant and the effect innocuous, but the insult roused the hot Irish blood of the leader of the English army. It "drew" him, in fact, precisely in the manner designed by Shér Singh. He at once directed his heavy guns to respond, from their position in front of Chiliánwálá, to the fire of the enemy. The distance from the enemy's advanced guns was from fifteen to seventeen hundred yards. Yet the density of the jungle prevented the English gunners from getting any sight of the Sikhs, and they had to judge their distance by timing the seconds between the report and the flash of the hostile guns. Their fire failed to silence that of the enemy, for Shér Singh, determined to complete the drawing operation he had so well begun, sent the whole of his field artillery to the front, and, the Sikhs, excellent gunners, maintained an equal contest with their foe.

This was more than Gough could stand. A thorough believer in the bayonet, and looking upon guns as instruments which it was perhaps necessary to use but which interfered with real

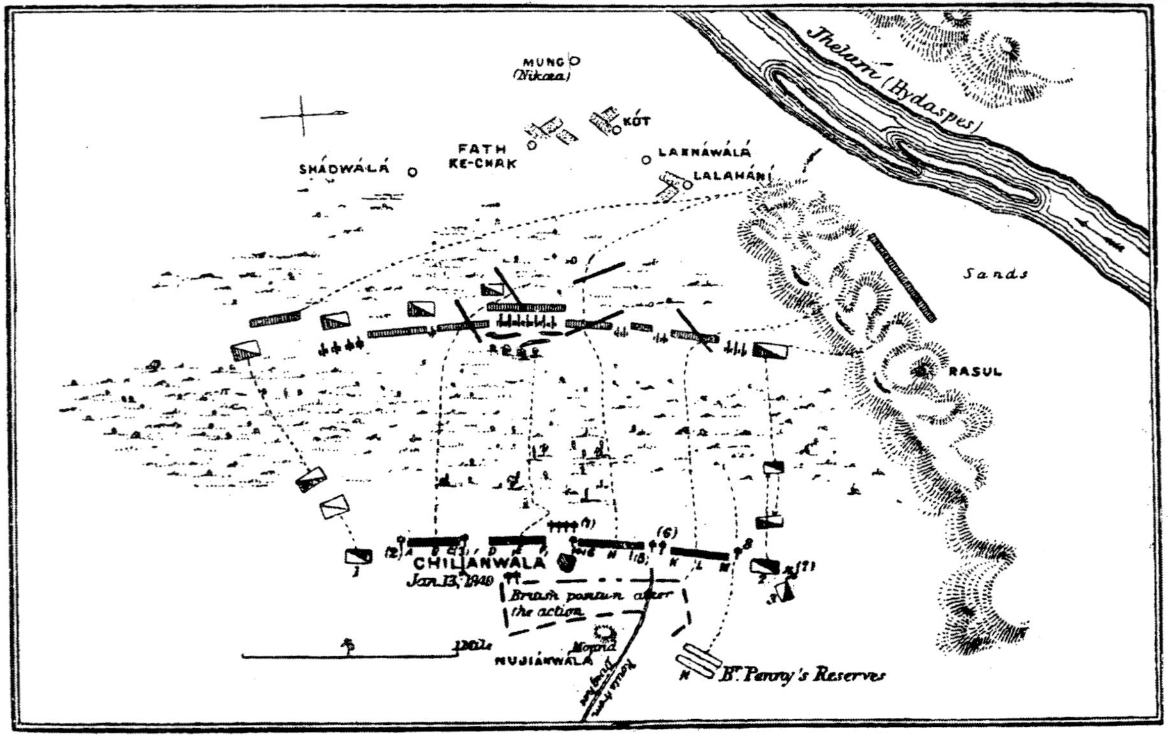

Cavalry.		Infantry.	
1. White's Brigade (3rd Lt. Drags., 5th and 8th Light Cavalry).	A 36th N.I. / B H.M. 61st / C 46th N.I. — Hoggan's Brigade.	G 30th N.I. / H H.M. 24th / I 56th N.I. — Mountain's Brigade.	
2. Pope's Brigade (14th Dragoons, squadron of 9th Lancers, &c.)	D 45th N.I. / E H.M. 24th / F 25th N.I. — Pennicuick's Brigade.	K 31st N.I. / L 2nd Europeans / M 70th N.I. — Godby's Brigade.	

Cavalry.

1. White's Brigade (3rd Lt. Drags., 5th and 8th Light Cavalry).
2. Pope's Brigade (14th Dragoons, squadron of 9th Lancers, &c.)

Artillery.

1. Heavy guns.
2, 3, 4, 5, 6, 7, 8. Field Bat. & H.A.

Infantry.

A 36th N.I.
B H.M. 61st } Hoggan's Brigade.
C 46th N.I.

D 45th N.I.
E H.M. 24th } Pennicuick's Brigade.
F 25th N.I.

G 30th N.I.
H H.M. 24th } Mountain's Brigade.
I 56th N.I.

K 31st N.I.
L 2nd Europeans } Godby's Brigade.
M 70th N.I.

fighting, he, wild with excitement, ordered his infantry to advance and charge the enemy's batteries.

The order of the English line was as follows:—Of the infantry, Sir Walter Gilbert's division occupied the right, but he was flanked by Pope's brigade of cavalry, strengthened by the 14th Light Dragoons, and three troops of artillery under Lieutenant-Colonel Grant. In the centre were the heavy guns under Major Horsford. The left was formed of General Colin Campbell's infantry division, flanked by White's brigade of cavalry and three troops of horse artillery under Lieutenant-Colonel Brind. The field batteries were with the infantry divisions, between the intervals of brigades. The reserve was commanded by Brigadier Penny, and Brigadier Hearsey protected the baggage.*

The reckless nature of the order given by the Commander-in-Chief—viz. to carry the guns in front at the point of the bayonet—may be judged from the fact that between those guns and the troops on the British left who were to carry them was very nearly a mile of dense and unknown jungle. However, British soldiers, well led, shrink from no impossibility; and on this occasion the divisional commanders, at all events, were men of tried experience and ability. Gough's orders, then, were obeyed. The British line pressed on. I propose first to accompany the left, led by Colin Campbell.

I have stated that Campbell's left brigade (Hoggan's) overlapped the right of Shér Singh's centre, and faced, therefore, in the original formation, a blank space. Pushing on towards the enemy, the right brigade then naturally came full in front of Shér

* Lawrence-Archer, pp. 44, 45. Gilbert's division was composed of Mountain's brigade (29th Foot, 30th and 56th N. I.), and Godby's brigade (2nd Europeans, 31st, 45th, and 70th N. I.). Campbell's division consisted of Pennycuick's brigade (24th Foot and 25th N. I.), and Hoggan's brigade (61st Foot, 36th and 46th N. I.). Penny's reserve was composed of the 15th, 20th, and 69th N. I. Hearsey had some irregular cavalry to guard the baggage. The total number of the British combatants was between fifteen and sixteen thousand.

Singh's right centre, which had been strengthened by many guns. Though the fire of these guns had been rapid,* the brigade had suffered comparatively little, until, breaking out of the jungle, it came to a more open space in front of the guns. Now the storm of shot and grape thickened, and the gallant brigade charged; but the jungle had necessarily disordered the formations, and, having to charge over about three hundred yards, the men were winded before reaching the guns, and broke from the charging pace at the moment that it was most important to have continued it. The brigade fell, then, unavoidably into some confusion; more especially as the pools of water in front of the enemy's battery obliged some of the men to make a detour. In doing this many of them began to load and fire. The result was that in a very brief space all order had disappeared. After a short interval of time, however, the scattered groups, finding themselves within reach of the guns, charged home as if with one mind, bayoneted the gunners, and for a moment held them!

But only for a moment. As the smoke cleared away, the Sikhs, noticing the small number of the men who had made that desperate rush, rallied; and, reinforced by infantry from the rear, recovered the battery; then, aided by their cavalry, drove back the brigade almost to the point which it occupied at the beginning of the action.

Colin Campbell, all this time, was with the left (Hoggan's brigade). That brigade, facing, as I have said, the long gap between the left of the right division of the Sikh army, commanded by Atar Singh, and the right of the centre division, with which was Shér Singh, had, pushing on without meeting with opposition, penetrated the gap, and, wheeling to the right, had placed itself on the flank of the Sikh centre. This position,

* *Vide* Sir Henry Durand's article, *Calcutta Review*, vol. xv, pp. 270, 271. Compare it also with the equally graphic account, confirming it in all main essentials, of another eye-witness, Captain Lawrence-Archer, in his excellent work, *Commentaries on the Panjab Campaign, 1848–9.*

however, was not so advantageous as it would at a first glance seem to be; for, whilst the right of the Sikh centre, wheeling in an incredibly short space of time, opposed a firm front to the British brigade, the entire right division, breaking from the opposition offered to their advance by the cavalry of Thackwell and the guns of Brind, wheeled to their left and fell on the rear and the left flank of Campbell. The latter, then, soon found himself engaged in front, flank, and rear—his sole chance of success resting on the courage and discipline of his men. The faith which Colin Campbell ever possessed in the British soldier was proved on this occasion to be well founded, for never did men deserve better of their country than, "during that mortal struggle, and on that strange day of stern vicissitudes," did the gallant 61st.*

Leaving Campbell thus making head against considerable odds, I must proceed with the reader to the British right. There Gilbert had to encounter difficulties not less great than those which the other divisional leader had encountered. He, too, had to storm batteries, supported by infantry, and covered by jungle, in his front; and, what was worse, when he was deeply engaged with the enemy, he had to see his flanks uncovered—the left by the defeat of Pennycuick's brigade, the right by the repulse of the cavalry, presently to be related. Nor had his own front attack been entirely successful. The left regiment of his right brigade, the 56th Native Infantry, after making head with great gallantry against superior numbers, and losing eight officers and three hundred and twenty-two men killed and wounded, had been forced back. The Sikhs, availing themselves of the gap thus produced, had separated the two brigades the one from the other, and these found themselves now, like Hoggan's brigade on the left, assailed, each on its own account

* *Calcutta Review*, vol. xv. p. 271. Lawrence-Archer, pp. 61, 62. It deserves in justice to the old native army to be recorded that the 30th and 46th N. I. "supported the 61st Foot with steadiness and courage."

on front, rear, and flanks. In this crisis, when everything seemed to frown on the British army, the behaviour of the Bengal Horse Artillery was superb. Splendid as is the record of that noble regiment, it may be confidently asserted that never did it render more valuable, more efficacious service to its country, never did it tend more to save a rash and headstrong general from the defeat he deserved, than on that memorable 13th January. The battery of Dawes attached to Gilbert's division was, at the crisis I have described, of special service. "In spite of jungle and every difficulty," records Durand, "whenever, in a moment of peril, he was most needed, Dawes was sure to be at hand; his fire boxed the compass before evening, and Gilbert felt and handsomely acknowledged the merit and the valour of Dawes and his gunners."*

I have stated that whilst Gilbert's left had been uncovered by the defeat of Pennycuick's brigade, and his centre broken by the crushing in of the 56th Native Infantry, his right had been exposed by the repulse of the British cavalry. It happened in this wise.

The cavalry on the right was commanded by Brigadier Pope, an officer in infirm health. It included a portion of the 9th Lancers, the 14th Light Dragoons, the 1st and 6th Light Cavalry. "Either by some order or misapprehension of an order," † this brigade was brought into a position in front of Christie's horse artillery—on the right of Gilbert's division—thus interfering with the fire of his guns and otherwise hampering it. Before Pope could rectify his mistake, a body of the enemy's horsemen, suddenly emerging from the jungle, charged his brigade, and one of them singling out Pope, cut him across the head with a tulwár. The brigade, taken by surprise, had halted, waiting for orders. In consequence of the

* "Dawes's battery was the saving of us."—*Journal of a Subaltern* (written by an officer of the 2nd Europeans).

† Lord Gough's despatch.

severe wound of the commander, no orders came, and the brigade, left to itself, and threatened by another body of horsemen, dashed, panic-stricken, to the rear, rushing over and upsetting guns, gunners, and gun-wagons in their headlong rout. The Gúrchuras, whose inferior numbers did not justify this scare pursued their flying enemy closely, dashed amongst the guns, cut down Major Christie, completely taken by surprise, and many gunners with him, captured all the guns of Christie's troop and two of Huish's, and would have penetrated to the general staff but for the gallantry of the 9th Lancers. These rallied behind the guns and checked the body of Gúrcharas. A few of the latter, however, did advance to within a short distance from the Commander-in-Chief—so near, indeed, that his escort of cavalry prepared to charge. They were, however, dispersed by a few rounds of grape.

Up to this point the battle had gone badly for the British. We have seen the left brigade of the left division fighting for dear life, surrounded on three sides; the right brigade of the same division driven back almost to its starting point; the two brigades of the right division separated from each other, and each surrounded; the cavalry and horse artillery, which should have covered the extreme right, defeated, and six guns captured. Lord Gough must have been very sensible of the critical state of affairs when he ordered up Penny's reserve to replace Pennycuick's brigade. But all order had disappeared; the several regiments, it might in some cases be said the several groups of each regiment, were fighting for themselves, and Penny's brigade, sent to reinforce Campbell, somehow found itself attached to Gilbert's division.

Gough had now to depend mainly upon his infantry; and the stout men who composed that infantry did not fail him. On the right the pertinacity and the high courage of the 29th Foot and the 2nd Europeans (now 104th Regiment) gradually wore down the enemy; on the left, Campbell, repulsing every attack, succeeded at last in forcing the Sikhs to give ground. On both flanks these successes were followed by a final charge, and the British cheer, sounding exulting even over the roar of artillery and the rattle of musketry, borne by the breeze to the ears of the Commander-in-Chief, was the first announcement to that gallant soldier that he might cease his anxiety, for that the day, if not won, was saved.

There was time yet even to win the day. The cavalry on the left, led by Thackwell, and the horse artillery on that flank were still intact. They had performed the great service of keeping in check the entire right division of the enemy. Unett, with a squadron of the 3rd Dragoons and three squadrons of the 3rd Light Cavalry, had made a most brilliant and successful charge, piercing the compact masses of the enemy; and the danger in that quarter being far less pressing than on the uncovered right, Brind had been despatched with his guns, and White with his brigade of cavalry, to the right flank. Thus strengthened, the cavalry there had re-formed. This took place just before the British cheer I have referred to announced the final repulse of the enemy's infantry.

"We feel convinced," writes Durand, in the article from which I have so largely quoted,* "that, had Lord Gough ridden up at that moment to H.M.'s 14th Dragoons, spoken a few words to the corps, and bid them retrieve the lost guns and strike for the bright fame of their Peninsular honour, they would have swept on like a whirlwind, and dashed upon the retiring confused masses of the enemy, as heedless of numbers as Unett's squadron of the 3rd had done on Atar Singh's compact, unshaken troops. It would have saved many a bitter pang, many a reproach, and silenced for ever the mention of the unhappy and unaccountable retreat which gave our guns and gunners to the enemy. It would, too, have prevented the with-

* *Calcutta Review*, vol. xv. pp. 272, 273. More than one officer who has fought in that battle has pronounced a similar opinion.

drawal of the infantry from the ground so hardly won; and all the guns taken from the Sikhs, and all the wounded, of whom we had many, would have been saved."

But it was not to be. The words were not spoken. The thought to speak them never probably entered the head of the infantry commander, who believed he had been saved by his infantry. Heedless of the other branches which, well managed, might have more than retrieved all the faults of the day, he rode forward to his exhausted but victorious infantry, who were close in front of him. The guns and re-formed cavalry were left in the position in which they had re-formed, as though they had been useless!

The mistake in this respect was the more glaring and the more disastrous in its consequences, as Gough was brought to the conclusion, after he had reached his infantry, that it was inadvisable for them to hold the ground they had won. It was 5 o'clock, and darkness was approaching. Campbell and other influential commanders then urged him to fall back, pointing out to him that the enemy, though repulsed, had not been broken, and that it was absolutely necessary to retire on a position where water could be procured, and where the baggage would be ensured protection. The nearest approach to such a position was Chiliánwálá, where, too, the ammunition was stored, and food would be obtainable. Gough yielded to these reasons, and gave the necessary orders.*

The British army then retired from the well-fought field, to win which had cost them, in killed and wounded, eighty-nine officers and two thousand three hundred and fifty-seven fighting men, leaving on the field many standards—lost, not captured—

* Sir Henry Durand contends, and in my opinion with justice, that this giving up the field of battle was a mistake. He would have had the infantry bivouac where they had fought, supported by guns. By daylight the wounded and captured guns would have been secured. He even ventures to think that the resumption of hostilities in the early morn would have been attended with success.—*Calcutta Review*, vol. xv. pp. 274, 275.

six guns, and all their dead.* It cannot be said of this battle that "it was a famous victory." Indeed, it can only technically be called a victory, and most certainly it was of a Pyrrhœan character.

The judgment formed after a lapse of more than thirty years, when time and death have assuaged all the passions of the period, is that no British general ever fought a battle so badly as Lord Gough fought Chiliánwálá. It was, throughout, a day of blunders.

The original conception, inspired by another, was masterly. Carried out exactly as it had been planned, it would have taken the long line of the enemy in flank and have rolled it up. There would have been no heavy jungle, nothing in the shape of natural obstacles to impede him.† But it was in the nature of Gough that the news of the vicinity of a body of the enemy, however small, should make him cast to the winds all his projects, however well conceived. It was something of this sort which caused him to make his first mistake, and leave the road to Rasúl.

When, however, he had quitted that road, and, marching to the left, had taken up a position in front of Chiliánwálá, Gough, instead of hurling his infantry blindly against the enemy's line, should have attempted to take advantage of the faults of their formation. The long gap between the Sikh right and the Sikh centre was the most conspicuous of those faults. A skilful general might have so thrust his army into that gap as to sever the two wings of the enemy and roll them up in opposite directions. It must be admitted that this would have been a very delicate operation, requiring very skilful handling, and quite beyond the powers of the actual British commander. But this is only to admit that Lord Gough was not a skilful general.

* Lawrence-Archer, pp. 78, 79.

† *Calcutta Review*, vol. xv. p. 275.

The attack, in the manner in which it was made, was one which required neither military knowledge nor military experience to order. One can understand how a general, in the crisis of a great battle, when the supreme moment for a decisive advance of his infantry had arrived, should launch forward his reserves with the command, "Up, Guards, and at them." But what is not comprehensible is that a general, leading an army composed of the three arms, facing an enemy about a mile distant from him, whose long line overlapped his own, and between whose position and his was a belt of dense jungle, should, before he had exhausted, or even seriously used, the fire of his artillery, turn to his infantry and exclaim, "Up, men, and at them"! And yet this is positively the gist of the directions which Lord Gough gave at Chiliánwálá. To give such an order, what experience, what knowledge, what education were required? A competitor for the army course could have said as much: probably, having the benefit of the long examination of the enemy's position from the mound of Chiliánwálá, he would have done far better! *

Whilst, after the battle, the English retired to the village of Chiliánwálá, the Sikhs on the other side, after gathering up

* On this point I cannot forbear to quote the striking criticism of Durand "Our attack," he writes, "fair upon the centre of the enemy, gave the latter the full advantage of his very extended position; and, as his centre was covered by thickish bushy jungle, which dislocated all formations in line, and inevitably produced confusion in the brigades, besides offering difficulties to the movements of the guns and to bringing them into action, the troops were sure to come in contact with the Sikh infantry and guns in the most unfavourable position, their organisation disturbed, and nothing but their own courage and the example of their officers to compensate for every conceivable disadvantage. Verily, British infantry, British officers, and British bayonets are of such a character, so entirely to be relied upon, that it is no wonder that British generals will dare and risk much. The dauntless valour of the infantry rectifies the errors of its commanders, and carries them through what would otherwise be inevitable defeat and disgrace. But it redeems their errors with its blood; and seldom has there been more devotion, but *alas!* more carnage, than on the hard-fought field of Chiliánwálá, a field fairly won, though bravely contested by the Sikhs of all arms."—*Calcutta Review*, vol. xv p. 276.

the trophies won, alas! from their enemy, fell back three miles, and re-occupied their position at Rasúl. It was the policy of the Sikh commander to await in his position the arrival of the troops led by his father and of the cavalry contingent expected from Afghánistán. The junction with these once effected, he had two courses before him; the first, by a rapid movement across the Chináb, to turn Lord Gough's position and fall upon Láhor; the second, to strengthen his position at Rasúl, and to tempt the English leader to attack him. His knowledge of Lord Gough's character, and the ease with which that general had always succumbed to similar temptations, misled Shér Singh on this occasion. It will be seen by the narrative that Gough, implored not to attack till he should be reinforced by the troops set free by the fall of Multán, was not to be drawn a second time. Shér Singh would still willingly have awaited him in the position he had greatly strengthened, but, forced by the impossibility of obtaining supplies for his increased army to quit it, he put into operation the second alternative, just one week, fortunately for the English, too late.

Meanwhile, Gough, on the morrow of Chiliánwálá, had taken up for his army a position between the village of that name and Mujiánwálá—a position far too cramped and confined, for it left all the roads open to the Sikh army, and the country free to their foraging parties. When Gough recognised this error it was too late to repair it, for the Sikhs, intellectually quicker than he, had occupied the points which dominated the plain.*

* "Much," says Durand, "was thrown away of the fruits of the victory by withdrawing from the ground which the infantry had so nobly won at Chiliánwálá; but when this had been done, much more was lost and thrown away, in our opinion, by failing to perceive the strategical importance of the position, which, for several days after the battle, the enemy left optional to Lord Gough to take up or not, as he pleased. Afterwards, when our own timidity had restored their confidence, the Sikhs saw the momentous importance of what we had neglected. They became exceedingly jealous of the hill-top looking down on Kotri, and any demonstration on the part of Gough to seize it would have been stoutly contested."—*Calcutta Review*, vol. xv. p. 285.

In this position Gough awaited the fall of Multán. That event occurred on the 21st January, eight days after Chiliánwálá. The troops engaged in the operation, consisting of three brigades, and numbering about nine thousand men, of whom one third were British, led by General Whish, set out at once for Rámnagar, but before that general could join the Commander-in-Chief circumstances had forced Lord Gough to break up his camp at Chiliánwálá.

I have stated that Shér Singh, after his well-contested battle, had retired on Rasúl, there to await the arrival of reinforcements led respectively by his father and by one of the sons of the Amír of Kábul. Chattar Singh reached him on the 16th and assumed the nominal command in chief. The Afgháns arrived two days later.

The arrival of Chattar Singh had increased the Sikh army by a third, and, when joined by fifteen hundred Afgháns, it numbered about thirty-four thousand fighting men.* The temptation to march upon Láhor was great; but, in the first place, the army had not yet recovered from the shaking at Chiliánwálá, and, in the next, it was still hoped that Lord Gough might be tempted.

The increased number of mouths in the Sikh position began, about this period, to cause them great inconvenience. Provisions had for some time been scarce, even for the Sikhs, and it was now found impossible to provide for many days longer for the greatly augmented army. On the 3rd February, then, in pursuance of a resolution arrived at the previous day, the Sikh leader, without quitting his position, thrust, as a tentative measure, his cavalry through the Khúri pass, thus threatening the road to Dinghí, a place in rear of the British army, and commanding a passage across the Chináb.

Gough was informed of this change, but, clinging to his

* The number given by some writers—sixty thousand and even more—is ridiculous. The trained army of the Sikhs never, in their best day, reached sixty thousand.—*Vide* Cunningham's *History of the Sikhs*.

good advisers, and brought to feel that in his actual position—the centre of the circle of which the enemy would have to traverse the arc—he could fall upon the Sikhs at a disadvantage should they attempt to cross the river, he kept a vigilant look-out and remained motionless. This was the more creditable to him, as he had to resist not only his own longings but the suggestions of influential men about him.

The thrusting of the Sikh cavalry through the Khúri pass was, in fact, one of the temptations of Shér Singh. This having failed, he pushed the horse (6th February) to Dinghí, at the same time holding Rasúl. Again, however, did Gough stand firm and refused to be drawn.

On the 11th the Sikh leaders tempted him once again, and, this time, in a manner which, they hoped, he could not resist. Advancing their cavalry in some force to Barra Amrá, they formed line of battle in front of Khúri, their right resting on the strong hill ground, a prolongation of their position of Rasúl—their left refused, and the Khúrí pass and road in their rear. It was a magnificent position, for if Gough had attacked them, as they hoped he would, he must have exposed his flank and rear. But again was Gough a very St. Anthony, and refused to move.

But even a St. Anthony must sometimes sleep. That afternoon, Shér Singh, baffled in his intentions, led back his army to its original position. But during the night he withdrew his left wing from Rasúl to Púran, thus bringing it in close communication with the right, which already occupied that line. The following day he completed all his preparations for a decisive move, and that night, whilst Gough was sleeping, succeeded in turning the English position, and in gaining a march towards the Chináb.

When this movement was reported the next morning to the veteran leader, it did not take him by surprise. Notwithstanding the march gained by the Sikhs, it was in the power of the English general greatly to harass them, had that general only so chosen. But the morning of the 14th February found Gough undecided how to act. Councils were held and dismissed. Orders were first given to the army to march at 11 o'clock, and then those orders were recalled. Finally, Gough contented himself with sending orders to Whish, who had reached Rámnagar, to push up a detachment to Vazírábád along the left bank of the Chináb, so as to prevent the crossing of that river. Whish had anticipated these orders, and it was the knowledge that such a detachment guarded the fords which brought conviction to the minds of the Sikh leaders that their turning movement was stamped by the motto ruinous in war—by the fatal "Too late." They marched, then, on the town of Gujrát and there took up a position. They did not despair. Their great object, still, was to bring Gough to action before he could be reinforced. They used every means to accomplish this result except the one which could not have failed. With a faint-heartedness which, to us looking back, seems unaccountable, they did not dare to attack him. They had many opportunities. They knew, as soldiers, that, with Whish marching to join him, Gough would not be mad enough to remain in his position—that he would stretch out a hand to the friendly supports. To strike him before that hand had been grasped was, then, their true policy, their only chance of success. They had the opportunity, because now the positions were reversed, and they occupied the point in the centre of the circle. But they could not nerve themselves to the enterprise. It may well be conceived that the splendid valour of the British infantry at Chiliánwálá had at least produced that result!

On the 15th Gough broke up from his position, and, without hindrance from the enemy, marched to Lasúrí, a position which secured, though it did not effect, a junction with Whish, and was yet near enough (the distance was twenty miles) to the Sikhs to prevent any attempt on their part to cross the Chináb. On the 16th indecisive councils again prevailed, some urging upon Gough to march to Kúngah, within five miles of the Sikh position, others, more wisely, to push on to Sadúlapúr. The advantages of the latter course were too obvious to be resisted, for whilst the march to Kúngah would most certainly have brought on a battle before Gough could be reinforced, that to Sadúlapúr was free from the risk of collision with the enemy, and gave time for the reinforcements to come up. Gough decided, then, upon the march to Sadúlapúr.

The day of the 16th had been spent in council. On the 17th, making a short march towards the enemy—his right on Golí and his left behind Ishárah—Gough was joined by one brigade of Whish's force. On the 18th he made another short march—halting with its left on Kúngah—five miles from the enemy. Here, on the 19th, he halted, to be joined by the second brigade of Whish's force, under Markham. On the 20th, joined by the third, or Bombay brigade, under Dundas, he marched in battle array to Shádíwálá. This march brought him face to face with the enemy.

The Sikh leaders had expected to receive the attack that very day. To meet it they had posted their army in the following manner:—Their centre was formed behind the village of Kálrá; their left rested on the Kátelah, a rivulet which flows into the Chináb at a point above Vazírábád; their right, refused, was covered by the Dwárah, a dry, sandy-bedded rivulet of some breadth, which, after passing to the west of Gujrát, takes a bend eastward, before striking south to Haríawálá and Shádiwálá. In rear of the position was the town of Gujrát. They maintained this order on the 21st.

Gough and his most trusted officers examined the position thoroughly on the 20th. It was not a strong one. The Dwárah, on which the Sikhs relied to protect their right, presented nowhere any real obstacle to men or guns. The Kátelah, a small stream easily crossed, was even less formidable. In resting upon that it might be said with truth that the Sikh left rested on the air, for it afforded no protection against attack. Gough, then, decided to attack the Sikh left and centre and drive them back on their right. To carry out this plan he directed an advance of the heavy artillery, placed in his centre, and of the right wing, composed of the divisions of Whish and Gilbert, and supported by the greater part of the field artillery. When these should have doubled on the Sikh right its left and centre, the British left wing, composed of Campbell's and Dundas's divisions, was to complete the work of destruction. The cavalry would then render the defeat one from which there should be no rallying. The Dwárah, up to the enemy's position, was to be the regulator of the advance of the British line.

Such was the general programme. It deserves, however, to be added that the British being very superior to the enemy, alike in the weight of metal and in the number of their guns, it was decided that the infantry should not advance to close quarters until the artillery had made itself felt. A strong feeling prevailed that the British could not afford another Chiliánwálá.*

"The morning of the 21st February," writes Durand, in the article so often quoted from, "was clear and bright, and, as the enemy's masses had very early taken up their position, there was no dust of moving columns to cloud the purity of the air and sky. The snowy ranges of the Himálaya, forming a truly magnificent background to Gujrát and the village-dotted plain, seemed on that beautiful morning to have drawn nearer, to gaze on the military spectacle. A looker-on might have thought the

* A story was current immediately after the campaign, which, though resting on no foundation, yet, from the conviction that it ought to have been true, found general acceptance. It was to the effect that Lord Gough's staff, knowing his excitability under fire, and his passion for employing infantry before the guns had done their work, induced the gallant veteran to mount, by means of a ladder—the only mode of access—to the top storey of an isolated building which commanded a complete view of the battle-field. They then quietly removed the ladder, and only replaced it when the artillery had done its work. *Se non è vero, è ben trovato.*

army drawn out on some gala occasion; for, the baggage being packed in safety at Shádiwálá, the force moved free of incumbrance, and the whole had the appearance of a grand review."

Exactly at half-past 7 o'clock the British army, formed up in the order I have mentioned,* marched to the pre-arranged positions. When the centre had reached Haríwálá, on the Dwárah, the distance from the Sikh centre and left, and from the village of Kalrá, which they held in force, was about two thousand yards. Upon the British line halting in line with this village the Sikh guns opened fire. The distance, however, was too great to allow it to have effect, and, when the heavy artillery of the British replied, it was found absolutely necessary to move forward to closer quarters. The British advanced, then, to a nearer but still too distant position. Just at that moment the horse artillery of both wings, displaying that splendid daring which gave the regiment of which it formed a part the title to the proud motto of *Ubique*, galloped to the front, and, careless of the prompt return fire from the enemy's guns, made their presence felt on the enemy's infantry. The heavy guns meanwhile steadily advanced, supported by the right, and, unlimbering within telling range, poured forth shot and shell with rapidity and precision upon the Sikh batteries and masses. So great was the effect, that the enemy, unable to stand before it, yielded ground, and retired behind the line of

* To enter more into detail, I may state that the exact order was as follows: On the extreme left was Dundas's Bombay column, covered by Blood's troop of Horse Artillery, and supported by Thackwell with White's cavalry brigade, the Sindh Horse, and Duncan's and Huish's troops of Horse Artillery. On its right was Campbell's division, covered by Ludlow's and Robertson's light field batteries; in reserve, Hoggan's infantry brigade.

In the centre were the heavy guns, eighteen in number, drawn by elephants. Next to the heavy guns, on their immediate right, was Gilbert's division; and on his right Whish's division, covered by Fordyce's, Mackenzie's, and Anderson's troops of Horse Artillery, with Dawes's—Dawes of Chiliánwálá renown—light field battery; Lane's and Kenleside's troops of Horse Artillery being in a second line in reserve, under Brind. The right flank was protected by Hearsey's and Lockwood's cavalry and by Warner's troop of Horse Artillery. – *Vide* Lawrence-Archer, p. 94.

Kalrá villages, which they still, however, held in force, and which served as a protection to them. Gough, all this time, had been anxiously waiting for the moment when he could use his infantry. That moment seemed to him now to have arrived, and, though it would have been far wiser, and, as it turned out, would have saved much expenditure of blood,* had he held them back for another quarter of an hour, he could restrain himself no longer, but ordered Gilbert and Whish to storm the villages in front of them.

Gallantly did the two British divisions advance to carry out their orders; but the resistance was determined, the bearing of the Sikhs heroic. They met the advancing foe face to face, and strove with undaunted courage to drive him back. Vain, however, were their efforts. Step by step did the British troops make good their footing, until at last they forced the enemy, still fronting them, to fall back on his second line. The gallant nature of the defence may be gathered from the loss inflicted by the Sikhs on their assailants. In carrying the village of Barra Kalrá the 3rd Brigade (2nd Europeans, 31st and 70th Native Infantry) lost upwards of three hundred killed and wounded; whilst in storming Chota Kalrá, the 1st Brigade (10th Foot, 8th and 52nd Native Infantry) lost in a few minutes more than half that number. But in addition to the loss of the infantry, that of the Horse Artillery who supported them was extremely heavy. Anderson's troop suffered severely, their leader himself falling, whilst Fordyce's troop was nearly annihilated!

Whilst affairs were thus progressing on the right, Colin Campbell and Dundas on the left were not the less rendering splendid service. True to the programme they advanced very gradually in alignment with the right wing, in columns at

* "Had Shakspear been permitted to expend a few minutes' attention and a few rounds upon Burra Kalra and its supporting batteries, the loss would have been less, or altogether avoided."—*Calcutta Review*, vol. xv. pp. 289, 290. Shakspear commanded the heavy guns.

deploying distance, taking no heed of the ineffective fire of the Sikh artillery in their front. It happened that two villages in their front, the villages of Lunpúr and Jamná, which, if defended, might have given them some trouble, had not been occupied by the Sikhs. On passing these, Colin Campbell, finding his men well within range, deployed, and, moving up to within about a thousand yards of the Sikh batteries, made his men lie down, and pushed forward Ludlow's and Robertson's light field batteries. These, commanded and worked by Major Mowatt, trotted rapidly forward before the Sikh gunners could get the range, unlimbered, and, at a distance of about eight hundred yards, opened a crushing fire on the battery opposed to them and on the infantry supporting it.

Under the fire of these guns, which steadily advanced, Campbell gradually pushed forward his infantry, making the men lie down whenever they halted. At last, the enemy's artillery fire gradually slackening, two of the British guns succeeded in taking up a position whence they could sweep the head of the Dwárah. This position was fatal to the enemy. In a few minutes the Dwárah was cleared of living Sikh infantry, "and Campbell, with very trifling loss, by good management of the guns under his command, occupied the position, from which he had forced his opponents to retire, without firing a musket-shot." *

So concluded the first phase of the fight. The British advance had been successful along the whole line. On the right, two important positions had been gained; on the left, the enemy had been forced back from the nálá (rivulet) on which they rested. It would be a mistake to suppose, however, that the Khálsa troops, though maltreated and forced back, were beaten. Driven though they had been from their first line, their hearts were still strong, their courage still resolute, their heads still clear; and, just at the moment when Gough was congratulating

* Durand, *Calcutta Review*, vol. xv. p. 289.

himself that the difficulties of the day had been overcome, the gallant Sikh infantry was preparing to make another bid for victory.

In taking up the line of the Dwárah, the English left—the divisions of Campbell and Dundas—had thrown itself on the right of the Sikhs. This manœuvre, extremely efficacious in forcing the Sikh line to quit its grasp on its first position, had yet been attended by his inconvenience, that it had produced a large gap between the English left and its centre. The Sikh leaders, unwillingly forced back, were not slow in detecting from their new alignment this defect in the English formation, and they prepared, with skill and courage, to take advantage of it. They recognised it was their last chance, for already their line of retreat was menaced. Not only had the Afghán cavalry succumbed to a gallant charge of the Sindh horse, but Thackwell was pushing forward White's brigade in a manner dangerously threatening to their right and rear. If, however, at this terrible crisis they could pierce the British centre, laid so invitingly open, all might yet be well. Full of these desperate hopes, the Sikh leaders, re-forming their right division, sent their men on this forlorn enterprise. It was indeed a bold push for victory. For a moment it seemed as though it might succeed; for when the English general, perceiving the danger, despatched in haste two troops of Horse Artillery to fill up the gap, he discovered that their shot and shell had been expended, and that they must await a fresh supply from the rear. The silence of these guns encouraged the Sikhs, and their advance assumed for a moment quite a dangerous character. That it would have proved so had the commander of the British division nearest the gap been other than a man of great readiness, of watchful coolness and of capacity, is quite certain. But, from his post on the Dwárah, Colin Campbell suddenly became aware of the danger. With a true military instinct, he at once turned the fire of a portion of his artillery upon the advancing mass.

The Sikhs, realising on the instant that they could not proceed without exposing their flank to an artillery fire, and that Campbell would be able to throw himself upon them as they pushed forward, unwillingly renounced the movement, and, covered by their cavalry, fell back in good order. It was time, indeed, that they should; for the English right was rapidly advancing, and the Sikh left and centre were retiring fast, in heavy columns, covered by cavalry, over the open country, passing to the east of Gujrát. Their right—completely turned by Dundas and Campbell, cut off from their natural line of retreat on the Jhelam by Thackwell, and driven upon the centre—was forced then to retire by the line taken by the other masses. "By 1 o'clock in the afternoon"—to use the exact words of the warrior-statesman whose criticism on the campaign is a masterpiece of fair and sound argument*—"Gough had overthrown the Sikh army, and had crowded it in heavy masses upon a line of retreat which offered no hope of support, provision, or escape for the disheartened soldiery, if properly followed up."

Followed up it was. Cavalry and Horse Artillery were launched in pursuit of the enemy. During the remaining hours of the day the beaten army was subjected to all the horrors and all the inconveniences of constant and repeated assaults. It gave way under the pressure. Many Sikhs quitted the ranks and rid themselves of their uniform. For miles the country was strewn with guns, bullocks, waggons, tents, and standards, abandoned in hot haste. Darkness at length put a stop to the pursuit. At a distance of some fourteen miles from the battle-field, Thackwell, who conducted it, halted his men, intending to bivouac for the night and renew the pursuit in the morning. But Gough, unwilling, apparently, to commit so important a

* Sir H. Durand, *Calcutta Review*, vol. xv. pp. 290, 291. The reader who may refer to this article will see the large extent to which I have been indebted to its author.

business to his cavalry unsupported by infantry, recalled him to camp.

The next morning two British columns were launched in pursuit of the enemy. One, the smaller, under Colin Campbell, proceeded to the Bimbir pass to secure any guns which might have taken that route;* the other, the more important, led by Gilbert, proceeded by Dinghí to the Jhelam, and, crossing that river, followed up the enemy with so much vigour, that on the 14th March the entire Sikh army unconditionally surrendered.†

Thus ended the second Sikh war. The army, which had considered itself betrayed at Firúzshahar and at Sobráon, had never thoroughly submitted to the conqueror. In 1848–9 it selected its own time of outbreak, it chose its own field, and again it was beaten. This time, certainly, there was no suspicion of treachery.

And yet it is beyond question that the main cause of the failure of the national rising was the inefficiency of the national leaders. No troops could have fought better than the Sikhs fought, no army could have been worse led than the Sikh army was led. Shér Singh's leadership was a leadership of lost opportunities. A great general—a general even of the average run of intellectual men—would have massed his whole army against Thackwell at Sadúlapúr and have crushed him. Such a general would have attacked the British army in its position on the morrow of Chiliánwálá: such a general would not have

* It returned a few days later, with no results.

† The English prisoners with the Sikh army, George St. Patrick Lawrence, Bowie, and Herbert, were released by Chattar Singh on the 6th March. Two days later, Shér Singh, at an interview with Gilbert, was informed of the only terms which could be accorded to him, viz. unconditional surrender. On the 14th Chattar Singh, Shér Singh, and the principal Sikh leaders delivered their swords into the hands of the British general. At the same time forty-one pieces of artillery were surrendered, and the remnant of the Sikh army, reduced to a moiety of that which had fought at Gujrát, laid down their arms in the presence of British troops. *Vide* also Lawrence-Archer, pp. 107, 108.

waited at Rasúl till the British reinforcements from Multán were within easy hail, but, turning Gough's position, or fighting him if he had placed himself in his path, would have recrossed the Satlaj and fallen upon Whish's army wherever he could have found it. All these things having been neglected, such a general, emerging at the eleventh hour, as Shér Singh emerged, from Rasúl, would have forced the English general to fight, even at the risk of attacking him. Gough had not been reinforced, and to fight him then would have been better policy than to wait for him at Gujrát.

Turn we now to the English general. Gough, at the outset of the campaign, committed as many faults as his opponent; but he redeemed them towards its close. Never was a campaign ushered in by so much vacillation. "At the very outset," to use the language of an officer who served throughout it,* "orders and counter-orders succeeded each other so rapidly, that a state of feverish excitement, prejudicial to the public interests, was unnecessarily kept up; and regiments showed the effects of varying and harassing rumours in their hospital returns."

It was, perhaps, in consequence of the vacillating air he breathed, that Gough, when he sent Thackwell across the Chináb, committed the grave strategical fault of dividing his army in the presence of an enemy superior to it when united. It does not exculpate him that Shér Singh missed the offered opportunity. Again, I have pointed out the serious tactical error he committed on the 13th January, in abandoning, on the spur of the moment, the matured plan to march on Rasúl. Chiliánwálá was a severe lesson to him. It taught him caution —for the moment, too great caution. On the morrow of the battle he contracted his army within a position, in which, had he been attacked, he would have fought at great disadvantage. He gave up his touch on the surrounding country, thus yielding

* Lawrence-Archer, p. 111.

to the enemy an advantage which, fortunately for Gough, he did not adequately appreciate. But from this time his errors ceased. His conduct in refusing the temptations laid in his way by Shér Singh cannot be too much appreciated, for, to his nature, such temptations must have been almost irresistible. Not only did he resist them, but he resisted likewise the pernicious advice of men of high position to manœuvre in a manner which must have precipitated a combat before his army had been reinforced. At Gujrát, too, he adhered steadily and wisely to a well-considered programme. In fact, Chiliánwálá had been a lesson from which he had known how to profit.

Chiliánwálá was, indeed, a lesson to both armies, and on both it produced different effects. Paradoxical as it may appear to pronounce in a manner so categorical regarding a battle, of which it may be said that, if the English won the field, the Sikhs carried off all the trophies of the fight, it is yet true that, morally, Chiliánwálá decided the issue of the campaign. Whilst, as we have seen, it produced an excellent effect on the English Commander-in-Chief, the Sikh leaders never recovered from the impression produced upon them by the splendid daring of the British infantry. It was that impression which induced vacillation in the Sikh camp at Rasúl, which prevented Shér Singh from attacking Gough before he had been reinforced, which hindered a bold strategic movement across the Chináb. Whatever, then, the faults of the English general, Chiliánwálá was not fought in vain. Gujrát was to it what Sobráon had been to Fírúzshahar.

One word as to the consequences of the national uprising. The reader who has accompanied me so far will recollect that by the agreement made with the Láhor Darbár, on the 16th December 1846, the British Government assumed, and delegated to a special officer, "full authority to direct and control all matters in every department" of the Sikh state, until such time as the Maháràjah Dhulíp Singh should attain the age of sixteen. This contract, whilst it made the British Government responsible for order in the Panjáb, constituted it also the guardian and protector of the young Mahárájah. Against the British protectorate, so constituted, the Sikh army rose, the interpreters of the national feeling against foreign overlordship. The British army subdued that rising, and conquered the Panjáb. The question then arose, For whom? The answer of Sir Henry Lawrence was clear and precise. "We have conquered the Panjáb," he said, in so many words, "for the young chief of whom we are the guardian." But other answers were given, displaying the aggressive nature of the Anglo-Saxon. These had the most weight with Lord Dalhousie, and he decided that the Panjáb had been conquered for England.

The Panjáb, consequently, was annexed. Against the annexation I do not venture a single word. It must have come sooner or later, and it was better to take it after a fair fight than to steal it in the manner we adopted towards Awadh (Oudh) some five years later. But for the guiltless boy, for the young Mahárájah, of whose interests we were the guardian, for Dhulíp Singh, surely some fitting provision should have been made. Granted that we did well to take his kingdom, by what right did we annex his private estates? This is a question in which the honour of the country is concerned. It behoves it also to demand whether a pension for one uncertain life is sufficient compensation for the loss of a great position and the forfeiture of inalienable private property!

INDEX.

A.

C.

F.

G.

H.

I.

J.

K.

L.

M.

N.

S.

T.

Y.